THE SABLE ARM

Modern War Studies

Raymond A. Callahan
Jacob W. Kipp
Jay Luvaas
Theodore A. Wilson
Series Editors

THE SABLE ARM

Black Troops in the Union Army, 1861-1865

DUDLEY TAYLOR CORNISH

With a New Foreword by Herman Hattaway

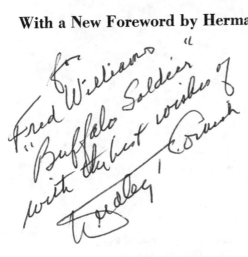

University Press of Kansas

FOR
EUSTACE
SERGEANT ANDERSON
AND THE
MEN OF D COMPANY
WHEREVER THEY MAY BE

Published by the University Press of Kansas (Lawrence, Kansas 66045), which was
organized by the Kansas Board of Regents and is operated and funded by Emporia State
University, Fort Hays State University, Kansas State University, Pittsburg State
University, the University of Kansas, and Wichita State University

Library of Congress Catalog Card Number: 87-50106

Printed in the United States of America
10 9 8 7 6

CONTENTS

And then there will be some black men who can remember that with silent tongue and clenched teeth and steady eye and well-poised bayonet they have helped mankind on to this great consummation.

—ABRAHAM LINCOLN

The giving of praise or blame is always easy but the understanding of anything is difficult; it is a truth which applies to this story.

—S. L. A. MARSHALL

During the thirty years since its original publication *The Sable Arm* has become known and respected by virtually all Civil War scholars. The book is a classic, a standard, and it justly earned for Dudley Taylor Cornish status as a master in this subfield of history. Reviewers hailed the book as "well documented," "thorough, meticulous, conscientious" and lauded its "extensive research . . . attested to by the very complete and helpful bibliography." It still stands today as the most valuable book ever written on its topic.

The original bibliography for *The Sable Arm* was assessed as "replete with ideas and thoughts for further investigation," and Cornish supplemented it in 1967 with the publication of his chapter "The Negro" in *Civil War Books: A Critical Bibliography*, edited by Allan Nevins, James I. Robertson, Jr., and Bell I. Wiley. No one has done more than, and few have done as much as, Cornish during his long career to enhance and facilitate inquiry in this area.

The Sable Arm traces the development of Union policy on the use of black troops in the Union army and analyzes the problems connected with the implementation of that policy. The idea of using black troops was a daring one at the time. "It is hard to realize," Cornish tells us, "how revolutionary the experiment of permitting Negroes to bear arms was considered, how fraught with imagined dangers to the Union cause, how galling to white pride."

Cornish is one of the many thousands of World War II veterans who benefited from the G.I. Bill, thereby attaining higher education that otherwise would have been impossible. He long has pointed out proudly that this infusion of a wider variety of "sorts and conditions of men" into the ranks of professional scholars led naturally to their consideration of more nonelitist topics—and in turn also to the consideration of those topics with less of an elitist-oriented methodology—than had typically been the case. Cornish was correct, of course, but it was the high standard of craftsmanship that he applied, his sparkle as well as his originality, that gave his book a timeless value. The volume "sheds a good deal of light on a rather obscure chapter of American military history," wrote one of the original reviewers, but the general story was not one that always had been entirely ignored. As Williston Loftin of Howard University observed, Cornish's treatment "clears up many heretofore shadowy aspects of the picture." Cornish's work has not since been superseded.

Among the many shortcomings of the earlier treatments that touched on the subject, one of the most troublesome was a distorting stress on the use of black troops in eastern armies. Cornish earned an early and honored place among those significant scholars, mostly of the past quarter century, who rightfully shifted some of the emphasis in Civil War studies to the happenings west of the Appalachians, and in Cornish's case even to the Missouri and Kansas frontier. His discussion of black soldiers who served in this neglected theater opened new avenues for further scholarly inquiry. (And Cornish himself made an additional contribution—his distinguished 1953 article in the *Kansas Historical Quarterly,* which was republished in 1969 by the State of Kansas Commission on Civil Rights as the pamphlet *Kansas Negro Regiments in the Civil War.*)

Readers who are looking for a plethora of gory details about the actual combat experiences of black troops may be somewhat disappointed. Cornish does answer, with an unqualified affirmative, the oft-asked question whether the black troops made good combat soldiers. But the greater strengths in *The Sable Arm* lie in the book's probing of background and underpinning. For example, one of the more significant and interesting stories Cornish recounts is that of the exemplary program formulated and executed by the Union army to educate white troops to accept their black comrades. It is striking that the United States government apparently did a better job in this regard during the Civil War than it did during either World War I or World War II. Still another well-handled subtheme is the occasional Southern threats to re-enslave any captured blacks and to summarily execute their white officers. It was a pathetic and ineffective program of attempted intimidation, engaged in by a few misguided Confederates, that resulted only in the black units' fighting all the harder and may even have had the backlash effect of striking fear into the hearts of rebel units when they had to face the tough and determined black outfits.

An officially recorded number of 178,892 black men served in the Union armies, including some 7,000 noncommissioned officers and about 100 commissioned officers, virtually all at company-grade levels (a token few making it to field-grade level). The regiments all were racially segregated and were commanded and otherwise staffed by whites. Black troops comprised 120 infantry regiments, 12 heavy-artillery regiments, 10 batteries of light artillery, and 7 cavalry regiments, constituting by the end of the war slightly more than 12 percent of the Union's land forces. (Some black sailors served in the Union navy; Benjamin Quarles, in his assessment of Cornish's book in the *Mississippi Valley Historical Review,* suggested that it was unfortunate that Cornish did not say much about them, or about civilian black military laborers, because "the existence of each of these groups . . . substantially reduced the army's black potential." Doubtless that is true, but the story of these men is not part of Cornish's subject.) Quite significantly, the number of black troops in the Union army toward the end approximately equaled the total number of Confederate soldiers still present for duty; surely this ratio had some psychological impact upon Southerners. Blacks took part in 449 engagements, 39 of them major. More than one-third of the black volunteers died in service.

Wood Gray correctly noted in his review of *The Sable Arm* in the *Journal of Southern History* that Cornish was "primarily concerned with finding answers to three major problems: (1) the steps by which the policy of enlisting Negroes was achieved; (2) the recruitment, organization, and training of such units; and (3) their employment and effectiveness in combat and the guarding of supply lines." Cornish does these things in an exemplary manner, his effort enhanced by his own experience in, and knowledge of, war. The truly great contributions to military history seem always to have been written by persons with that degree of intimate understanding. *The Sable Arm* remains an inspiring example of the best in Civil War scholarship of the post–World War II era. Cornish explored important and neglected matters, and his work suggests that there remains a good deal of further investigation, along similarly fresh pathways, that the rest of us should be attempting to get done.

HERMAN HATTAWAY

University of Missouri–Kansas City

PREFACE

On March 7, 1864, the New York *Times,* a newspaper with a reputation for sober and reliable reporting and policy, published this editorial:

"There has been no more striking manifestation of the marvelous times that are upon us than the scene in our streets at the departure of the first of our colored regiments. Had any man predicted it last year he would have been thought a fool, even by the wisest and most discerning. History abounds with strange contrasts. It always has been an ever-shifting melo-drama. But never, in this land at least, has it presented a transition so extreme and yet so speedy as what our eyes have just beheld.

"Eight months ago the African race in this City were literally hunted down like wild beasts. They fled for their lives. When caught, they were shot down in cold blood, or stoned to death, or hung to the trees or the lamp-posts. Their homes were pillaged; the asylum which Christian charity had provided for their orphaned children was burned; and there was no limit to the persecution but in the physical impossibility of finding further material on which the mob could wreak its ruthless hate. Nor was it solely the raging horde in the streets that visited upon the black man the nefarious wrong. Thousands and tens of thousands of men of higher social grade, of better education, cherished precisely the same spirit. It found expression in contumelious speech rather than in the violent act, but it was persecution none the less for that. In fact the mob would never have entered upon that career of outrage but for the fact that it was fired and maddened by the prejudice which had been generated by the ruling influences, civil and social, here in New York, till it had enveloped the City like some infernal atmosphere. The physical outrages which were inflicted on the black race in those terrible days were but the outburst of malignant agencies which had been transfusing the whole community from top to bottom year after year.

"How astonishingly has all this been changed. The same men who could not have shown themselves in the most obscure street in the City without peril of instant death, even though in the most suppliant attitude, now march in solid platoons, with shouldered muskets, slung knapsacks, and buckled cartridge boxes down through our gayest avenues and our busiest thoroughfares to the pealing strains of martial music and are everywhere saluted with waving handkerchiefs, with descending flowers, and with the acclamations and plaudits of countless beholders. They are halted at our most beautiful square, and amid an admiring crowd, in the presence of many of our most prominent citizens, are addressed in an eloquent and most complimentary speech by the President of our chief literary institution, and are presented with a gorgeous stand of colors in the names of a large number of the first ladies of the City, who attest on parchment, signed by their own fair hands, that they 'will anxiously watch your career, glorying in your heroism, ministering to you when wounded and ill, and honoring your martyrdom with benedictions and with tears.'

"It is only by such occasions that we can at all realize the prodigious revolution which the public mind everywhere is experiencing. Such developments are infallible tokens of a new epoch."

The "prodigious revolution" which the *Times* found manifest in New York's ovation to its first colored regiment was the acceptance of the Negro as a soldier capable of fighting for the preservation of the Union and for the freedom of the slave. What made this a revolution was far more than the sharp turn of attitudes and events in New York in the eight months between the draft riots of July, 1863, and the public honors for the 20th U.S. Colored Troops in March, 1864. This revolution involved a broadening of the war aims of the Lincoln administration from preservation of the Union to abolition of human slavery. It involved also the gradual recognition of the Negro's right to fight for those war aims, of his ability to perform as a soldier— recognition, in short, of the Negro's manhood.

Now, Negroes had fought in nearly every American war

before the outbreak of the Civil War. They had fought in the colonial wars, in the Revolution, and in the War of 1812. But until the American Civil War the American Negro was never an official part of the military establishment of the United States. He helped out in times of crisis, but after the crisis he reverted to what he had been before, slave or free colored. The regular army was closed to him; state laws generally prevented his belonging to the militia because militiamen bore arms. It was during the Civil War that the American Negro permanently won the right to fight. Ever since that war he has served in the regular army and in the militia of some of the states. The Korean War saw the final achievement of integration, of an end to segregated service in the several branches of the armed forces of the United States.

In his long struggle from Bunker Hill to Battle Mountain, the American Negro won his most important victories by participating in and contributing to the Civil War. Without Battery Wagner, Brice's Cross Roads, Deep Bottom, Honey Springs, Nashville, Petersburg, and Port Hudson, the American Negro must have been excluded indefinitely from the rights and responsibilities of American citizenship. For him the Civil War was indeed a prodigious revolution. Had he not fought his way into the Union Army, had he remained passive observer instead of active participant, the history of the American people in general and of the American Negro in particular must have been far different from what it has been.

While the history of the American Negro soldier began long before 1861, he did not become an officially recognized and permanent part of the United States armed forces until the Civil War. The story of the Negro soldier in that struggle is therefore a logical point of departure for a study of the Negro in the United States army. Everything that the Negro soldier had done before 1861 was merely preliminary and, in the opinion of the vast majority of the contemporaries of Abraham Lincoln, of little or no value in solving the thorny problem of the employment of Negroes as soldiers in the Union Army. During the Civil War the problem was met and in part solved. The Negro was used as a soldier, and, in Northern estimation at least, he made a good soldier. He proved himself sufficiently to warrant recognition by the Congress of the United States as a part of the regular army.

The history of the Negro soldier in the Union Army has remained an obscure chapter in American history. The reasons for this are twofold. First, the subject has never been completely examined and described: only three book-length studies have appeared, all before 1890, and before publication of the voluminous and basic *Official Records* was half completed. There have been regimental histories, pamphlets, essays, articles by the score, all of them partial treatments of the total subject. There have been volumes on the general history of the Negro during the war, but all of them treat his military experiences as only a part of a larger story. Secondly, so much misconception, misunderstanding, and misinformation has grown up around the Negro soldier that his true history has been twisted and mutilated. Although War Department records show that 178,895 Negro soldiers served, one biography of Ulysses S. Grant states that there were "about one hundred thousand negroes in the Union Army," while the *Dictionary of American History* gives an approximation of 300,000. The Grant biography also asserts that Negroes were first used as soldiers in 1863 "in an experimental way, at the siege of Vicksburg," and further declares that Grant usually "kept them in the rear, guarding his wagon trains." Negro troops were in fact used in an experimental way in Louisiana, Kansas, and Missouri, and along the Atlantic coast, in the fall of 1862. In May of 1863 the War Department established the Bureau for Colored Troops to regularize their recruitment and organization. Of the colored troops at Milliken's Bend, Louisiana, in June, 1863, General Grant wrote the adjutant general: "Their conduct is said . . . to have been most gallant, and I doubt not but with good officers they will make good troops." In the Wilderness numerous Negro regiments fought at the very front; at Petersburg they fought again and again, and in the final drive toward Appomattox Negro soldiers constituted the entire XXV Corps of Grant's army. Battle records indicate that not all of this corps were detailed to guard wagon trains.

Nor were these all of the inaccuracies and gross errors in fact in the treatment of the Negro soldier problem in Mr. Lincoln's army. Standard histories and some of the best specialized studies of the war make no more than passing reference to the subject. Some scholars have charged that there has been "a conspiracy of silence" designed to hide the Negro's military accomplishments. When there is wide lack of agreement on ascertainable facts, a fresh examination of the record seems required. It has been the object of this volume to make this fresh examination, to attempt to fill this historical hiatus.

While it has been difficult to reconstruct the story "as it actually happened," there are sufficient reliable materials and authentic records of the recruitment, training, officering, and military use of Negro troops to make possible a near approach to the truth of the matter. This volume attempts to do that. It has not been the purpose of this study to prove that Negro troops won the Civil War or even that the war might have been lost to the Union if Negro troops had not been used by the Lincoln administration. The purpose has been to examine and describe the slow advance of the movement to arm the Negro; to follow that movement through the maze of difficulties and obstacles that had to be overcome, circumvented, or ignored before the Negro was permitted to do more for the freedom of his race than drive a supply wagon, cook for white soldiers, or labor on fortifications; and, finally, to show the gradual emergence of the Negro soldier as a member of the Union Army and to assess his contribution to that army and to the outcome of the war.

The history of the Negro soldier in the Union Army involves far more than the Negro himself, although certainly he is its central figure. Involved also are military and civil leaders: cabinet officers, governors of states, senators and congressmen, newspaper editors, intellectuals, regular and volunteer army officers, abolitionists, old friends of John Brown, politicians, and just plain people. No major segment of the American people escaped involvement. There were those, like Frederick Douglass and Martin Delany, who were primarily interested in Negro participation in a military role as a first step toward the elevation of their race to full participation in American life. There were those, like James H. Lane of Kansas and Owen Lovejoy of Illinois, who were interested in putting arms into the hands of all who would help support the Union and crush the rebellion.

There were those, like Benjamin F. Butler, who saw the Negro soldier as a potent agent for personal advance. There were those also, like Thomas Wentworth Higginson and James Montgomery and James Beecher, who because of their personal abolitionist convictions could no more ignore the opportunity of striking hard blows against slavery than they could have stopped breathing by an act of will. And then there was the great mass who waited on more dedicated men to show the way and prove the practicality of the Negro soldier before themselves participating; General Godfrey Weitzel was one of these, firmly opposed to arming the Negro in 1862, commanding the all-Negro XXV Corps in 1865. There were the radicals who led the way, and there were the moderate and the cautious who joined the movement after it had taken on respectability and even a degree of popularity.

This is far more than military history. American military history, by the very nature of our society and the organization of our government and of our army, is more nearly social and political history than mere military analysis. This is especially true of our Civil War, as indeed it must be of any civil conflict. The problem of the Negro soldier was a complex of complexities difficult to confine to any one plane. The problem was only superficially a military one; it was social and economic; it was ethical and psychological. The fact that the army served as an agent of social change in helping to reach a solution to the problem does not simplify the history of the problem. This book traces the broad outlines of administration policy and army practice toward the problem of the Negro soldier in the Union Army, a problem which, then as now, was only one facet of a much greater problem. If historical examination of the past can illumine the problems of the present and so help toward their final solution, this book may be a contribution toward the solution of the American dilemma of the integration of the American Negro into American society.

DUDLEY TAYLOR CORNISH

Pittsburg, Kansas

ACKNOWLEDGMENTS

While research and writing are primarily individual functions, I am under the happy obligation of acknowledging encouragement and substantial help from my family, friends, associates, librarians, and archivists. My wife Maxine has borne heavy burdens through revision after revision, galley proof, and index; it is to her that I owe the greatest debt. Certainly the Shakeshafts—Marion, Jerry, and Dick— have been deeply involved in the work from the start, and to Jerry especially I am grateful for interest, continued encouragement, promotional activity, and valuable assistance in finding lost or strayed material. My old friend Andrew N. Borno lent a needed and appreciated hand in tracking down John Cochrane.

My colleagues at Kansas State Teachers College, Pittsburg, have demonstrated patience and forbearance, and I am particularly grateful to Elizabeth Cochran and Alvin H. Proctor for counsel and encouragement. These former students—Thomas J. Boyd, William L. Dunn, Thurston M. Graham, Eugene Jackson, and Walter A. Meeks—gave me inestimable help toward an appreciation and understanding of the American Negro. Friends at the University of Colorado helped in several ways: Colin B. Goodykoontz by counsel and precept, Robert G. Athearn by the example of his prodigious production. The Beta Epsilon Chapter of Phi Alpha Theta made possible my research in the National Archives and Library of Congress.

I am under heavy obligation to many archivists and librarians: to R. Paul Bartolini, formerly librarian of Porter Library here, now in the Philadelphia Public Library; to Gilbert Fites, formerly of the Porter staff, now librarian at Fairmont State College, West Virginia; to Bryant Harvey Jackson of Porter Library; to C. Jane Titus of the Baltimore and Pittsburgh, Pa., public libraries; to Paul Angle of the Chicago Historical Society for permission to use material from its collections; to V. L. Bedsole and his helpful staff in the Department of Archives, Louisiana State University; to Kirke Mechem and Nyle H. Miller of the Kansas State Historical Society, a rich storehouse of Civil War material; to

Robert T. Quarles, Jr., of the Tennessee Historical Society; and to Elizabeth Drewry in the War Records Division of the National Archives.

Authors and publishers have graciously granted me permission to use copyrighted materials; gratefully I acknowledge the following obligations—

To the Bobbs-Merrill Company, Inc., for permission to quote from Bell Irvin Wiley, *The Life of Johnny Reb, the Common Soldier of the Confederacy* (Indianapolis, 1943).

To the Arthur H. Clark Company for permission to quote from Fred A. Shannon, *The Organization and Administration of the Union Army, 1861-1865,* 2 vols. (Cleveland, 1928).

To Doubleday & Company, Inc., for permission to use material from David C. Mearns, ed., *The Lincoln Papers,* 2 vols. (New York, 1948).

To Henry Holt and Company, Inc., for permission to quote from Ralph V. Harlow, *Gerrit Smith, Philanthropist and Reformer* (New York, 1939).

To Houghton Mifflin Company for permission to use material from W. C. Ford, ed., *A Cycle of Adams Letters, 1861-1865,* 2 vols. (Boston, 1920); from C. F. Adams, *Charles Francis Adams, an Autobiography* (Boston, 1916); from Edward W. Emerson, *Life and Letters of Charles Russell Lowell* (Boston, 1907); and from Henry Greenleaf Pearson, *The Life of John A. Andrew, Governor of Massachusetts, 1861-1865,* 2 vols. (Boston, 1904).

To the Illinois State Historical Society for permission to quote from John Hope Franklin, ed., *The Diary of James T. Ayres, Civil War Recruiter* (Springfield, 1947).

To Allan Nevins of Columbia University for permission to quote from his *Frémont, Pathmarker of the West* (New York, Longmans, Green and Co., Inc., 1955).

To Rutgers University Press for permission to quote from Benjamin P. Thomas, *Theodore Weld, Crusader for Freedom* (New Brunswick, 1950).

To the World Publishing Company for permission to quote from Roy P. Basler, ed., *Abraham Lincoln: His Speeches and Writings* (Cleveland, 1946).

To Yale University Press for permission to quote from John W. DeForest, *A Volunteer's Adventures, A Union Captain's Record of the Civil War* (New Haven, 1946).

To all others who have, directly or indirectly, helped the work along, I wish to express my general but deep-felt thanks. It should go without saying that the writer accepts full responsibility for the substance of the book.

D. T. C.

Pittsburg, Kansas

I. *"We are ready and would go ..."*

> ... I warn southern gentlemen, that if this war is to continue, there will be a time when ... [it will be] declared by this free nation, that every bondsman in the South—belonging to a rebel, recollect; I confine it to them—shall be called upon to aid us in war against their masters, and to restore this Union.
>
> —THADDEUS STEVENS, August 2, 1861

"Our cry now must be emancipation and arming the slaves." So wrote young Henry Adams in the first November of the Civil War.[1] To an Adams of Massachusetts the argument was logical. Henry had been born into opposition to slavery and brought up in the ferment of abolitionism. Now that the irrepressible conflict had finally come, it seemed to offer the great opportunity, once and for all, to end the institution out of which the sectional struggle had in large measure grown. Free the slaves and let them fight to preserve the Union and thus ensure their own freedom. There was hard New England logic about the idea. But Henry Adams was three thousand miles away from New England and just about as far from expressing the majority opinion of the American people.

As secretary to his father, Charles Francis Adams, the United States minister to Great Britain, Henry had been out of his native state since the second month of the war, and he was somewhat out of touch with the realities of civil war in America. The realities were liable to make a mockery of logic. In the long run, of course, Henry was right. But November of 1861 was too early

1

in the history of the struggle for his cry to stir thunderous echoes. There were certain men who had already learned that; there would be others who would in the course of time learn it for themselves. And then there was Abraham Lincoln, who would at length make emancipation and arming the slaves his policies. But the Lincoln logic was different from the Adams variety; it was softer, more accommodating, adjustable, conciliatory; it was the pragmatic logic of the political leader. It was exasperating to men of the Adams temper, but in the long run it caught up with the Adams logic and its resilience made it wear better and win more support in the American market place.

There were certain men named Tilmon and Dodson and Burr Porter and Edward Vernon and a Michigan doctor named G. P. Miller, all of whom had earlier suggested in part what Adams suggested in November, and they had found out that they were far ahead of the Lincoln administration. Four days before old Edmund Ruffin had fired the first shot at Fort Sumter, Levin Tilmon of New York wrote the president, "if your Honor wishes colored volunteers, you have only to signify . . ." [2] There is no evidence that Lincoln gave any sign. On April 16, four days after the shooting began, Burr Porter, who signed himself "Ex-major, Ottoman Army (three campaigns)," wrote Secretary of War Simon Cameron to suggest that "the Government raise as soon as practicable two regular regiments of infantry from the free colored people of the border States," because, in Porter's opinion, "the [white] volunteers dread the night vedette and kindred duties in the aguish localities of Western Florida." The secretary's answer, however, dealt only with the major's further suggestions for the organization of white regiments. [3] A week later Dodson, a colored attendant "about the Senate chamber," made his offer of some "300 reliable colored free citizens of this city who desire to enter the service for the defense of the city." Jacob Dodson was no ordinary custodian: he had been "three times across the Rocky Mountains in the service of the country with Frémont and others." But despite his unusual qualifications his offer was declined. "This Department," Cameron informed him, "has no intention at present to call into the service of the Government any colored soldiers." [4]

The qualifying "at present" may have salved Dodson's disappointment. At any rate, the time had not yet arrived.

Nor had it arrived five months later when Edward Vernon twice wrote Simon Cameron urging his acceptance of a regiment of New York Negroes to be led by "efficient and accomplished white officers." Cameron merely directed Vernon to Governor Morgan of New York, since the War Department had "referred the organization of additional forces to the Governors of the several States." [5]

Toward the end of October, Dr. Miller wrote the secretary to "solicit the privilege of raising from 5,000 to 10,000 freemen to report in sixty days to take any position that may be assigned us (sharp shooters preferred)." There was no mistaking the seriousness of the proposition: if it was not accepted, Dr. Miller assured Cameron, he and his friends would, "if armed and equipped by the Government, fight as guerrillas." Their proposed organization was not to be exclusively Negro: "A part of us are half-breed Indians and legal voters in the State of Michigan." There was nothing half-bred about their determination. "We are all anxious to fight for the maintenance of the Union and the preservation of the principles promulgated by President Lincoln," Miller asserted, "and we are sure of success if allowed an opportunity. In the name of God answer immediately." The opportunity was not allowed, as the immediate answer from the War Department made clear in the involved phraseology of official language: "The Department fully appreciates the patriotic spirit and intelligence which your letter displays, and has no doubt that upon reflection you will perceive that there are sufficient reasons for continuing the course thus far pursued in regard to the important question upon which your letter is based." [6] In short, the war would continue to be a white man's war, as Dr. Miller probably perceived upon reflection.

*   *   *

On April 6, a week before the bombardment of Fort Sumter, the New York *Times* had argued editorially that "the question which we have to meet *is precisely* what it would be if there were not a negro slave on American soil. ... The issue is between

anarchy and order,—between Government and lawlessness,—
between the authority of the Constitution and the reckless will
of those who seek its destruction." A great many Americans,
Abraham Lincoln among them, could have endorsed the *Times*
statement. Six months later, on October 8, the *National Intelligencer* could put the situation accurately in almost the same
language: "The existing war has no direct relation to slavery.
It is a war for the restoration of the Union under the existing
Constitution."

But what a war is in October is not necessarily what it will be
in November or what it may become by another October. Forces
were let loose by the war, and men moved with those forces.
While the war officially had no direct relation to slavery, there
were those who stubbornly persisted in misunderstanding its
nature. Most stubborn and eloquent was Frederick Douglass,
former Maryland slave and spokesman of the free colored people
of the North through *Douglass' Monthly*, which he edited and
published at Rochester, New York. In a lengthy May editorial,
"How to End the War," Douglass took sharp issue with the "soft"
policy of the Lincoln administration.

"A lenient war is a lengthy war," he argued, "and therefore
the worst kind of war." To stop the war effectively before its
evils spread through the whole nation, to stop it on the soil where
it had begun and among those who had begun it, he advocated
"carrying the war into Africa." To do this he would "LET THE
SLAVES AND FREE COLORED PEOPLE BE CALLED INTO
SERVICE, AND FORMED INTO A LIBERATING ARMY, to
march into the South and raise the banner of emancipation
among the slaves." If this seemed radical and extreme, Douglass
was convinced that the circumstances of the war justified it. "The
South having brought revolution and war upon the country," he
reasoned coolly, "and having elected and consented to play at
their fearful game, she has no right to complain if some good as
well as calamity shall result from her own act and deed." [7]

The Rochester Negro leader echoed the charge (already
widely circulated in the North) that the Confederates were not
hesitating to use their slaves and free colored men as a labor
force to construct fortifications. He went further, to maintain that

the Confederates would not scruple to use colored men "on the field of battle ... with guns in their hands, to shoot down the troops of the United States Government." For his part, Douglass was certain that "ten thousand black soldiers might be raised [by the Union] in ... thirty days to march upon the South." He argued that "One black regiment alone would be, in such a war, the full equal of two white ones. The very fact of color in this case would be more terrible than powder and balls. The slaves would learn more as to the nature of the conflict from the presence of one such regiment, than from a thousand preachers."

Frederick Douglass's point of view was that of an American Negro, an articulate Negro, a former slave with a lash-scarred back. To him it was clear in May of 1861 that "Every consideration of justice, humanity and sound policy confirms the wisdom of calling upon black men just now to take up arms in behalf of their country." [8] What he considered "the nature of the conflict" did not become apparent to the mass of Northern and Union men until nearly two years later.

Douglass was painfully aware that their country had not yet seen the wisdom of calling on black men to help. He recalled that white friends had asked him what his people would do in the crisis facing the nation. His answer was a mixture of hope and despair. "Would to God you would let us do something. We lack nothing but your consent. We are ready and would go, counting ourselves happy in being permitted to serve and suffer for the cause of freedom and free institutions. But you won't let us go." As proof of this, Douglass reminded his readers of Benjamin F. Butler's offer of Yankee troops to put down a rumored slave insurrection in Maryland and of the refusal of Negro recruits offered by the free colored people of Boston. While the South marshaled its slaves to help wage war against the Union, Douglass saw in the North "weak and contemptible tenderness toward the bloodthirsty slaveholding traitors, by the Government and people of the country." With the furious eloquence of an Old Testament prophet, he castigated the Union: "Until the nation shall repent of this weakness and folly, until they shall make the cause of their country the cause of freedom, until they shall strike down slavery, the source and center of this gigantic rebellion, they don't deserve the support of a single sable arm, nor will it succeed in crushing the cause of our present troubles." [9] So did the leader and spokesman of American Negroes diagnose the cause of the war, and so did he prescribe a speedy cure for it.

The news columns of *Douglass' Monthly* were written in the same biting, militant language, with the point of view of the editor never for a moment obscure. Regiments of colored men were being formed in New York, Boston, Syracuse. "It now remains for the Government to accept their services," Douglass commented, with the sorrowful admission that their acceptance was "very doubtful." In giving his wholehearted support to the proposed formation of Negro regiments in New York City, Douglass urged the free colored men of the North "to drink as deeply into the martial spirit of the times as possible: [to] organize themselves into societies and companies, purchase arms for themselves, and learn how to use them." This was dangerous advice for anyone to publish in 1861, let alone a Negro, but Frederick Douglass was convinced that the war would probably "reach a complexion where a few black regiments will be absolutely necessary." In such a contingency, he wanted his people not only ready but "casting about for an opportunity to strike for the freedom of the slave and for the rights of human nature." [10]

No vain imaginings were these recruiting activities among Northern Negroes. Some New York colored men in May, catching what Horace Greeley described as the city's "fervid though not very profound enthusiasm" after Sumter, began drilling in a privately hired hall. They had to give up their project, however, when the chief of police warned them that "they must desist from these military exercises, or he could not protect them from popular indignation and assault." [11] While the military exercises in this instance seem to have come to an end, other New York Negroes were not so easily discouraged, and on July 26, 1861, three regiments of colored men were offered to the governor of New York to serve for the duration of the war. The colored population of the state guaranteed not only the arms, clothing, and equipment of these troops but also their pay and provisions! The governor, however, felt compelled to decline this extremely generous offer, "There being no authority to enroll colored men . . ." [12] The soul of old John Brown may have been marching on, but it marched in exclusively white company.

* * *

During the early months of the war, both North and South were troubled with rumors of Negro regiments being raised by their opponents, and various spokesmen, official and unofficial, tried to quiet these rumors and the fears they naturally inspired. As early as April 1, 1861, the New York *Times* had denied a charge by the Charleston (S. C.) *Mercury* that the Lincoln administration was planning to arm "the free blacks of the North to aid insurgent negroes in the South." The *Times* decried "a journalism that inculcates and a people who believe such monstrous inventions" and lamented the fact that Northern newspapers contradicting such nonsense were excluded from the South so that Southern minds were "poisoned systematically, while rigid care is taken that no antidote of truth shall be administered." The New York paper's discussion of the matter ended on this ominous note: "Sooner or later the truth must become known to the people of the Cotton States, and on their own plantations will arise the Nemesis that is to exact full retribution."

Again on April 12, the very day on which the war began, the *Times* berated the New York *Journal of Commerce* for insinuating that the administration approved William Lloyd Garrison's suggestion that slave insurrections be stirred up in the South. Indignantly the *Times* denied any such approval and concluded, "Whatever may be the course or the issue of the war that seems to be impending, we trust it will not be accompanied by the unutterable horrors of a servile insurrection." In like manner, on May 10, the Nashville (Tenn.) *Republican Banner*, a Union paper, tried to scotch rumors of Northern regiments of fugitive slaves by reprinting a dispatch from the New York *Tribune*. Apparently, "a person formerly in the diplomatic service" had offered to raise a brigade of runaway slaves in Canada. Administration reaction was unequivocal: ". . . under no circumstances whatever would the Government listen to any such proposition."

On May 12 the *Times* in a lighter vein discussed Southern newspaper reports of the raising of Negro troops by the South, in Virginia, Alabama, and Louisiana specifically. The *Times* editorial writer was wryly amused at these indications of "the delirious devotion to the revolutionary cause of the free darkies . . . who loll in luxury on the plantations of Alabama, or linger over their *paté de fois gras,* or Chateau Lafitte, by the romantic swamps of the Savannah." The *Times* suggested that Northern Negroes were eager to meet their Southern counterparts in arms halfway: some had even proposed "to Jeff. Davis that if he will rendezvous the whole of his black warriors somewhere on the coast of South Carolina, they will be delighted to meet them and him *there,* on any day he may name—he to general the black revolutionary cohorts, and Fred. Hannibal Douglass to lead the enemy." In a more serious tone, the *Times* summed up arguments in favor of the use of Negro troops by the North, particularly in the semitropical regions of the South, and pointed out that Negroes had long served in both the French and British armies. These arguments aside, the New York paper admitted that "for the present at least, the revolutionists must have the monopoly of the negro element in their army."

In Washington on May 20 the *National Intelligencer* discounted a story credited to the New Orleans *Picayune* of a meeting of the free colored population of the Crescent City to organize for military purposes. The *Intelligencer* had seen nothing in New Orleans newspapers "which would authorize the announcement that the services of colored troops had been accepted," and went on to comment with acid sarcasm on the failure of a movement in Massachusetts to open the Bay State militia to Negroes.

Whatever the disclaimers of the *National Intelligencer,* however, newspapers in the Deep South did not uniformly disapprove of efforts to enlist the aid of free colored men for the States' Rights cause. On May 2 the Shreveport (La.) *Daily News* reprinted the *Picayune* item referred to by the Washington paper: "A very large meeting of the free colored men" of New Orleans had been held "to take measures to form a military organization, and to tender their services to the Governor of Louisiana." John Dickinson, proprietor of the Shreveport paper and a Confederate leader of some stature in his part of the South, made no editorial criticism of this news, and on the following day he reprinted a more extensive story from the Baton

Rouge *Gazette & Comet.* This reported that "our honored and respected friend and fellow citizen Capt. H. B. Favrot, is at work mustering into service the free colored men of the city and has already about thirty of them enrolled." Far from disapproving, the Baton Rouge paper had nothing but praise for the captain and his project. "We count on [the free colored people] as a host in any emergency; their lives and property; the laws under which they live and receive protection from tyranny and despotism, are all in jeopardy in this perilous hour. The recollections of the 8th of January 1812 [1815], and their important part, bravely and honorably maintained in that action, nerves them now to emulate the heroes of the olden time. For his patriotic move, in this direction, Capt. Favrot deserves the lasting gratitude of a generous people." Certainly in Shreveport, Baton Rouge, and New Orleans there seems to have been little reluctance to call on Negroes, free men of color, to help in the war for Southern independence.

For the suggestion that Negroes be used as soldiers by the Union, however, John Dickinson of the Shreveport *Daily News* had only bitter scorn. In mid-May he warned colored men of what he considered the deceitful motives of Northern advocates of Negro regiments. "How the colored portion of the North can be such fools as to believe the strong profession of love for them by the Black Republicans," John Dickinson could not conceive. "Repeatedly," he charged, "have they been humbugged by these monsters in human shape, in all manner of ways; yet they still, strange to say, seem to place implicit confidence in all that is poured into their ever eager ears by that class of men, who have proved a curse to this country."

As evidence of Northern rascality, the Shreveport editor selected this extract from the Boston *Traveller* of May 8: "New Orleans should be occupied, and a strong chain of positions established along the Mississippi. *As it would be a great sacrifice of life to occupy these positions with white men during the summer months, it may become necessary to enlist a certain number of black regiments for this purpose. . . .* There are a great number of free blacks at the North desirous of responding to the call and we hope now they will be enlisted, organized, *and prepared to occupy the yellow fever posts in the enemy's country, during the SUMMER MONTHS.*" The italics and capitals are of Louisiana rather than Massachusetts origin.

"If the federalists can succeed in getting *Black Regiments* for this purpose," Dickinson commented, "we are greatly mistaken, for in the North are to be found persons of the black class, who are well educated, and fully capable to form their own opinions on the subject; they, if we mistake not, will be the very worst regiments to controle [*sic*], for in all probability they will see into the cunning of their pretended friends and sympathizers and revolt; thus instead of being used as tools against us, they will be of material benefit to us of the South." How would the tables be turned? "They will commence the fight among themselves," John Dickinson believed, "rather than be subjected to such treatment at the hands of the Abolitionists." And he had some further word for his opposite number in Boston: "if the editor of the Traveler imagines that the free blacks of the North, do not fear *yellow jack,* he knows very little about their character, for they fear it more than the whites . . ." Finally, Dickinson concluded, Northern Negroes, having become "disgustingly impudent, and intractable," would not make good soldiers. The Black Republicans had "spoilt that class of their population, and soon, we opine, they will rue the day they ever dabbled in the negro question." [13]

*   *   *

Whatever policies the newspapers discussed, the official policy of the Lincoln administration had been made clear in the early months of the war: this was no abolitionist war, and servile insurrection had no place in it. To the dismay of the abolitionists, Union soldiers seemed to be doing more to protect the institution of human slavery than they were to put down the Confederacy. In late April, Brigadier General Benjamin F. Butler, commanding Massachusetts troops in Maryland, offered those troops to Governor Thomas H. Hicks to help suppress a rumored slave uprising. [14] Here for once Ben Butler's action and attitude were in keeping with administration policy. Lincoln's great concern during the first third of the war was to keep the sensitive Border states—Maryland, Kentucky, Missouri, and parts of Virginia— loyal to the Union, or at the very least to prevent their secession.

One good way to retain the loyalty of Union men and slave-holders in those states was to quiet their fears of invading abolitionist armies bearing emancipation on their bayonets.

Other Union officers in May and June of 1861 did their part to make administration policy clear. Brigadier General William S. Harney, commanding the Military Department of the West, was "not a little astonished" when Thomas T. Gantt of St. Louis asked him whether the federal government intended "to interfere with the institution of negro slavery in Missouri or any slave State or impair the security of that description of property." In answering Gantt, Harney pointed out that since the beginning of the war fugitive slaves coming into Union lines had been returned to their owners, and he referred to Butler's offer to Hicks. "Incendiaries have asked of the President permission to invade the Southern States," Harney advised Gantt, "and have been warned that any attempt to do this will be punished as a crime." [15] This was the very reverse of radicalism.

In late May, when young General George B. McClellan began his campaign to capture Grafton in what is now West Virginia, he made it plain that his Northern armies would have no part of any abolitionist crusade. "Preserve the strictest discipline," he ordered his colonels; "See that the rights and property of the people are respected, and repress all attempts at negro insurrection." Here was no John Brown. To the Union men of Western Virginia, McClellan proclaimed that his soldiers would "with an iron hand, crush any attempt at insurrection" on the part of their slaves.[16]

General Robert Patterson, commanding the Department of Pennsylvania, also emphasized this policy in an address to his troops about to march south in early June. "You must bear in mind you are going for the good of the whole country," he cautioned his men, "and that while it is your duty to punish sedition, you must protect the loyal, and, should occasion offer, at once suppress servile insurrections." [17] With the best reason in the world the *National Intelligencer* remarked on June 12 that the "commanders of the federal forces seem to have vied with each other in repelling all suspicions of an unfriendly purpose toward the peculiar domestic institution of the Southern States." This same editorial showed how baseless were Southern apprehensions, maintaining what should have been perfectly obvious: "the war now waging is certainly not directed against slavery . . ."

*   *   *

While such observations must have made enjoyable reading for many Americans, North as well as South, there were others to whom they were anathema. One such was Frederick Douglass, who stubbornly and indignantly insisted that the Union ought to "Send no more slaves back to their rebel master; offer to put down no more slave insurrections *'with an iron hand,'* reject no more black troops; release no more slaveholding rebels on their word of honor; hang or imprison for life all pirates; and henceforth let the war cry be, down with treason, and down with slavery, the cause of treason." [18] And on July 9 ninety-two members of the House of Representatives voted with Owen Lovejoy of Illinois, brother of the martyred abolitionist editor Elijah Lovejoy, to support his resolution asserting that "it is no part of the duty of the soldiers of the United States to capture and return fugitive slaves." [19]

Not all Union generals were as faithful as Harney and McClellan and Patterson in carrying out the lenient Lincoln policy. Toward the end of the summer Major General John Charles Frémont, commanding the Western Department at St. Louis, took matters into his own hands and tried to revise policy in a new direction. Frémont was a powerful figure in the West and in the Republican party. He had carried the Republican standard in the presidential campaign of 1856, and in 1861 he was a prominent member of the party's antislavery wing. In August of that year Frémont found his position a desperate one, especially after the Union defeat at Wilson's Creek in southwestern Missouri. However difficult his position in Missouri, however broad and indefinite Lincoln's instructions to Frémont, the Pathfinder certainly overstepped the bounds of the politically practical in his proclamation of August 30. [20] He ordered martial law over the entire state, which the military situation probably justified. But then he went beyond martial law, beyond even the First Confiscation Act passed by a Congress smarting under the humiliation of the Union disaster at Bull Run, and proclaimed that "The property, real and personal, of all persons in the State of Missouri who shall take up arms against the United States, or who shall be directly proven to have taken an active part with their enemies in the field, is declared to be confiscated to the public use, and their slaves, if any they have, are hereby declared freemen." [21] This position was, as Horace Greeley put it, "in advance of any that had yet been sanctioned at Washington." [22]

Owen Lovejoy was one of the political advisers in the picturesque Frémont entourage, which helps to explain the general's emancipation order, particularly since Lovejoy's determination had been encouraged in July by a letter from Gerrit Smith in which the New York abolitionist had urged the propriety and practicality of freeing the slaves. [23] But whether urged to his radical step by Lovejoy or by his own strong antislavery convictions, Frémont presented the Lincoln administration with a serious problem. To sustain the proclamation and widen the application of its principles would convert the war for the preservation of the Union into a war for the extermination of slavery. Lincoln was a long way from this, however much support for the change rallied behind Frémont. Accordingly, the president made it clear that the general must alter his proclamation. Frémont, once committed to a line of action, was difficult to move; he required a direct presidential order in addition to Lincoln's original personal dispatch written "in a spirit of caution, and not of censure." With this requirement the president "very cheerfully" complied on September 11, and the proclamation was altered "to conform to, and not to transcend" the provisions of the First Confiscation Act. [24]

So was the lightning withdrawn from the Frémont thunderbolt. But the nation had seen and heard the flash and the roll. In the Middle West and all across the North the press had been quick to commend what Frémont had done. Even Secretary of War Cameron had been moved to telegraph his congratulations, only discovering afterward that the president disapproved. [25] When the president had asserted his authority and the general had changed his order, a storm of consternation, disbelief, and frustrated rage swept the country even as jubilation had swept it less than a fortnight earlier. William Lloyd Garrison, never any respecter of persons or institutions, published the presidential order enclosed in the black bands of mourning and charged Lincoln with "a serious dereliction of duty." [26]

For a few days it had seemed as if the Civil War was about to become more than a struggle to bring the eleven wayward sisters back into the family. For a few days the prospects had seemed bright for a crusade against the institution that lay at the base of the sectional conflict. The hopes of the abolitionists had been raised high. Now, with the war already five months old, administration policy had once more been clearly asserted— the old lenient, conciliatory policy.

The *National Intelligencer* of September 23 expressed reasonable criticism of Frémont's radical action and sustained Lincoln's position. "It must be obvious to all who pause to reflect on the relations of slavery to this conflict," the *Intelligencer* editorial suggested, "that, so far as they may be suspended or destroyed by war, it must be mainly due to such incidental effects as are likely to result from the exigencies of military movements made in States 'wholly or partially under insurrectionary control.' Even if the liberation of slaves were an avowed object of the war, it could be accomplished only in the track of a liberating army, as mere edicts of emancipation would be utterly powerless except so far as they are carried into effect by the law of force, against the wishes and interests of the parties concerned as slaveholders . . ." The Washington paper should have held the type over to run again one year later. The editorial concluded with a reasonable appeal to "the patriot, equally with the humanitarian, to sustain the hands of the President in the just and legal attitude he has taken, in conformity with the Constitution and the laws under this head."

But the time for reasonableness was growing short. Certainly there were reasonable men who could understand how important Border state loyalty was to the Union, but how long could the sentiments of slaveholders in Maryland, Kentucky, and Missouri, no matter how loyal, stand in the way of the growing antislavery feeling of the North? James Russell Lowell struck responsive chords in many Northern hearts when he asked, after Lincoln had vetoed Frémont's order, "How many times are we to save Kentucky and lose our self-respect?" [27]

John Charles Frémont was not long to play a prominent role

in the war. Short weeks later he was relieved of command in
the Western Department and replaced by a regular army officer,
Major General David Hunter. Regular officers, products of the
military academy at West Point, were, in Horace Greeley's
opinion, "educated . . . in a faith that identified devotion to
Slavery with loyalty to the Federal Constitution and Government . . ." [28] David Hunter was presumed to be safely conservative in the fall of 1861. Certainly he was more capable and experienced in military affairs than Frémont. Of his personal
loyalty to the president, Lincoln could have no doubts. Not until
the spring of 1862, as commanding general of the Department
of the South, would this West Pointer violate at last the Greeley
stereotype.

*   *   *

While the question of emancipation was temporarily settled
with the withdrawal of Frémont's proclamation, another matter
pregnant with controversy now pushed insistently to the fore.
This was the question of what role, if any, the Negro might play
in the war—the Negro soldier question. While the North hesitated, the South acted.

Certainly the Confederacy as such, the central government of
the Confederate States of America, did nothing conclusive about
enrolling Negro soldiers until March, 1865, too late to be of any
value. But individual Southern states were recruiting free
Negroes even before First Bull Run. In June of 1861 the legislature of Tennessee authorized the use in the "military service
of the State [of] all free male persons of color between the ages
of fifteen and fifty." [29] Newspaper reports, North and South,
show that active steps were taken to enforce this law. The
National Intelligencer on August 6 credited the Cincinnati
Gazette with this dispatch: "A number of colored people have
arrived in Cincinnati from Tennessee, having fled to escape the
conscription ordered . . . of all free colored men . . . for the Confederate Army, and all women who are fit for service for camp
and hospital service. They state that the impressment was without previous notice, and so sudden that few escaped. Those who
came here had to abandon everything, some of them considerable
property. They state that . . . if they serve faithfully through the

war they shall be made citizens." The report ended with the observation that "In the North colored companies have been offered to the Government and rejected."

The Memphis *Avalanche* of September 3 reported a "procession of several hundred stout negro men" marching through that West Tennessee city "in military order, under command of Confederate officers." Instead of the usual weapons they carried "shovels, axes, blankets, &c." According to the *Avalanche,* "A merrier set were never seen. They were brimful of patriotism, shouting for Jeff. Davis and singing war songs." Four days later the same newspaper declared that "Upwards of 1,000 negroes, armed with spades and pickaxes, have passed through the city within the past few days. Their destination is unknown; but it is supposed that they are on their way to the 'other side of Jordan.' " [30] Beneath the jocular surface of these reports, under the minstrel-show language typical of Southern comment on Negro participation in the Civil War, some hard facts are discernible. Accustomed to using Negroes for their heaviest manual work, Southern states were mobilizing their slave and free Negro manpower. While not armed as soldiers, these Negroes were nevertheless under military command and equipped to do essential military labor.

There were reports, too, of Confederate use of Negroes as soldiers as well as laborers. The scouts of the 1st Vermont Infantry reported a Richmond howitzer battery manned by Negroes at Newmarket Bridge, Virginia, in August. The regiment's colonel, J. W. Phelps, commenting on his scouts' report, considered their estimate of Confederate numbers exaggerated, but, he added, "with regard to their artillery, and its being manned in part by negroes, I think the report is probably correct." [31]

During the fall of 1861, as talk of the use of Negro soldiers by the Union increased, the primary argument was that the South had already set the precedent. With his usual directness Frederick Douglass stated the case. "It is now pretty well established," he asserted, "that there are at the present moment many colored men in the Confederate army doing duty not only as cooks, servants, and laborers, but as real soldiers, having muskets on their shoulders, and bullets in their pockets, ready to shoot down loyal troops, and do all that soldiers may do to destroy the Federal Government and build up that of the traitors and rebels. There were such soldiers at Manassas, and they are probably there still. There is a negro in the army as well as in the fence, and our Government is likely to find it out before the war comes to an end. That the negroes are numerous in the rebel army, and do for that army its heaviest work, is beyond question." [32]

The Chicago *Tribune* summed up the question even more succinctly. After reporting the successful use of Fortress Monroe fugitive slaves as gun crew of a 32-pounder aboard one of the ships of the Union expedition against the Hatteras forts, the *Tribune* asked, "What great reason is there for not allowing more contrabands to lend a hand in defense of the Stars and Stripes? Negroes are employed by the thousands in the rebel armies, to fight against the Union. Why not let 'nigger' fight 'nigger'?" [33] For that matter, if the Union Navy could use the "strong black arm," why could not the army do likewise?

Both army and navy had employed Negro laborers, cooks, and servants on a rather extensive scale by the end of 1861, and, thanks in some measure to Ben Butler, the word "contraband" had passed into common usage as meaning a fugitive from Southern slavery. [34] But the Union Navy had decided to go all the way and enlist Negroes with a directness completely lacking in the army approach to the question. As naval vessels accumulated fugitives from Virginia plantations up and down the Rappahannock through the summer months, the problem of their status in the service demanded solution. On September 25, Secretary of the Navy Gideon Welles solved the problem. "The Department finds it necessary," he wrote, "to adopt a regulation with respect to the large number of persons of color, commonly known as contrabands, now subsisted at the navy yard and on board ships of war." They could hardly be sent away, Welles reasoned, "nor can they be maintained unemployed, and it is not proper that they should be compelled to render necessary and regular services without a standard compensation. You are therefore authorized, when their service can be made useful, to enlist them for the naval service, under the same forms and regulations as apply to other enlistments. They will be allowed, however, no higher rating than 'boys,' at a compensation of $10 per

month and one ration per day." [35] That was it. They would be
underpaid, and their naval careers could describe no glorious
arcs in the sky, but Gideon Welles had decreed that the United
States navy would enlist Negroes to help man the ships and guns
of the Union. This Welles regulation stands as a forgotten milestone in the Negro's fight for the right to participate in the Civil
War on the side of the Union.

*   *   *

Perhaps it was the example of Gideon Welles that led Simon
Cameron into a series of acts that helped to end his cabinet
career. The secretary of war was slowly moving toward the
abolitionist position. His enthusiastic and impolitic congratula-
tion of Frémont's abortive emancipation order is evidence of the
change. Other evidence is not hard to find. While Cameron hesitated to grant authority for the raising of Negro soldiers to
private individuals outside the army, such as Vernon and Miller,
his department issued orders of a revolutionary nature on October 14, 1861: Brigadier General Thomas W. Sherman was
authorized to employ fugitive slaves as Union soldiers in South
Carolina! [36]

This General Sherman, a Rhode Islander and West Point
graduate, class of 1836, an almost forgotten man in Civil War
histories, commanded the Port Royal Expedition against the
coast of South Carolina in November of 1861. The expedition,
like its general, has been almost lost to history. Planning for it
began under the direction of Secretary of the Navy Welles in the
days immediately following the federal defeat at First Bull Run.
After a series of top-level strategy meetings, the decision was
made to assemble naval craft, transports, an army force of
13,000 men, and a battalion of Marines in Long Island Sound
and at Annapolis, Maryland. The objective was to secure a
beachhead on Hilton Head Island and adjoining bits of mud and
sand in the Sea Islands off South Carolina. [37] This combined
operation was a serious gamble, but it provides some measure of
Union determination to carry the war south into the home of
secession. While its immediate object was to establish an auxiliary base for the Atlantic blockade of Confederate shipping, it

was not merely incidental that Hilton Head was thirty miles from Savannah and fifty miles from Charleston.

Since General Sherman, a veteran of the Seminole and the Mexican War, was leading a small expedition into hostile country, it seemed prudent to instruct him to use whatever assistance he might find once he got ashore. Hence the General Instructions of October 14. "You will. . ." the orders ran, "avail yourself of the service of any persons, whether fugitives from labor or not, who may offer them to the National Government. You will employ such persons in such services as they may be fitted for— either as ordinary employes, or, if special circumstances seem to require it, in any other capacity, with such organization (in squads, companies, or otherwise) as you may deem most beneficial to the service . . ." Although the words "Negro" and "soldiers" did not appear, here was authority for the military organization of colored men. But it was hardly intended as blanket authority; the next line proved that: "this, however, not being a general arming of them for military service." It was "well understood," by Horace Greeley at least, "that this sentence was inserted by the President in revising the order." [38]

The rest of the instructions were more nearly in accord with administration policy. "You will assure all loyal masters," the orders ran smoothly, "that Congress will provide just compensation to them for the loss of the services of the persons so employed." Justification of the policy followed: "It is believed that the course thus indicated will best secure the substantial rights of loyal masters, and the benefits to the United States of the services of all disposed to support the Government, while it will avoid all interference with the social systems or local institutions of every State, beyond that which insurrection makes unavoidable and which a restoration of peaceful relations to the Union under the Constitution will immediately remove." [39]

This was policy based on military expediency and the limited administration view of the war. Lacking the men to give Sherman forces sufficient to do more than secure a peripheral position on Hilton Head and Port Royal islands, the secretary of war felt it necessary to include in his orders authority to use as auxiliaries any persons available "whether fugitives from labor or not." Lincoln, for his part, was apparently willing to permit Cameron's orders to be issued with the specific limitation that no general arming of "them" was authorized, contemplated, or desired.

With the navy under Flag Officer Samuel F. DuPont pre-empting the glorious task of bombarding and reducing Forts Walker and Beauregard at the entrance of Port Royal Sound, the best harbor available between Hatteras and Florida, the Sherman expedition secured a beachhead on November 7.[40] Once ashore, Sherman issued a proclamation to the people of South Carolina reminiscent of McClellan's proclamation on the eve of his invasion of Western Virginia. In apologetic tones, the general explained his forcible intrusion upon the Palmetto State, the state in which secession had first flowered and from whose soil the first shots of the war had been fired. "In obedience to the orders of the President of these United States," Sherman began, "I have landed on your shores with a small force of National troops." Were it not for his 25-year record of loyal service to the nation, one might suspect that Sherman was in-viting the rebels to capture or push into the ocean his "small force."

With obviously mingled emotions and loyalties colored by memories of his years at Fort Moultrie in Charleston, the in-vading general continued: "The dictates of a duty which, under the Constitution, I owe to a great sovereign State, and to a proud and hospitable people, among whom I have passed some of the pleasantest days of my life, prompt me to proclaim that we have come among you with no feelings of personal animosity; no desire to harm your citizens, destroy your property, or interfere with any of your lawful rights, or your social and local insti-tutions, beyond what the causes herein briefly alluded to may render unavoidable." [41] It should surprise no literate person that General Sherman never availed himself of the opportunity his instructions provided to raise Negro troops.

However conciliatory Sherman's proclamation, the people of the immediate locality seem not to have been reassured by it. John B. Lance, a young Confederate soldier in Beaufort District, wrote his family three days after the Union landings, and his message was not a happy one. "I have bad news to rite to you," he scribbled, "the Yankies have taken Beaufort Island . . . it is a great loss to the South [.] I saw a man that knows all about it this morning [.] . . . they say it was one of the fines[t] harbors for Ships that is in the South [.] the people are verry Badley sceard down here[;] they think we will have hot times here." [42] How well founded were their fears they could not have known, nor was Thomas the Sherman to bring them any speedy realization.

*   *   *

As 1861 drew to a close, Simon Cameron moved fatally toward public support of the radical notion of arming Negroes. On November 20, Attorney General Edward Bates recorded his displeasure with the secretary of war: the secretary at a social gathering which included newspapermen had had the bad taste to come out openly in favor of organizing Negro soldiers in the South, as he had in a cabinet meeting a few days earlier. With Secretary of the Interior Caleb Smith, Bates had "opposed it vehemently," as he had in the cabinet meeting. Bates was the more upset that "some prying letter writer communicated the whole affair to the N. Y. papers (the *Times*) and so, the matter took the open air." [43]

The attorney general may have been displeased with Cameron's advocacy of Negro soldiers, but he should not have been surprised. The secretary of war had been making his position increasingly clear. He had congratulated Frémont in September; he had issued the Sherman orders in October; and in mid-November, on the occasion of an official visit to the camp of a New York infantry regiment near Washington, he had openly suggested arming Negroes. This regiment, the 65th New York Volunteers, was commanded by Colonel John Cochrane, nephew of Gerrit Smith and a former States' Rights Democrat who had turned radical Unionist with the fall of Sumter.

On November 13, Colonel Cochrane's regiment received new uniforms, and, according to the New York *Tribune* of the following day, "On the occasion the Colonel made a speech in which he distinctly enunciated the doctrine of emancipation. Secretary Cameron followed in a stirring address strongly endorsing the remarks of Col. Cochrane, and especially the sentiments expressed by the eloquent soldier touching the slave question. He declared that the time for timidity had gone by." Cameron's "address" appeared on the same page of the *Tribune* and did not contain the word "timidity." The secretary did, however, stress using the Negro for reasons of military necessity, and he asserted that "every means which God has placed in our hands it is our duty to use for the purpose of protecting ourselves."

Perhaps the New York *Times* of November 14 gave a more accurate account of what happened at the camp of the 65th New York. A *Times* correspondent wrote: "Col. John Cochrane made a speech . . . in which he took strong grounds for emancipation as a military necessity. He contended that the duty of the Government . . . is to take the negro by the hand, place in it a musket, and set him loose upon his master. Col. Cochrane's speech being concluded, Secretary Cameron was called upon. He responded in a few remarks, understood to express a concurrence in the general tenor of Col. Cochrane's sentiments."

Since it was still the expressed policy of the government to conciliate the South and to play down emancipation and any hint of arming Negroes, Cameron, as a member of Lincoln's cabinet, might better have reprimanded Cochrane than pronounced agreement with him. But Cameron went further than that. When the colonel made a speechmaking tour toward the close of November, a tour chiefly devoted to advocating the arming of Negro soldiers, Simon Cameron accompanied him to New York and to Springfield, Massachusetts, and sat on the platform, lending his tacit support to the radical doctrine of John Cochrane.[44]

In December, Cameron overplayed his hand and stretched the president's patience to the breaking point. In the only "annual" report Cameron ever made as secretary of war he devoted much space to the Negro question, concluding with a strong recommendation that the slaves of rebels should be armed or at least declared free. "If it shall be found that the men who have been held by the Rebels as slaves are capable of bearing arms and performing efficient military service," Cameron argued, "it is the right, and may become the duty, of this Government to arm and equip them, and employ their services against the Rebels, under proper military regulations, discipline, and command." [45]

Not only did Simon Cameron here urge more radical action than any of his cabinet colleagues or any other high officer of the administration had dared openly, but he compounded the felony by ordering copies of his report printed and distributed to the postmasters of key Northern cities with instructions that these copies be handed to the press as soon as Lincoln's annual message had been read to Congress. And Cameron dared make these arrangements even before the president had seen his report!

Gideon Welles described the denouement as he saw it unfold. Lincoln, he wrote, "was displeased with portions of the report . . . and quite as much displeased that it had been printed, and to some extent distributed without its first being submitted to him. He was especially displeased with that part which assumed to state or enunciate the policy to be pursued by the Administration in regard to slaves." As presidential displeasure burst about him, Secretary of War Cameron attempted to justify his action "on the ground that there was nothing novel in his report—that it was the course pursued by the Army which had been acquiesced in and he supposed approved by the President and Cabinet," a probable reference to the Sherman orders of October. That Lincoln was hardly impressed by this defense is clear from Gideon Welles's record: "The President ordered that part of the report which he deemed instrusive and objectionable to be expunged, and thus expurgated it was transmitted with the other documents that accompanied the President's message to Congress." [46]

There was little time left for Cameron as a member of Lincoln's cabinet. The secretary had already come under attack for the confusion that reigned in his department and, more damaging, for his purchases of army supplies. His handling of the Negro soldier issue, his persistence in repeatedly bringing up the matter and maintaining a position widely at variance with the policy of his president, sealed Cameron's fate. Lincoln apparently decided in early December to rid himself of the embarrassment of the Pennsylvanian's presence in his official family. In early January the occasion presented itself when Cassius M. Clay requested release from his post as minister to Russia.

Quietly Lincoln accepted Clay's resignation, and on January 11,
1862, he appointed Simon Cameron to represent the United
States at the court of the czars.[47]

*   *   *

Meanwhile Union generals were developing individual variations of administration policy as they applied that policy in their
individual commands. Wherever Union forces touched slave
territory, fugitives made their way to Union camps and ships,
thus providing a continuing problem and raw material for more
problems. By and large, the generals followed what had come to
be known as the "Butler" policy of using contrabands as teamsters, cooks, officers' servants, and laborers. This policy seems to
have been favorably enough received in the North. The *National
Intelligencer*, hardly an abolitionist sheet, admitted on October
8 that in using Negro labor "the National Government will only
follow the example of the Confederate rebels." The Albany
(N. Y.) *Journal* described Butler's contraband policy as "the
true one" and argued that "it is just as clearly right to transfer
these slaves as fast as possible from the corn fields to the trenches
as it is to appropriate a drove of the enemy's beeves from his to
our own shambles." [48]

Major General John E. Wool, in command at Fortress Monroe,
followed the Butler example.[49] But that example was not uniformly accepted by the armies of the North. Major General John
A. Dix, commanding in Accomac and Northampton counties,
Virginia, discovered a method of avoiding the fugitive problem
altogether. "Special directions having been given," he pointed
out, "not to interfere with the condition of any person held to
domestic service; and, in order that there may be no ground for
mistake or pretext for misrepresentation, commanders of regiments and corps have been instructed not to permit any such
persons to come within their lines." [50] Butler and Wool never
prevented fugitives from entering their lines, and, once they
were in, they made good use of them. Dix would not go that far.
His area of Union control was not going to become a branch line
of the underground railway. Then, in November, a comparatively little-known general named Halleck went Dix one better
and ordered fugitives already within his lines to be ejected.

On the same day that Edward Bates confided his disgust with
Cameron's conduct to his vinegarish diary, Major General Henry
W. Halleck issued General Orders, No. 3, November 20, from
his St. Louis headquarters. The order became widely known,
and as widely hated, by radicals and abolitionists across the
entire North. It is hard to imagine a greater contrast than that
between Halleck and Frémont, especially in their understanding
of the nature of the war. Frémont had run far ahead of administration policy; Halleck ran far behind, and ordered a complete
reversal of the Butler policy. Moreover, what he ordered was in
utter disregard of the Lovejoy Resolution of July 9. Halleck's
Order No. 3 tersely directed that no fugitives "be hereafter permitted to enter the lines of any camp or of any forces on the
march, and that any now within such lines be immediately excluded therefrom." [51] Halleck argued in defense of his order that
it was purely military and not political in nature. He had merely
taken what he considered were elementary precautions to prevent
conveyance to the enemy of "important information respecting
the number and condition" of his forces.

While it is difficult to refute Halleck's insistence that "un-
authorized persons" ought to be prevented from entering and
leaving his lines, it is hard to quarrel with Horace Greeley's
opinion that the practical effect of Order No. 3 was "the re-
manding of all slaves to their masters—seven-eighths of whom
were most envenomed, implacable Rebels—by depriving them of
refuge within our lines from these masters' power." [52] Guided
only by narrow military considerations, Halleck had overlooked
what was more and more to be shown as Union forces moved
south,—the fact that in many regions the best friends, even the
only friends, to the Union were the slaves themselves. Small
wonder that a storm of protest burst about the head of "Old
Brains" for this reversal of the Butler contraband policy.

Perhaps Halleck actually helped in the over-all development
of a broadening war policy. Certainly Order No. 3 became
a popular talking point, a rallying point for radicals in the army,
in the Congress that assembled in December, and in various
centers of abolitionist sentiment. With his habitual lack of understanding of political matters, Halleck made an issue of the reception of fugitives by the armed forces of the Union. As a result,

the whole subject of slaves and slavery was brought into sharp focus only a few days before the second session of the Thirty-seventh Congress convened.

When Congress assembled on December 2, 1861, it quickly showed a disposition to come to grips with the badly tangled problem of what to do with the slaves of rebels. As the radicals followed up their beginnings of July and August with more definite efforts to take control of the conduct of the war, both House and Senate were soon jammed with bills at striking variance with Lincoln's policies. Lyman Trumbull of Illinois, author of the First Confiscation Act, announced on the first day of the session that he would introduce a new bill for confiscating rebel property and freeing "the persons they hold in slavery." Good as his word, Trumbull introduced such a bill three days later, and in presenting it he set forth the sentiments of the radicals. "They who deny their allegiance to the Government," he maintained, "have no right to claim its protection. Let the Government cease to afford it; deal with them and their property as their crimes deserve; prosecute the war with vigor, and it will soon be brought to a successful issue." [53]

Owen Lovejoy, true to form, introduced a bill to make it a penal offense "for any officer or private of the Army or Navy to capture or return, or aid in the capture or return, of fugitive slaves." When that bill dropped out of sight in the maze of legislation before the session, Lovejoy introduced a resolution to require the secretary of war to revoke the first section of Halleck's Order No. 3. After long and heated debate this resolution was tabled on December 13.[54] In the Senate, Henry Wilson of Massachusetts took up the cudgels for similar ends, and on December 18 the resolution of his colleague, Charles Sumner, was adopted, directing the Committee on Military Affairs "to consider the expediency of providing by additional legislation that our national armies shall not be employed in the surrender of fugitive slaves." [55] This led directly to an additional Article of War in the following March. While the temper of the new Congress was clearly shown to be fractious and restive, there was little progress in either house until the middle of 1862, when legislation looking to a change in the nature of the war was passed. By that time the use of Negro troops had passed from the realm of radical possibility into the shape of uniformed fact.

*   *   *

The end of 1861 found the Lincoln administration still far from accepting the radical interpretation of the war and just as far from using Negro soldiers in prosecuting it. Lincoln's annual message to Congress had nothing more to suggest in the premises than a plan to colonize all slaves brought to freedom by the operation of the First Confiscation Act or who might be freed by the action of individual states. "It might be well to consider, too," the president continued, "whether the free colored people already in the United States could not, so far as individuals may desire, be included in such colonization." [56]

Some Americans found this the next thing to no solution at all. The Emporia (Kan.) *News* of December 21 editorialized on the subject "What Shall Be Done with Slavery?" and argued, "Set the slave free, and you deal a blow at the Rebellion which will hurt it worse than anything which has yet been done." The Kansas paper would not stop with emancipation. "We believe with Cameron, Butler [what foresight!], and Cochrane," it asserted, "that they should also be armed, and made to fight for the Union. If the South uses them to shoot down our brave sons, ought we not to retaliate by using them to subdue the enemies of the Government?"

Three months earlier Frederick Douglass had made a more dignified and considered recommendation. "Let it be known," he had written in September, "that the American flag is the flag of freedom to all who will rally under it and defend it with their blood." Once more Douglass had urged, "Let colored troops from the North be enlisted and permitted to share the danger and honor of upholding the Government. Such a course would revive the languishing spirit of the North, and sickly over with the pale cast of thought, the now proud and triumphant spirit of the armed slaveholding traitors of the South." More than that, the Negro leader was convinced that his proposal would "lift the war into the dignity of a war for progress and civilization, and save it from the reproach of being merely a war for retaining under one

rule a people who think they can govern themselves. It would
bring not only Garibaldi and his twenty thousand Italian braves
to our side, but what is more important still, our own sense of
right, and the sympathy of enlightened and humane men throughout the world." [57]

Frederick Douglass's thought carried far beyond the mere retaliation suggested by the Emporia *News*. As he was later to
record, he saw in the war "the end of slavery"; and his "interest
in the success of the North was largely due to this belief." [58]
Winning the war was an empty concept for the Rochester editor
if it was to mean only the defeat of the Southern Confederacy.
Winning the war for him meant also the winning of freedom for
his people.

At the end of 1861 Douglass and his people could look back
over nine months of war and find little solid accomplishment.
The South still held the Union at bay. The slaves were still slaves.
The enthusiastic efforts of American Negroes to contribute some
share of the war effort had been declined on almost every hand.
Only in the Union Navy had they been granted any opportunity,
however limited, to prove their worth as men. The Confederacy
went ahead using its colored population when and where it
wanted. The North continued the policy dictated by discretion
and Lincoln's hope of conciliating the Border States and perchance the South itself. Only in Congress were there signs of a
change in that policy. For the American Negro and his white
friends the first year of the war was empty of harvest. But the
soil had been prepared.

II. *"The ultras in their eagerness have spoilt all."*

> ... the side which first summons the negro to its aid
> will conquer ... the South will emancipate and arm her
> slaves sooner than submit to defeat ... the abolition of
> slavery is no longer a question. The only question left
> to be answered is, whether they or we shall abolish
> it—on which side the four million blacks shall fight—
> whether they or we shall inscribe on our banner "Justice
> to the negro," and under it advance to success.
>
> —FREDERICK DOUGLASS, February, 1862

Two days after First Bull Run, Charles Francis Adams, Jr.,
wrote his father, "this defeat tends more and more to throw the
war into the hands of the radicals, and if it lasts a year, it will be
a war of abolition." [1] The war lasted the year, and in 1862 it
became a war of abolition as well as a war to preserve the Union.
The revolt of the radicals in Congress mounted and moved from
success to success: the military rendition of fugitive slaves was
forbidden in March; slavery in the District of Columbia was
ended in April, and in July the Second Confiscation Act gave the
president discretionary power to use Negro soldiers. [2] In September, Lincoln announced his emancipation plans, full of promise
for the American Negro, however empty of immediate practical
effect.

Meanwhile the movement to use the Negro as a Union soldier
passed from thought and discussion to action as military men of
enterprising and crusading spirit recruited, armed, drilled, and
fought colored troops in Kansas, Louisiana, and South Carolina.
These leaders took matters into their own hands regardless of

War Department orders and administration policy. The road they thus surveyed and opened was a rough one for both leaders and their colored troops. But by the fall of 1862 Negro soldiers were being raised, equipped, and used against the rebels by War Department order and as a part of administration policy.

*　　*　　*

The first definite signs of a change in the nature of the war came in Congress. There the radicals steadily consolidated their early gains and stiffened their attacks. And they did so with demonstrable popular support. On January 6, Senator Charles Sumner of Massachusetts presented eight petitions from various groups of citizens in New York, New Hampshire, Pennsylvania, and his own state, "praying for the total abolition of slavery throughout the country." Senator William Fessenden presented a similar petition from his constituents in Hancock County, Maine. Senator Jacob Collamer presented another with 312 signatures from Hinesburgh, Vermont, asking for abolition and "calling on all the inhabitants of the United States, bond and free, to aid in suppppressing rebellion." Preston King of New York presented a petition from the mayor and citizens of Frederick Douglass's city of Rochester arguing that "negroes are capable of enduring all seasons of a southern climate" and urging therefore "that the example of Washington and Jackson in using them for war purposes be followed." [3] With that kind of support and urging from the people, the radicals were not slow to get to their work. On January 15 no less than seven different bills dealing with rebels and their property were reported out of committee.[4] There was no mistaking the spirit and intent of Congress as the new year began.

Outside of Congress, however, little occurred in the first quarter of the year to indicate what was to happen before it was three-quarters gone. Edwin McMasters Stanton had replaced Simon Cameron as secretary of war, but it was not at once apparent that Stanton would soon be riding with the radicals. As the new secretary buckled down to the Herculean task of bringing order out of the chaos of contracts that Cameron had made, generals in the field continued much as they had in the past. Despite heated Congressional debate on the subject, Halleck continued to enforce Order No. 3 in the West. A rising brigadier named Grant held his regimental commanders responsible for the enforcement of Halleck's order in his district of West Tennessee, and another brigadier named Buell, commanding the Department of the Ohio, found it necessary to direct one of his divisional commanders, General O. M. Mitchel, to arrest and hold for their masters some fugitives supposed to be in Mitchel's camp.[5]

A decided change for the better, from the point of view of those interested in giving Negro soldiers a chance, came about in early April when the new secretary of war considered the possibility of using colored men for garrison duty in the malarial regions of the South. The New York *Times* of April 9 approved the idea, reasoning that "The blacks, thoroughly acclimated, will be saved from the risks of the climate; while in the well-defined limit of fortifications they will be restrained from the commission of those revengeful excesses which are the bug-aboos of the Southern people." The *Times* was not inclined to be overcareful of Southern sensitivity on that score, "seeing the merciless readiness of the rebels to turn upon us the Indian savages of the Southwest." The New York paper considered the Negroes' "rare merit in the handling of artillery" a strong argument for their military use "sufficient to acquit Mr. Stanton of sympathy with Garrison Abolitionism." To support this contention, the *Times* insisted that Negroes had proved excellent artillerymen in "both the British and American service," and continued, "They are proof to the heat and smoke of the casemate, unendurable by whites in a warm climate, while the ardor of their labor and courage throws the utmost energy into their gunnery. It is also asserted that their practice is quite as accurate as that of white artillerists. Other considerations equal, and the expediency of arming the blacks in any circumstances once determined—a subject we are sure the Secretary will weigh very carefully before deciding—this faculty of the negro as a gunner would go far to commend his employment."

The Leavenworth (Kan.) *Conservative* on April 16 tacitly endorsed the proposal by reprinting a paragraph from the New York *Evening Post* in favor of the proposition "to garrison the recaptured Southern forts with negro regiments during the sickly season." The *Post* did not discuss the merits of colored artillery-

men after the manner of the *Times* but instead fell back on the
old chestnut, "The rebels have set the example in this respect."

While the question was debated in the papers, there were reports of more definite moves toward making soldiers of Negroes.
On May 7 the Nashville *Dispatch* disclosed that the New York
Commercial had proclaimed, "There is no longer any doubt as
to the intention of Mr. Stanton to have contrabands uniformed,
armed and equipped at the forts on the Southern coast." A correspondent had learned "from high authority" that supplies had
already been ordered. "The Zouave style of uniform has been
selected, with the baggy red trowsers and braided jackets." The
fact that General David Hunter issued red Zouave trousers to
colored men later that same month rather substantiates the newspaper story. It was in fact Hunter who had initiated the whole
project on April 3 in a letter to Stanton asking for 50,000
muskets and "authority to arm such loyal men as I can find in
the country" around his headquarters on Port Royal Island,
South Carolina. In addition, Hunter requested "50,000 pairs of
scarlet pantaloons," maintaining curiously "This is all the clothing I shall require for these people." [6]

For his part, Edwin M. Stanton was slowly maturing his attitude toward Negro troops although four months would elapse
before that attitude would be clarified in War Department orders.
Aware of the mounting success of the radicals, perhaps Stanton
decided that the future belonged to them and that if he wanted
to share in that future he would have to move with the growing
sentiment for arming the Negro. Nor was David Hunter the only
regular army officer to urge upon the secretary of war the military value of the Negro. From General O. M. Mitchel at Huntsville, Alabama, Stanton received a dispatch in early May which
must have helped him to decide on the wider use of Negro auxiliaries. "The negroes are our only friends," Mitchel told the
secretary, "and in two instances I owe my own safety to their
faithfulness. I shall very soon have watchful guards among the
slaves on the plantations bordering the [Tennessee] river from
Bridgeport to Florence, and all who communicate to me valuable information I have promised the protection of my government." [7]

Stanton's reply to Mitchel is significant. "The assistance of slaves is an element of military strength," the secretary wrote, "which, under proper regulations, you are fully justified in employing for your security and the success of your operations. It has been freely employed by the enemy, and to abstain from its judicious use when it can be employed with military advantage would be a failure to employ means to suppress the rebellion and restore the authority of the Government." [8] David Hunter might have written that letter, so well did it represent his own matured views on the question of using Negroes to help sustain the Union.

*   *   *

David Hunter was a regular army officer and a graduate of the military academy at West Point, class of 1822. After a long and undistinguished career, he had attained the rank of major before the crucial election of 1860. He had first attracted the attention of Abraham Lincoln during the summer and fall of that fateful year, and Lincoln had invited him to accompany the official party from Springfield to Washington early in 1861. Like many another regular officer, Hunter rose rapidly in the first months of the war. He became colonel of the 3rd Cavalry on May 14, 1861, a brigadier general of volunteers three days later, and a major general of volunteers on August 13 while recovering from a wound received at First Bull Run. [9] He followed Frémont in command of the Western Department in the fall of 1861 and was in turn replaced by Halleck at McClellan's nomination. On March 31, 1862, Hunter took command of the Department of the South, the somewhat grandiloquent label given the Sea Islands under tenuous Union control since the DuPont-Sherman expedition of November, 1861. Hunter was then sixty years old but still something of the beau sabreur with a blunt, direct countenance hung with long mustaches. For a few weeks he moved about his new command cautiously, feeling his way, familiarizing himself with the people and problems of his amphibious department spread along the level islands and across the sluggish tidal rivers of South Carolina, Georgia, and northernmost Florida. Then, suddenly, it became apparent that there was a new man in the headquarters at Hilton Head.

Hunter's predecessor, Thomas W. Sherman, had come to Hilton Head in November, 1861, with War Department authority to

arm the slaves "if special circumstances seem to require it."
Sherman had never found circumstances sufficiently special.
Instead, the thousands of fugitives who came into the Union lines
had been organized by plantations and put to work for the
Treasury Department growing long-staple cotton in the fields
abandoned by their rebel masters. To supervise this vast and
ambitious project, Secretary of the Treasury Salmon P. Chase
had appointed his old friend and former secretary, Edward L.
Pierce, a Boston lawyer with liberal ideas. Not content with
merely working the ex-slaves in the cotton fields under conditions
somewhat similar to those prevailing before their masters fled,
Pierce had recruited with his assistant superintendents a number
of teachers, among them "the choicest young men of New England, fresh from Harvard, Yale, and Brown and from the divinity
schools of Andover and Cambridge" and a few young women
from Newport, Philadelphia, and Massachusetts. This missionary
band had arrived in Beaufort, an exclusive resort in antebellum
days, on March 9 to begin the challenging work of teaching the
illiterate black population.[10] This was the civil situation when
Hunter arrived three weeks later.

The military situation was not nearly so promising nor so
well in hand. The Union expeditionary forces held only the Sea
Islands and a few outposts on the Florida mainland. In addition
to holding the excellent harbor at Port Royal as a major base for
the Atlantic blockading squadrons, the main Union objective was
Charleston, strongly protected by a growing system of forts and
earthworks. Union arms were inadequate to the task of reducing
either these rebel works or those ringing the ocean side of
Savannah. Indeed, the federal troops were barely sufficient to
maintain their precarious peripheral positions along the coast.
The demands of Union armies operating in defense of the capital,
struggling toward Richmond under McClellan on the Peninsula,
or working with increasing success up the Tennessee and Cumberland rivers and down the Mississippi prevented the strong re-
inforcement of the Department of the South.

General Hunter surveyed his little theater of war, considered
the tactical situation of his troops—infantry, artillery and a battalion of the 1st Massachusetts Cavalry—spread out among the
cotton plantations and under the live oaks on the flat, sun-

drenched islands. Little wonder that in less than a week he had
written the secretary of war for the authority and means to arm
the Negroes. While he waited for word from Washington he put
his plans into operation.

On April 13 he made his first important move: he declared
that "All persons of color lately held to involuntary service by
enemies of the United States in Fort Pulaski and on Cockspur
Island, Georgia, are hereby confiscated and declared free, in
conformity with law, and shall hereafter receive the fruits of
their own labor." To ensure them such fruits, Hunter further declared that the hiring policies earlier initiated by General
Sherman would continue in force with the same rates of pay for
able-bodied Negroes.[11] On April 25, Hunter put the three Southern states lying under the shadowy control of his department
under martial law. On May 8 he extended his proclamation of
April 13 beyond the limits of the First Confiscation Act, on which
it had been based. "Slavery and martial law in a free country are
altogether incompatible," he decreed; "The persons in these
three states, Georgia, Florida, and South Carolina, heretofore
held as slaves are therefore declared forever free."[12]

This had the Frémont ring, and it met the same fate that the
Pathfinder's proclamation of August 30, 1861, had found at the
president's hand. Lincoln had submitted his plan for compensated emancipation by state authority to the Congress in early
March, and two months later he was still hoping for some
affirmative sign from the loyal slave states.[13] He was in no mood
to entertain favorably any proclamation which might jeopardize
his own conciliatory aims, and his reaction to Hunter's effort at
policy making was stiff with impatience, disapproval, and disappointment.

On May 19, Lincoln issued a proclamation of his own. He
declared that "the Government of the United States had no knowledge, information, or belief of intention on the part of General
Hunter to issue such a proclamation; nor has it yet any authentic
information that the document is genuine." Not only had Hunter
operated without prior consultation with his commander in chief,
he had failed to observe the simple courtesy of informing him
of his action, and Lincoln had learned of it only by way of the
newspapers. In emphatic language admitting of no misunder-

standing, the president declared that "neither General Hunter nor any other commander or person has been authorized by the Government of the United States to make proclamations declaring the slaves of any State free; and that the supposed proclamation now in question, whether genuine or false, is altogether void, so far as respects such declaration." Having thus crushed Hunter, Lincoln attempted to repair whatever damage might have been done by the general in a moving appeal to the loyal men of the Border states to take advantage of his liberal offers of federal aid to finance gradual emancipation.[14]

The *National Intelligencer* of May 17 had discussed the Hunter proclamation in an editorial two and a half columns long, lamenting the lack of unity in political and military action so revealed and taking Lincoln to task with the question: "What hopes of reconstruction can survive if the President, neglecting to restrain his subordinates . . . should tamely acquiesce in the parcelling out of the national authority into as many Major Generalships as we have Major Generals in the field?" The same Washington newspaper was able to report contentedly on May 22, three days after Lincoln had restrained Major General Hunter, that the president's proclamation had been received "by the loyal press with universal expressions of assent and approbation." This the *Intelligencer* supported with citations from the *Times,* the *World,* the *Sun,* and the *Commercial Advertiser* of New York, and the Newark (N.J.) *Daily Advertiser.* It was a little too early, however, for celebrations over the end of David Hunter's independent actions. This became clear with startling swiftness.

On May 6, three days before Hunter had issued his short-lived emancipation proclamation, he set on foot his project to arm the slaves, the project underlying his April request for arms and colorful uniforms. Brigadier General H. W. Benham, commanding the Northern District of the Department of the South on Edisto Island, explained this new departure to Jules de la Croix, one of Pierce's Treasury Department agents, in this manner: "General Hunter, as he is authorized to do by the War Department [on the basis of the Cameron instructions to T. W. Sherman], desires to organize in squads and companies, and perhaps into a regiment, a portion of the negroes that have escaped bondage and have come into our lines." Carefully and reasonably Benham delineated Hunter's plan: "He intends to have them paid, fed, and clothed, as well as drilled, in the same manner with our other troops, and would desire to receive for this purpose all able-bodied volunteers of proper age and fitness in other respects, and he would be glad to have you, as the principal agent under the Treasury Department on this island, examine the negroes to this end, laying the matter and the General's proposition fully before them. And then he would wish you to take the names of, and forward to him at Hilton Head, all such negroes as may volunteer for this purpose." [15]

The plan was reasonable enough. After full explanation of the "proposition," the Negroes were to have an opportunity to volunteer their services. Hunter's selection of de la Croix to begin the work on Edisto Island was reasonable, too. The agent in charge of the Negroes working the Treasury's cotton fields was close to the people, far closer than any military man in the department. But this approach, however well conceived, seems not to have been successful, if, indeed, it was ever given a trial.

On May 9, the very day on which Hunter declared all slaves in three states forever free, he "requested" General Benham and five other district commanders to "order the commanding officers in your district to send immediately to these headquarters, under a guard, all the able-bodied negroes capable of bearing arms within the limits of their several commands." [16] This was "laying the matter and the General's proposition fully before them" with a vengeance. This was not Hunter's first mistake, but it was a major mistake in the long tragic series of efforts to organize the first Negro regiment in the Union Army.

Had Hunter followed the reasonable and liberal plan laid down in Benham's letter to de la Croix, had he patiently sought *volunteers* instead of dragooning the terrified Negroes and forcing them willy-nilly into baggy red trousers, his progress must have been far smoother than it was. He might even have been sustained in his efforts to augment the federal forces in his department. Certainly Chase and Stanton would have stood by him and his project if he had carried it out intelligently. But patience was not a primary virtue of the advocates of abolition

and arming the Negro. Too impatient to wait on volunteers,
Hunter stirred distrust, resentment, and opposition.

The sorry tale of how this 1st South Carolina Colored Regiment was manned is told in full in the letters Edward Pierce
received from his agents on the cotton plantations. Pierce then
sent a fully detailed report to the secretary of the treasury. The
Negroes, Pierce protested, "were taken from the fields without
being allowed to go to their houses even to get a jacket, this, however, in some cases, being gone for by the wife. The inevitable-
ness of the order made many resigned, and there was sadness
in all. It is hard to imagine how the order could have been
executed without arousing both fear and indignation, but
Pierce's account indicates that no effort whatsoever was made
to soften the blow of this wholesale impressment. "As those on
this plantation were called in from the fields," Pierce wrote
indignantly, "the soldiers, under orders, and while on the
steps of my headquarters, loaded their guns, so that the negroes
might see what would take place in case they attempted to get
away. . . . Wives and children embraced the husband and father
thus taken away, they knew not where, and whom, as they said,
they should never see again." [17]

The effect on the colored population of this callous and
ill-considered action was immediate and lamentable. L. D. Phillips, Treasury superintendent at Dr. Pope's plantation, spoke
his mind freely. "The plea of military necessity," he wrote
heatedly, "has been stretched to cover up many a mistake and
some acts of criminal injustice, but never, in my judgment, did
major-general fall into sadder blunder and rarely has humanity
been outraged by an act of more unfeeling barbarity." [18]
Another agent, G. M. Wells, wrote from Mrs. Jenkin's plantation on St. Helena Island: "This conscription, together with
the manner of its execution, has created a suspicion that the
Government has not the interest in the negroes that it has pro-
fessed, and many of them sighed yesterday for the 'old fetters'
as being better than the new liberty." [19]

Time, it is said, heals all wounds. Time also provides perspective. While the factual content of the reports of Pierce and
his agents cannot be questioned, a later and more complete report came out of Port Royal less than a week after Hunter's

conscription order was executed. The Nashville *Dispatch* of
May 24 reprinted from the New York *Evening Post* an extensive eyewitness account from Hunter's headquarters. Under a
Port Royal dateline of May 14, the *Post*'s correspondent told
of the collection of all able-bodied Negroes "who submitted
in considerable alarm, having the fear of Cuba and of a forced
conscription held up to them!" This sounds like the earlier
reports, but the newspaperman continued, happily, "It soon
came out, however, that the General's intentions were eminently
humane and judicious." The Negroes, he explained, were taken
to a "comfortable camp, well fed, and informed that they were
to be registered and have free papers for them and their
families." This must have put a rather different complexion on
the whole unfortunate business. After this start at reassurance,
a rather belated explanation of the procedure of their impressment was made to the Negroes with the news that they would
have "their free choice to enlist or return to the plantation."
Certainly this must have seemed a curious and baffling turn
of events to the people involved.

The *Post* correspondent had visited the "comfortable camp"
a few miles from Hunter's headquarters. He maintained that
he had never seen "a happier looking crowd" than he had
found there. "They were busy at clearing more camp ground,"
he wrote, "cooking food and other necessary work, and all
seemed activity and cheerfulness." Commanding the enterprise
was Acting Colonel Arthur M. Kinsey, Hunter's nephew, who
had been a first lieutenant on the general's staff short days
earlier. "The company officers and privates of our army," the
correspondent continued, "and those I saw there headed by
Captain Trowbridge of Company A, seemed well chosen and
full of the right spirit, and very sanguine of success, both in
recruiting and in making a good regiment." Everywhere was
optimism. "One officer ventured the opinion that when they got
their music going, and a few of the Zouaves dressed in uniform,
all would enlist who were fit to serve." [20]

This report puts a different light on the manner in which
Hunter tried to begin his colored regiment, but the first impression on the Negro population was to be difficult to change. Of
even greater significance for Hunter personally and for his

ultimate failure to win War Department approval and support
was the fact that the damning letters from the plantation superintendents to Edward Pierce and from Pierce to Chase were
already on their way north. By the time the newspapers had
printed the rest of the story, Chase had forwarded "the Port
Royal papers" to the secretary of war.

General Hunter had done a great service to the cause of the
Negro soldier, however outrageous the means he had used. He
had forced the issue into the open, and from the middle of May
on through the rest of 1862 the question of arming the Negro,
slave or free, occupied column after column of newspaper
space and stirred the expression of every kind of opinion, conviction, and reaction. In the last paragraph of his report on
the new experiment at Hilton Head, the New York *Post* correspondent indulged in discussion of a sort soon to be typical of
newspaper writers all over the nation: How would the experiment work? "Among military men," this reporter wrote, "great
differences of opinion prevail, but it is believed that, both with
soldiers and officers, the movement will be popular when it is
seen how completely it is in the interest of the white soldier as
well as the black—by furnishing a force for those kinds of
duty and those locations in which the black is safe, while the
white soldier can only serve at a great hazard." [21]

Not all correspondents were so sanguine in their expectations. A New York *Times* man was convinced that enrolling
Negro soldiers could "mean nothing else than a determination
to exterminate the white population" of the South. Southerners
might submit to the domination of the Union, he thought, but
to ask them to yield to their own slaves, "armed by our Government and quartered in their midst, is an error, the folly of
which is only exceeded by the devilish malignity that suggests
it." The *Times* writer looked into the future and thought he
saw "a number of military consequences" sufficient in his
opinion "to excite the disgust of the country." One such dis-
gusting consequence was the eventuality of Negro officers commanding white troops.

"The man that fights in the ranks and distinguishes himself," the *Times* correspondent reasoned, "is entitled to applause and promotion. A regiment of negroes will claim black

officers, and will, if the qualities of command are found to exist, be entitled to them. And when regiments are brigaded, and brigades are consolidated into divisions, we shall, by the exigencies of battle, be liable to have black Colonels converted into Generals on the field, and to see portions of our army of white men under the command of negroes." The *Times* man, having conjured up this bogeyman, was convinced that there were no "white citizens of the United States willing to serve under a negro commander . . ." [22]

A Boston *Journal* report, reprinted in the *National Intelligencer* of May 30, detailed a number of criticisms of Hunter's experiment in addition to those already aired. Because numbers of former slaves had run off and hidden from Union recruiters, the *Journal* maintained, the agricultural operations of the Treasury Department had been seriously interrupted. And, the Boston paper asserted, there was no "encouraging alacrity" among the Negroes to exchange "the cotton patch for the 'tented field' " or the "bucolic hoe for the death-dealing musket." Quite the contrary: "To those who are acquainted with the negroes' proclivity for decided colors, no other evidence need be adduced to prove the strong repugnance betrayed for the new vocation of the caparisoned soldier when it is known that the contrabands at Port Royal, in their profound disrelish for 'soldier's life,' actually renounce the felicity of enduing themselves in nether integuments of scarlet." Or, in other words, not even Hunter's baggy red Zouave pantaloons drew many takers.

The Boston paper had more serious arguments against the conscription of Negroes and their use as soldiers against the South. On conscription, the *Journal* pointed out that thus far it had been "the pride of the loyal States that, while the insurgents are compelled to resort to conscription, all *our* soldiers were volunteers. Let us not lose this distinction." The paper also called attention to the grave danger threatening Negro soldiers if taken prisoner. Considering the "infuriated temper of the Southern insurgents, called to fight their own slaves, it is to be feared that the latter . . . would be treated even worse than our white prisoners of war." The *Journal* expressed the hope that in the remote event that contrabands were enrolled as soldiers, the government would not expose them "to the brunt of battle and the liability of capture." [23] This was indeed to become a problem of alarming proportions and with widespread consequences.

From the Middle West the strident voice of the Chicago *Tribune* was raised in reply. "He who imagines that these blacks are being organized *to be put in the forefront of battle,* or because of any inability to crush the rebellion without their assistance, *insults the loyal millions of the North,* and the *gallant army of the North; and none but a malignant traitor will entertain such a thought.* They will be armed," the word came down from Olympus on the shores of Michigan, "*if at all, only as auxiliaries should be*—as they have been indeed by the rebels from the beginning of the war. Their employment at this time and during the summer is a military necessity. We only wish our armies everywhere could have them. And the movement in New York to organize a colored brigade looks as if it was the purpose of the Government to make this an element in the service, *greatly to the relief of our own troops* from the drudgery of a summer campaign." [24]

This New York movement received some public attention in mid-May just as the furor over Hunter's emancipation order reached its height. The Nashville *Dispatch* of May 18 reported that "recruiting has been secretly going on for the past three weeks, and the rolls exhibit nearly 16,000 names." But the *National Intelligencer* of the next day discounted the rumors, reprinting a wholesale denial from the New York *Commercial Advertizer.* There had been a small movement in New York "prior to the date of Gen. Frémont's [Hunter's?] celebrated proclamation," the *Advertizer* admitted; some three hundred men had been enrolled. The list of their names had been given to "a responsible gentleman and thus the matter remains."

For its own part, the *National Intelligencer* of May 30 expressed doubt of the ability of the "rude negro of Southern plantations" to learn to handle a musket "though that very implement may with entire safety be placed in his hands if he is to be kept out of battle, as the *Chicago Tribune* suggests." Pushing its point further, the *Intelligencer* argued that John Brown had been wise in selecting pikes rather than muskets to hand the slaves in Virginia; "he knew that in the clumsy hands of the unskilled negro the savage pike would be vastly more effective than the civilized carbine." The paper hoped that "when our government is reduced to the necessity of imitating his example, (which we do not anticipate) . . . it will at least imitate his shrewdness in the choice of weapons."

By the middle of June progress reports on the Hunter experiment were showing a pronounced lack of agreement. The Nashville *Dispatch* of June 22 disclosed, on the basis of the Hilton Head correspondence of the New York *Herald*, a decidedly anti-administration paper, that "enlisting . . . is going on . . . with no great success." The company "formed here three or four weeks since" numbered nearly a hundred and fifty "when the intensity and zeal of the 'innocents' culminated," and since then "the contrabands' courage like that of Bob Acres', has oozed out at their fingers' ends, and the company could scarcely turn out a corporal's guard." On the other hand, the *National Intelligencer*, a more impartial journal than the *Herald*, on June 28 printed a more encouraging report although in some details it was surprisingly at variance with the testimony of men on the spot.

The *Intelligencer* described the uniform of the organization as consisting of a "dark blue coat, blue trousers, conical broadbrimmed black hat, and black haversack—no stripes or trimmings of any sort and no bright buttons." There was no mention of the widely advertised red trousers and braided jackets. The soldiers enrolled were being "used for the most part in the quartermaster's department, unloading vessels and performing other labor of this sort." Details of requisitioning working parties from the regimental commander were described with the final observation that the "regiment never appears with arms, and it is said that none have been issued to it as yet." This statement hardly accords with General Hunter's own information prepared for the secretary of war on June 23, information requested by Stanton because he had received a Congressional request for it.

With all the publicity Hunter's project enjoyed, it is not surprising that Congress should eventually have taken an interest in the general and his regiment. Over radical objections, Representative Charles Wickliffe of Kentucky on June 9 secured

passage of a resolution calling on the secretary of war to provide some official information on Hunter's activities. Wickliffe
wanted to know whether Hunter had organized a regiment of
fugitive slaves, whether he had done so with War Department
authority, and whether the War Department had furnished him
with uniforms, arms, and equipment for his recruits.[25] Stanton
replied on June 14 that his department had "no official information" on Hunter's regiment, that the general was not authorized
to raise Negro troops, and that the department had not furnished
Hunter with arms "to be placed in the hands of 'those slaves.'"
The secretary denied the House access to the correspondence
between the War Department and Hunter for security reasons,
but he informed the House that he had ordered the general to
report at once.[26] On June 13, Stanton forwarded the House request to Hunter. Ten days later the general set to work drafting
a suitable reply.

The suitability of what David Hunter finally sent north to
Stanton and eventually to the House of Representatives depends
in great part on the point of view of the reader. The tone of
Hunter's composition was challenging, not to say flippant, in
the extreme. To Wickliffe's first question, whether he had
organized a regiment of fugitive slaves, the general wrote pro-
vocatively: "no regiment of 'fugitive slaves' has been or is being
organized in this department. There is, however, a fine regiment
of persons whose late masters are 'fugitive rebels'—men who
everywhere fly before the appearance of the National flag, leaving their servants behind them to shift, as best they can, for
themselves. So far, indeed, are the loyal persons composing this
regiment from seeking to avoid the presence of their late owners
that they are now, one and all, working with remarkable industry to place themselves in a position to go in full and effective pursuit of their fugacious and traitorous proprietors."[27]

To the Kentuckian's second question, whether he had War
Department authority to raise his regiment, Hunter replied by
pointing to Cameron's instructions to Sherman of the previous
October. In this portion of his letter, the general again indulged
his penchant for the whimsical in further comments on "fugitive
masters." He reasoned that "In the absence of any 'fugitive
master law' the deserted slaves would be wholly without remedy,

had not the crime of treason given them the right to pursue, capture, and bring back those persons of whose protection they have been thus suddenly bereft." [28]

As to the matter of uniforms, arms, and equipment for his new soldiers, Hunter replied that, while he lacked specific authority to outfit them, still had it seemed "that liberty to employ men in any particular capacity implied with it liberty also to supply them with the necessary tools." In that belief, he wrote, he had "clothed, equipped, and armed the only loyal regiment yet raised in South Carolina."

In the closing paragraphs of his letter Hunter wrote what was clearly calculated to stir the War Department and the Congress to support his project. Giving the excuse of "many other diversified and imperative claims" on his time, he apologized for having raised only one rather than "at least five or six" Negro regiments. "The experiment of arming the blacks," he stubbornly insisted, "so far as I have made it, has been a complete and even marvelous success. They are sober, docile, attentive, and enthusiastic, displaying great natural capacities for acquiring the duties of the soldier. They are eager, beyond all things, to take the field and be led into action; and it is the unanimous opinion of the officers who have had charge of them that in the peculiarities of this climate and country they will prove invaluable auxiliaries, fully equal to the similar regiments so long and successfully used by the British authorities in the West India Islands." In conclusion Hunter expressed the hope that "there appearing no possibility of other re-enforcements, owing to the exigencies of the campaign in the Peninsula," he might have "organized by the end of next fall" and ready to "present to the Government from 48,000 to 50,000 of these hardy and devoted soldiers." [29]

The beauty of Hunter's reply was definitely in the eye of the beholder. The radicals enjoyed it hugely, and it was read before the House on July 2 "amid roars of laughter . . ." [30] It was ordered printed, whereupon Isaac N. Arnold of Illinois moved for 10,000 extra copies and Harrison G. Blake of Ohio expressed his hope that "the gentleman will make it a hundred thousand." On the following day Owen Lovejoy asked the consent of the House for a second reading "Inasmuch as the gentle-

man from Kentucky [Wickliffe] was absent attending a secession meeting when General Hunter's reply to his resolution was
received." This brought more laughter from the House, but
Wickliffe objected that he did not want it read for his benefit.
His colleague from Kentucky, George W. Dunlap, found
Hunter's sentiments "clothed in discourteous language . . . an
indignity to the American Congress, an insult to the American
people and our brave soldiers in arms," but Dunlap's resolution of "condemnation and censure" was lost as Elihu B. Wash-
burne of Illinois moved successfully for adjournment.[31]

On July 5, Wickliffe himself launched into a long attack on
Hunter and his letter in particular and the arming of Negroes
in general. While in a parliamentary sense Wickliffe's object
was to force the House to reconsider its motion to order the controversial letter printed, his practical effect was to provide
opportunity for Lovejoy and Stevens and other radicals to air
their views on the practicality, justice, and wisdom of arming
the slaves. In the end his motion to reconsider was laid on the
table by the conclusive vote of 74 to 29.[32]

Two weeks later the Second Confiscation Act became the law
of the land. Although it provided special authority for arming
Negroes, it fell short of approving Hunter's experiment. Section
11 of the new legislation authorized the president "to employ
as many persons of African descent as he may deem necessary
and proper for the suppression of this rebellion," and to that
end to "organize and use them in such manner as he may judge
best for the public welfare." Another bill that became law on
the same day went even further. Sections 12, 13, and 15 of the
Militia Act of July 17, 1862, authorized the employment of
Negro soldiers, the emancipation of individual Negro soldiers
and their families—providing that the former masters of such
families were rebels—and the payment of these soldiers at a
rate $3 a month below that granted white privates in the Union
armies.[33] This last section regarding pay was to become a
storm center for the two years following its passage.

But even the Militia Act, radical though it was, did not give
David Hunter the full and specific support his experiment
needed. Section 12 of the act authorized the president "to receive into the service of the United States, for the purpose of

constructing intrenchments, or performing camp service, or any other labor, or any military or naval service for which they may be found competent, persons of African descent, and such persons shall be enrolled and organized under such regulations, not inconsistent with the Constitution and laws, as the President may prescribe." [34] This merely shifted the problem from Congress to president. It was no solution to the pressing problems that Hunter faced, the practical military problems of appointing officers to whip the new regiment into shape and to lead it in the field, and of paying the black companies. Lincoln had the authority Hunter needed, but the president showed no inclination to use that authority himself or to delegate it to his erstwhile friend at Hilton Head. The *National Intelligencer* of July 26 with customary irony probably presented an accurate reflection of Hunter's frame of mind when it observed: "The President, it is doubtless thought by the progressive school of political Generals, betrays an amazing degree of stupidity in not at once judging it best to promise to put arms into the hands of all the slaves who shall be encouraged by his promise of freedom to escape from their masters."

On July 30 the *Intelligencer* ended a lengthy editorial debate with Horace Greeley's *Tribune* with this rebel opinion set forth by the editor of the New Orleans *Picayune*, an opinion with which the Washington paper was in general agreement: *"We don't think it would be so bad a thing to let Hunter try the experiment of making soldiers of these people.* It would give another illustration of the 'engineer hoisted with his own petard.' Nothing better could be desired to disgust the Federal officers and soldiers with all intermeddling with our slave population, or the slaves with the hypocrisy and falsity of the professions of sympathy and kindness for them on the part of these new friends, than the practical operation of such a scheme." The irony of this Louisiana point of view was not immediately apparent.

*   *   *

Hunter was nearing the end of his rope as July passed into August and still no help came from the War Department. He wrote the secretary of war on August 4 begging for authority to

commission officers in his regiment and to make some arrangement for paying his colored troops. He desired "earnestly to
have a speedy and favorable decision upon the organization of
the regiment" and admitted that recruiting had slowed down.
But even in gathering adversity Hunter was sanguine of the
ultimate worth of his project. "I make no doubt whatever," he
wrote, "that half a dozen colored regiments can be placed in
the field within two months after my plan shall have received
official countenance; and once the regiments are reorganized
and regularly paid as soldiers, it will require but a few additional posts to be established along the shore of the mainland
. . . to bring many thousands of these loyal persons flocking
around the standard of the Union." [35]

Official countenance of his plan was not forthcoming, and
for this Hunter had no one to thank but himself. His original
impressment of the Negroes was not forgotten, and while his
reply to Wickliffe's resolution had pleased the radicals it had
shocked the more conservative element in the North. Worst of
all, Hunter had alienated the support of the white officers and
men of his own command.

Lieutenant Charles Francis Adams, Jr., serving with Massachusetts cavalry at Hilton Head, described the situation to his
father in strong terms. "Our ultra-friends, including General
Hunter," he wrote, "seem to have gone crazy and they are
doing the blacks all the harm they can. On this issue things are
pretty bad. General Hunter is so carried away by his idea of
negro regiments as, not only to write flippant letters about his
one to Secretary Stanton, but even to order *their exemption*
from *all* fatigue duty; so that while our Northern soldiers work
ten hours a day in loading and unloading ships, the blacks never
leave their camp, but confine their attention to drill." This
development must have been the more disappointing to the overworked white soldiers since they had been prepared by public
discussion of the Negro soldier question to expect them to bear
a heavy share of the hard work required of forces in the field.
"There may be reasons for this," young Adams admitted, "but
it creates intense feeling here and even I cannot see the justice
of it." [36]

Supporting Adams's assertions, the Baltimore *American*'s

Port Royal correspondent made this bitter comment toward the end of July: "It seems that the war in this department is carried on solely for the benefit of the negroes, that expensive transports are set aside exclusively for transporting from place to place idle and decrepit negroes; that wherever the Union forces go the negroes must be carried, fed, and clothed. Everything is for the nigger. . . ." [37]

To his brother, Henry, Lieutenant Adams made even more plain than he had to his father the unpopularity of Hunter and the rising tide of anti-Negro sentiment in the rank and file of Northern forces under his command. Adams called Hunter "arbitrary and wholly taken up with his negro question," and the young officer was convinced that the colored regiment was a failure. Earlier Henry had written a letter bursting with enthusiasm for Hunter and his project and urging Charles Jr. to seek a commission in the new organization. Charles laughed bitterly at the idea: "after all my assertions of principles to become a 'nigger driver' in my old age, for that is what it amounts to, seeing that they don't run away, or shirk work or fatigue duty." [38]

Charles Adams was extremely pessimistic about the future of Negro soldiers. He saw only a limited role for them in the Union's struggle. "Hunter and you are all wrong," he told Henry, "and, for once, the War Department was right. The negroes should be organized and officered as soldiers; they should have arms put in their hands and be drilled simply with a view to their moral elevation and the effect on their self-respect, and for the rest they should be *used* as fatigue parties and on all fatigue duty." This opinion foreshadowed Adams's later theories on the role of the army as a training school for future Negro citizens, theories which Adams developed as lieutenant colonel of the 5th Massachusetts Cavalry, a Negro regiment. [39] But in the summer of 1862 Adams had no enthusiasm for Negro soldiers. "As to being made soldiers," he told Henry, "they are more harm than good. . . . Under our system and with such white officers as we give them, we might make a soldiery equal to the native Hindoo regiments in about five years. It won't pay and the idea of arming the blacks *as soldiers* must be abandoned." [40]

Lieutenant Adams was a disturbed young man. He came from a long line of New England and national leaders interested in freedom for the slaves, and he was deeply resentful that Hunter's well-intentioned but shortsighted radicalism had injured the cause of abolition. Adams was particularly resentful of the effect Hunter's stubborn concentration on his pet project had had on the white officers and men in the Department of the South. "To my mind the ultras are doing all the harm they can," he wrote out of his disturbance and resentment. "As to the army, so far as I see it, it is completely demoralized on this question by the conduct of these men, and it makes me sick to hear New England men talk on the subject of the negroes here and all who would aid them. Such prejudice and narrow bigotry I never met in Southerners. There is no abolitionism or, I fear, even emancipation in the army here. The ultras in their eagerness have spoilt all." [41]

*   *   *

The final blow to Hunter's hopes came on August 6 when President Lincoln made it clear that, despite the acts of July 17, he was not yet ready to enroll Negroes as soldiers although he would continue to use them as laborers with the army. The New York *Times* announced the president's policy statement and the circumstances around it: "A deputation of Western gentlemen waited upon the President this morning to offer two colored regiments from the State of Indiana. . . . The President received them courteously, but stated to them *that he was not prepared to go the length of enlisting negroes as soldiers. He would employ all colored men as laborers, but would not promise to make soldiers of them.*" Charles Adams, Jr., must have read the news with grim satisfaction.

"The deputation," the *Times* continued, "came away satisfied that it is the determination of the Government *not to arm negroes,* unless some new and more pressing emergency arises." The Peninsular campaign had just ended in costly failure, and the second disaster at Bull Run was still three weeks away. Once again it had been Lincoln's concern for the Border state problem which had determined his policy. "The President argued," the *Times* reported, "that the nation could *not afford to lose Kentucky at this crisis, and gave it as his opinion that to arm the negroes would turn 50,000 bayonets from the loyal Border States against that were now for us.* Upon the policy of using negroes as laborers, the confiscation of rebel property, and the feeding of the National troops upon the granaries of the enemy, the President said there was no division of sentiment." [42]

Lincoln promised the "Western gentlemen" that he would continue a vigorous prosecution of the war. He simply stopped short of arming the slaves or attempting to foment slave insurrections in the South. He would carry out the confiscation and emancipation clauses of the Second Confiscation Act; he had, after all, signed the bill after changes had been made to avoid his contemplated veto. The *Times* admitted that "This policy will not meet the demands of a very large and very active public sentiment in the loyal states," but argued that human nature as well as reason entered into considerations of the Negro soldier question. There was no doubt in the mind of the *Times* writer that the Union had a right to arm the slaves. The question was the expediency of doing so. Was there evidence that the slaves wanted to fight for the Union? Could they be trusted? There were, besides, two obvious disadvantages in using colored troops: the effect in the sensitive Border states, certainly, plus the danger of dissension in the North. All in all, the *Times* man concluded that arming the slaves was unnecessary. The Union had strength enough to win without black help.[43] So did the cautious and conservative *Times* support the president's decision of August 6.

Lincoln could expect no such support from the Chicago *Tribune,* and he got none. In a front-page editorial that paper stated its position, loud and clear. "Assuredly, the most rejoicing," the *Tribune* maintained, "will not be among loyal men at the decision of the President against arming the negroes. Lukewarm patriots, 'fire in the rear' sympathizers with the rebellion, men who love slavery more than the Union, will openly exult at the evidence that the Government is not yet ready to use every loyal arm in the restoration of its power and destruction of its enemies." There would, of course, be those who could not hail the policy statement with joy. "With men who have no

wish but that the country shall be saved," the *Tribune* declaimed
self-righteously, "and who believe of all its evils slavery is the
worst, the regret will be sincere, that our national trials thus
far have not sufficed to do away with the prejudice which will
consult hues and complexion when what is wanted are laborers
at the fire." As for the future, the newspaper saw revolutionary
change in the making: "the hand on our national dial is steadily
moving to the end that must come, too resistless to be stayed by
old time prejudices, or held back by President or Congress.
Destiny has forced it. The people will it." [44] Vox populi, vox
Dei, vox Chicago *Tribune*.

The Buffalo (N.Y.) *Commercial Advertizer* of August 7 expressed a more reasonable attitude. The Buffalo paper had been
working editorially for arming the Negro as a military necessity, but it was able to accept the president's arguments in good
grace. "The declared policy of the Government to employ the
negroes as laborers will effect the same purpose as if they were
armed," the *Advertizer* maintained. "It will dignify the position and protect the health of our Northern troops, by relieving
them from menial service and exhausting fatigue." One can
imagine Lieutenant Adams reading this and uttering a fervent
"Amen!"—at the same time pushing to the back of his mind a
desire to mark the lines of type and send the newspaper to
Hunter's headquarters.

To the Buffalo paper it is plain that using Negroes as labor
battalions with the armies would "add vastly to the efficient
fighting strength of the army by sending into the ranks thousands of men who have been hitherto employed as cooks,
hostlers, teamsters, and upon entrenching, fatigue, and pioneer
duty." It was plain also that necessity did not demand the arming of the Negro. "We shall be spared," the editorial concluded, "the humiliating admission that this great people were
compelled to ask the aid of slaves, and draw from the South an
element of strength to enable us to maintain and preserve our
liberties." [45]

David Hunter was beaten.

His wound at First Bull Run never hurt him so much as the
letter he addressed to Stanton on August 10, 1862: "Failing
to receive authority to muster the First Regiment of South Caro-

lina Volunteers into the service of the United States, I have disbanded them." Again he told the secretary of war what he had hoped from the experiment, "that not only would this regiment have been accepted, but that many similar ones would have been authorized to fill up the decimated ranks of the army and afford the aid of which the cause seems now so much in need." But the authority he required to establish the work had failed him, and he had at length "deemed it best to discontinue the organization." [46]

Edwin M. Stanton's attitude during July and August of 1862 is not clear. In view of the positive opinion he had expressed on the military use of Negroes to General Mitchel, and in view of assurances Secretary of the Treasury Chase had given Ben Butler of a gradual coming around in the thinking of the administration in June,[47] it is hard to understand why Stanton consistently ignored Hunter's appeals for War Department approval of his course of action in South Carolina. Especially is it hard to understand in view of the authorization Stanton gave General Rufus Saxton to raise Negro soldiers a bare fortnight after Hunter had disbanded his regiment.

Were it not for that particular reversal of policy, the whole question might be dismissed on the basis of the cabinet discussions of July 21 and 22, discussions chiefly taken up with Lincoln's proposal of emancipation. On both days the question of arming Negroes had come up, and Lincoln had "expressed himself as averse" to that revolutionary move.[48] The president's statement of August 6 merely consolidated his position on the subject. It might be concluded that Stanton as a loyal member of the administration simply followed the presidential lead in letting Hunter's experiment die on the vine. But there still remains the irrevocable fact that on August 25 Stanton gave to Rufus Saxton authority he had denied David Hunter.

Stanton must have read some of the reports coming out of Port Royal; he should have been acquainted with the conflicting stories and opinions on what and how Hunter's red-trousered men were doing. While some of these stories must have made Stanton dubious of the value of Negro soldiers, there were others which must have encouraged the secretary to think well of their military potential. A correspondent of the usually reli-

able New York *Times* wrote from Hilton Head in early July of
the progress of Hunter's troops in learning military drill and
precision. The correspondent maintained that he was only
"echoing the opinion of every naval and military officer without exception who was present" at a formal review of the regiment in reporting that the troops "presented an efficiency in the
manual of arms and the evolutions of parade such as I have
never seen surpassed by any regiment of equal time under
tutelage." This should surprise no one who has worked with or
observed Negro soldiers on parade. "To every order given,"
the *Times* man wrote with evident amazement, "the response
was quick and simultaneous . . . with a silent obedience and
accuracy hardly to be surpassed by any white regiment at
Hilton Head." Perhaps Hunter's concentration on drill and
military instruction to the exclusion of all fatigue details for
his troops was justified after all.

The civilian reporter was not the only impressed observer.
"Commodore DuPont expressed himself to the effect," he wrote,
"and almost in the words I have used. He arrived in the South
a thorough believer in the hopelessness of elevating the negro
race, but, like Paul on his journey to Damascus, he has seen a
great light. His honest and capacious mind has been opened to
the convictions of evidence." [49] Perhaps the evidence had not
been sufficient to convince Stanton. Perhaps he was considering
more than the evidence of smart parade ground appearance.
Certainly the secretary of war had to consider larger issues than
how the Negro recruits were taking to drill.

A reasonable solution to the problem presented by Stanton's
permitting Hunter to fail on August 10 and then directing Saxton to resume the work on August 25 is that the secretary of
war had decided that Hunter was not the man to carry the work
forward. Chase had shown Stanton the correspondence from
Edward Pierce on Hunter's initial recruiting efforts and their
effects on the colored population of the Sea Islands. Stanton
must have been aware, too, of the mounting unpopularity and
distrust of Hunter among the white troops of his department.
While his later actions indicate that Stanton was ready to use
Negro soldiers—indeed, he had so expressed himself in the
cabinet meetings of July 21 and 22—it is probable that his

willingness to let Hunter fail was motivated by the conviction that Hunter was not suited to the work and that, on the other hand, Rufus Saxton was. Subsequent events lend strong support to this conclusion.

Lieutenant Charles Adams watched the breakup of the first attempt to organize the 1st South Carolina Colored Volunteers with mingled emotions. To him there was more in that failure than a rebuff to an ambitious major general or a check to an ultra-abolitionist scheme. "General Hunter's negro regiment was disbanded yesterday," he wrote his father in London, "and now they have all dispersed to their old homes. Its breaking up was hailed here with great joy, for our troops have become more anti-negro than I could have imagined." But there was more than joy: " ... for myself, I could not help feeling a strong regret at seeing the red-legged darkies march off; for, though I have long known that the experiment was a failure, yet it was a failure of another effort at the education of these poor people and it was the acknowledgment of another of those blunders which have distinguished all and every our experiments on slavery throughout this war. ... Why could not fanatics be silent and let Providence work for awhile. The slaves would have moved when the day came and could have been made useful in a thousand ways. As it is, we are Hamlet's ape, who broke his neck to try conclusions." [50]

III. *"And who better to begin the work . . ."*

> Suppose that the day the ordinance of secession was declared ... some one had said, that as a result of that insane action in less than two years a regiment of free negroes, under the command of a 'Massachusetts Yankee,' would appear in the streets of New-Orleans, what kind of a reception would such a prophecy have called forth? Why, jeers, ridicule, or possibly hanging to the nearest lamp post.
>
> —New York *Times*, October 14, 1862

While David Hunter's ill-starred experiment in South Carolina held the center of the stage, another act of the drama was shaping up in the wings in Louisiana. There, two other Union generals—one a regular army man from Vermont and a fervid abolitionist, the other a political adventurer from Massachusetts—disagreed profoundly on the subject of Negro soldiers. As a result of this disagreement the abolitionist resigned from the army while the politician mustered in the first colored regiment to become an official part of the Union armies.

John W. Phelps, a graduate of the military academy in Thomas Sherman's class of 1836, had risen to the rank of captain by 1850, resigned from the service in 1859, and come back in May of 1861 as colonel of the 1st Vermont Volunteers. Almost immediately, on May 17, Phelps had been made a brigadier general of volunteers, and as a brigadier he accompanied Admiral David Farragut and General Benjamin Butler up the Mississippi to capture New Orleans in April of 1862.[1]

Benjamin F. Butler of Massachusetts had already made a

name for himself, several names in fact. He had first won the condemnation of Northern abolitionists by offering his Yankee troops to Governor Hicks of Maryland in the first weeks of the war to help put down a slave insurrection. Then a month later, in Virginia, it had been largely Ben Butler who had pioneered the Union practice of confiscating fugitive slaves as contraband of war and putting them to work in the Union engineer and quartermaster departments. While Butler had been enthusiastic about employing Negroes as a labor force with the armies, he had not been long in New Orleans before he made clear to the War Department his position on Negro soldiers.

While Hunter and his officers drilled red-trousered ex-slaves at Hilton Head, Butler wrote the secretary of war that "The military necessity does not exist here for the employment of negroes in arms in order that we may have an acclimated force." Rather than use colored men, Butler would use loyal Louisiana whites and, once given War Department permission, he was convinced, he would have "five thousand able-bodied white citizens enlisted within sixty days," many with previous military experience and "commanded by intelligent loyal officers." Butler hoped and believed, he wrote Stanton, "that this war will be ended before any body of negroes [can] be organized, armed, and drilled so as to be efficient." [2]

Ben Butler in May placed a low estimate on the value of Negroes as soldiers. In his customary discursive fashion he gave the secretary of war the benefit of his expert opinion formed after a month in Louisiana. The Negro there, Butler wrote, "by long habit and training has acquired a great horror of fire-arms, sometimes ludicrous in the extreme when the weapon is in his own hand." The Yankee general was inclined to agree that "John Brown was right" in arming the slaves with pikes or spears instead of muskets. By a curious reading of early Louisiana history, Butler attributed the British defeat by Andrew Jackson's forces in January of 1815 to the failure of a colored regiment brought with the attacking army of the crown from the West Indies. More cogently, he argued that if the North were to admit "the proposition that white men cannot be soldiers in this climate," such admission would "go far toward asserting the dogma that white men cannot labor here, and therefore establish the necessity of exclusively black labor, which has ever been the cornerstone of African slavery." [3]

As for newspaper reports of "the free negro corps" of New Orleans organized by the rebel Louisiana government "for the defence of the South," Butler thought that these might have given Stanton "a very erroneous idea" as to the worth of Negro soldiers. But, curiously, Butler himself seems to have been favorably impressed by his first contact with that organization, despite his derogatory comments. Some of the officers of the free colored militia had called on him to discuss "the question of the continuance of their organization, and to learn what disposition they would be required to make of their arms." Butler wrote Stanton that "in color, nay, also in conduct they had much more the appearance of white gentlemen than some of those who have favored me with their presence claiming to be the 'Chivalry of the South.' " All this aside, Ben Butler was satisfied that "no military necessity exists to change the policy of the Government in this respect within my command." [4] That was the Butler position in May.

Meanwhile John W. Phelps, commanding at Camp Parapet, a few miles west of New Orleans, rather quickly became a sharp Green Mountain thorn in the side of the general commanding the Department of the Gulf. Although Butler had issued on May 23 precise orders on the exclusion of Negroes from Phelps's lines,[5] reports began to come in almost at once indicating the brigadier's abolitionist turn of mind. Not content merely to welcome fugitive slaves at the picket lines, Phelps's command provided the basis for charges that they were enticing Negroes away from surrounding plantations and had even gone so far as to free from the stocks a Negro convicted of barn burning. Plantation owners complained to Butler: "Our negroes, heretofore quiet, now feeling under no restraint commit burglary and other depredations, and then seek refuge in [Phelps's] camp where they are received and protected." [6] Secretary of the Treasury Salmon P. Chase hit the nail squarely on the head when he wrote Butler in June: "It is quite plain that you do not find it so easy to deal with the contraband question [in Louisiana] as at Fortress Monroe." [7]

In something like desperation, Butler on June 18 reported

to the War Department the growing severity of the fugitive slave problem, aggravated by Phelps. Several weeks later, in early July, Stanton stated the government position in language not widely different from what Butler had used in stating his "contraband" policy in the first months of the war. The president, Stanton told Butler, "is of the opinion that, under the law of Congress [of March 13, 1862, forbidding military rendition of slaves], they cannot be sent back to their masters; that in common humanity they must not be permitted to suffer for want of food, shelter, or other necessaries of life; that to this end, they should be provided for by the Quartermaster's and Commissary's Departments; and that those who are capable of labor should be set to work and paid reasonable wages." The secretary further assured the general that in giving these directions Lincoln had not intended to "settle any general rule in respect to slaves or slavery, but simply to provide for the particular case under the circumstances in which it is now presented." [8]

Ben Butler was not satisfied; the presidential provision was not adequate for the particular Louisiana case. Late in July the Massachusetts general complained in a letter to his wife that "The Government have sustained Phelps about the negroes, and we shall have a negro insurrection here I fancy. If something is not done soon, God help us all." Butler was afraid that the Negroes were getting "saucy and troublesome," but, he asked Mrs. Butler, "who blames them?" [9]

General Phelps, too, had the feeling that something needed to be done about the Negro situation, but he was unwilling to wait on a Washington solution. On his own initiative he began the organization of five companies of Negro soldiers, and on July 30 he sent to Butler's headquarters his requisitions for "arms, accoutrements, clothing, camp and garrison equipage, etc., for three regiments of Africans," which he proposed to raise for the defense of Camp Parapet and the neighborhood. To support his project, Phelps pointed out that his position was swampy and unhealthy, that his white soldiers were "dying at the rate of two or three a day," and that Southern loyalists were not furnishing their quota of men. "An opportunity now offers of supplying the deficiency," he optimistically informed his

commanding general, "and it is not safe to neglect opportunities in war." The Vermonter thought he could probably have
three colored regiments raised in a short time; he had with
little difficulty organized three hundred Negroes into five companies. "These men," he maintained, "are willing and ready
to be put to the test. They are willing to submit to anything
rather than slavery." [10]

Phelps had more than exclusively military reasons for want-
ing to organize Negro regiments. He considered Southern
society "on the point of dissolution" and thought the best way
to keep the Negro from becoming part of "a general state of
anarchy" was "to enlist him in the cause of the Republic" and
thus remove him from the temptation of listening to "any petty
military chieftain . . . offering him freedom" with the intention
of using him rather for "robbery and plunder." Phelps had
given some serious thought to methods of organizing Negro
troops and had specific recommendations on the subject. To
"organize and discipline our African levies," he suggested the
establishment of a training center on the coast of South Carolina
to which the current graduates of the military academy would
be sent to ensure a leaven of well-trained officers in supervisory
capacities. He thought that line officers for colored companies
could be secured from "the more promising noncommissioned
officers and privates of the Army." Phelps was very much in
earnest. "Prompt and energetic efforts in this direction," he
urged, "would probably accomplish more towards a speedy
termination of the War, and early restoration of peace and
amity, than any other course which could be adopted." [11] But
his timing was wrong.

Even before he had seen Phelps's bold and comprehensive
plan, Butler had sent an order to Camp Parapet directing that
the fugitives there be put to work cutting timber and building
fortifications. Phelps's reply was immediate and outspoken.
"While I am willing," he wrote furiously, "to prepare African
regiments for the defense of the Government against its assail-
ants, I am not willing to become the mere slave driver which
you propose, having no qualifications that way." And he tendered his resignation and requested a leave of absence until
the resignation could be accepted. [12]

On August 2, Butler bent to the task of replying to these two communications from Phelps. To his request for arms and equipment for the proposed colored troops, Butler stated that the president alone had authority to employ Negroes as soldiers, according to the acts of Congress approved two weeks earlier, on July 17. Butler was entirely correct in asserting that "The President has not as yet indicated his purpose to employ the African in arms." Besides, the harried commanding general explained, he could not issue the supplies Phelps had requested because what he had on hand were "by the letter of the Secretary of War, expressly limited to white soldiers, so that I have no authority to divert them however much I may desire to do so." Butler could not sanction Phelps's course of action, but he would send his application to the president. In the meantime, he instructed Phelps, "you must desist from the formation of any Negro Military Organization."

As for the resignation, Butler refused to accept it. At great length he reasoned with his disgruntled subordinate, pointing out the necessity of the work he had ordered. "It must be done," he maintained, either by the five hundred fugitives at Camp Parapet or by Union white soldiers. Forgetting for the moment what he had earlier written Stanton on the subject, Butler argued that the Negroes could stand hard work in the oppressive atmosphere of Louisiana in August far better than white troops could. He reminded Phelps that Union soldiers "of the Army of the Potomac did this very thing last summer in front of Arlington Heights," and he asked, "Are negroes any better than they?"

Having dealt with the order that had precipitated the resignation, Butler then turned to that subject itself. He was particularly sharp on the point and read Phelps a harsh lecture. "To resign in the face of the enemy has not been the highest plaudit to a soldier," the volunteer informed the regular, "especially when the reason assigned is that he is ordered to do what a recent act of Congress has especially authorized a Commander to do, i.e., employ the Africans to do the necessary work about a camp or upon fortifications." Brusquely Butler concluded his peroration: "General, your resignation will not be accepted by me; leave of absence will not be granted, and you will see to it that any orders, thus necessary for the defense of the City, are faithfully and diligently executed, upon the responsibility that a soldier in the field owes to his superior." [13] Having done that, Butler did the only thing left to him as commanding general: he referred the whole matter to the War Department for final disposition.[14]

Then the Massachusetts general did what many another man, military or civilian, has done when faced with problems too great for himself alone: he wrote to his wife. He told her what he had probably wanted to tell the secretary of war: "Phelps has gone crazy. He is organizing the negroes into regiments and wants me to arm them. . . . I told him he must set the negroes to work and not drill them and he thereupon has resigned." [15]

If Butler had supposed for an instant that Phelps would quietly forget the whole incident and settle down to the military business of following the orders of his superior, the commanding general was in for a shock. Phelps lost no time in replying, and he left no room for doubt in Butler's mind. It can be of but little consequence to me," the Vermont brigadier wrote indignantly, "as to what kind of slavery I am to be subjected, whether to African slavery or to that which you so offensively propose to me, giving me an order wholly opposed to my convictions of right as well as of the higher scale of public necessities in the case . . . I cannot submit to either kind of slavery." Phelps appealed to Butler's "sense of justice to reconsider" his decision and to grant "the quiet, proper, and customary action upon my resignation." Still undaunted by Butler's double rebuff, Phelps included the information that "several parties of the free colored men of New Orleans have recently come to consult me on the propriety of raising one or two colored regiments of Volunteers from their class of the population for the defense of the Government and good order." It must have given Butler some relief to learn that Phelps had directed these parties to "propose the measure" to department headquarters.[16]

Less than two weeks later Butler wrote the secretary of war that he had "determined to use the service of the free colored men who were organized by the rebels into the 'Colored Brigade,' of which we have heard so much. They are free, they have been used by our enemies, whose mouths are shut, and they will be loyal." [17] As Horace Greeley put it, "The current of events soon carried Gen. Butler along with it." [18]

Phelps alone had not convinced Butler of the military necessity and political expediency of Negro troops. On the contrary, the evidence points to the conclusion that Butler was converted to the cause in spite of his difficulties with Phelps. *Butler's Book* is notable not so much for the light it throws on the question as for the manner in which it demonstrates the worst characteristics of memoirs. Either Butler's memory played him tricks when he finally got around to writing his *Book*, or he deliberately and mendaciously reconstructed the history of his administration of affairs in the Department of the Gulf to give the impression that he individually and independently made the decision to use Negro troops as auxiliaries to the white forces under his command.[19] He did make such a decision, but the manner in which the current of events led him to that decision is widely at variance with his own version.

A number of pressures were brought to play upon Ben Butler for about two months before he finally made his decision to muster Negro regiments. The malleable character of the general and his willingness to shift with the tide of popular sentiment did the rest. Toward the end of June, Secretary of the Treasury Chase had indicated in a long discursive letter that administration policy was coming around slowly to the contingency of emancipation and arming the slaves. A later and even longer letter from Chase to Butler must have arrived in New Orleans between August 2, when Butler denied Phelps's plan for the organization of colored troops, and August 14, when he wrote Stanton of his determination to use them. In this letter Chase reviewed for the general's edification the whole slavery problem. The secretary of the treasury suggested that a military solution to this problem in the Department of the Gulf might "contribute largely to settle the negro question in the free states" by siphoning Negroes from the North to freedom in the South. Chase indicated, too, that Lincoln's earlier dissatisfaction with Hunter's course in South Carolina had abated markedly during July.

If Butler had entertained any doubts of Chase's intentions in the first few pages of this letter, those doubts should have been dispersed by what its closing paragraphs contained. There was a great opportunity down there on the Gulf, Chase was convinced, "And who better to begin the work than my friend Gen. Butler?" The secretary suggested that Butler "simply see that the acts of Congress are carried out in good faith," meaning that he cease altogether to return fugitive slaves to their masters. Then, in his most cajoling tones, Chase came directly to the point: "It would hardly be too much to ask you to call, like Jackson, colored soldiers to the defence of the Union; but you must judge of this. Of one thing be assured—you can hardly go too far to satisfy the exigency of public sentiment now." Chase knew his man. There were a few closing lines to hide the point slightly, some generalities about the "exercise of your own good judgment" and the redundant statement that "as far as prudence allows you may certainly go." [20] This may have been the deciding pressure.

There is another letter, one from Mrs. Butler at home in Massachusetts, that may have helped her soldier husband to his decision to ride the rising tide of sentiment. Certainly it must have strengthened Butler's determination. In one short paragraph Mrs. Butler summed up abolitionist spirit in the North and pointed the way political winds were blowing. "Emancipation, and arming the negroes is held in check for a little," she told her husband, "the border states will not submit to it, soon as there is a plausible hope of success it will be brought forward again. . . . If you look at Port Royal you will see that Hunter is kept in his place, and carries out all his Proclamation put forth. The President's veto was not decisive. Phelps' policy prevails instead of yours. The abolitionists will have this a war to free the slaves at once if possible, nothing else is thought of. The Administration will assent to it just as fast and as far as the Country will sustain it." [21]

Meanwhile, in keeping with current War Department practice, Phelps's resignation was accepted, and he left the service on August 21, 1862. Butler protested that he "loved General Phelps very much," insisting that "He was a crank upon the slavery question solely; otherwise he was as good a soldier and commander as ever mounted a horse." Butler also insisted that "in the strongest language of which [he] was capable [he had] represented to the President [his] great desire to have Phelps remain" under his command.[22] But in the Department of the Gulf and especially among Phelps's own officers, it was the feeling that their Vermont brigadier had been "bullied out of the service." [23]

In an editorial entitled "The Enrollment of Negroes" the *National Intelligencer* of August 15 discussed the Phelps-Butler controversy and sustained Butler's position, not knowing that he was shortly to outdo Phelps at his own game. In the same editorial the *Intelligencer* discussed a new Massachusetts law which directed public officials "in preparing the new enrollment" for military service "to include the names of *all* citizens, *white or colored* . . . between the ages of eighteen and forty-five years." The Washington newspaper had a word for that sort of thing, and the word was "fanaticism." The editorial expressed the fervent hope that Lincoln would meet such "pressure" with good common sense.

Before that newspaper had reached Louisiana, Ben Butler had taken the final plunge. On August 22, the day after Phelps's resignation became effective, Butler published his General Orders, No. 63, calling on the free colored militiamen of Louisiana to enroll in the volunteer forces of the Union.[24]

He had taken the plunge, but only after having been convinced by the importuning letters of Salmon P. Chase and a cautious weighing of the tactical situation in the North as well as in Louisiana. Confederate pressure on Baton Rouge and abolitionist pressure on the administration made for a powerful combination. And even in the act of plunging Ben Butler displayed characteristic shrewdness. He issued no general invitation to all the colored men of the Pelican State. His invitation specified only those free colored men who had been enrolled in Louisiana militia units by the Confederate state government. Butler was not yet the man to arm slaves openly. The Confederate government in Richmond gave credit where credit was due in its order of August 21, 1862, outlawing David Hunter and John Phelps for having "organized and armed negro slaves for military service against their masters, citizens of this Confederacy." [25]

Butler was careful to make clear in his order of August 22 that it applied only to "a military organization, known as the 'Native Guards' (colored)," which had been "duly and legally enrolled as a part of the militia" of Louisiana in the spring of 1861, "its officers being commissioned by Thomas O. Moore, Governor and commander-in-chief of the militia of the State of Louisiana." [26] Thus, by a technicality, Butler escaped for a time the opprobrium of having armed "slaves." So successful was this piece of Butler shrewdness that even the *National Intelligencer* on September 5 published his order with no comment beyond the introductory statement that "Gen. Butler, having discovered that the present Governor of Louisiana had organized a body of free negroes as soldiers in the service of the Confederate States, has issued an order inviting them into the service of the United States . . ."

George S. Denison, acting surveyor of customs at New Orleans, reported to his chief, Secretary Chase, on the hidden joker in Butler's hand. "By accepting a regiment which had already been in Confederate service," Denison wrote, "he left no room for complaint (by the rebels) that the Government were arming the negroes." That much seems clear enough. But Denison saw more. "But, in enlisting," he disclosed, "nobody inquires whether the recruit is (or has been) a slave. As a consequence, the boldest and finest fugitives have enlisted, while the whole organization is known as the Free Colored Brigade."

Denison had more to say on Butler's whole project, and his testimony seems to be substantially supported by other evidence. "Gen. Butler's opposition to the enlistment of negroes by Gen. Phelps," he charged, "was not a matter of principle. Gen. Phelps had the start of him, while Gen. B. wanted the credit of doing the thing himself, and in his own way. And he is doing it, shrewdly and completely, as he does everything." [27]

The colored men, slave and free, responded to Gen. B.'s invitation in gratifying numbers. No explanation is necessary for the eagerness of the fugitives to enlist. As Phelps had told Butler earlier, "They are willing to submit to anything rather than slavery." As for the free colored men who had previously been enrolled to fight for the South, there is evidence that they were motivated in part by the treatment they had received at the hands of their white neighbors before the coming of the Yankees. In September of 1861 the colored citizens of New Orleans had offered their services "as an escort for the prisoners of war," but this offer had been declined, albeit with thanks "for the promptness with which they answered the call." Then, in March of 1862, when the Crescent City was in peril of Yankee conquest, the free colored militia had been called upon to "maintain their organization and to hold themselves ready prepared for such orders as may be transmitted to them." [28] Apparently the orders were never transmitted. At any rate, New Orleans had capitulated without the colored soldiers' having seen any action in her defense. While the white Confederate forces withdrew, the free colored men had remained in the city, feeling "left" in more ways than one. [29] For whatever reasons, a desire to fight for the Union and an end to slavery or a desire to fight against the rebellion which had treated them rather shabbily, recruits came in rapidly.

In high good spirits on the first day of September, Ben Butler wrote Stanton: "I have succeeded wonderfully well in my enlistments of Volunteers here. A full regiment, three companies of cavalry—Six hundred to form a new regiment and more than 1200 men enlisted in the old regiments to fill up the ranks." Then, as a sort of afterthought: "I shall also have within ten days a Regiment 1000 strong of Native Guards (Colored), the darkest of whom will be about the complexion of the late Mr. Webster." [30] So did the War Department learn officially of the outcome of the Phelps-Butler controversy. On September 27, 1862, the 1st Regiment Louisiana Native Guards was mustered into federal service. It was followed on October 12 by the 2nd Regiment and on November 24 by the 3rd. [31] The news must have given a kind of bittersweet satisfaction to Brigadier General John W. Phelps in retirement in the Green Mountains of Vermont.

On October 1 the New Orleans correspondent of the New York *Times* wrote enthusiastically of the reception there of the emancipation news. He commented in the same dispatch on "the additional wonder of the first appearance of the Guardes de Afrique, the regiment of free colored people called out by Gov. Moore, but not put into the field until the arrival of Gen.

Butler." He had just seen a squad of these new troops, he told his Northern readers, "bearing their bayoneted muskets proudly, marching down Camp Street, in charge of some half-dozen prisoners of their own color. As trifling as these things appear to the superficial observer, they really mark momentous eras in the history of this revolution." [32]

It must have been with considerable satisfaction that Frederick Douglass published a report sent north by an officer in one of the new Louisiana colored regiments. "You would be surprised," the officer began, "at the progress the blacks make in drill and in all the duties of soldiers. I find them better deposed [sic] to learn, and more orderly and cleanly, both in their persons and quarters, than the whites. Their fighting qualities," he admitted, "have not yet been tested on a large scale, but I am satisfied that, knowing as they do that they will receive no quarter at the hands of the Rebels, they will fight to the death." This was not the report of an abolitionist visionary but of a military realist, as the closing lines of the letter indicate: "As an old Democrat, I felt a little repugnance at having anything to do with negroes, but having got fairly over that, am in the work. They are just as good tools to crush rebellion with as any that can be got." [33]

Henry Adams's hope of November, 1861, "emancipation and arming the slaves," was well on the road to high fulfillment. The muscles of the sable arm Frederick Douglass had urged so long were finally beginning to be flexed by the Union.

IV. *"Soon have an army."*

... I have been reflecting upon [Lane of Kansas], and
have concluded that we need the services of such a man
out there at once; that we better appoint him a brigadier-
general of volunteers today, and send him off with such
authority to raise a force ... as you think will get him
into actual work quickest. Tell him when he starts to
put it through. Not be writing or telegraphing back here,
but put it through.

—ABRAHAM LINCOLN, June 20, 1861

Out in the West, out beyond the Mississippi, the step from
contraband laborers with Union armies to Negro soldiers in
those armies was neither so long nor so difficult as it seemed to
be in the East and in the South. A paragraph in the Leavenworth *Daily Conservative* of October 6, 1861, describing some
of James H. Lane's cavalrymen, showed that the color line was
no insuperable barrier in Kansas. The *Conservative*'s correspondent wrote: "One peculiarity of this mounted force is
curious enough to be noted down. By the side of one doughty
and white cavalier rode an erect well-armed and very black
man: his figure and bearing were such that, without any other
distinguishing characteristic he would still have been a marked
man. It is well known that negroes and Indians serve in the
rebel army but this is the first instance which has come to our
personal knowledge—although not the only one in fact—of a
contraband serving as a Union soldier."
Strange that the *Conservative*, Senator Lane's own paper,

69

should have found this circumstance at all curious. More than
a fortnight earlier, on September 14, the paper had discussed
the plans of Colonel Charles R. Jennison, a Lane henchman,
for raising a regiment at Leavenworth. In the course of the story,
the *Conservative* had observed without adverse comment:
"There seems to be a good prospect just now to organize a regiment of colored fugitives in these parts. Thirty-five . . . have
transferred themselves to this town and are now enjoying the
privileges of free men. . . . The Colonel proposes to organize a
company of contrabands for the service. He has them drilling
already and says they promise to make fine soldiers and thinks
they will make spendid 'Home Guards.' "

What was afoot in Kansas was the result of a mixture of circumstances peculiar to that strife-torn region. The struggle
between proslavery forces and free-soil men had been sporadi-
cally enriching Kansas soil with human blood since passage of
the Kansas-Nebraska Act in 1854. That struggle had attracted
the attention of John Brown and a train of radical abolitionists
including James H. Lane, James Montgomery, and Charles
Jennison. John Brown slept in an Adirondack grave, but Lane
and the others were alive and active in Kansas. They were men
who could be relied on to act with ruthless, primitive energy in
the Brown manner whenever occasion for destroying slavery
should offer. From the beginning of the Civil War they displayed an easy disregard for the feelings and property rights
of their "neighbors" across the Missouri border. Not only were
fugitive slaves encouraged to seek sanctuary in the free state
of Kansas; the Jayhawkers took peculiar delight in expeditions
of liberation into the slaveholding state lying conveniently
along the eastern flank. To them the Civil War was only a con-
tinuation of their earlier battles. Their theater of war was so
far removed from the center of government that they could
disregard administration policy and War Department orders
with impunity. With Senator Lane, a brigadier general commissioned at Lincoln's personal direction,[1] to provide some
cloak of respectability for their actions, the Jayhawkers operated like border chieftains out of some feudal past.

That Negroes should have been openly enrolled as Union
soldiers in Kansas in the fall of 1861 was entirely consonant

with the logic of radical abolitionism and Kansas territorial history. Lane summed up the Kansas attitude in a letter to General Samuel D. Sturgis in early October: "The institution of slavery must take care of itself. Confiscation of slaves and other property which can be made useful to the Army should follow treason as the thunder peal follows the lightning flash." [2]

In the Senate, as 1862 began to unfold, Lane introduced a resolution to authorize field commanders in Kansas to muster into service all persons who presented themselves for that purpose. Although in debate on the question Lane hedged somewhat to maintain that his resolution would not give the power to arm Negroes, he drew cheers from the gallery when he declared that he would say to Negroes, "I have not arms for you, but if it is in your power to obtain arms from rebels, take them, and I will use you as soldiers against traitors." [3]

Back in Leavenworth, toward the end of January, Lane was more characteristically outspoken. While he declined to "call in the Comanches" to help the Union cause, it would give him no pain, he said, "to see a negro handling a gun." A Negro might "just as well become food for powder," said the Great Jayhawker, "as my son." As long as rebels carried guns, he continued, he would not "propose to punish the negro if he kills a traitor." A master of bombast, he went on, warming to his subject as his audience began to catch his enthusiasm: "Now, I may lose my standing in the Church, but I tell you I take stock in every negro insurrection, and I don't care how many there are." If Southerners objected to being killed by Negroes, Lane suggested, with what passed for humor on the frontier, "let them lay down their arms."

To charges that the slaves lacked native intelligence sufficient to make good soldiers, he had this to say: "The negroes are much more intelligent than I had ever supposed. I have seen them come into camp (occasionally)"—his broad hint that fugitives merely strayed into his camp "occasionally" brought roars of knowing laughter from his listeners—"looking down as though slaves. By-and-by they begin to straighten themselves, throw back their shoulders, stand erect, and soon look God straight in the face. . . . After a long day's march, after getting supper for the men, after feeding and cleaning the horses, I have seen them out, just back of the tents, drilling. And they take to drill as a child takes to its mother's milk. They soon learn the step, soon learn the position of the soldier and the manual of arms. You can see that in the innermost recesses of their soul the 'devil is in them.' " To Jim Lane the course of action was clear. "Give them a fair chance," he cried, "put arms in their hands and they will do the balance of the fighting in this war." To him it was a matter of large indifference whether traitors were punished "on the battlefield, on the gallows or from the brush by a negro." [4]

Here was a man formed for the work of radicals, a giant in stature and in standing among his friends in the West, and well acquainted, as the New York *Times* put it, with "the warfare peculiar to the borders." Further, the New York paper declaimed, "His restless activity—his fertility of resource—his personal magnetism—mark him with the most important qualities of a military leader." [5] The almost legendary tale of Lane's operations in the trans-Mississippi West during the summer and fall of 1862 runs like a leitmotif through the grim history of that second year of war. Making friends by the hundreds as easily as he mad enemies, Lane bludgeoned and cajoled his way along, with and without War Department authority, carrying problems as lightly as he carried debts, depending more on his personal eloquence and magnetism than on the force of logic, magnificently undisturbed at reports against him that would have ruined a lesser man.

Around him Lane gathered a coterie of abolitionists and friends of old John Brown, Jayhawkers in the border tradition, men with John Brown's fanatical eyes, men careless of the little amenities of comfortable society and careless, too, of personal loyalties. Foremost among Lane's lieutenants were Charles Jennison and James Montgomery, each fighting the other for personal advancement and neither giving any more loyalty to Jim Lane than the expediency of the moment dictated. Behind each other's backs they connived and plotted, and it is a tribute to the personal ability of Lane that he ever reached the point of having a Negro regiment drilled and disciplined and assembled in one camp.

On August 3, Montgomery wrote Governor Charles Robinson

to blast Jennison as "an unmitigated *liar black leg and Robber*";
Montgomery was urging his own candidacy as colonel of the
colored regiment then being recruited. A few days later George
H. Hoyt, a friend of Jennison's, wrote the governor that, while
Jennison was working with Lane, "he takes hold of this work
not as a Lane man, but altogether on the *Jennison* basis . . ."
Jennison had his eyes on that colonelcy, too. On August 22,
Jennison himself wrote to Robinson to disclose that he had dis-
covered "at all points in Southern Kansas a general feeling
that Lane is a great humbug." [6]

Humbug or Jayhawker, the imperturbable Lane went grandly
ahead. In early August he opened a recruiting office in Leavenworth for the enlistment of both white and colored men, although the latter were technically enrolled as laborers.[7] To
recruit Negroes north of the Kansas River, Lane appointed
Captain James Williams, and he selected Captain H. C. Seaman
to enroll colored volunteers south of the river. Both captains
were known abolitionists.[8] On August 5, Lane wired Stanton of
prospects in Kansas. "Recruiting opens up beautifully," he
reported with typical optimism, "good for four regiments of
whites and two of blacks." The next day Lane wired the secretary again: "I am receiving negroes under the late act of Congress [of July 17, 1862]. Is there any objection? Answer by
telegraph. Soon have an army." [9]

Now there was an objection; the newspapers for August 6
were full of the news of Lincoln's opposition to the arming of
Negroes. But the Eastern papers had not yet reached Kansas.
On that same day the War Department informed the governor
of Wisconsin that "The President declines to receive Indians
or negroes as troops." [10] But Stanton did not get around to
telling Lane the policy until two weeks later. Meanwhile, in
blissful ignorance, Lane and his recruiters went ahead with
their work. The Emporia *News* of August 9 reported wholesale
progress, particularly by the devious Jennison, already called
"the Colonel." He, the *News* announced, had "tendered two
regiments of negroes to Gen. Lane," although these "regiments"
could have been only companies. On the same page of the *News*
was the report of a Mound City, Kansas, celebration of the
anniversary of British emancipation in the West Indies. The

high point of the celebration came when "a company of one hundred able-bodied contrabands enlisted, were mustered into the service of the United States and armed—all in a very short space of time." This particular company, the *News* continued, was "for immediate service in Missouri under Colonel Montgomery who will have a battalion of Indians, negroes, and white men under his command. The 'tri-colored brigade' will undoubtedly give a good account of itself."

The New York *Times* of August 17 published reports from its Kansas correspondent describing Lane's popularity with the Negroes, who "Under his direction . . . are enthusiastic to enlist and fight. Already about a hundred stalwart fellows are enrolled in Lawrence in two companies, both expected to be filled . . ."

Lane's successes seem to have disturbed Governor Robinson, and on August 20 he wired Stanton to report that "General Lane is recruiting a regiment of colored men in Kansas." Robinson wanted to know whether he should commission the officers of the organization in keeping with practice in white volunteer regiments. Stanton's reply raised no question of the propriety of Lane's recruiting Negroes; rather did he seem to give the movement his blessing by directing Robinson to send him the names of Lane's nominees for commissions and promising that "instructions will be given you on the subject." [11] Two days later the secretary of war wrote at length to Lane himself, congratulating him on the success of his recruiting but telling him that "regiments of African descent can only be raised upon express and special authority of the President. He has not given authority to raise such troops in Kansas, and it is not comprehended in the authority issued to you. Such regiments cannot be accepted into the service." [12] There is no indication that this information had any deterring effect on Jim Lane.

As August ended, colored men continued to be enrolled in Kansas, and in early September six leading Missouri citizens found it necessary to complain to the president of the depredations of armed bands of Negroes raiding into Missouri from their base in Kansas. After reciting the dangers to which they had been subjected, they insisted that Lane "should be instructed not to suffer the arming or enrollment of negroes" or

be replaced.[13] Perhaps as a result of this protest, Stanton wired
Lane again on September 23 to state flatly "you are not authorized to organize Indians, nor any but loyal white men." [14] This
was just as effective as his letter to Lane a month earlier.

The Great Jayhawker was having troubles nearer home. His
radical steps had not been taken without opposition. Many
Kansans and Missourians opposed the movement to arm Negroes
out of prejudice, it is true, but there were others whose opposition was based on honest doubt of the military value of colored
soldiers. Others, like the loyal slaveholders of parts of Missouri,
feared the loss of their valuable slave property as a result of
the impetuous activities of Lane's recruiters. Still others were
frankly in sympathy with the Confederate cause and opposed
all measures to recruit Union soldiers, white, Negro, or Indian.
Many colored men came forward to offer themselves quickly
and eagerly for service, sensing the importance of the opportunity. But there were others who were understandably reluctant
to volunteer for fear they would be badly used by the white
troops around them and by the Union government. There were
those, too, who were afraid to volunteer and leave their families
without support or protection in white communities where Negro
"rights" were liable to be a bad joke.

Lane's recruiting officers found obstacles in their paths, some
of them placed there by civil authorities. Some of his recruiters
were even charged with "unlawfully restraining persons of their
liberty." [15] Perhaps these charges were not completely without
foundation. Perhaps the word "volunteers" in the name of the
Kansas Negro regiment was slightly inaccurate. Jim Lane was
primarily interested in getting troops; they did not *have* to be
volunteers. At one Leavenworth mass meeting, as the recruiting
drive got under way, Lane declared that "the negroes are mistaken if they think white men can fight for them while they stay
at home." Lane warned the Negroes: "We have been saying
that you would fight, and if you won't we will make you." [16]

The men who filled up the companies of the 1st Kansas
Colored Volunteers seem to have been largely recruited from
among fugitive slaves out of Arkansas and Missouri. Some of
them were fugitives in a technical sense only; their former
owners complained bitterly, in some instances, that Lane's

marauders had stolen them out of hand, which was probably
true.[17] One entire company was raised by one man, Benjamin
F. Van Horn. Learning that a large number of fugitives had
taken refuge with the Sac and Fox Indians, Van Horn brought
this news to General James G. Blunt and Jim Lane. Those en-
thusiasts at once commissioned Van Horn a lieutenant and sent
him out to get a company after thoughtfully providing him with
several wagons loaded with supplies and equipment and even
a drillmaster! A few weeks later Van Horn returned triumphantly leading a full-strength company of eighty men. He
remained in the service as their company commander.[18]

On September 22, "Our Own Correspondent" at the headquarters of the 1st Regiment of Kansas Colored Volunteers,
"Camp Jim Lane near Wyandot," wrote the New York *Times* at
great length on the progress of that organization. He had good
words for the experiment and some observations that should
have been of interest to Union military leaders. "The regiment
encamped at this point is progressing finely," he reported.
"There are seven nearly full companies upon the ground, and
the aptitude of the men for acquiring the drill has already made
their progress more than equal any body of white men so new
to the service. Apart from this aptitude for acquiring the
manual, the negroes are decidedly the easiest managed, most
willing, and good-humored people it has been my fortune to see
massed since this war began." The *Times* correspondent had
an explanation for this: "The very first idea of a soldier's life,
subordination, to learn which our white citizens have to un-
learn nearly all their past experience has taught them, the
negroes, by the circumstances of their lives, have certainly to
a degree as great as the most strenuous martinet would insist
upon. An army is essentially a despotism; the only point is to
intelligently accept it, and, using the power thus acquired, our
army will be invincible." There was no doubt in this reporter's
mind "as to the capacity of the negroes to acquire the mechani-
cal part of the soldier's duty."

The dispatch went into great detail to describe the training
of the Negro soldiers, and he commented on their cooperation
with each other in correcting the usual recruit's errors at drill.
The men spent five hours a day drilling and learning the duties

of sentinels, and each day ended with a dress parade at which the men presented "quite a respectable appearance." The uniform in the West differed substantially from the red Zouave trousers and dark jackets of Hunter's men. Lane's command wore forage caps, gray trousers, and blue jackets. Their camp, the correspondent noted, was a model of neatness and order with both officers and men showing great pride in its appearance.[19]

These troops soon became more than recruits sweating at drill under the baking sun of Kansas and endlessly policing their company streets. Although there is no record of his ever having been given War Department permission to raise Negro soldiers, early October of 1862 found Lane sending his men raiding into Missouri in the finest Jayhawking tradition. A detachment of his troops, according to newspaper reports, was met "by a company of Missouri State Militia and driven back. Several shots were fired, but little damage was done to either party."[20] By the end of October, however, the 1st Kansas Colored was no longer being driven back. Some five companies met a large force of guerrillas near Butler, Bates County, Missouri, in "the first engagement in the war in which colored troops were engaged."[21] A Leavenworth *Conservative* correspondent waxed eloquent on the military prowess of these new additions to Union strength. "It is useless to talk any more about negro courage," he maintained. "The men fought like tigers, each and every one of them, and the main difficulty was to hold them well in hand. . . . Saddle and mount is the word. These are the boys to clean out the bushwhackers."[22]

Five companies later returned to Bates County and during a five-day expedition engaged a large force of rebels near Island Mound. After routing their enemies and capturing a large amount of stock, the Kansas troops continued on to Fort Scott, the hub of Union defense lines in the upper trans-Mississippi West.[23]

Their actual employment in combat, if only against rebel irregulars and Missouri bushwhackers, was good training for the Negro soldiers and good publicity, too. It seems to have helped reduce opposition to their recruitment, in Kansas at any rate, although the effect was quite otherwise in Missouri and

Arkansas. They had fought and with some success; they had
launched a career of three years of hard duty on the frontier
from Fort Leavenworth south to Fort Scott and beyond to Fort
Gibson and Fort Smith and Pine Bluff deep in Arkansas. On
January 13, 1863, six companies were mustered into federal
service as the 1st Regiment, Kansas Colored Volunteers, Lieutenant Colonel James M. Williams commanding.[24] The choice
of Williams to command the new regiment was a good one.
Lacking the glamor of the Jayhawkers like Jennison and Montgomery, he had nevertheless done a commendable, industrious,
and quiet job of organizing the companies. He was to lead the
organization well through many trials, yielding his command
temporarily only after he was severely wounded at the head of
his men at Honey Springs in June, 1863. Probably it was
Charles Jennison's rather unsavory reputation and selfish ambition that prevented his getting the command. For his part,
James Montgomery left Kansas in disgust in December, 1862,
and later became colonel of the 2nd South Carolina Colored
Volunteers, afterwards the 34th United States Colored Troops.

On the basis of official dates of muster-in, the 1st Kansas
Colored was the fourth Negro regiment to enter the Union
Army. Butler's three regiments of Louisiana Native Guards
stand first on the rolls. But Kansas was the first of the free states
to enroll Negro soldiers, and small units and companies of
Kansas colored troops fought in the first engagements in the
Civil War in which American Negroes were permitted to fight
for the Union.

V. *"No man can hender me."*

Events of no ordinary interest have just occurred in the Department of the South. The negro troops have been tested, and to their great joy, though not contrary to their own expectations, they have triumphed, not only over enemies armed with muskets and swords, but over what the black man dreads most, sharp and cruel prejudices.

—Chicago *Tribune*, November 19, 1862

The curtain had been rung down on David Hunter's attempt to raise Negro troops, but it was no final curtain. The spotlight of national interest had shifted to Kansas and Louisiana during August and September of 1862, but even as Negroes were being armed and organized by Lane and Butler, the 1st South Carolina Colored Volunteers began, like the phoenix, to rise from the ashes of Hunter's hopes. The movement to arm the Negro was too vital to die easily; Union needs for military manpower were too great to leave untouched forever the reservoir of free colored men in the North and the vast slave population of the South. Even before the War Department could learn of Butler's enrollment of Negroes along the Mississippi, even as Edwin M. Stanton tried to discourage the activities of Kansas radicals along the Kaw, the Marmaton, and the Missouri, orders went out for the enlistment of colored troops in the Sea Islands of South Carolina.

These orders were not addressed to Hunter but rather to Brigadier General Rufus Saxton, a regular army officer and West Pointer who had gone south as chief quartermaster with

Thomas W. Sherman and had been placed directly under War
Department orders in June of 1862.[1] Rufus Saxton was an excellent choice for the work. Where Hunter had been hasty and
shortsighted, Saxton was even-tempered, conciliatory, patient,
and aware of the importance of maintaining good relations with
the white army around him. Saxton's father was an abolitionist;
the son was not. General Saxton was interested in working out
a solution to the Negro problem, but he was no ultra. He seems
to have won the confidence of the white officers and men in the
Department of the South with almost the same ease as he won
the hearts of the Negroes, who were quick to recognize him as
a friend. He soon became "Gen'rel Saxby" all over the Sea
Islands.

The War Department orders to Saxton were almost all that
Hunter had begged for. Admitting the dearth of troops in the
Department of the South and the inability of the government to
provide reinforcements, Stanton authorized Saxton "to arm,
uniform, equip, and receive into the service of the United States
such number of volunteers of African descent as you may deem
expedient, not exceeding 5,000, and [you] may detail officers
to instruct them in military drill, discipline, and duty, and to
command them." The orders contemplated equal pay for equal
work: "persons so received into service and their officers [are]
to be entitled to and [will] receive the same pay and rations as
are allowed by law to volunteers in the service." [2]

So did the American Negro become an official part of the
Union Army. The authority was limited and showed no broad
policy looking toward the wholesale use of Negro troops. While
it granted equal pay and rations, that part of the order was for
almost two years to be treated as an error on the part of
Secretary Stanton and was not honored as the promise of the
War Department and Union government. There was no mention
of advance pay and bounties authorized to white recruits by
law. The importance of these orders of August 25, 1862, is that
by them Negroes were mustered into the service of the United
States by War Department authority rather than by some enterprising general officer acting on his own initiative. The orders
signify a major turning point in the war policy of the Lincoln
administration, foreshadowing the large-scale organization of

Negro regiments in 1863 and their broadening combat use throughout the rest of the war.

Lincoln had made it clear on August 6, less than three weeks earlier, that he was not in favor of arming Negroes as soldiers. Secretary Stanton had now authorized that very thing. Lincoln's frame of mind in this period is not readily discernible. He was making up his mind, indeed he had already made up his mind, to the necessity of emancipation as a military measure. Certainly various members of his cabinet, Chase and Stanton especially, had pointed out that emancipation and arming the Negro were complementary steps.[3] Military events during that terrible summer argued more persuasively than cabinet officers for the revolutionary step: McClellan's Peninsular campaign had ended in failure and withdrawal; Pope failed disastrously at Second Bull Run as August ended, and Lee's skirmishers were thrusting north of the Potomac. Further, mid-term elections loomed, and Lincoln's Republican party needed all the votes it could muster. The presidential announcement of August 6 had been designed to conciliate Border state sentiment. The Stanton order of August 25 may have been designed to conciliate abolitionist sentiment in the North and West. Whatever his personal attitude toward arming the Negro in late August, Lincoln at least permitted his secretary of war to issue the necessary orders. The president himself made no favorable public utterance until his final Emancipation Proclamation of January 1, 1863.

General Hunter, meanwhile, had left the scene of his failure, having been granted sixty days' leave of absence on August 22, the day on which Butler invited volunteers from the free colored militia of Louisiana. Hunter turned over command to the officer next in rank in the department, Brigadier General J. M. Brannon.[4] When Stanton sent his epochal orders to Saxton, Henry W. Halleck, now general-in-chief of the armies, sent a copy of these orders to General Brannon and ordered him to "give all possible assistance" to Saxton in carrying them out.[5] There was to be nothing halfway about the Saxton project.

It was just as well, too. Saxton found his situation difficult and his mission hedged about with obstacles. The *National Intelligencer* of September 16 discussed some of these obstacles and handicaps. "The arming of the negroes," the Washington

paper complained, "has hitherto proved not only unpopular with
the people, but especially among the volunteers. To again attempt the thing after its failure on Gen. Hunter's hands appears
to be unwise and injudicious; but if Mr. Lincoln gives us the
order to fight by the side of the negro, let us first find the
negro who will stand by us." Disregarding the fact demonstrated a thousand times over from the beginning of the war
that fugitives trooped into Union lines wherever federal forces
touched slave territory, the *Intelligencer* argued: "We must get
the blacks into our possession in order to make soldiers of
them, just as certainly as we must catch a hare before we cook
him; and to obtain the blacks will require a larger force and
bigger bounty than Uncle Sam has yet supplied to us or offered
the negro."

A few weeks later, on October 3, the *National Intelligencer*
replied to its own pessimistic arguments with a dispatch from
Port Royal announcing that "Contrabands are coming in here
daily by the hundreds. Gen. Mitchel will not let Pro-Slavery
and Breckinridge army officers keep them back." The latter
comment referred to Brigadier General Isaac Stevens, serving
in the Department of the South, who had been chairman of the
national committee to elect John C. Breckinridge of Kentucky to
the presidency in 1860. Although the dispatch disclosed that
there was "but little work for these poor devils to do," it
pointed out that "a brigade of five thousand will soon be
organized and ready to bear the brunt of any action, or do the
hard work of entrenching if necessary."

Brigadier General O. M. Mitchel took command of the Department of the South on September 17.[6] He quickly assessed
the situation and three days later sent a comprehensive report
to Stanton, a report which indicated that Saxton's job would
not be easy. The new commanding general saw trouble in the
dual command existing in the Sea Islands: Saxton, the military
governor of the islands, was under direct control from Washington, working independently of the Department of the South,
and Mitchel had discovered cases of "friction and raw collision
... between the officers of the two individual commands." He
was certain, he told Stanton, that no matter how harmoniously

the two generals might work together, "there will be trouble
constantly arising among the subordinates."

But more deep-seated than this jurisdictional difficulty was
the prejudice Mitchel found among white officers and men
"against the blacks, founded upon an opinion that in some way
the negroes have been more favored by the Government and
more privileges granted to them than to the volunteer soldiers."
General Mitchel was earnestly concerned with the problem and
working to find a solution to it.[7] And certainly this was the most
serious handicap Saxton had to overcome in his work of organizing Negro troops. The legacy of Hunter's shortsighted
radicalism was to plague him throughout the balance of the
year.

There were other problems, of course. Saxton's first report
to Stanton disclosed that the rebels were "moving all their slaves
back from the sea-coast as fast as they can" to prevent their
escape to join the Union forces. Disregarding the course of the
war in the North, where Lee had only recently been turned back
at Antietam Creek with heavy Union casualties, Saxton asked
that large reinforcements be sent south to secure Union positions on the mainland and thus simplify the Negro problem of
escaping and enlisting. Saxton, taking a leaf from Hunter's
book, argued that "the service of 50,000 effective men [could]
do more [in his department] than twice that number in any
other field," by building a fire in the rear of the Confederacy
and requiring the transfer of rebel troops from northern Virginia to keep Southern slaves in check.[8]

In his second report, Saxton discussed another problem: he
complained that his sphere of operations and supply of human
material were limited by the large numbers of able-bodied
Negroes already employed by the Quartermaster and Engineer
departments, by the navy, as officers' servants, and as free
laborers on the steamboats and with private traders. Those
available for rebuilding the 1st South Carolina were accordingly
few.

There was yet another serious difficulty: the Negroes who
had belonged to Hunter's regiment had served three or four
months without pay while their families had suffered. Meanwhile, as Saxton explained it, "Those who did not enlist . . .

were receiving wages all this time" for work in any of a half-
dozen occupations around the islands. The result was that
"Accustomed as these people are to having their rights disregarded, this failure to pay them for their service has weakened
their confidence in our promises for the future and makes them
slow to enlist." Saxton suggested that a small bounty might
help lower the Negroes' resistance to military service and re-
establish their confidence in the Union. That prejudice in the
white army was slowly melting is indicated by Saxton's comment that he was receiving "a great many applications from all
grades of officers and soldiers serving here for positions" in his
new organization.[9]

Meanwhile, as Saxton labored to overcome the bitter legacies
of Hunter's failure, the idea of Negro soldiers began to take
hold. It was helped somewhat by the preliminary announcement of Lincoln's emancipation plans on September 22. This
made clear to all who could read and understand an important
shift in Union war aims, a sharp swing away from a merely
restraining war to an antislavery crusade. Public opinion in
favor of Negro soldiers also was encouraged by an increasingly
good press. During the last quarter of 1862 Northern newspapers were crowded with news stories and editorial comment
on colored troops in the Union armies. From Kansas, Louisiana,
and South Carolina, correspondents filed dispatches describing
the appearance of the men and their camps, their ability to
learn drill quickly, their discipline, and their determination.
Certainly the newspapers did a great service to the cause of the
Negro soldier by keeping him constantly in the public eye. The
Negro soldier himself did the rest.

More convincing than editorial arguments were the reports
of the progress and actual military employment of Negro troops
in the South and West. From New Orleans, for example, came
encouraging word of the military appearance and discipline of
the 1st Louisiana. A New York *Times* correspondent attended
an inspection of that regiment, and by some accident the inspecting officer arrived before any warning of his approach
could be given. The response of the troops was worthy of
regulars. "A few moments only elapsed," the reporter wrote,
". . . before the men were in line, then broke into columns of

companies and went through inspection. There were ten companies on the ground, numbering ninety-six men each, and on
the whole, their conduct could not have been better; in fact, I
have seen older white regiments, with more regimental drills,
that are not their equal." The *Times* man was impressed with
the "happy arrangement of the men" which gave the appearance
of uniformity in height. So well did the old military device of
"sizing" the men by companies work that the correspondent did
not believe "there was an inch difference between the entire
regiment." He was also surprised and impressed by the attractive and soldierly appearance of the regiment's company officers, all colored but ranging in shade from nearly white to
"unmixed African." Perhaps the most significant revelation in
the dispatch came toward its close: the regiment had completed
its training and was about to leave camp "to take up their position in Algiers," just south of New Orleans, "to guard . . . a
line of railway." [10]

Although his regiment was far from having completed its
training (it was, in fact, far from filled up), General Saxton
decided to send his troops into action. This was no large-scale
operation, but a long-range raid by one company under the
personal direction of Lieutenant Colonel Oliver T. Beard of the
48th New York Infantry. The main purposes of the raid were
to feel out the rebel pickets along the coasts of Florida and
Georgia and up the Bell and Sapello rivers, to destroy salt-
works and whatever food and supplies could not be taken off,
and to bring in whatever slaves could be found. There was one
other important purpose: Saxton wanted to find out what the
fighting qualities of his troops actually were. The expedition
was, in fact—in modern military terminology—a reconnaissance in force, a commando raid, a recruiting drive, and a
training problem with live ammunition, all rolled into one.

In a busy week, from November 3 to 10, Colonel Beard took
Captain Trowbridge's Company A on a highly successful ma-
rauding expedition. Aboard a captured steamer and with occasional fire support from a small gunboat, the Negro soldiers
spread havoc along the coast of Georgia and Northern Florida.
They drove in rebel pickets at point after point, killed nine of
the enemy, took three prisoners, destroyed nine different salt-

works, destroyed also about $20,000 worth of horses, wagons, rice, corn, and other Confederate property, and they carried off over one hundred and fifty slaves. Colonel Beard reported to General Saxton on his return that "The colored men fought with astonishing coolness and bravery. For alacrity in effecting landings, for determination, and for bush fighting I found them all I could desire,—more than I had hoped. They behaved bravely, gloriously, and deserve all praise."

Casualties were surprisingly low; only four men were wounded. In fact, the force grew in strength as the operation advanced. "I started from Saint Simon's with sixty-two colored fighting men," Beard told Saxton proudly, "and returned to Beaufort with 156 fighting men (all colored)." The process was simplicity itself. "As soon as we took a slave from his claimant," Beard explained, "we placed a musket in his hand and he began to fight for the freedom of the others." In addition to these welcome recruits, the raiders brought off sixty-one women and children.[11]

Jubilantly General Saxton reported the success of this first use of his colored troops as a military force against the Confederacy. "It is admitted upon all hands," he wrote the secretary of war, "that the negroes fought with a coolness and bravery that would have done credit to veteran soldiers. There was no excitement, no flinching, no attempt at cruelty when successful. They seemed like men who were fighting to vindicate their manhood and they did it well." On the strength of this small experiment, Saxton optimistically spun out a detailed plan for bringing the Confederacy to swift ruin by a multiplication of similar raids by Negro troops with naval support all along the Atlantic coast. In conclusion, he told Stanton that the 1st South Carolina was filling up rapidly with 550 men already enrolled.[12]

On the other side of the line, reaction was far from jubilant. A letter signed "Cavalry" appearing in the Savannah *Republican* of November 14 sketched out this "abolitionist" vandalism on the Georgia coast. "At the residence of Reuben King, Esq., they forced some fifty negroes to accompany them," the letter writer declared, "in spite of their piteous cries and lamentations, 'to free, clothe and educate' as they stated. The com-

mander of the [steamer] ordered those shot who refused to go
... " The author of the letter had only contempt for Yankees.
"They next visited the residence of Col. D. McDonald," he
wrote, "where they succeeded in capturing Col. M., breaking
up his salt-works and stealing a few things, when hearing that
some cavalry was approaching, the cowardly wretches fled to
their boats. These *philanthropic, noble* friends of the black
man, at each of these places, sent *armed negroes* ahead to bear
the brunt and receive our bullets, should any soldier be present.
How Yankee! How brave!"

The comment of the New York *Times* was somewhat briefer,
less critical, but certainly to the point. "Very late advices from
Kansas and Florida," the account began, referring also to the
1st Kansas Colored's encounter with irregulars near Butler,
Missouri, "give details of engagements between the rebels and
United States negro troops in which the latter behaved with distinguished coolness and brave courage, and achieved decided
success." Even to the cautious *Times* this was news of tremendous significance: "The result of these experimental fights is
such as inspires the rebels with indescribable horror, and bids
fair to work important changes in the policy of the Government
toward the negroes." [13]

While the country was still buzzing over these demonstrations of the practical value of Negro soldiers, General Saxton
sent Colonel Beard out again, this time with three companies
instead of one, up the Doboy River in Georgia "in quest of
lumber and other articles needed for the department." This
second expedition provided opportunity for the men of the 1st
South Carolina to show how they could stand up in a sharp
rifle skirmish and hold a position stubbornly against the gun-
fire of a concealed enemy.

A small unit of thirty-odd men, reconnoitering near their
sawmill objective, ran into a Confederate ambush. After a
momentary panic, they rallied and "opened a brisk fire on the
places occupied by the concealed enemy." They kept up this
fire until Colonel Beard ordered them to retire. And their withdrawal was no rout. "They retired," Beard reported, "firing as
they went with a slowness and deliberateness that could not
have been surpassed by veteran troops." The Department of the

South was the richer by nearly 300,000 board feet of "superior boards and planks" in addition to the saws and belting found in the raided sawmill. The cost was low: only four men wounded. "On the last expedition," Colonel Beard asserted in his report to General Saxton, "the fact was developed that colored men would fight behind barricades; this time they have proved, by their heroism, that they will fight in the open field." [14]

There were no more raiding parties for the 1st South Carolina for two months. The new colonel of the regiment arrived in Beaufort on November 24. He was strong on drill, discipline, instruction, and military appearance, and so the men who had already been under enemy fire had perforce to settle down to the routine of drill, guard mount, loading by nines, and dress parades. General Saxton had made a superb choice in the man to lead the 1st South Carolina: he was Thomas Wentworth Higginson of Massachusetts, abolitionist and old friend of John Brown, a man with an excellent reputation throughout the North because of his intellectual and literary attainments. He had been captain of a crack company in the 51st Massachusetts Infantry when Saxton's invitation reached him in mid-November. He could have been no more surprised, he wrote later, "had an invitation reached [him] to take command of a regiment of Kalmuck Tartars," but he "had been an abolitionist too long and had known and loved John Brown too well, not to feel a thrill of joy at last on finding [himself] in the position" where John Brown "only wished to be." [15] Higginson left his Massachusetts company and went south immediately.

He found his new regiment over half full but lacking the precision and uniformity of drill and bearing habitual in his former command, and he went to work at once to make the 1st South Carolina a well-drilled, smoothly functioning, military machine. Higginson was exactly what the situation demanded. He lent the enterprise a respectability it had previously lacked and he quickly brought the regiment into a state of training and morale equal to that of any white regiment of similar experience. His intelligence, imagination, devotion to duty, and military experience provided the right mixture. He had soon won the confidence and affection of his men, and he gradually

restored the regiment and the whole enterprise of arming
Negroes in the opinion of the white officers and men of the
department by seeing that his men did their fair share and
more of the fatigue duty and unloading supply ships. Higginson was not the one to repeat Hunter's mistakes.

The new colonel found nothing to complain of in his men.
He especially liked their spirit. The first Negro soldier he spoke
to had been wounded on the expedition after lumber. Pointing
to the soldier's injured arm, Higginson asked:

"Did you think that was more than you bargained for, my
man?"

"I been a-tinking, Mas'r," the Negro replied, *"dat's jess
what I went for."*

For Higginson, the entire experience was novel and challenging, and he gave it his best. He was aware more than
anyone else of the signal importance of making the regiment a
good one, aware that the organization "was watched with mi-
croscopic scrutiny by friends and foes." He admitted later that
"It was no pleasant thing to live in this glare of criticism; but
it guarantied [sic] the honesty of any success, while fearfully
multiplying the penalties, had there been a failure." [16] It was
as if Higginson had taken for his personal motto the chorus of
a spiritual popular with the Sea Island Negroes:

> Jesus make de blind to see,
> Jesus make de cripple walk,
> Jesus make de deaf to hear,
> Walk in, kind Jesus!
> No man can hender me.[17]

That spirit seemed to imbue the entire regiment.

The obstacles to success grew for the most part from "the
legacy of bitter distrust bequeathed by the abortive regiment
of General Hunter,—into which they were driven like cattle,
kept for several months in camp, and then turned off without a
shilling, by order of the War Department." There were men in
his organization who had originally enlisted under Hunter,
particularly in Captain Trowbridge's Company A, and while
they were "the best soldiers we have in other respects," they

struck Higginson as "the least sanguine and cheerful" in the
regiment. "Were this a wholly new regiment," he recorded in
his journal on December 2, "it would have been full to overflowing . . . ere now." [18]

By the end of the year the new colonel was well established
in his headquarters tent at Camp Saxton and with growing
numbers of soldiers manning the companies of his regiment. He
was pleased with their appearance, ability, and attentiveness,
proud of their performance as sentinels, and at all times fas-
cinated by their language, games, songs, stories, and humor.
Their training had advanced far more rapidly than he had
hoped. And on the first day of the new year there was a celebration at Camp Saxton.

There had been other holidays in the camp. Thanksgiving,
three days after Higginson's arrival at Beaufort, had had its
extra rations, oranges, and prize shoots. Christmas, the greatest
festival in the slaves' calendar, had had to pass almost unnoticed except for the omission of taps to permit the men to
"sit up and burn their fires and have their little prayer meetings
as late as they desired." The celebration on January 1, 1863,
however, was unique. It signified more than the beginning of a
new year. For the American Negro it was the first day of a
new era.

Everything was in readiness by ten o'clock in the morning.
Ten beeves had been spitted and roasted over huge fires during
the night. Ten barrels of molasses-and-water, one for each
company, had been prepared (to one barrel of water, add three
gallons of molasses, half a pound of ginger, and one quart of
vinegar; stir well; serve), "destined to cheer but not inebriate."
The band of the 8th Maine had volunteered for the occasion
and was on hand early. By midmorning a multitude began to
converge on Camp Saxton in its grove of magnificent, shining
live oaks, their beards of Spanish moss stirring gently in the
fresh ocean breeze. The people came by land and by sea;
colored women with bright handkerchiefs on their heads, their
menfolk in sober Sunday best, and white visitors also, in car-
riages and on horseback or ferried to the place of meeting in
Union steamers—plantation superintendents, teachers, officers
and soldiers from nearby islands. And the men of the 1st South

Carolina, resplendent in their red pantaloons and blue jackets, made the bright center of the varicolored throng.

The regimental chaplain, the Rev. Mr. Fowler, began the services with prayer. Then Dr. W. H. Brisbane, a former resident of the Sea Islands who had freed his slaves long before the war, read the president's Proclamation of Freedom. There were cheers, and then the Rev. Mr. Mansfield French, who had accompanied the first Beard expedition, presented Colonel Higginson with a magnificent stand of colors for the regiment, the gift of Dr. George B. Cheever's Church of the Puritans in New York. As the colonel received the colors, but before he could begin his acceptance speech, an unscheduled and altogether unexpected incident took place: spontaneously a handful of Negroes began to sing, strongly and clearly, "My Country, 'tis of thee, sweet land of liberty, of thee I sing." Other voices took up the words; some of the whites joined in, but Higginson waved them to silence. On through all the verses the Negroes sang. Higginson had never seen or heard "anything so electric; it made all the other words cheap; it seemed the choked voice of a race at last unloosed."

When the singing was done, the colonel made his speech, and witnesses said it was inspired. Then he in turn handed the stiff new flags to the regimental color-bearers, Sergeant Prince Rivers and Corporal Robert Sutton, who made their own speeches, articulate and suitable. There were other speeches, by General Saxton, by Mrs. Frances D. Gage of New York, by a Judge Stickney from Florida. There was special music—an ode had been composed especially for the occasion by Professor John C. Zachos of Cincinnati—and the men of the regiment sang the John Brown song "with much spirit." But, as Higginson set it down in his journal, "the life of the whole day was in those unknown people's song." The thing had hit him hard. "Just think of it!—the first day they had ever had a country, the first flag they had ever seen which promised anything to their people, and here, while mere spectators stood in silence, waiting for my stupid words, these simple souls burst out in their lay, as if they were by their own hearths at home!" [19]

The dress parade was "brilliant and beautiful"; the whole scene had a barbaric splendor all its own: the black companies in scarlet and blue, their bayonets gleaming in the sunlight, their new colors snapping proudly in the wind, marching to the Maine band's music; the throngs of colored people looking on as their men did themselves honor in the sight of white men and women; the sunlight glinting on the bright leaves of the live oaks and shimmering on the blue water beyond. It was a glorious day, full of promise for the future. One of the spectators later described her feelings: "Our hearts were filled with exceeding great gladness; for, although the Government had left much undone, we knew that Freedom was surely born in our land that day." [20]

*   *   *

On the basis of dates of muster-in, the 1st South Carolina Colored Volunteers was the fifth regiment of Negro soldiers to join the ranks of the Union Army. It was made an official part of that army on January 31, 1863.[21] But official dates and data can be misleading, as Colonel Higginson pointed out in his classic history of the regiment. While there were reports of the enlistment of Negro soldiers in Kansas and Missouri from late 1861 on through the spring and summer of 1862, the first large-scale, organized effort to arm the Negro was Hunter's experiment at Beaufort. From the beginning, the enterprise attracted national attention; it became a sort of test case for the movement, eclipsing in importance the successes of Butler and Lane. When Rufus Saxton took up the unfinished work, he inherited at least one company, Captain Trowbridge's Company A, which had remained somewhat intact, although on an unofficial basis, throughout the hiatus after Hunter had failed. This company was officially mustered into service by General Saxton in November, 1862,[22] and in point of actual service, steady and unbroken, with and without official sanction, it deserves the palm as the first organization of Negro soldiers.

In popular imagination Hunter's regiment, matured under Saxton and Higginson, remains the first of all Negro regiments, despite the fact that official records put it in fifth place. In justice to Hunter and Trowbridge and in recognition of the patient fortitude and sacrifice of their red-trousered men, the 1st South Carolina deserves to be called the first American Negro regi-

ment. The survival of the regiment through the summer and
fall of 1862 contributed immeasurably to the ultimate success
of the movement to permit the American Negro to fight for his
own freedom.

In early April of 1863 an incident occurred on Port Royal
Island that demonstrated graphically the acceptance of the
Negro soldier by his white comrades-in-arms. Colonel Higginson's regiment was assigned to picket duty, relieving the
55th Pennsylvania Volunteers. Edward L. Pierce, superintendent of the Treasury's plantations in the Sea Islands, observed
the arrival of the colored soldiers at an advanced picket station.
Over two hundred Pennsylvanians were lounging about awaiting the orders that would send them back to rest camps well
out of range of probing Confederate patrols. As they waited,
the Northern whites eyed with casual and noncommittal interest
the Negro troops resting in ranks after their ten-mile march
out to the station. A question occurred to Pierce, who had a
sense of history, and he turned to a private of the 55th and
asked:

"Isn't this rather new, to be relieved by a negro regiment?"

"All right," the white soldier answered; "They've as much
right to fight for themselves as I have to fight for them." [23]

So, however laconically and ungenerously, the white Union
Army began to accept the revolution going on around and
within it.

VI. *"The very air seemed to be filled with obstacles."*

... this is nothing but an experiment after all; but it is an experiment that I think it high time we should try, —an experiment which, the sooner we prove fortunate the sooner we can count upon an immense number of hardy troops that can stand the effect of a Southern climate without injury; an experiment which the sooner we prove unsuccessful, the sooner we shall establish an important truth and rid ourselves of a false hope.

—WILLIAM H. SIMPKINS, early 1863
Captain, 54th Massachusetts Infantry
Killed in action, July 18, 1863

"I am told you have at least thought of raising a negro military force. In my opinion the country now needs no specific thing so much as some man of your ability and position to go to this work. When I speak of your position, I mean that of an eminent citizen of a slave State, and himself a slaveholder." Thus Abraham Lincoln wrote on March 26, 1863, to Andrew Johnson, military governor of Tennessee. "The colored population," Lincoln urged, "is the great available, and yet unavailed of, force for restoring the Union. The bare sight of 50,000 armed and drilled black soldiers upon the banks of the Mississippi would end the rebellion at once. And who doubts that we can present that sight if we but take hold in earnest? If you have been thinking of it, please do not dismiss the thought." [1] Nothing seems to have come of this appeal; there is no record that Johnson ever replied to the presidential proposal. The letter stands, however, as clear evidence that the movement which had painfully struggled for its existence in 1862 had finally won a permanent place in the war policies of the administration and of the president.

The first seven months of 1863 were crucial to the success of this movement to arm the Negro. With the publication of the Emancipation Proclamation on January 1, the idea of using the "strong black arm" which Frederick Douglass had been advocating since the first month of the war received limited presidential endorsement. By the end of July more than thirty Negro regiments had been organized. Some of these regiments had already seen heavy action and had won national recogniton of their fighting worth. One of them, the 54th Massachusetts Infantry, had won a permanent place on the roster of distinguished American regiments. In fact, by the middle of 1863 the administration and the nation were thoroughly committed to the use of Negro troops. In the army, the new policy had been announced and put into practice, and it had won increasing acceptance as white soldiers saw that their black comrades-in-arms could make an effective contribution to the war effort.

The Lincoln administration committed itself to this new policy in a cautious, hesitating, fits-and-starts manner. It is significant that of the first five Negro regiments raised or raising in 1862, only one—the 1st South Carolina Volunteers —had full War Department authorization. There simply was no official reprimand to Butler's activities in Louisiana, nor were any effective steps taken to halt Jim Lane's work in Kansas and Missouri. Lincoln's preliminary emancipation proclamation of September 22, 1862, had made no mention of Negro troops, and in his second annual message to Congress in December of that year the president devoted about a third of that paper to full discussion of his favorite schemes of compensated emancipation and colonization. He even suggested an amendment to the Constitution to provide for the implementation of those programs.[2] Not until his final proclamation of January 1, 1863, did Lincoln publicly endorse the use of Negroes as soldiers and definitely reverse his stand of August 6, 1862, when he had agreed only to their use as laborers with the armies.

Even in his great proclamation Lincoln indicated little enthusiasm for the widespread use of Negro soldiers. He issued
no sweeping invitation welcoming Negro Americans into full
participation in the war. His proclamation stated merely: "such
persons of suitable condition will be received into the armed
service of the United States to garrison forts, positions, stations,
and other places and to man vessels of all sorts in said
service." [3] This was hardly unqualified endorsement of the tactical use of Negro soldiers successfully carried out in November by the 1st South Carolina or of the work to which they had
been put by both Butler and Lane. Lincoln was still cautiously
considering the extreme sensitivity of the Border states and of
loyal slaveholders who, as well as Southerners, feared widespread slave insurrections. Union colored troops would be kept
within the definite confines of fortifications and aboard the
ships of Secretary Welles's navy.

Once committed to the revolutionary step of emancipation
as a military measure, however, the Lincoln administration
found it more and more impossible to reject the logic of permitting the Negro to help secure his own freedom. The very
application of emancipation depended on the advance of Union
armies into slave territory. To exploit the military advantages
of emancipation, to deprive the Confederacy of the vital services of its slave population, more and more Union reinforcements were needed. And as administration officials tabulated
the losses of the Peninsular campaign, of Second Bull Run, of
Antietam, and of Fredericksburg as 1862 drew to a bloody
close, it must have been painfully obvious that the Union could
no longer afford to neglect or refuse any possible source of
manpower. As the exuberance of the first white volunteering
disappeared and as calls for more and more men went out
from Washington, arguments in favor of using the Negro manpower of both North and South took on new force.

Typical of the more cautious Northern press, the New York
Times of January 9, 1863, carefully weighed the question of
arming the Negro and almost gingerly concluded that, under
certain conditions, the experiment might be attempted. The
Times found "insuperable objections to raising a negro army
for the mere purpose of proving that negroes can fight," and

maintained that "the time is past when we could afford to carry
out this war for the purpose of elucidating a theory, or loosen-
ing an ethnological knot." The prime question to be considered
in making soldiers of Negroes was "its immediate effects . . .
on the fortunes of war." If it proved impossible to secure
enough white soldiers to meet Union military requirements,
then Negroes ought to be used if they could make "even
tolerable soldiers," providing their use would not produce "a
stronger spirit of resistance in the South and of discontent in the
North, than their aid will counterbalance." The *Times* asserted:
"In all wars, invasion of the feelings of the people are worthy
of the closest study, in a military point of view, as they
materially affect the success and duration of the operations."
But the New York paper was chiefly concerned with Northern
rather than Southern reaction. "There was a time," the editor
admitted, "when it might have seemed advisable to consult
Southern prejudice for other and more sentimental reasons.
But no one but a fool or a visionary will deny that that time is
now past. The state of Southern feeling or opinion is for us, at
this supreme crisis, simply a question of strategy. If we try to
look at it any longer in any other way, we shall simply seal
our own fate. Nobody will pity us." So the *Times* published its
obituary notice of Lincoln's statesmanlike but unsuccessful
efforts at conciliation.

There were, the *Times* maintained, "numerous and weighty"
reasons for using Negro soldiers. They were physically hardy
and could stand the Southern climate better than Northern
whites. They possessed intimate knowledge of the South and
could find their way where Northern strangers would become
hopelessly lost. They were deeply discontented with their lot as
slaves; this would lead them to serve "for less pay and with
fewer comforts than white men." They were accustomed to
discipline. Further, Negro troops had already been used by
the British with some success in the West Indies and in Africa.
"The last and crowning reason" in favor of arming the Negro,
the *Times* argued, was that "there has as yet been no race discovered, however effeminate or weak or pusillanimous or
degraded, that will not make at least tolerably good soldiers
under officers whom they fear or respect." As proof, the *Times*

offered the "Russian serfs, bred under the lash, bought and
sold like horses," who had fought heroically at Eylau, Boro-
dino, and Sebastopol; the "timid and debased Bengalee"
converted into "a soldier who has proved himself, under British
officers, more than a match, on many a hard-fought field, for
the most war-like races of Upper India"; and "even the
Chinese" made by General Frederick Townsend Ward of
Salem, Massachusetts, "into soldiers at whose head he marched
as fearlessly against battery and entrenchment as if they belonged to the flower of martial races." The *Times* urged that
"Discipline and good leading will . . . make, not the best kind
of soldiers, but good soldiers of any men. To make the best
kind of soldiers we need religious and patriotic fervor in a
degree rarely seen. It is not every age or generation which has
the glory of sending men to stand fast with Riding at Morgar-
ten, or charge behind Cromwell at Naseby." It would be another
six months before the *Times* would find in American Negro
soldiers that rare fervor that makes men attempt and even accomplish the impossible. Port Hudson and Milliken's Bend had
not yet been heard of in New York, and Robert Gould Shaw
was only a captain in the 2nd Massachusetts Infantry.

*   *   *

While the question of Negro troops occupied the attention
of the Northern press, the practicality and advisability of their
use were being debated in the halls of Congress also. On December 9, 1862, Representative John Hickman of Pennsylvania
introduced a bill to authorize Lincoln to raise one hundred
Negro regiments. Two weeks later James H. Lane, temporarily
in Washington in the role of Kansas senator, "gave notice of
his intention to ask leave to introduce a bill authorizing the
President to call into the field two hundred regiments of infantry composed of persons of African descent." [4] While it would
be surprising to find Jim Lane asking leave to do anything, it
is characteristic of him that he should have planned to double
Hickman's figure for Negro regiments.

Apparently Lane never carried out his intention. At any rate,
Congressional debate on the subject was chiefly confined to
the House and arose over a bill introduced by Thaddeus Stevens

on January 12 calling for the enlistment of 150,000 Negro soldiers or one hundred and fifty regiments. This Stevens bill was hotly debated during the closing days of January and passed the House on February 2 by a vote of 83 to 54. It went to the Senate the next day and was referred to the Committee on Military Affairs. On February 13, Senator Henry Wilson of Massachusetts, acting for that committee, reported the bill back with the recommendation that it not pass "because the authority intended to be given by it" was "sufficiently granted in the twelfth and fifteenth sections of the act approved July 17, 1862," which had empowered the president to use Negro soldiers at his discretion.[5] To support its position that further legislation was unnecessary, the committee had only to point to the five regiments already mustered into federal service and to authorizations granted by the War Department for more such organizations. For, while editors wrote eloquent disquisitions and while congressmen orated on the Negro soldier question, president and War Department had gone quietly ahead to initiate the recruitment of Negro regiments in the North as well as in the South.

No integrated policy emerged at once. For the first quarter of 1863 the president and his War Department seemed to grapple with the Negro soldier policy on a sort of catch-as-catch-can basis, granting authority for Negro enlistment and organization to individual civil and military officers without any obvious effort to standardize that policy. By the end of March authorization for eight regiments, in addition to the half dozen already in being, had been given by the War Department, with Lincoln's approval and even hearty endorsement. As if to emphasize the lack of over-all plans, these authorizations had gone to a New York politician, a Kansas Jayhawker, and two New England governors. These were variously authorized to recruit in Louisiana, South Carolina, Rhode Island, and Massachusetts. The wonder is that out of these piecemeal beginnings there was born a flaming legend that deeply stirred the North and more than any other single fact or act made the Negro soldier a full-fledged participant in the Civil War.

*   *   *

Daniel Ullmann, lawyer and Know-Nothing candidate for governor in New York in 1854, commander of the 78th New York Volunteers in the Peninsular campaign and briefly a prisoner of the rebels, called on President Lincoln in October of 1862 and "urged upon him the overruling necessity of arming the liberated slaves." When addressing a group of Empire State veterans shortly after the war, Ullmann described the interview uninhibited by either modesty or reluctance to play a major role in shaping Union policy. "You arm the Blacks, and enlist them into the Armies of the United States," Ullmann said he urged Lincoln. The president had interrupted to argue that the step could not be taken because it "would drive many of our friends from us. The people are not prepared for it."

"I am by no means sure of that, Mr. President," Ullmann had answered, "besides, events, now-a-days, follow each other in such quick succession, and public opinion changes with such astounding rapidity, that, in these great exigencies, it appears to me, the path of duty is sometimes to lead as well as to follow ... pardon a man just out of a Rebel prison for being strenuous on this point. . . . As I laid [sic] sick in Libby, I resolved that, if my life was spared, and I ever had opportunity, I would, again, to the utmost of my ability, press this course upon you."

Lincoln, accustomed as he must have been to listening to the advice of men certain of their superiority in wisdom and policy, broke in upon the rush of words with the simple question: "Ullmann, would you be willing to command black soldiers?"

Even his recollection of five years later indicates that Ullmann was momentarily stunned by the question, but his reply was worthy of his profession: "Mr. President, that is a home question. I do not know that I would, of choice, but I am a soldier, it is my duty to obey, and I confess that I would glory in aiding to strike what, I am sure, will be the most effective moral blow of the war." [6]

Whatever reluctance Colonel Ullmann may have had in October seems to have been overcome by early January. Armed with "a paper to hand to the Secretary of War" from Lincoln and attended by Vice-President Hannibal Hamlin of Maine, Ullmann called on Stanton on January 12 to discuss the subject of Negro soldiers "at considerable length." Next morning the New Yorker received a letter of appointment making him a brigadier general of volunteers [7] with orders to raise a brigade of four regiments of "Louisiana volunteer infantry, to be recruited in that State, to serve for three years or during the war." [8]

The new general, the first to owe his star to the new Union policy, opened headquarters in New York City and began the hard work of organizing the cadre of his Louisiana brigade. His initial optimism was somewhat dampened by the discovery that, contrary to his October feeling, public opinion was "far from being ripe on the subject" of Negro soldiers. His friends, aware of the tensions in New York society that were to produce the great draft riots of July, thought it necessary to warn him of the dangers of mob action. Ullmann found some Northern governors, especially Coburn of Maine and Andrew of Massachusetts, willing to help him find "officers of the right stamp," but, he related afterward, "Not a few officers and men of the volunteer army refused promotion in this [Negro] service." And these were not the sum of the new brigadier's troubles: "the work of organizing moved more slowly than was agreeable," he wrote, "because of the delay in some of the Government Bureaus in filling requisitions &c. It required sharp letters from the Secretary of War ... to stimulate the action of several of them, especially the Paymaster and Medical Bureaus." Without the consistent support of Stanton, Ullmann's venture must have died aborning at No. 200 Broadway. "It is not easy to understand or appreciate ... the difficulties which met this movement at every step of its early stages," he recalled nearly a quarter of a century later. "The very air seem[ed] to be filled with obstacles. They came from the most unexpected quarters. I can never sufficiently express my grateful thanks to Mr. Secretary Stanton for the ready support which his strong arm gave me in those trying times in New York, Washington, and Louisiana." [9]

Vice-President Hamlin, a man with a long record of antislavery activities, also provided steady assistance to Ullmann, especially in his efforts to get seasoned officers for the work. The *National Intelligencer* of February 25 reprinted a para-

graph from the Washington *National Republican* reporting
that Hamlin had gone to Maine "to confer with Governor Coburn" about officering the Ullmann brigade of "Chasseurs
D'Afrique." The officers, according to the dispatch, were "to be
from Maine and the principal ones were selected by prominent
gentlemen from that State and in this city, viz.: The first regiment is to be commanded by Captain [John F.] Appleton of the
12th Maine, son of Chief Justice Appleton [of Maine] . . . The
second regiment is to be commanded by Captain Cyrus Hamlin," one of the sons of the vice-president. "Nearly all the other
officers are to be selected from Maine regiments in the field."
Captain Hamlin assisted Ullmann in his work of organizing the
expedition in New York, but not until April 10 did the brigade
cadre take ship for New Orleans and the theater of operations.[10]

Elaborate preparations had been made for Ullmann's arrival
in the Department of the Gulf. His orders directed him to report
to General Nathaniel P. Banks, commander of the department
since December, 1862, when he had replaced Butler. Not only
Stanton and Halleck but President Lincoln himself instructed
Banks to assist Ullmann as much as he could. The president
spoke directly to the point in his letter to Banks. "Hon. Daniel
Ullmann, with a commission of a brigadier general," Lincoln
wrote, "and two or three hundred other gentlemen as officers,
goes to your Department and reports to you, for the purpose
of raising a colored brigade. To now avail ourselves of this
element of force is very important, if not indispensable. I therefore will thank you to help General Ullmann forward with his
undertaking, as much and as rapidly as you can; and also to
carry the general object beyond his particular organization if
you find it practicable. The necessity of this is palpable if, as I
understand, you are now unable to effect anything with your
present force; and which force is soon to be greatly diminished
by the expiration of terms of service, as well as by ordinary
causes. I shall be very glad if you will take hold of the matter
in earnest." [11]

Banks was in a peculiarly advantageous location for taking
hold of the matter in earnest and with good results. Louisiana,
of all the slave states under partial or total Union control, had
the largest number of male slaves between the ages of eighteen

and forty-five—75,548—in addition to 3,205 free colored men in the same military age group.[12] The arming of Negroes had won its first successes in Louisiana, and on February 12, 1863, Banks reported to the War Department that he had some 3,251 Negro troops enrolled in his command. In addition to the three regiments of Native Guards mustered by Ben Butler in the fall of 1862, Banks disclosed that a company of artillery had been organized and that a fourth regiment of infantry was "progressing favorably." [13] And even before Lincoln and the War Department had urged Banks to help Ullmann, the general commanding the Department of the Gulf had, on March 20, issued orders for the organization of a fifth colored regiment "for service for Three (3) years or during the war as Engineers, Sappers, Miners and Pontoniers, to have the organization prescribed by law for a regiment of Engineer troops." These orders seemed to blueprint not so much combat as service troops. "Competent officers will be detailed," Banks ordered, "for their discipline and instruction in the various trades incident to this arm of the service as Carpenters, Blacksmiths, Wheelwrights, Miners[,] Masons[,] Boatmen[,] Bridge Builders, Harness makers etc., etc." [14] Certainly Banks was aware of the need for auxiliary troops in his department and particularly aware of the demand for labor battalions to lighten the drudgery of his white troops. His proposed 1st Regiment of Louisiana Engineers, however, was destined to take its place in the forefront of Negro combat troops a bare two months after its organization had been ordered.

* * *

Colonel James Montgomery of Kansas, disgusted with his three-cornered feud with Jim Lane and Charles Jennison, had left Kansas for Washington in December of 1862 to seek a better fortune than had been his on the Border. At the national capital the bearded Jayhawker pulled all the political strings he could find, as his correspondence with George L. Stearns of Boston plainly shows. Montgomery found that Senator Pomeroy of Kansas was willing to help him, but he told Stearns that Senator Lane was doing all he could against him. Stearns, a wealthy Boston ship-chandler who had helped finance John Brown, was

a man of considerable importance in his own state, and Montgomery sought his assistance. "I think I can depend on
Pomeroy," the old Border chieftain told Stearns, "and I am
making friends, quite fast, among the members [of the Senate];
but Lane is a member of the *nominating Committee* [selecting
individuals for elevation to star rank], and this gives him an
opportunity for mischief that he would not otherwise have." But
all was not lost: "Mr. [Henry] Wilson is chairman of the
Committee, and, I fear, will be guided by Lane, in his actions,
unless a strong influence can be brought to bear on him from
his own State." The implication is plain that Montgomery expected Stearns to bring his own strong influence to bear on
Senator Wilson. In any case, the Jayhawker was not putting all
his eggs into the Stearns basket; far from it. "I had a short
interview with the President," his letter continued, "and am
promised a longer one, at a more convenient season. He received me very kindly." Whether Lincoln helped Montgomery
is not clear, nor is it certain that Stearns was able to swing
Wilson out of the Lane influence. But Montgomery had found
a new friend: "Genl Hunter is here, and is doing what he can
for me. He wants me to go South with him. . . ." [15]

The channels through which Montgomery operated his one-
man lobby were devious, but the results of his efforts became
quite clear on January 13, 1863, when he was authorized by
the War Department "to raise, subject to the approval of the
general commanding the Department of the South and under
his direction, a regiment of South Carolina volunteer infantry,
to be recruited in that State, to serve for three years or during
the war." [16] Ever an advocate and practitioner of direct action,
Colonel Montgomery wasted no time organizing a cadre in the
North but went immediately south with Hunter. General Saxton
reported to Stanton on January 25 that the organization of the
1st Regiment of South Carolina Volunteers had been completed and that he had "commenced the organization of the
Second Regiment, which is to be commanded by Colonel Montgomery." [17] The New York politician and the Kansas Jayhawker had received War Department authority for their recruiting enterprises on the same day, but before Ullmann had

even reached Louisiana, Montgomery had led his Negro soldiers into action in Florida.[18]

* * *

Governor John Albion Andrew of Massachusetts, long a zealous abolitionist, had been among the first to see the value to the Union and to the Negro himself of arming colored men. With Lincoln's proclamation of emancipation as 1863 opened, Andrew recognized that the hour of opportunity had arrived. After consulting with Stanton in early January, Andrew first considered the possibility of recruiting Negroes in North Carolina and even proposed Benjamin F. Butler, then at liberty, as the man to take up the work. But Butler, lately returned from Louisiana under something like a cloud, was out of favor with the War Department, and the proposal came to nothing. John Andrew, no man to let disappointments crush him, then asked for and received authority to raise colored troops in his own state.[19] The *National Republican* of January 28 announced the granting of this authority as "the secret of the late mission of Gov. Andrew, Wendell Phillips, F. W. Bird, Dr. [Samuel Gridley] Howe, and a host of others of the radical school of politics in Massachusetts to this city, and [it] accounts for the[ir] many and frequent interviews with the president." Two days earlier, on January 26, the secretary of war had ordered "That Governor Andrew, of Massachusetts, is authorized, until further orders, to raise such number of volunteer companies of artillery for duty in the forts of Massachusetts and elsewhere, and such corps of infantry for the volunteer military service as he may find convenient, such volunteers to be enlisted for three years or until sooner discharged, and may include persons of African descent, organized into separate corps." [20] So the 54th Massachusetts Infantry was conceived. If ever a military organization was dedicated to high purpose even before a single soldier had been enlisted or a single officer commissioned, it was the 54th. If ever a regiment of fighting men lived up to the expectations of those who conceived and directed its recruitment and organization, it was the 54th.

On January 15 the adjutant general had informed the governor of Rhode Island that "the President will accept into the

service of the United States an infantry regiment of volunteers
of African descent, if offered by your State and organized
according to the rules and regulations of the service." This communication was followed on February 10 by another from the
adjutant general declaring that Rhode Island had been "authorized to raise a colored regiment of infantry or heavy artillery,"
and as a result the 14th Rhode Island Heavy Artillery was
organized. By the end of the following October the regiment had
recruited some nine hundred men, "about half the maximum
number for an artillery regiment." [21] Three months before that
time the 54th Massachusetts Infantry had made itself immortal.

Governor Andrew knew what he wanted in the way of a regiment of Negro soldiers, and he lost little time in getting it. He
wanted to make "a model for all future Colored Regiments,"
and he was convinced that, as the first Negro organization to be
raised in the North, "its success or its failure [would] go far
to elevate or to depress the estimation in which the character of
the Colored Americans will be held throughout the World." [22]
Within a few days after he had received Stanton's order,
Andrew had selected the regiment's colonel, Robert Gould
Shaw, then a captain in the 2nd Massachusetts Infantry, and its
lieutenant colonel, Norwood P. Hallowell, a captain in the 20th
Massachusetts. Hallowell accepted at once and reported for duty
within a week.

Shaw was at first reluctant to accept the colonelcy, doubting
his capacity to handle well the large responsibilities it entailed.
Besides, as William James pointed out at the dedication of the
Shaw Monument in 1897, he "loved the Second Regiment, illustrious already, and was sure of promotion where he stood. In
this new negro-soldier venture, loneliness was certain, ridicule
inevitable, failure possible; and Shaw was only twenty-five;
and, although he had stood among the bullets at Cedar Mountain and Antietam, he had till then been walking socially on the
sunny side of life. But whatever doubts may have beset him,
they were over in a day, for he inclined naturally toward difficult resolves. He accepted the proffered command, and from
that moment lived but for one object, to establish the honor of
the Massachusetts 54th." [23]

The selection was a happy one, perhaps the happiest possible.

His contemporaries were as one in hailing Shaw's appointment; Henry Lee Higginson spoke for them all in 1897: "He had a singularly simple, direct, earnest, true mind and character. He held strong opinions and beliefs which governed him, and was not tortured with doubts as so many people are. He took things as they came, and did the plain duty ready to his hand. He thought for himself; revolted at the sight of injustice or cruelty; was full of courage and manliness, and enriched and warmed his own life and that of others by his sympathy and affection. Not a sign of fanaticism or of sentimentality, but a deep, true and warm reverence for goodness and nobility in men and women, was always present and expressed." [24]

Charles Russell Lowell, who would have been Shaw's brother-in-law, wrote his mother in February of 1863: "You will be very glad to hear that Bob Shaw is to be Colonel and Norwood Hallowell Lieutenant-Colonel of the Governor's Negro Regiment. It is very important that it should be started soberly and not spoilt by too much fanaticism. Bob Shaw is not a fanatic." Lowell, writing to Henry Higginson a week later, expressed some doubts as to the success of the enterprise. "I have no idea," he wrote, "that they can get a full regiment in New England, but think they can get enough intelligent fellows here to make a *cadre* for one or more regiments to be raised down South." But, he concluded, "this is likely to be a success, if any black regiment can be a success." [25]

Young Colonel Lowell's doubts were soon realized, and Andrew's recruiters found that raising a full regiment in New England, let alone Massachusetts, was next to impossible. The number of free colored males of military age in Massachusetts by the census of 1860 was 1,973, and Joseph Kennedy, superintendent of the census, figured that if they came forward as volunteers in the same ratio "wherewith the whites have been supplied" Massachusetts might count on 394 Negro soldiers.[26] But Andrew went ahead as optimistically as if he had fifty thousand men to draw on. Boston yielded scarcely one company, New Bedford another; once more Andrew looked to North Carolina and Virginia, but Stanton was unwilling. The Massachusetts governor soon concluded that his recruiting officers would have to go beyond the boundaries of his state.

This, of course, was impossible, but an organization of private individuals was formed and thrown into the breach. That old friend of John Brown and James Montgomery, George L. Stearns, one of the foremost of Massachusetts abolitionists and advocates of arming the Negro, came forward to serve as chairman of a committee to raise men and money. Technically, his biographer has pointed out, "Andrew sent no Massachusetts recruiting-officers outside the State; practically, Stearns' agents went everywhere through the Middle States and even penetrated beyond the Mississippi." [27] The *National Intelligencer* of March 16, 1863, jokingly reported that Andrew had "opened recruiting offices at New York, Philadelphia, Fortress Monroe, and even as far southwards as Key West." A New Yorker, the *Intelligencer* related, had expressed "fear that his crimping sergeants will shortly turn up in Egypt, competing with Napoleon for the next cargo of Nubians."

The roster of those who assisted in raising the 54th Massachusetts reads like the index to a history of abolitionism: Amos A. Lawrence, John M. Forbes, Dr. LeBaron Russell, Richard P. Hallowell, and William I. Bowditch in and around Boston; Francis G. Shaw, the colonel's father, in New York City; Gerrit Smith in the Mohawk Valley. Out in Rochester, Frederick Douglass heard the cheering news. Here was the realization of all that he had hoped, prayed for, and preached for nearly two years, and he threw himself into the work. George L. Stearns stopped in Rochester en route to Buffalo to establish his recruiting headquarters there, and he enlisted the Negro leader to encourage enlistments in the Massachusetts regiment. Stearns' first recruits in New York were Douglass's two sons, Charles and Lewis. The latter became the 54th's first regimental sergeant major. [28]

Douglass spoke out in a call to arms that was soon echoed and re-echoed in newspaper columns all across the land. Out of his own deep conviction and indignation he wrote eloquently to his fellow Negroes, urging them to seize the opportunity to fight their way to American citizenship. "When first the rebel cannon shattered the walls of Sumter," he began, "and drove away its starving garrison, I predicted that the war then and there inaugurated would not be fought out entirely by white

men. Every month's experience during these dreary years has
confirmed that opinion. A war undertaken and brazenly carried
on for the perpetual enslavement of colored men, calls logically
and loudly for colored men to help suppress it. Only a moderate
share of sagacity was needed to see that the arm of the slave
was the best defense against the arm of the slaveholder. Hence,
with every reverse to the national arms, with every exultant
shout of victory raised by the slaveholding rebels, I have im-
plored the imperiled nation to unchain against her foes her
powerful black hand. Slowly and reluctantly that appeal is
being heeded."

What was the Negro's course, now that he was finally to be
permitted to lend a hand to save the Union? "Stop not now to
complain," Douglass urged; leave discussion to the future.
"When the war is over, the country is saved, peace is established, and the black man's rights are secured, as they will be,
history with an impartial hand will dispose of that and sundry
other questions. Action! Action! not criticism, is the plain duty
of this hour. Words are now useful only as they stimulate to
blows. The office of speech now is only to point out when, where,
and how to strike to the best advantage. There is no time to
delay. . . ." [29]

Following his own advice, Douglass traveled throughout the
North making speech after speech urging Negro audiences to
enlist in the 54th Massachusetts and later, as other organizations
got under way, in a variety of colored regiments recruited in
the free states. He had a warm spot in his heart for the regiment
in which his sons were serving, and with pardonable parental
pride he pointed out to the crowds who came to hear him that
Charles and Lewis Douglass had been the first Empire State
men to join the 54th. American Negroes generally, Douglass
argued, owed a special debt to Massachusetts. "We can get at
the throat of treason and slavery through the State of Massachusetts," he maintained. "She was first in the War of Independence; first to break the chains of her slaves; first to make
the black man equal before the law; first to admit colored
children to her common schools. She was first to answer with
her blood the alarm-cry of the nation when its capital was
menaced by the Rebels. You know her patriotic Governor, and

you know Charles Sumner. I need add no more. Massachusetts now welcomes you as her soldiers." [30]

Not all of Frederick Douglass's neighbors shared his enthusiasm for arming Negroes. The Rochester *Daily Union and Advertiser*, a Democratic paper much given to criticism of the administration and its war policies, consistently disparaged Douglass's crusade. On February 9, 1863, the *Union and Advertiser* discounted the idea that Negro soldiers would actually fight, especially since they would not be treated as prisoners of war. The editorial concluded that it was not "contemplated to send the colored regiments, if raised at the North, to the post of danger. They will probably be used to garrison forts not liable to attack, and to aid United States Marshals in making arrests of editors and others suspected of disloyalty, and for police duty. We shall doubtless have a colored regiment stationed in Rochester some day," the paper cynically remarked, "to see that no demonstrations of disloyalty are manifested."

Regardless of criticism, Stearns quickly assembled a far-flung organization for collecting Negro volunteers. Stations were opened from Nantucket to Pittsfield, from Albany to Buffalo, from Elmira to Philadelphia, and as far west as Chicago. Mass meetings were held to explain the movement and to encourage volunteers to come forward; the speakers included abolitionists like Wendell Phillips and William Lloyd Garrison, officers of the regiment, and prominent Negroes like Martin Delany and O. S. B. Wall. And the volunteers came forward, slowly at first and then in a steady flood. Four companies of the 54th were full and ready for muster by the end of March, and recruits were coming into Readville, the Massachusetts training camp just outside Boston, at the rate of one hundred a week during April. Small wonder that with the Stearns organization functioning as it was, it was decided to organize the 55th Regiment in May, and Norwood Hallowell was transferred from the 54th to command the sister organization.[31]

As the first companies were formed at Readville, and as Colonel Shaw and his officers went to work to make soldiers of the raw recruits, the War Department moved to put the organization of Negro troops on a regular basis. As Ullmann's cadre made its last preparations for moving to Louisiana, the secretary of war dispatched Brigadier General Lorenzo Thomas to the Mississippi Valley on an inspection trip. Thomas, the adjutant general of the Union Army, was directed to examine the military situation at the various posts in the valley. He was to give careful attention to the condition of "that class of population known as contrabands," and he was to confer with General Grant and other officers out there on the manner in which the proclamation of January 1 was being executed. Most important of all, Stanton ordered Thomas: "You will ascertain what military officers are willing to take command of colored troops; ascertain their qualifications for that purpose, and if troops can be raised and organized, you will, so far as can be done without prejudice to the service, relieve officers and privates from the service in which they are engaged, to receive commissions such as they may be qualified to exercise in the organization of brigades, regiments, and companies of colored troops. You are authorized in this connection to issue in the name of this Department letters of appointment for field and company officers, and to organize such troops for military service to the utmost extent to which they can be obtained in accordance with the rules and regulations of the service...." [32]

This was to be no routine inspection mission. It presaged the full-scale organization and employment of Negro soldiers. It initiated the new Negro soldier policy of proceeding not by the parceling out of authority to selected individuals and states but by decree and direction of the War Department acting through the army. This step was the great turning point in the development of the movement to arm the Negro as a soldier.

VII. *"I am here to raise as many regiments of blacks as I can."*

Adjutant General Thomas was brought home on Sunday, in easy stages from the hospital in Louisville, saved literally from the jaws of death. The North will be interested to hear that Gen. Thomas has organized 20 negro regiments in Lower Mississippi, has put under cultivation 60 abandoned Louisiana, Mississippi, and Arkansas plantations, and, better than all, has totally changed in all the armies of the West and South the pro-slavery feeling. The services rendered by this veteran officer to the Government, in organizing and pushing forward the enrollment of the contrabands of the Southwest, ought never to be forgotten.

—Washington *Daily Morning Chronicle,* June 23, 1863

Lorenzo Thomas is usually remembered, when he is remembered at all, as the adjutant general whom President Andrew Johnson appointed secretary of war to replace Edwin M. Stanton in the cabinet crisis of 1868 just preceding Johnson's impeachment. That fact is unfortunate. Lorenzo Thomas deserves better from the hands of history and historians. His role in the circumstances of Johnson's impeachment was neither a happy nor a creditable one. His great contribution had been made five years earlier, and his tragedy is that the events of 1868 eclipsed what he had done during the war years.

In the early spring of 1863 Thomas was on the eve of sixty, a career officer who had been graduated from the military academy at West Point forty years before. His military career had been chiefly distinguished by the amount of paper work he had presumably accomplished—for over fifteen years he had served in the office of the adjutant general and since March of 1861 as the adjutant general of the United States himself. In the first summer of the Civil War he had finally attained star rank. On the face of things, it is hard to imagine a more unlikely choice for the enormous task that Stanton's order of March 25 thrust upon him.

The secretary of war had at least two reasons for selecting Thomas to go west and organize Negro regiments in the Mississippi Valley. If Negro troops were to be raised on a scale that would provide them in sufficient numbers to be of any significance in the war, then the War Department would have to do more about the matter than parcel out authority for their organization to a general here and a governor there. What was needed was an integrated, centralized policy initiated and pushed by the War Department itself. By March of 1863 seven months had passed since the initial orders had been sent to Rufus Saxton, and in those months only five Negro regiments had been mustered. Four or five more were in process of organization, but the pace was much too slow to make the practical application of Negro strength of any real value to Union arms. Perhaps some hint of Stanton's impatience with the situation is his reply to an offer made by one William A. Adair of Pittsburgh on March 13. Adair had asked, "Can the colored men here raise a regiment and have their own company officers?" Stanton had been adamant in his opposition to Negro officers in Andrew's 54th Massachusetts, but he wired Adair on March 21: "If a regiment of colored men can be raised in Pittsburg I will authorize them to have their own officers." [1] The War Department was determined, by the fourth week of March in 1863, to push the Negro soldier's recruitment and employment. The large question was how to do this.

Relations between Stanton and the adjutant general had never been cordial; indeed, Stanton had "promised," on his appointment to the War Department, to pick Thomas up "with a pair of tongs" and drop him into the Potomac. Thomas was variously referred to as "lukewarm," "incompetent," "probably dishonest," and yet over a year after Stanton had taken over the department and cleansed it of the corruption and incompetence of the Cameron regime, the adjutant general was still there.

Suddenly the lightning struck. With only twenty-four hours'
warning, Thomas was dispatched to the Mississippi with sweeping
authority and huge responsibilities. Stanton probably found in
the policy problem presented by the Negro soldier a solution
to his personal problem. With the one stone of his orders of
March 25 he killed the two birds: the organization of Negro
troops was initiated by a high officer of the War Department and
the secretary of war was freed of the presence of that officer in
Washington.[2]

Certainly Lorenzo Thomas and Edwin Stanton were extremely
unlike in habit, temperament, and training. Thomas seems to
have been infatuated with paper work and regulations. Stanton,
one of the most brilliant legal minds of his generation, on many
occasions showed a disposition to disregard military channels,
protocol, and regulations and to slash red tape with what must
have seemed reckless abandon to the adjutant general. If Stanton
did send Thomas west "in what was probably an effort to be rid
of him," this was one of the most fortunate pieces of spite work
in the long history of the Civil War.

On the day after Stanton issued his sweeping orders to Thomas,
Lincoln wrote Andrew Johnson in Tennessee suggesting that "the
bare sight of 50,000 armed and drilled black soldiers upon the
banks of the Mississippi would end the rebellion at once." Who
doubts, the president asked, "that we can present that sight if we
but take hold in earnest?" Lorenzo Thomas, adjutant general
turned recruiting sergeant, career officer sent to do abolitionists'
work, did "take hold in earnest." By the end of 1863 he had
organized twenty Negro regiments. By the end of 1864 he could
report that he had initiated the organization of fifty regiments.
He had even exceeded Lincoln's optimistic forecast of 50,000
Negro soldiers by six thousand, in round numbers. By the end
of the war, Thomas had been instrumental in the recruitment and
organization of over 76,000 Negro soldiers, in round numbers,
or about 41 per cent of the total number of Negroes who served
in the ranks of the Union armies.[3]

*   *   *

"You undoubtedly recollect," Thomas reminded Stanton in
October of 1865, "that the determination to send me on this

duty was a sudden one, and the purpose was only unfolded to me the day prior to the date of the instructions, and you urged expedition in the matter. The subject was new to me, and I entered upon the duty by no means certain of what I might be able to effect. Still, as more of my military service was performed in the slave States, and I was perfectly familiar with plantation life—I felt that I knew the peculiarities of the colored race—I could, with the blessing of Divine Providence, at least do something to alleviate the condition of the numerous thousands who would come within our military lines for protection." [4] In spite of the suddenness of his orders and the novelty of the mission, Thomas displayed the "expedition" Stanton urged. His progress down the Mississippi is easily traced in the communications he sent almost daily to the War Department. On April 1, one week after his orders had been handed to him, he wrote Stanton from Cairo, Illinois, to report on the condition of the colored population and to urge that they "be employed with our armies as laborers and teamsters, and those who can be induced to do so, or conscripted if necessary, be mustered as soldiers." Regiments of Negroes, Thomas believed, would give protection to the free colored people working abandoned plantations along the Mississippi. "They could garrison positions," he concluded, "and thus additional [white] regiments could be sent to the front." [5] Lorenzo Thomas was not gifted with prophetic vision, but he did foresee with considerable accuracy the important role Negro troops would play in the Mississippi Valley. In March of 1865, a scant month before the end of the war, Major General E. R. S. Canby's report to Washington showed that of nearly 28,000 Union troops "serving on the Mississippi River" over 18,000, or very nearly two-thirds, were Negro. [6]

On April 2, Thomas telegraphed Stanton that General Samuel R. Curtis had told him of "a well drilled regiment of blacks at Fort Leavenworth," the 1st Kansas Colored Volunteers commanded by Colonel James Williams, then performing garrison and fatigue duty at Fort Scott, Kansas. The adjutant general thought that if the 1st Kansas Colored "could be sent on the Mississippi it would have a good effect upon the contrabands and facilitate enlistments." [7] The idea had merit, but active participation in the bloody civil war on the Border kept

the Kansas Negro soldiers from helping Thomas in his recruiting.

It was on April 2 that Thomas (or "subject general officer,"
as he might have put it) really began his work in the valley. At
Columbus, Kentucky, he "announced the policy of the Government with regard to the contrabands, which was hailed with
delight by the troops" there. Proceeding down the river, he
addressed some seven thousand Union troops at Helena, Arkansas, on April 6, and again he reported that his announcement
of the "policy respecting the blacks was most enthusiastically
received." This new policy, he assured Stanton, "infused new
life into the troops, and . . . now they see that the rebellion will
be crushed." [8] A week later, on April 13, the *National Intelligencer* reprinted a special dispatch from Helena to the New
York *Tribune* which described in detail the arrival of the adjutant general at the Arkansas encampment. "His speech was received with rapturous applause," the correspondent reported;
"the immense audience of soldiers uncovered their heads and
gave cheer after cheer in rapturous approval of all that had
been said."

That Lorenzo Thomas was doing more in the valley than
make speeches is indicated by his telegram of April 7 to the
assistant adjutant general, Colonel E. D. Townsend: "Send
immediately blanks to muster in two Regiments to Memphis, for
two Regiments to Helena, and for six Regiments to General
Grant's headquarters. This position is destitute of blanks of almost every description—" how his adjutant's heart must have
burned under his blue coat at the thought—"Send a full supply
direct," he ordered. He was being aided at Helena, he told
Colonel Townsend, "in every way by General [Benjamin M.]
Prentiss; and the officers and men have new life infused into
them since the grand affair of yesterday," the assembly at which
Thomas had addressed the troops. The adjutant general was
warming to his work. "If the troops below do half as well," he
wrote enthusiastically, "my mission will be a success. I authorized a regiment this morning and at noon three companies of
100 each were ready for muster." [9]

On April 8, Thomas reached Lake Providence in northeastern Louisiana, and there again he addressed the Union troops

to explain the new Negro soldier policy. There again, he reported to the secretary of war, the "troops received it with great enthusiasm, and many speeches were made by officers of different ranks, fully endorsing the policy." General Thomas asked each division he visited to raise two colored regiments, but, he confidently predicted, "the difficulty will be to restrict them to that number, for at least ten regiments can be obtained" from John MacArthur's and John A. Logan's divisions of James B. McPherson's army corps. Against this possibility, Thomas ordered "one thousand pair of negro shoes, large sizes" forwarded to Memphis, with arms for the same number. On April 14 he telegraphed Washington from Milliken's Bend, Louisiana, that he would require "altogether, muster-rolls for twenty regiments." By April 18, with his mission barely three weeks old, Thomas was halfway to that goal: he had authorized the raising of ten Negro regiments, and they were filling up with encouraging speed.[10]

The adjutant general's April 8 address to the troops drawn up under the live oaks at Lake Providence was typical of all the addresses he made and was to make at Union camps up and down the Mississippi. His mission was twofold in nature. He had not only to initiate the organization of Negro regiments, but even before that could be successfully begun he had to combat and allay the rather strong anti-Negro sentiment of the white soldiers. There was nothing subtle or devious in the Thomas approach to this dual problem. To the officers and men assembled around him, the old soldier spoke directly and simply.

"I come from Washington clothed with the fullest power in this matter," he told them, ". . . I can act as if the President of the United States were himself present. I am directed to refer nothing to Washingon, but to act promptly—what I have to do, to do at once—to strike down the unworthy and to elevate the deserving." He reminded the troops of the value of the slaves and their labor to the Confederacy, and he announced the determination of the Lincoln administration to use that labor for the preservation of the Union. Recalling the Emancipation Proclamation for his audience, Thomas spoke sternly of reports that some Union troops had turned fugitive slaves away from their picket lines instead of welcoming them. That sort of thing would no longer be tolerated. Fugitives "are to be encouraged to come to us," the general proclaimed. "They are to be received with open arms; they are to be fed and clothed; they are to be armed." [11]

Then Thomas delivered what was to many ambitious officers and men of the Union the most attractive part of his message. "This is the policy that has been fully determined upon," he declared: "I am here to raise as many regiments of blacks as I can. I am authorized to give commissions, from the highest to the lowest, and I desire those persons who are earnest in the work to take hold of it." One can imagine the electric effect of this announcement on the audience: quickening pulses and new enthusiasm for the whole Negro soldier program as sergeants mentally became lieutenants and captains and as lieutenants saw themselves wearing the oak leaves and even the eagles of field rank. "I desire only those whose hearts are in it," Thomas continued, "and to them alone will I give commissions. I do not hesitate to say that all proper persons will receive commissions." [12]

Since every new colored regiment required a commissioned staff of about thirty-five officers, the Thomas goal of twenty regiments meant in the neighborhood of seven hundred commissions to white soldiers, the great bulk of them noncommissioned officers—all who could qualify and whose hearts were in it. In addition, every Negro regiment required ten company first sergeants, plus quartermaster, drill, and platoon sergeants. In some instances, Negro regiments were organized with almost exclusively white noncommissioned staffs. Here was wide opportunity for military advancement thrown open to hundreds of ambitious and enterprising white soldiers. Here also was an intelligent counterblow to army sentiment against the use of Negro soldiers: white soldiers were given a substantial stake in the success of the new government policy.

As for those who persisted in maltreating the colored population, General Thomas made it clear that he had "the fullest authority to dismiss from the army" all such persons. "This part of my duty," he warned, "I will most assuredly perform if any case comes before me. I would rather do that than give commissions, because such men are unworthy the name of soldiers." The adjutant general meant precisely what he said. He did later find it necessary to dismiss from the service a number of officers who refused to accommodate their prejudices to the Union's Negro soldier policy.[13]

Thomas announced his intention to raise twenty regiments of Negro troops in the valley and expressed his conviction that every Negro regiment raised would free a white regiment from garrison duty to "face the foe in the field." "This, fellow soldiers," the adjutant general concluded, "is the determined policy of the administration. You all know full well when the President of the United States, though said to be slow in coming to a determination, when once he puts his foot down, it is there, and he is not going to take it up. He has put his foot down; I am here to assure you that my official influence shall be given that he shall not raise it." [14]

Some indication of the effectiveness of this particular speech is provided by the report of a correspondent of the Cincinnati *Commercial,* reprinted in the *National Intelligencer* of April 20. According to the dispatch, which included Thomas's address in full, "The rush for offices in the contemplated negro regiments is great. The Seventh Missouri alone offers to furnish from its rank and file efficient officers for one regiment." The Ohio correspondent was convinced that there would be "no difficulty as far as the officers are concerned," but he found that the Negroes were not very favorably inclined toward the project. He thought, however, that if they were "impressed with the fact that they must accept one of two alternatives—slavery or soldiery—they [would] readily choose the latter."

The newspapers of the country discovered General Thomas and his mission by the middle of April, and as the news spread it was inevitable that David Hunter should have heard it even at remote Hilton Head. A thousand miles to the west of the Sea Islands the policy that Hunter had pioneered a year earlier was being put into effect. His policy had finally become administration policy, but it was being announced and initiated by another and in a theater of war far removed from his. Swallowing his frustration, Hunter wrote Lincoln to thank him "for the comfort and hope conveyed in the speech of Adjutant-

General Thomas, delivered in Louisiana on the arming of the negroes." Hunter found this not only an indication of "a thoroughly vigorous war policy" but assurance, he told the president, "that you have at length done that which it would be well for the country if you had done much earlier—taken the control of affairs into your own strong, honest hands, compelling all the resources of the country to move together to one definite and glorious object under the guidance of a single will."

The bitterness of his disappointments lay close to the surface of Hunter's mind as he reviewed the glacial slowness of the policy shift that had produced the Thomas mission, but he did not put the blame for that slowness on Lincoln alone. "That you should long have hesitated," the radical regular carefully told his president, "before assuming the responsibility of this step I do not wonder. Arrayed against you were all the clique prejudices of the two professions, Army and Navy; and . . . it was but natural that you should first prefer trusting to those who claimed to be oracles in the science of making war. These oracles failing, however, to realize their predictions, and you having now two years experience to guide the innate sagacity and clear purposes of your mind, I believe with my whole heart that you will prove your own best adviser; and I hail the emphatic speech of General Thomas, made by your authority and in your name, as the first clear ray from a brighter dawn that lies before us." But the general commanding the Department of the South had not written Lincoln for the sole purpose of congratulating him for having finally come around to his own way of thinking. The flames of Hunter's old hope leaped high in his heart, although the year's experiences had taken the fire and fight of his "fugitive masters" days out of his style. Choosing his words with obvious care, Hunter begged Lincoln for "the same powers given to General Thomas." [15] There was still some time for his 50,000 black troops on the coasts of South Carolina and Georgia. But Hunter's star was setting as the Negro soldier marched forward into an increasingly brighter dawn. Never was Hunter to enjoy the powers given to Lorenzo Thomas; his policy had been right, his execution and timing wrong, and he was granted no second chance.

Hunter's star was setting—he was never to be as adept at

handling his department and the troops in it as he was at devising major policy—but a new star was rising in the West. Henry W. Halleck, now in Washington as general-in-chief, thought it necessary to warn Ulysses S. Grant, a fighting general with no claims to policy making, about the new administration policy before the adjutant general arrived on the Mississippi. In a long discursive letter written while Lorenzo Thomas was posting west, Halleck gave the rising major general friendly advice in unofficial but nonetheless persuasive tones. Where Hunter had been in advance of the administration in handling the Negro problem, Grant had dragged his feet. As late as February 12, 1863, he had issued a sort of watered-down version of Halleck's notorious Order No. 3 of the first November of the war, excluding Negroes from his picket lines.[16] Halleck pointed out that this was not only "a bad policy in itself, but ... directly opposed to the policy of the Government." In his usual pompous style, the general-in-chief read Grant a short lecture on the duties of generals in the field: "Whatever may be the individual opinion of an officer in regard to the wisdom of measures adopted and announced by the Government, it is the duty of every one to cheerfully and honestly endeavor to carry out the measures so adopted."

Having emphasized that particular—and elementary—point, Halleck got to the crux of the situation. "It is expected," he told Grant, "that you will use your official and personal influence to remove prejudices on this subject, and to fully and thoroughly carry out the policy now adopted by the Government. That policy is to withdraw from the use of the enemy all the slaves you can, and to employ those so withdrawn to the best possible advantage against the enemy." Carefully Halleck explained to Grant how the character of the war had changed, how earlier visions of reconciliation with the Southern states had faded away. Again and again he repeated that the government had adopted a definite policy and that the army "must cheerfully and faithfully carry out that policy." Halleck was not reprimanding Grant for his earlier activities and for those of his subordinate officers, some of whom had even returned fugitive slaves to their masters; that would have been a difficult task for the author of Order No. 3 to perform gracefully. "I

write you this unofficial letter simply as a personal friend," he
assured the field commander, "and as a matter of friendly
advice. From my position here, where I can survey the whole
field, perhaps I may be better able to understand the tone of
public opinion and the intentions of the Government than you
can from merely consulting the officers of your army." [17] It
should surprise no one that when Lorenzo Thomas reached the
Mississippi Valley and announced the new policy of the Lincoln
administration, he found General Grant most attentive and co-
operative. Whatever doubts Grant may have had on the wisdom
of that policy were to be largely removed by military events of
the next few months.

Obviously stirred by his letter from General Halleck, Grant
instructed his divisional commanders to support the new policy.
In sharp contrast to his orders of February 12 were those he
sent on April 11 to Major General Frederick Steele, commanding the 11th Division of the Army of the Tennessee. "General
L. Thomas is now here with authority to make ample provision
for the negro," Grant told Steele, and he directed the division
commander to provide for all Negroes he had "where they are,
issuing to them necessary rations until other disposition is made
of them." No more fugitives were to be turned away by Union
pickets: Steele was ordered to "encourage all negroes . . . to
come within our lines." [18] Halleck had instructed Grant ex-
plicitly, and the pupil had absorbed the instruction thoroughly.

Grant wrote Halleck himself on April 19 to report that at
least three of his commanders had taken "hold of the new policy
of arming the negroes and using them against the enemy with a
will." These officers were at any rate, Grant wrote, "so much
soldiers as to feel themselves under obligation to carry out a
policy which they would not inaugurate[,] in the same good
faith and with the same zeal as if it was of their own choosing."
For himself, Grant assured the general-in-chief that he could
be relied on to carry out "any policy ordered by proper authority to the best of [his] ability." In token of his support of
this particular War Department policy, Grant issued a general
order directing all corps, division, and post commanders to
"afford all facilities for the completion of the negro regiments
now organizing in this Department." Commissary officers were

directed to issue the necessary supplies, and quartermasters to furnish stores "on the same requisition and returns as are required from other troops." Halleck must have been pleased and even a little amused at the last sentence of the order: "It is expected," Grant decreed, "that all commanders will especially exert themselves in carrying out the policy of the Administration, not only in organizing colored regiments and rendering them efficient, but also in removing prejudice against them." [19] Not even David Hunter could have put it better.

* * *

While the major generals wrote letters and orders, Brigadier General Thomas continued on his mission in the valley. His activities and speeches attracted wide attention throughout the nation as spring moved north and burgeoned into summer. While many reports were critical of Thomas, still he trudged ahead with his work, moving from the Deep South to Washington and back again, pausing only when sickness and exhaustion nearly cost him his life during the first hot weeks of June. Charles A. Dana, assistant secretary of war, was on an investigatory trip in the Mississippi Valley in the spring of 1863, and he observed some improvement in the attitude of army officers on the Negro soldier question. "Officers in this army," Dana wrote Stanton on April 20, "who, three months ago, told me they would never serve along with negro regiments, now say that Adjutant-General Thomas makes bad speeches to troops, but that they shall obey orders, nevertheless." [20] By the middle of May, the misanthropic attorney general, Edward Bates, was confiding to his diary that "abolition seems to be the strongest rallying point . . . even Adjt Genl L. Thomas has become a very zealous proselyte—he is out on the Missi. straining his little powers in the effort to organize black battalions, but thus far, with little success, tho' the raw material is abundant, all around him." [21]

Thomas himself seems to have been oblivious to the criticism his efforts attracted. He continued to "address the troops, and impress upon them the policy of the Government respecting blacks." He was convinced, he reiterated, that his announcements were received with enthusiasm and that the army "fully recognizes the necessity of using the negroes in any way to assist in crushing the rebellion." Further, Thomas told the secretary of war in late April, "the negroes themselves are beginning fully to comprehend the purposes of the Government with regard to them, are well satisfied, and eagerly seek to enter military organizations." [22] Contradicting the adjutant general's optimistic reports, the *National Intelligencer* of April 22 commented in a paragraph on the organization of what it called "the First African" regiment at Helena, Arkansas, that "The negroes don't manifest much enthusiasm, and some of them have to be impressed."

While his contemporaries in the War Department, in the Lincoln administration, and in the newspapers belittled Thomas's efforts, the perspective of ninety years suggests more sympathetic treatment. The biographer of Governor Andrew of Massachusetts, writing more than a generation after Appomattox, was probably more just to Thomas than were his critics in 1863: "He did his business with dispatch if not with thoroughness, moving rapidly from point to point; by the end of the year he could report twenty thousand negroes under arms as a result of his initiative." [23] What many of the adjutant general's contemporaries misunderstood was what Lorenzo Thomas had been sent to do. He was, after all, no mere recruiting agent. Rather was his task that of initiating Union policy on a grand scale, of breaking down white opposition to the use of Negro soldiers, of educating Union troops in the valley on this one subject, of starting the work of organization and then moving on to begin it anew at the next Union position while other officers took up the actual details of recruiting and organizing and carried them forward to completion. These things Thomas did and did well.

Perhaps he did make "bad speeches" from the lofty point of view of a Dana or from the narrow point of view of prejudiced regular and volunteer officers. Read today, however, those speeches demonstrate many of the characteristics of good propaganda, of a fairly well thought-out educational or promotional campaign. Thomas appealed to the soldiers who made up his audiences on the basis of patriotism, humanity, and self-interest. He clearly told them his message; he simply gave them the reasons for that message; he asked cooperation, and he held out rewards and punishments. He repeated himself often; to the more sophisticated he must have been something of a bore. But the fact remains that the Thomas speeches were effective. His order and letter books are crammed with special orders creating regiments of Negro troops—at Helena, Arkansas, at Columbus, Kentucky, at Milliken's Bend and Young's Point, Louisiana, at Corinth, Mississippi, at Memphis and Nashville, Tennessee. By the end of 1863 his original goal of twenty regiments had been reached. By the end of the war he had had a hand in the organization of seventy Negro regiments. Lorenzo Thomas was responsible for initiating the organization of better than 40 per cent of all the regiments of United States colored troops who bore arms in the Civil War.

That fact alone ought to be sufficient argument for a re-evaluation of the role of Lorenzo Thomas in the history of American Negro soldiers and their role in the Civil War. However pedestrian, regulation-bound, and uninspiring his contemporaries may have found him, the adjutant general undertook the cause of the Negro soldier long before service with Negro soldiers became popular. He helped make that service popular by his steady, stubborn devotion to duty. The very fact that Thomas was not a radical or a zealot probably aided him in his work. David Hunter had made bitter enemies and had increased anti-Negro feeling in the Union Army by his myopic enthusiasm for his personal crusade. Lorenzo Thomas was simply the agent of the War Department, the spokesman of the president, a career officer carrying out an assignment, a professional soldier with no discoverable political aspirations or connections. As such he stirred up a minimum of suspicion and opposition to his efforts. Because of his conservative background, experience, and reputation, he had the effect of helping to make the movement to arm the Negro "respectable" and acceptable.

Examination of his letters and orders and reports shows that Thomas was not content with mere surface fulfillment of his instructions. He was thorough in the attention he gave to every detail of the work. He organized divisional boards of officers to examine candidates for commissions in colored regiments. He gave time and concern to the problem of caring for the families of Negro soldiers and fugitives generally. He became almost a radical in insisting on equality of treatment for the Negro regiments he organized. Time after time he took a strong position on this subject: he objected strenuously to the tendency to have colored troops do more than their fair share of fatigue duty, and he urged that they be permitted to do "the work of soldiers." [24] He gave continuing attention to the officers appointed over Negro soldiers; he saw to it that the deserving were rewarded when possible, and in other cases his wrath was often swift and sure. "By means also of frequent inspections by myself and two officers of my staff," he reported to Stanton, "the careless and indifferent officers were gotten rid of and more zealous ones appointed." [25]

Whatever Lorenzo Thomas may have felt when he first learned of his mission to the Mississippi Valley, he gave his best to that mission. Far from being an "indifferent" officer, he gave the new policy his wholehearted support; indeed it must have amazed some of his contemporaries to see a regular become so thoroughly zealous in the interest of a despised race. With his usual perspicacity, Abraham Lincoln accurately stated the case in a letter to Stanton in late July of 1863: "I think the evidence is nearly conclusive that General Thomas is one of the best (if not the very best) instruments for this service." [26]

*   *   *

Encouraged by letters from President Lincoln, Secretary Stanton, and General Halleck toward the end of March and undoubtedly stimulated by the activities of other general officers farther up the Mississippi, Nathaniel P. Banks launched his own Negro soldier program on May 1, 1863. General Orders, No. 40, issued from the headquarters of the Department of the Gulf, Opelousas, Louisiana, announced Banks's proposal to organize "a corps d'armée of colored troops, to be designated as the 'Corps d'Afrique.' " This corps was to "consist ultimately of eighteen regiments, representing all arms—Infantry, Artillery, and Cavalry, organized in three Divisions of three Brigades each, with appropriate corps of Engineers and flying Hospitals for each Division." Arguing that "with a race unaccustomed to military service, much depends on the immediate influence of officers upon individual members, than those that acquired more or less of warlike habits and spirit by centuries of contest," Banks limited the size of his proposed regiments to five hundred men rather than the regulation thousand, at the same time retaining the full number of commissioned and non-commissioned officers.

No fanatic, Banks announced that his Corps d'Afrique was not to be "established upon any dogma of equality or other theory, but as a practical and sensible matter of business. The Government makes use of mules, horses, uneducated and educated white men, in the defense of its institutions. Why should not the negro contribute whatever is in his power for the cause in which he is as deeply interested as other men? We may properly demand from him whatever service he can render." Critical of the regiments mustered into service under Butler's command, Banks by implication blamed their alleged short-comings on their Negro officers.[27] Nowhere in Banks's lengthy and verbose order was there any mention of Daniel Ullmann, with whom he was supposed to be cooperating in his efforts to raise a Negro brigade in Louisiana. Small wonder that Ullmann, nearly a quarter of a century after the war, should have commented bitterly on the behavior of the general commanding the Department of the Gulf. He charged that Banks had been strongly influenced by local planters who were definitely opposed to the recruitment of Negro troops. Ullmann himself was "beset" by those planters, who resorted to "all kinds of devices ... to obstruct the execution" of his orders. Nor was this all. Ullmann's officers, he complained, "met with difficulties at every step. These came not only from Planters. With a few honorable exceptions, the whole mass of the officers, not only of the regular army, but where we did not expect it, of the volunteers, had an implacable prejudice, which led them to say and do many foolish things. These latter, however, finally abated their highly wrought feelings when they thought they discovered an opportunity for *promotion* in this direction."[28]

Ullmann's charge that Banks was influenced by the prejudices of the planting gentry of Louisiana seems to fall under the weight of the regiments of Negro troops raised under orders from Banks's headquarters. As for personal prejudice, Banks

seems to have been opposed only to Negro officers. His orders
were explicit in regard to the policy of organizing Negro regiments. "Officers and soldiers," he directed, "will consider the
exigencies of the service in this Department, and the absolute
necessity of appropriating every element of power to the support of the Government. The prejudices or opinions of men are
in nowise involved." [29] Perhaps Ullmann's accusations were
motivated in great part by Banks's independent action in organizing his own Corps d'Afrique without regard to Ullmann's
activities. Adding insult to injury, Banks in early June consolidated Ullmann's troops with his own organization: "The regiments now being raised under the direction of Bridagier General
Daniel Ullmann, and at present known as the First, Second,
Third, Fourth, and Fifth Regiments of Ullmann's Brigade, will
be respectively designated as the Sixth, Seventh, Eighth, Ninth,
and Tenth Regiments of Infantry of the Corps d'Afrique." [30]
The same orders designated the Louisiana Native Guard regiments mustered by Ben Butler as the 1st, 2nd, 3rd, and 4th
Regiments of Infantry of the Corps d'Afrique. In fact, of the
first ten regiments in his corps, Banks had organized only one.

Joseph T. Wilson, a Negro soldier who served first in the 2nd
Louisiana Native Guards and afterward transferred to the 54th
Massachusetts, criticized Banks after the war and charged that
his "treatment of the negroes was so very different from that
which they had received from Gen. Butler,—displacing the
negro officers of the first three regiments organized,—that it
rather checkmated recruiting . . ." [31] Banks, however, had an
antidote for slow recruiting—conscription—and he used it
freely. He had, as a matter of record, ordered conscription of
all unemployed Negroes in March when the organization of his
1st Engineers had been launched. David Hunter had established
a precedent for conscripting Negroes: not only his original attempts in the spring of 1862 but more recently in a general
order of March 6. [32] In 1863 the Union turned to the draft as
a means of securing white soldiers, so that conscription of
Negroes was not so great an inequality as it might at first appear. Conscription continued to be used in a variety of forms,
with and without any color of law, wherever Union officers
found or imagined a need for it.

Whatever the means he used, Banks could report to Lincoln in mid-August that he had in his department "twenty-one regiments nearly organized, three upon the basis of a thousand men each, and eighteen of 500 men, making in all 10,000 or 12,000 men." [33] Two weeks later, on September 1, Brigadier General George L. Andrews, whom Banks had appointed to command his Corps d'Afrique, reported that he had "twenty regiments of infantry organized . . . and nearly all filled to the required numbers," and "in addition . . . four regiments of engineers . . . three of which are full" and the other nearly so. General Andrews, encouraged by the "facility with which these regiments have been raised," saw "no obstacle to raising within three months from six to ten additional infantry regiments." He had already begun to recruit a cavalry regiment, which he proposed "to fill with picked men, selected from those accustomed to riding on horseback and to the care of horses; they should also be active, robust men. From their knowledge of the country," Andrews assured Banks, "it is thought that such a body of men, well-officered, cannot fail to be of great service." [34]

Quick to realize the practical value of the Negro soldier, both military and political, quick to take credit for regiments which other men had raised in his department, Banks used his Corps d'Afrique throughout his long and speckled command of the Department of the Gulf. His activities in the spring of 1863, far from lending support to Ullmann's charges of truckling to slaveholders' prejudices, seem rather to justify the opinion of ex-Native Guard Joseph Wilson that Banks "endeavored to out-Herod Gen. Lorenzo Thomas . . ." [35]

*　　*　　*

The first seven months of 1863 were crucial to the cause of the Negro soldier in the Union Army. In that period the Lincoln administration became thoroughly committed to the use of colored troops. While the adjutant general went ahead with his work in the Mississippi Valley, the War Department carried on similar work on a small scale in the East. Late in April, Colonel E. A. Wild of Boston was authorized by the secretary of war, on Governor John Andrew's nomination, to organize a brigade of colored troops in the Department of North Carolina, and in the middle of that month the new brigadier reported to Major General John C. Foster, commanding that department, and went to work. General Foster, encouraged by Halleck, enjoined the officers and men of his command to give Wild "every facility and aid in the performance" of his mission.[36] With Negro soldiers being recruited and organized nearly everywhere north and south, the evolution of Union war policy was almost complete.

Probably discouraged with the slow results of its piecemeal practice of authorizing specific individuals to raise Negro soldiers, certainly encouraged by General Thomas's reports of success in the Mississippi Valley, the War Department put the whole program of employing Negro soldiers on a higher plane of organization and standardization by establishing a separate bureau in the adjutant general's office "for the record of all matters relating to the organization of colored troops." General Orders, No. 143, May 22, 1863, regularized the method of raising Negro soldiers with full control centralized in the Bureau for Colored Troops under the adjutant general. Major Charles W. Foster was appointed chief of the bureau with the title of assistant adjutant general, and he set up headquarters at No. 531 17th Street. Field officers were detailed as inspectors of the activities under bureau jurisdiction. Boards of officers were established to examine candidates for commissions in colored regiments, and the main outlines of the work sketched out authoritatively for the first time. With the publication of this order, the whole movement to arm the Negro moved off its original amateurish, haphazard, and volunteer basis to a new footing of professional, organized, regularized activity under central control from Washington.[37]

On June 30, 1863, as Union and Confederate patrols scouted in the vicinity of Gettysburg, a regiment "designated the First U.S. Colored Troops" was mustered into service in Washington, the first raised under the "immediate supervision" of the new bureau. It signified the coming of age of the American Negro soldier and presaged the disappearance of such exotic and fanciful titles as Zouaves d'Afrique, Louisiana Native Guards, Corps d'Afrique, and 1st Arkansas Volunteers of African Descent. With the exception of the two Massachusetts colored regiments, the 54th and 55th, colored troops were mustered directly into federal service and were organized and led by officers acting under the authority of the United States and not of any particular state.[38] Negro soldiers were not fighting for any particular state; they were fighting for the United States, the government of which had promised them freedom. There was justice as well as logic in changing the designation of Higginson's "Fust Souf" Carolina Volunteers to the 33rd U.S. Colored Troops, Thomas's 1st Arkansas to the 46th U.S.C.T., Butler's 1st Louisiana Native Guards to the 73rd U.S.C.T., Jim Lane's 1st Kansas Colored Volunteers to the 79th U.S.C.T.

The establishment of the Bureau for Colored Troops was a milestone in the history of the Negro in the Civil War. For the balance of the war the organization of Negro regiments was on a uniform national basis whether those regiments were raised in New York, Maryland, Ohio, or Illinois or in Southern regions under Union control. No longer was the movement to depend on individual ambition or radicalism.

Just as the proof of any pudding is in its eating, so the final proof of the Negro soldier came not so much from War Department orders and the clarification of administration policy as from the demonstrated fighting qualities of that soldier. The organizational achievements of Lorenzo Thomas and the regularization of Negro regiments by the Bureau for Colored Troops must have been hollow indeed without the final battle proof offered as those troops found opportunity to do "the work of soldiers." In the last analysis, the Negro soldier won the right to fight not by virtue of decisions made in Washington by president or secretary of war or Congress. He won it by his own performance as a soldier in action.

VIII. *"But the high soul burns on . . ."*

Many persons believed, or pretended to believe, and confidently asserted, that freed slaves would not make good soldiers; that they would lack courage, and could not be subjected to military discipline. Facts have shown how groundless were these apprehensions. The slave has proved his manhood, and his capacity as an infantry soldier, at Milliken's Bend, at the assault upon Port Hudson, and at the storming of Fort Wagner.

—EDWIN M. STANTON, December, 1863

In July of 1862, Charles Francis Adams, Jr., had written from Hilton Head, South Carolina, his emphatic conviction that "the idea of arming the blacks *as soldiers* must be abandoned." One year later, in the decisive month of July, 1863, he wrote his father confidently: "The negro regiment question is our greatest victory of the war so far, and, I can assure you, that in the army, these are so much a success that they will soon be the fashion." [1] What had happened in those twelve months of war to change young Adams's mood from condemnation and despair to admiration and jubilation?

Much had happened. But the proof of the value of the American Negro as a soldier of the Union had not come from the final clarification of administration policy, nor from the activities of Lorenzo Thomas, Nathaniel Banks, Daniel Ullmann, and John Andrew. These had been important, of course; without them the whole movement to arm the Negro must have died on the vine, even as Hunter's efforts had come to nothing but frustration and despair in August of 1862. No matter what force and encour-

132

agement the administration and the War Department applied to the Negro soldier policy, complete acceptance of the Negro as a soldier depended ultimately on his performance as a soldier. Lorenzo Thomas and Daniel Ullmann had labored in vain if the regiments they raised had failed to measure up as soldiers in battle. John Andrew's high purpose could never have been realized if the 54th Massachusetts had faltered before the earthworks of Fort Wagner. The test of the soldier is battle. No amount of talk can change the basic facts of war. No amount of talk could have won the Negro soldier his place in the Union Army. He had to win that place, soldier-fashion, by fighting and dying in battle. In the first seven months of 1863 the American Negro soldier did precisely that.

*   *   *

War in 1863 still had flags and parades with bands of music. It was not the same as the spring of 1861; the enthusiasm and optimism of those first months had been bled out by nearly two years of war. The exuberant volunteers who had blithely swung south to hang Jeff Davis to a sour apple tree had become veterans by the spring of 1863. Volunteers were fewer in number and new regiments were slow to appear. There were new regiments in 1863, but many of them were of colored troops, and they did not always have an opportunity to parade proudly before marching south. Many of them were already south, recruited in the enemy's country and with small room or time for the pomp and circumstance of war. Still, there were a few parades, and two of them are worth watching as the blue ranks march past. One took place in Beaufort, South Carolina, in January, the other in Boston in May.

January is a changeable wench in the Sea Islands. Although the previous week had been "like May," with bluebirds and even a butterfly, Monday, January 19, was a cold and disagreeable day. For the officers and men of the 1st South Carolina Volunteers, however, the weather was of small importance. For on that day Colonel Higginson paraded the whole regiment through the streets of Beaufort and back again—"the first appearance of such a novelty on any stage." How the ghosts of Beaufort, prewar watering place of the planting aristocracy of the coast, must have stirred uneasily at the sight of this regiment of freed slaves, resplendent in red trousers and blue coats, carrying muskets and the colors given them on Emancipation Day. The band of the 8th Maine, which had played for them on that day, came to their assistance again, met them at the outskirts of town and played them through it. Color Sergeant Prince Rivers expressed the feelings of every last private when he ecstatically exclaimed afterward, "And when dat band wheel in before us, and march on,—my God! I quit dis world altogedder."

Colonel Higginson had made careful preparation for this public appearance, aware that not only Southerners, white and Negro, would be watching but also "throngs of officers and soldiers who had drilled as many months as we had drilled weeks, and whose eyes would readily spy out every defect." His men exceeded his greatest expectations. One of them commented afterward, "We didn't look to de right nor to de leff. I didn't see notin' in Beaufort. Eb'ry step was worth a half-a-dollar." Along the sandy streets of Beaufort they marched, under the spreading live oaks, stepping proudly to the Maine music, the chill wind snapping the stiff new flags. Then back they came again, past the shuttered mansions beyond the broad lawns, as if to show that their first smart appearance had not been accidental. The great occasion over, they marched the three miles back to camp. The Maine band had left them, but they made their own music, singing their favorite "John Brown Song" and "all manner of things,—as happy creatures as one can well conceive." To their Massachusetts colonel, the parade conjured up visions of "the many dusky regiments, [still] unformed ... marching up behind us, gathering shape out of the dim air." [2]

On the next day Major General David Hunter returned to command of the Department of the South after a four months' absence, and on January 21 he visited Higginson. With the perversity of generals, Hunter arrived at Camp Saxton during battalion drill rather than at dress parade, catching the regiment in its old clothes. But the men cheered both Hunter and Saxton lustily, particularly since Hunter promised them "pay when the funds arrive," Springfield rifles, and blue trousers.

This last was especially welcome to the colonel, who had never taken to the regiment's barbaric Zouave costume. Best of all, Hunter "graciously consented" to let the regiment make another parade—this one without music, and far beyond the streets of Beaufort—an expedition in force up the St. Mary's River between Georgia and Florida. Higginson's men had been on two earlier expeditions under Colonel Beard of New York, but for two months they had been kept in their camp, learning drill and discipline. Now, their colonel believed, they were ready. "Our success or failure," he wrote in his journal, "may make or mar the prospects of colored troops." [3]

Two days after Hunter had approved the project, Higginson was on his way at the head of a formidable force of 460 troops aboard three oddly assorted steamers, the *Ben de Ford,* the *John Adams,* and the *Planter,* which had been "liberated" from the rebels by Robert Small, a Negro pilot. The *John Adams* was the "chief reliance" of the expedition; she was an army gunboat converted from an old double-ender East Boston ferryboat but ideally suited to the narrow, tortuous St. Mary's. To negotiate some of the sharper bends in the river it was necessary to run the *John Adams* into the bank, let the current swing her around, reverse her engines, and so continue.

The St. Mary's expedition was no spur-of-the-moment enterprise. The Department of the South was in dire need of lumber; practically all building materials had to be shipped down from the North, although timber was plentiful on the mainland. The supplies brought in by the November expeditions were all used up by January. A recent expedition of four white companies had failed to secure material, but Corporal Robert Sutton of Higginson's regiment knew of vast quantities of lumber up the St. Mary's. Sutton had been a slave on the Alberti plantation at Woodstock on the river, and he was thoroughly acquainted with the region. In his official report, Higginson called Sutton "the real conductor of the whole expedition," and the ex-slave performed with intelligence and courage throughout the week-long action, despite three wounds.[4]

The affair was an unqualified success. The steamers returned deep-laden with 250 bars of railroad iron, 40,000 bricks, some lumber, a flock of sheep, and even a piano for the Negro school

near Camp Saxton. Higginson had led his men in action, and
he was enthusiastic about their behavior. "Nobody knows anything about these men who has not seen them in battle," he told
General Saxton. ". . . There is a fiery energy about them beyond
anything of which I have ever read, except it be the French
Zouaves. It requires the strictest discipline to hold them in
hand." But keep them in hand he did. "No wanton destruction
was permitted," he reported, "nor were any buildings burned
unless in retaliation for being fired upon, according to the
usages of war." The temptations had been great. At Woodstock
a vast store of household goods had been discovered, all just
as they had been packed and crated for removal from the
coastal plantations for safekeeping inland. But Higginson was
no Jayhawker, and the only trophies he carried off were a
cannon, a flag, and part of the equipment of a slave jail on the
Alberti plantation. There the colonel introduced Corporal
Robert Sutton to his former owner, but she, with "unutterable
indignation," turned to Higginson and exclaimed acidly, "Ah,
we called him Bob!" [5]

The expedition ran into resistance. There was a night engagement ashore in which the regiment gave better than it received. On the return trip from Woodstock the bluffs along the
St. Mary's were thick with Confederate sharpshooters, but by
keeping his men under hatches, Higginson came through with
only one casualty: Captain Clifton of the *John Adams* was
killed on his own hurricane deck. A New York *Times* correspondent at Fernandina, Florida, made a clean beat with his
enthusiastic report. He described the expedition as "a complete
success," declaring that "Our colored troops are more than a
match for any equal number of white rebels which can be
brought against them. With a few horse carts to transport ammunition, (for they will provide commissary and quartermaster
stores as they go), these free men are all-sufficient to snuff out
the rebellion." The *Times* of February 10 carried excerpts from
the reports of Colonel Higginson and Captain Charles Trowbridge of Company A along with its reporter's exuberant dispatch, but editorially it took a more cautious tack, criticizing
Higginson for his "entertaining official report." He "seems to
think it necessary," the *Times* commented, "to put his case

strongly, and in rather exalted language, as well as in such a way as to convince the public that negroes will fight." Given the colonel's literary bent and the controversial nature of the service in which he was engaged, it was impossible for him to write his report in any other way.

Still, the New York paper concluded that the Massachusetts abolitionist had sound plans for the future. "The Colonel puts forth the very good suggestion" that "a chain of forts" on the mainland and manned by Negro troops "would completely alter the whole aspect of the war in the seaboard Slave States, and would accomplish what no accumulation of Northern regiments can so easily effect." "This," the *Times* agreed, "is the very use for negro soldiers suggested in the Proclamation of the President. We have no doubt that the whole State of Florida might easily be held for the Government in this way, by a dozen negro regiments."

The *National Intelligencer*'s reaction to this further demonstration of the tactical possibilities of the Negro soldier was to reprint on February 13 a report from the Hilton Head correspondent of the Hartford (Conn.) *Times,* which maintained that the expedition had been a conspicuous failure. This dispatch asserted that the Negro soldiers, surprised at night by a small band of rebels, had *"fired in every direction, and then stampeded for the transports, throwing away their guns."* This was in direct contradiction of the facts of the case as set down by Colonel Higginson and others accompanying him. Here is the colonel's report of the engagement: "At Township, Fla., a detachment of the expedition fought a cavalry company which met it unexpectedly on a midnight march through pine woods and which completed surrounded us." Certainly, the situation called for firing in every direction. "They were beaten off," Higginson's report continued, "with a loss on our part of one man killed and seven wounded, while the opposing party admits twelve men killed, including Lt. Jones, in command of the company, besides many wounded. So complete was our victory that the enemy scattered and hid in the woods all night, not venturing back to his camp, which was five miles distant, until noon next day, a fact which was unfortunately unknown until too late to follow up our advantage."

To Higginson the expedition was proof positive that "the key to the successful prosecution of this war lies in the unlimited employment of black troops. Their superiority lies simply in the fact that they know the country, while white troops do not, and, moreover, that they have peculiarities of temperament, position, and motive which belong to them alone. Instead of leaving their homes and families to fight, they are fighting for their homes and families, and they show the resolution and sagacity which a personal purpose gives. It would have been madness to attempt, with the bravest white troops, what I have successfully accomplished with black ones." [6]

The St. Mary's expedition had, however, been a failure in one respect: few recruits were added to the roster of Negro soldiers. While Higginson's regiment was full, the 2nd South Carolina under Colonel James Montgomery needed men badly if it was ever to develop into an effective organization. Early in February, Montgomery was recruiting at Fernandina off northeastern Florida, but finding that most of the able-bodied freedmen of that place had already been enlisted in the 1st, he continued down to Key West. There he enlisted 130 men, all volunteers. But the pickings continued slim, and his regiment numbered less than one hundred and fifty at the beginning of March. It was in part to remedy this situation by tapping richer manpower resources that an ambitious expedition got under way in early March. General Saxton sent Colonel Higginson up the St. John's River in northern Florida "to carry the proclamation of freedom to the enslaved; to call all loyal men into the service of the United States; to occupy as much of the State of Florida as possible with the forces under [his] command." These forces numbered less than a thousand infantrymen. Higginson had left many of his own regiment "sick and on duty in Beaufort," and Montgomery's regiment was scarcely two full companies. Saxton gave Higginson a free hand in the management of the enterprise, specifying only that he occupy Jacksonville and entrench there. The town had twice been in Union hands earlier and twice evacuated.[7]

To send such a small force, however augmented by gunboats, on such a foray deep into enemy country seems at first to have been decidedly daring if not downright risky. But

Confederate forces were concentrated in the defense of Charleston, and Florida's isolation from the rest of the South made her a favorable field for the trial. Further, Saxton told Stanton, there were supposed to be "large numbers of able-bodied negroes" near Jacksonville "watching for an opportunity to join us." If they could not come to the Union lines, those lines would be extended to them. The operation moved smoothly and successfully from the start, despite Higginson's dissatisfaction with efforts to keep the movement secret. Up the St. John's went the amphibious force to occupy Jacksonville early on the morning of March 10 without firing a shot. Even Confederate Brigadier General Joseph Finegan, commanding the District of Florida, frankly admitted that the Union troops "had occupied the town with so much celerity and secrecy as to have surrounded it with [their] pickets before the people generally were aware of [their] presence." Correctly analyzing the purpose of the expedition and its potent threat, Finegan wrote "That the entire negro population of East Florida will be lost and the country ruined there cannot be a doubt, unless the means of holding the St. John's River are immediately supplied." [8]

Saxton reported to Stanton on March 14 with his usual enthusiasm: ". . . so far the objects of the expedition have been fully accomplished. The town is completely in our possession and many prisoners." Never one to miss an opportunity to praise the performance of colored troops, Saxton told the secretary of war that there had been "constant skirmishing going on for several days, and in every action the negro troops have behaved with the utmost bravery. Never in a single instance can I learn that they have flinched." Of the effect of the raid and seizure of Jacksonville on the South, Saxton had no doubts. "It is my belief," he wrote Stanton, "that scarcely an incident in this war has caused a greater panic throughout the whole Southern coast than this raid of the colored troops in Florida." [9]

Reports of Confederate officers largely bear out Saxton's belief. Letters and telegrams crisscrossed the lower South, from Florida to Richmond and back to Charleston, as the rebel forces rallied to drive out the invaders. But Confederate extremity was Higginson's opportunity. General Beauregard regretfully informed Richmond that he could spare neither men nor guns from Charleston or Savannah.[10]

Meanwhile the invaders dug in, built "formidable fortifications" in and about the town, held off rebel attacks with the help of gunboats in the river, and even extended their field of operations by raids farther up the St. John's. Higginson relished his command of the only Union post on the mainland in the Department of the South and watched with pleasure the conduct of his men in the role of victors occupying a white city. James Montgomery, for his part, developed the upriver raid "into a fine art." His notions of foraging were "rather more Western and liberal" than Higginson's: after his first sally the steamer carrying Montgomery's troops "seemed an animated hencoop."

The Jayhawker carried the war deeper into Florida, extending his activities seventy-five miles up the St. John's to Palatka and returning laden with wagons, mules, cotton, forage, freed slaves, and fifteen prisoners.[11]

For ten days Higginson and his little force held Jacksonville, skirmishing daily with Confederate forces on the outskirts of town. His men were wearing down from constant duty and watchfulness when the 6th Connecticut arrived from Hilton Head, to be followed in two days by a part of the 8th Maine. While Higginson was relieved of anxiety for the safety of the post, he now was confronted with worries of a different sort. He commanded parts of four regiments, "the first time in the war ... that white and black soldiers had served together on regular duty." How the mixed force would get along was a major question, but there were no incidents. Colonel John D. Rust of the 8th Maine cooperated well with Higginson; white soldiers replaced the Negro provost guard on town patrol, a concession Higginson was glad to make in the interest of good race relations, and all went well in Jacksonville. Plans were completed for the white regiments to hold the town while the Negro force moved into the interior following the lines already reconnoitered by Montgomery.

Higginson expected Hunter himself to visit Jacksonville, but on March 28 orders from Hunter recalled the entire expedition. Jacksonville was evacuated for the third time on the following day. War Department plans for the early reduction of the

Charleston defenses required more military muscle than Hunter had at Hilton Head. Colonel Higginson was never sure of the reason why his expedition was terminated just as it seemed to be moving ahead encouragingly, but he thought it "simply the scarcity of troops in the Department, and the renewed conviction at headquarters that we were too few to hold the post alone." [12] When Union forces returned to Jacksonville a year later, the expedition was 20,000 strong, roughly ten times Higginson's augmented command, and even that number proved insufficient to win the bloody battle of Olustee.

The burning of part of the town rather marred the Union withdrawal from Jacksonville. Fortunately for the reputation of the Negro troops, the fires were started by white soldiers, as many Northern newspapers were at pains to point out. The New York *Evening Post* laid the blame on the Maine troops, although Colonel Rust was credited with trying to stop the vandalism. A New York *Tribune* correspondent reported that the "Negro troops took no part whatever" in the lamentable outrage and were "simply silent spectators of the splendid but sad spectacle." According to this *Tribune* reporter, "The 6th Connecticut charge[d] it upon the 8th Maine, and the 8th Maine hurl[ed] it back at the 6th Connecticut." [13]

Before the sudden breaking off of the Jacksonville expedition, President Lincoln had been cheered by reports of its successes. "I am glad to see the accounts of your colored force at Jacksonville," he wrote Hunter. "I see the enemy are driving them fiercely, as is to be expected. It is important to the enemy that such a force shall not take shape and grow and thrive in the South, and in precisely the same porportion it is important to us that it shall." Accordingly, Lincoln urged that "the utmost caution and vigilance is necessary on our part. The enemy will make extra efforts to destroy them, and we should do the same to preserve them and increase them." [14] And they were preserved and increased as Lorenzo Thomas, Daniel Ullmann, and Nathaniel Banks pushed their recruiting in the Mississippi Valley, and as Governor Andrew and the recruiting organization of George Stearns built up the ranks of the 54th Massachusetts. It had seemed for a time that the Union must look only to the Department of the South for demonstrations of what

Negro soldiers could do for the cause of the Union but, as the spring of 1863 warmed into summer, Higginson and Montgomery's men lost their corner on martial glory.

*   *   *

The *National Intelligencer* of June 10 carried a notice of Montgomery's "latest expedition into the interior" in which "his forces destroyed a vast amount of cotton, rice, and other property, and brought off 725 slaves." This was the sort of foray the Jayhawker particularly enjoyed, but its importance was overshadowed by another story in the same issue of the *Intelligencer*, the official report of General Banks about the assaults by Louisiana colored regiments on the Confederate stronghold of Port Hudson. On May 27 the 1st and 3rd Regiments of Infantry of the Corps d'Afrique—Butler's 1st and 3rd Louisiana Native Guards—with Banks's 1st Engineers, a regiment barely two months old, went into the most important and terrific action of their lives. They distinguished themselves in the eyes of the entire country by showing outstanding bravery and determination against a strongly entrenched enemy, advancing over broken ground so covered with fallen trees as to make a tangled abattis.

General Ullmann, who was present on the spot, wrote that the Negro troops "made six or seven charges over this ground against the enemy's works. They were exposed to a terrible fire and were dreadfully slaughtered. While it may be doubted whether it was wise to so expose them, all who witnessed these charges agree that their conduct was such as would do honor to any soldiers." Ullmann was convinced that "the conduct of these regiments on this occasion wrought a marvelous change in the opinion of many former sneerers." [15] Nor was he alone in this conviction. An officer of engineers wrote after the assault: "Port Hudson is doomed. It would make a good iron mine now. Our negro troops are splendid, beat the French Zouaves. Who would not be a Niggadier General?" The engineer continued with the enthusiasm of a convert. "You have no idea," he told his correspondent, "how my prejudices with regard to negro troops have been dispelled by the battle the other day. The brigade of negroes behaved magnificently and fought splendidly; could not have done better. They are far superior in discipline to the white troops, and just as brave." [16]

Nathaniel Banks sounded more like Thomas Wentworth Higginson than a general supposed to have anti-Negro prejudices. For once, certainly, he and Ullmann were in solid agreement. "Whatever doubt may have existed heretofore as to the efficiency" of Negro regiments, Banks wrote Halleck, "the history of this day proves conclusively to those who were in condition to observe the conduct of these regiments that the Government will find in this class of troops effective supporters and defenders. The severe test to which they were subjected, and the determined manner in which they encountered the enemy, leaves upon my mind no doubt of their ultimate success." [17] Port Hudson also settled the question of Negro soldiers, once and for all, as far as the New York *Times* was concerned. That newspaper had cautiously refused to commit itself to enthusiastic support of the Negro soldier until he had been tested in a large-scale engagement. Events on the Sea Islands and up the St. Mary's and St. John's rivers had simply not been of sufficient magnitude to provide any real test. Reports from Port Hudson, however, satisfied the *Times*. On June 11 it printed extracts from Banks's report to Halleck and then commented editorially: "this official testimony settles the question that the negro race can fight with great prowess. Those black soldiers had never before been in any severe engagement. They were comparatively raw troops, and were yet subjected to the most awful ordeal that even veterans ever have to experience —the charging upon fortifications through the crash of belching batteries. The men, white or black, who will not flinch from that, will flinch from nothing. It is no longer possible to doubt the bravery and steadiness of the colored race, when rightly led."

That last phrase, "when rightly led," can be construed as an expression of the notion that Negro soldiers, to perform at the peak of bravery and steadiness, require white officers. Very probably that is what the *Times* intended. But the facts of Port Hudson hardly support that hoary myth. The 1st and 3rd Infantry of the Corps d'Afrique each had nineteen Negro company officers, nearly two-thirds of the total. And the records indicate that they gave their men the leadership the assaults demanded. Captain André Cailloux, commanding Company E of the 1st, stood out as the individual hero of the assaults, although at the cost of his life. His men tried several times to reach his body, but he lay too close to the Confederate works to be recovered until Port Hudson had surrendered. Then his friends and associates in New Orleans, where he had been prominent in free colored society, honored his memory with a state funeral complete with "all the rites of the Catholic church" and the military pageantry appropriate to the occasion. The band of the 42nd Massachusetts (white) played the long procession through the crowded streets of the Crescent City, and the 6th Infantry, Corps d'Afrique, provided the escort of honor. Joseph T. Wilson witnessed "the funeral pageant of the dead hero, the like of which was never before seen in that, nor, perhaps, in any other American city, in honor of a dead negro." [18]

Before the news of Port Hudson had reached New York and Washington, two other Louisiana Negro regiments had received their baptism of fire at a place called Milliken's Bend, and they had fought well. On June 7 a force of Confederates variously estimated at from 1,500 to 3,000 attacked the camp of the 9th and 11th Regiments of Louisiana Volunteers of African Descent. At the outset the attackers had the advantage and drove the Negroes back. These two regiments were very new. They had been organized by Lorenzo Thomas in his first month in the Mississippi Valley. Assistant Secretary of War Charles Dana reported that "the negro troops at first gave way, but hearing that those of their number who were captured were killed, they rallied with great fury and routed the enemy." General Elias S. Dennis, commanding the District of Northeastern Louisiana, disagreed with Dana in some details of his report but nevertheless praised the colored troops for their close-in fighting and bayonet work. Dana quoted Dennis as having said, "It is impossible for men to show greater gallantry than the negro troops in this fight." [19]

Whatever the details, Negro soldiers had once more proved their ability to stand up to Confederate infantry with the bayonet and clubbed rifle until forced by superior numbers to retire. A Confederate report gave the Negroes credit for showing more courage than their white comrades: the "charge was resisted by the negro portion of the enemy's force with considerable obstinacy, while the white or true Yankee portion ran liked whipped curs almost as soon as the charge was ordered."[20] In the opinion of Charles Dana, "the bravery of the blacks in the battle of Milliken's Bend completely revolutionized the sentiment of the army with regard to the employment of negro troops." Dana wrote that he had "heard prominent officers who formerly in private had sneered at the idea of negroes fighting express themselves after that in favor of it." Grant recorded in his *Memoirs* that Milliken's Bend was "the first important engagement of the war in which colored troops were under fire. These men were very raw, having all been enlisted since the beginning of the siege [of Port Hudson], but they behaved well." By all accounts, the action at Milliken's Bend was hard-fought throughout. General Dennis called it the hardest he had ever seen. Captain M. M. Miller of Company I, 9th Louisiana, who lost sixteen killed and fifteen wounded of his original thirty-three men, described it as "a horrible fight, the worst I was ever engaged in, not even excepting Shiloh. The enemy cried, 'No quarters,' but some of them were very glad to take it when made prisoners." [21] Milliken's Bend enjoyed a fame all its own—it remained a touchstone of Negro courage and determination.

Out on the border, where James Montgomery had learned to forage, the 1st Kansas Colored Volunteers filled up with recruits, labored on the defenses of Fort Scott, and, in early May, took up the line of march southward, along the military road to Fort Gibson. As Hooker's mauled Army of the Potomac pulled back from the smoldering underbrush about Chancellorsville, Colonel James Williams's regiment went into camp at Baxter Springs in southeast Kansas. There the 1st Kansas Colored began to build up their battle record—and extend their casualty list. On May 18 a foraging party of about fifty white and colored troops suffered a surprise attack from the notorious Missouri guerrilla fighter, Major T. R. Livingston. The Negro regiment lost twenty men killed in action, and several were taken prisoner. When one of these prisoners was murdered by

Livingston's men, Williams retaliated by ordering the shooting of one of his Confederate prisoners.[22]

Toward the end of June the regiment left Baxter Springs and moved on south as part of the mixed escort of a wagon train going to Fort Blunt in the Cherokee Nation. This march provided the Kansas Negroes with opportunity to show their fighting ability. At Cabin Creek the train was attacked by a large force of Texans and Indians, and after some preliminary skirmishing on July 1 the Confederates took up strong positions on the south bank of the creek. On the same day, in the East, Union and Confederate forces faced each other across the mile of ground between Cemetery and Seminary ridges south of a little Pennsylvania town called Gettysburg. The next morning, July 2, the Frontier troops attacked and in two hours of steady fighting drove the enemy with substantial losses from his position. This engagement was one of the first in the war in which white and colored troops fought side by side, and it is recorded that the white officers and men "allowed no prejudice on account of color to interfere in the discharge of their duty in the face of an enemy alike to both races." [23]

It was at Honey Springs, slightly over two weeks later, that the 1st Kansas Colored established its military reputation. On July 17, after an all-night march, Union troops under command of Major General James G. Blunt came upon a strong Confederate force under General Douglas Cooper. After a "sharp and bloody engagement of two hours' duration," Cooper's command fled from the field. During the fight the Negro regiment, which held the Union center, moved up under fire to within fifty paces of the Confederate line and there, still under fire, halted and exchanged volley fire for some twenty minutes until the Texans and their Indian allies broke and ran. The Kansas Negroes captured the colors of a Texas regiment, but the 2nd Regiment of Colonel Phillips's Indian Home Guards seems to have appropriated the trophies after the battle had ended.[24]

This was the most important battle in the regiment's entire history. It set to rest a great deal of Western criticism of the use of Negroes as soldiers. General Blunt wrote after Honey Springs: "I never saw such fighting done as was done by the negro regiment. They fought like veterans, with a coolness and valor that is unsurpassed. They preserved their line perfect throughout the whole engagement and, although in the hottest of the fight, they never once faltered. Too much praise cannot be awarded for their gallantry." James G. Blunt was convinced: "The question that negroes will fight is settled; besides they make better soldiers in every respect than any troops I have ever had under my command." But possibly the most expressive opinion, perhaps somewhat unsuitable for an official report, was uttered after Cabin Creek by an officer of the 3rd Wisconsin Cavalry, identified as an Irish Democrat: "I never believed in niggers before, but by Jasus, they are hell for fighting." [25]

* * *

"I know not, Mr. Commander, where, in all human history, to any given thousand men in arms there has been committed a work at once so proud, so precious, so full of hope and glory as the work committed to you." So spoke Governor John Andrew to Colonel Robert Gould Shaw of the 54th Massachusetts Infantry at the regiment's Readville camp. It was May 18, a fine cloudless day, and Readville was crowded with the friends and relatives of the men who made up the 54th. Fifteen hundred miles to the west, a detachment of the 1st Kansas Colored was fighting desperately near Sherwood, Missouri, to survive a surprise attack by guerrilla forces. At Readville, the 54th formed in line and moved into regimental square. The dignitaries gathered within the square of Negro companies, and the governor presented the colonel with four silken flags: a national emblem, the state color, a regimental banner of white silk bearing the figure of the Goddess of Liberty, and another bearing a white cross in a field of blue and the Christian motto, *In Hoc Signo Vinces*. More than a thousand spectators, white and colored, thronged the parade ground, among them Frederick Douglass, Wendell Phillips, Samuel May, Professor Louis Agassiz, and William Lloyd Garrison. On that same fair day the secretary of war telegraphed Andrew to have the new regiment report to General David Hunter at Hilton Head.[26]

Ten days later, as the battered regiments of the Corps d'Afrique recovered some of their dead and wounded during a

few hours of truce before Port Hudson, the 54th moved out of
Readville, entrained for Boston, and there formed to march
triumphantly through flag-hung streets. Past Wendell Phillips's
house the Negro regiment marched, reviewed by Garrison himself dramatically standing on a balcony, "his hand resting on a
bust of John Brown." At the State House the governor and his
staff joined the regiment, and they marched together to the
Common. There Colonel Shaw led his men in review past the
cream of Massachusetts society. After a rest, the regiment moved
on again from the Common to Battery Wharf, the band playing
John Brown's hymn as the blue ranks marched down State
Street "over ground moistened by the blood of Crispus Attucks,"
a Negro victim of the Boston Massacre, "and over which An-
thony Burns and Thomas Sims," fugitive slaves, "had been
carried back to bondage." At Battery Wharf the regiment em-
barked on the steamer *Demolay*; late in the afternoon the lines
were cast off and the 54th moved south into action and immor-
tality.[27]

"No regiment on its departure," the Boston *Evening Journal*
said that night, "has collected so many thousands as the Fifty-
fourth. The early morning trains from all directions were filled
to overflowing, extra cars were run, vast crowds lined the streets
where the regiment was to pass, and the Common was crowded
with an immense number of people, such as only the 4th of
July or some rare event causes to assemble."

General Hunter reported to Governor Andrew that the 54th
arrived safely at Hilton Head on June 3. He promised the
governor that his regiment would "soon be profitably and
honorably employed." [28] After a few days at Beaufort the
Massachusetts men were ordered south to St. Simon's Island,
Georgia, where Colonel Shaw reported to Colonel James Montgomery on June 9. The latter had been making forays along
the coast of Georgia and Florida, and he lost no time in intro-
ducing the young Massachusetts colonel to amphibious raiding,
Western style. On June 10, while the 54th was still pitching
tents and settling into its new camp, Montgomery came to the
wharf on a little steamer and, without even coming ashore,
called out to Shaw:

"How soon can you be ready to start on an expedition?"

"In half an hour," Shaw replied, correctly reading the challenge implicit in Montgomery's question. Eight companies were readied for the raid, two remaining behind as camp guard. After picking up the old *John Adams* with five of Montgomery's companies aboard, the expedition set out, running up the coast to Doboy Sound, where two gunboats joined the party on June 11. The objective was the pretty little town of Darien, Georgia, on the Altamaha River. The gunboats "searched it with their shells," and the troops landed unopposed. The town was deserted. Montgomery gave orders for foraging parties to go to work, and in a short time the men returned burdened with "every species and all sorts and quantities of furniture, stores, trinkets, etc." That was not all. "After the town was pretty thoroughly disembowelled," Shaw reported afterward, Montgomery turned to him with "a sweet smile" on his bearded face, and said in a quiet voice:

"I shall burn this town."

The Jayhawker had his reasons. "Southerners must be made to feel that this is a real war," he explained to Shaw, "and that they [are] to be swept away by the hand of God like the Jews of old."

Shaw interpreted neither the Bible nor the war so literally. He questioned the correctness and legality of such action under the laws of war. Montgomery had a simple answer to that argument.

"We are outlawed," he declared, "and therefore not bound by the rules of regular warfare." And by his express order, Darien was destroyed.

Shaw indignantly wrote Governor Andrew of the affair. He sent a second letter to Hunter's adjutant, Colonel Halpine, trying to find out if Montgomery was under orders to pillage and burn. The Darien expedition was the worst possible beginning for the career of the 54th. The regiment had been promised "honorable" work. The men had come south to fight rebels, not to burn the homes of defenseless civilians. The memory of Darien plagued Shaw for the rest of his short life.[29]

His friends in the North were as shocked and disappointed as the young colonel. Charles Lowell wrote his fiancée, Shaw's sister: "I don't wonder Rob feels badly about this burning and plundering,—it is too bad. Instead of improving the negro character and educating him for a civilized independence, we are re-developing all his savage instincts." Not content merely to sympathize, Lowell wrote William Whiting, solicitor of the War Department, arguing strongly against any repetition of the Darien outrage. "If burning and pillaging is to be the work of our black regiments," Lowell warned, "no first-rate officers will be found to accept promotion in them,—it is not war, it is piracy more outrageous than that of Semmes." Further, Lowell maintained, the results would be harmful in a strictly military sense. "Expeditions to help off negroes and interfere with corn crops," he wrote, "are too important a mode of injuring the rebels to be neglected: if made by well-disciplined blacks, kept always well in hand, they could be carried far into the interior and made of great service; but troops demoralized by pillage and by the fear of retaliation . . . the natural consequence . . . will not often venture out of sight of gunboats." [30]

Colonel Higginson himself could not have argued the point better. He had been at great pains to keep his men "well in hand" and to discourage all pillaging and needless destruction of property. James Montgomery was a primitive patriarch uninhibited by any effete Eastern notions of the rules of civilized warfare, and his Old Testament kind of warfare was completely at odds with the Harvard tradition of fair play. To New England romantics, war was a kind of game, played according to definite rules. Montgomery, with fanatic realism, made his own rules. Higginson, the romantic, had raised money to send Sharps rifles to Kansas in the fifties. Montgomery, the realist, had used them.

For whatever reasons, the 54th went on no more raids with Montgomery. The regiment settled into easy, pleasant camp life on St. Simon's, the island made famous by Fanny Kemble, whose husband, Pierce Butler, owned a large plantation there. The tropical idyll ended on June 24, when the regiment shipped north to St. Helena, across Port Royal Sound from Hilton Head. Hunter had been relieved, and Brigadier General Quincy A. Gillmore commanded the Department of the South. Preparations were under way for active operations against Charleston. As more and more regiments left St. Helena for Folly Island in

the first days of July, Shaw became fearful that his men would
have no chance to show what they could do. On July 6 he wrote
Brigadier General George C. Strong, who had briefly commanded at St. Helena, expressing his disappointment at being
"left behind," especially since he "had been given to understand that we were to have a share in the work of this department." Convinced that his regiment was "capable of better service than mere guerrilla warfare," Shaw told Strong that it
was "important that the colored soldiers should be associated
as much as possible with the white troops, in order that they
may have other witnesses besides their own officers to what they
are capable of doing." [31] Shaw's anxiety was eased on July 8
with the arrival of orders to have the regiment ready to move at
an hour's notice.

General Gillmore was launching an offensive to seize Morris
Island and with it control of the entrance to Charleston Harbor.
The 54th was part of Alfred H. Terry's division, which was
assigned to make a diversionary demonstration on James Island, west of Morris and due south of Charleston. With Folly
Island as a jumping-off place, the main offensive got under way
on July 10. The presence of Terry's 4,000 men on James Island
made General G. T. P. Beauregard, commanding at Charleston,
anxious for the safety of the city. He reduced his force on
Morris to concentrate more men and guns on James. Terry's
diversion had been more successful than Gillmore had hoped,
and all of Morris Island south of Fort Wagner fell into Union
hands. An assault on Wagner failed on July 11. The position
was too strongly entrenched and heavily gunned.

Beauregard continued to mistake Terry's demonstration for
the main Union attack, and in the gray dawn of July 16 he
pushed his forces forward to remove what he considered dangerous pressure toward Charleston. So it was that on James Island the men of the 54th had their first taste of battle, of
honorable soldier's work. Massachusetts pickets on the right of
the Union line caught the brunt of the Confederate attack. If
they had broken, the line must have been rolled up, the 10th
Connecticut on the left of the 54th cut to pieces, and the rest of
Terry's division caught off balance. Under fire for the first time,
the companies of the 54th gave ground slowly, fighting desper-

ately. Their action gave the Connecticut troops time to move
from their dangerous position and gave the rest of the division
time to form in line of battle and brace for the Confederate
assault. It never came. The success of the dawn attack had depended on surprise, and the stubborn resistance of the Negro
pickets on the Union right had spoiled what might otherwise
have been an effective attack. As the Confederates withdrew,
Shaw re-established his old picket line, and General Terry sent
him word that he was "exceedingly pleased" with the conduct
of the 54th. The men of the 10th Connecticut were appreciative,
too, and a newspaper correspondent wrote north a few days
later, "probably a thousand homes from Windham to Fairfield
have in letters been told the story how the dark-skinned heroes
fought the good fight and covered with their own brave hearts
the retreat of brothers, sons, and fathers of Connecticut." [32] For
this praise the 54th Massachusetts had paid with fourteen men
killed in action, eighteen wounded, and thirteen missing, probably captured.

His demonstration on James Island accomplished, Terry was
ordered to evacuate it that night. Through blinding rain and
with lightning flashes as their only illumination, the men of
the 54th marched painfully back, literally feeling their way
through the tangled marshland of James Island until, early in
the morning of July 17, they reached a beach across from Folly
Island. There, with no rations and little water, they waited
through the day for transportation. They were under orders to
report to General George Strong on Morris Island without delay. But there were delays. The transport *General Hunter* finally
came for them, but there was no wharf, and they spent the
entire night shuttling from beach to transport in a leaky long-
boat, thirty men at a time. It rained all night, and there were
still no rations. On the morning of July 18 the *General Hunter*
set them ashore on Folly Island, and they marched some six
miles across the island and up the beach to Light House Inlet.
There the tired and hungry men waited again for transport to
Morris Island. It was five o'clock in the afternoon before they
were carried over.

Colonel Shaw went forward at once to report to General
Strong. Fort Wagner had been under bombardment all day and

was to be stormed that evening. Strong, undoubtedly thinking of Shaw's letter and his wish for "better service than mere guerrilla warfare," offered the 54th the honor of leading the assault. Shaw might have refused. His men had gone two nights without rest and two days without rations; they had been on the march most of the day. But the young colonel moved fatally and fatalistically. In a sense he could not refuse this supreme chance to prove the valor of his regiment. For two days he had had a presentiment of death; he seems to have moved like a man caught by Destiny. He had to discharge the duty committed to him and his thousand men in arms by Governor Andrew, his state, and the cause of the Union. He sent Adjutant Wilkie James back to bring up the regiment. This was to be their ordeal by fire.[33]

The assault column, commanded by General Truman Seymour, was composed of three brigades, the first and heaviest under General Strong. Seymour afterwards defended the choice of the 54th to lead the first brigade, maintaining that the regiment "was in every respect as efficient as any other body of men, and as it was one of the strongest and best officered, there seemed to be no good reason why it should not be selected for the advance." [34] After the assault columns had been formed, Strong and Shaw spoke briefly to the men of the 54th. Tensely the regiment stood there in the deepening twilight. The western sky was still bright with sunset afterglow, but a heavy sea fog was gathering over the Atlantic. Indistinct in the darkness ahead, the scarred and battered earthworks of Fort Wagner crouched, waiting. Three-quarters of a mile of level sand lay between the 54th and the defiant flag on those earthworks. To the left lay a salt marsh. On the right the long waves rolled in and broke on the hard-packed sand. There was no danger that the men would lose their way this night.

The signal was given.

As cool and straight as on parade at Readville but a little pale, Colonel Shaw threw away his cigar, took position in the center of the head of the column, and called his men to attention. The dark ranks stiffened on the narrow sands. The flags were lifted up into the ocean breeze. The guns growled hungrily in the distance.

"Move in quick time until within a hundred yards of the fort," Shaw told his men, "then, double-quick and charge!"

"Forward!" he commanded, and the 54th Massachusetts Infantry moved up the beach to meet its destiny. Behind came the 6th Connecticut, the 48th New York, the 3rd New Hampshire, the 9th Maine, and the 76th Pennsylvania. Colonel Haldimand S. Putnam held his second brigade of four regiments in support.[35]

Wagner had been under artillery fire most of the day. Now came the Confederates' turn, and as the column moved forward to the attack, "the guns of Wagner, Gregg, Sumter, and also those on James and Sullivan's Islands opened upon it rapidly and simultaneously." The infantrymen in Wagner held their fire. As the 54th reached the narrowest part of the beach only two hundred yards from Wagner—the right flank men were up to their knees in sea water—"the firing from the navy and that of our own mortars and the gun batteries on the extreme left had to be suspended," General Gillmore reported, and "a compact and most destructive musketry fire was instantly delivered from the parapet by the garrison which, up to that moment, had remained safely ensconced in the bomb-proof shelters."[36]

Into the storm of fire the 54th moved, at the double now, past the southeastern salient of the fort, into the deep ditch before it, up and over the curtain, into Wagner itself. For a time the national and state flags waved on the parapet as the men of the regiment died under them. They fought with bayonet and clubbed rifle against artillery and rifle fire and grenades. Connecticut and New York troops clawed their way into the southeastern salient, but in the darkness their efforts were futile. Seymour sent in the supporting brigade, and although the salient was held for nearly three hours, the net result was an increased number of casualties, Colonel Putnam among them. It is more to be wondered that any men should have lived to gain the interior of Wagner than that the assault should have failed.

In military logic there had been some reason for the effort. The day-long artillery and naval bombardment of the fort had seemed effective. But the correct moment for assault probably came and passed in the afternoon. The hours between five and

seven gave the Confederates time to brace for the attack. There
was no possibility of surprise: preparations for the assault,
every movement of Union troops, were observed from Wagner
and other Confederate works in the vicinity. It was the kind of
operation that can be justified only by success. It had failed.
Colonel Shaw and three other officers of the 54th were killed;
eleven other officers and 135 men were wounded; nearly a
hundred were missing or taken prisoner. From a narrow military point of view the assault was without value. In a broader
view, it was a valuable sacrifice.

Hardly another operation of the war received so much
publicity or stirred so much comment. Out of it a legend was
born. As a result of it Robert Gould Shaw came as close to
canonization as a New England Puritan can. It took another
New Englander to put it into words. The lines of James Russell
Lowell on the Shaw Monument on Boston Common sum up the
meaning of the assault of the 54th on Fort Wagner:

> Right in the van on the red rampart's slippery swell
> With heart that beat a charge he fell
> > Foeward as fits a man.
> But the high soul burns on to light men's feet
> Where death for noble ends makes dying sweet.

Colonel Shaw and the 54th became symbols of the best that any
troops, white or Negro, could do. "That a gentleman should
leave a congenial place in the Second Massachusetts," James
Ford Rhodes wrote a generation after the war, "and part from
brothers in friendship as well as brothers in arms because his
antislavery sentiment impelled him to take a stand against the
prejudice in the army and in the country against negro soldiers;
that he brought his regiment to a fine degree of discipline; that
when the supreme moment came his blacks fought as other soldiers have always fought in desperate assaults—all this moved
the hearts and swayed the minds of the Northern people to an
appreciation of the colored soldier, to a vital recognition of the
end which Lincoln strove for and to the purpose of fighting out
the war until the negro should be free." [37] Colonel Charles Russell Lowell tried to comfort Shaw's sister with words that few

women and not all men can understand. "The manliness and
patriotism and high courage of such a soldier," he wrote, "never
die with him; they live in his comrades . . . That is the time to
die when one is happiest, or rather I mean that is the time when
we wish those we love to die: Rob was very happy too at the
head of his regiment where he died . . ." [38]

He was buried at the head of his regiment, too, whether by
malevolent design is beside the point. The North believed that
Shaw was buried by the Confederates, as a gesture of contempt, in a ditch "with his niggers." The news swept across the
North, and indignant reaction was swift and sure. Plans were
made to attempt to recover his body, but a letter from Colonel
Shaw's father to General Gillmore put a stop to the enterprise.
"We hold," Francis Shaw wrote Gillmore, "that a soldier's
most appropriate burial-place is on the field where he has
fallen." [39] Fort Wagner became not only the pinnacle of
Colonel Shaw's short life, but also his abiding place for
eternity.

After the assault on Fort Wagner on July 18 there was no
longer any doubt about using Negro troops to crush the rebellion. In July of 1863, the turning point of the war, there
were some thirty Negro regiments being organized or already
in the field. By the end of the year the number had doubled,
and the work was gathering momentum and even popularity.
Joseph Holt, judge advocate general and former secretary of
war, wrote Edwin M. Stanton in August of 1863: "The tena-
cious and brilliant valor displayed by troops of this race at
Port Hudson, Milliken's Bend, and Fort Wagner has sufficiently
demonstrated to the President and to the country the character
of the service of which they are capable. . . . In view of the
loyalty of this race," Holt continued, in words which could
have been borrowed from Frederick Douglass, "and of the ob-
stinate courage which they have shown themselves to possess,
they certainly constitute, at this crisis in our history, a most
powerful and reliable arm of the public defense." [40]

IX. *"The difficulty is not in stating the principle . . ."*

... the darkies fought ferociously, and, as usual, the cruelty of Fort Pillow is reacting on the rebels, for now they dread the darkies more than the white troops; for they know that if they will fight the rebels cannot expect quarter. Of course, our black troops are not subject to any of the rules of civilized warfare. If they murder prisoners, as I hear they did, it is to be lamented and stopped, but they can hardly be blamed.

—CHARLES FRANCIS ADAMS, JR., 1864

Brigadier General Johnson Hagood, Confederate commander at Secessionville on James Island, had a problem. "Thirteen prisoners Fifty-fourth Massachusetts, black," he reported on July 16, 1863, "What shall I do with them?" Headquarters promptly instructed Hagood to send them to Charleston "under a strong guard, without their uniform."

Although Captain W. H. Peronneau, prison commander at Castle Pinckney in the harbor, maintained that the Northern Negro prisoners were "willing to submit to the State laws" and "to go to Battery Bee and work," General G. T. Beauregard, commanding at Charleston, had qualms about treating captured Northern freedmen as slaves. Three days after the great assault on Fort Wagner, Beauregard wired Richmond for instructions. "What shall be done with the negro prisoners who say they are free?" he asked. Confederate Secretary of War James A. Seddon wasted few words in his reply: "The joint resolutions of the last Congress control the disposition of all negroes taken in arms. They are to be handed over to the authorities of the State

157

where captured to be dealt with according to the laws thereof."
On July 23, Beauregard confessed ignorance of such Congressional action, but six days later he wrote the governor of South
Carolina that he had been furnished a copy of the resolutions
and was "prepared to turn over" his Negro prisoners "to be
dealt with according to the laws of the State of South Carolina." [1]

*   *   *

Long before the Union had begun to use Negroes as soldiers,
it should have been clear what the Southern reaction to such a
policy would have to be. The great and abiding fear of the
South was of slave revolt. Nat Turner and Denmark Vesey were
names to blanch the Southern cheek and haunt the Southern
dream. For many Southerners it was psychologically impossible
to see a black man bearing arms as anything but an incipient
slave uprising complete with arson, murder, pillage, and rapine.
The South was haunted throughout the war by a deep and
horrible fear that the North would send—or was sending—agi-
tators among their slaves to incite them to insurrection. That
no such barbarous scheme was resorted to by the Union is a
credit to the humanity and good sense of the Lincoln administration, although it was urged enough by some radicals.
    In the South the absence of slave uprisings was considered
proof of the fundamental felicity of the Negro in slavery.
"History has no parallel to the faith kept by the negro in the
South during the war." Henry W. Grady of Atlanta wrote afterward. "Often five hundred negroes to a single white man, and
yet through these dusky throngs the women and children walked
in safety, and the unprotected homes rested in peace. Un-
marshalled, the black battalions moved patiently to the fields
in the morning to feed the armies their idleness would have
starved. . . . A thousand torches would have disbanded every
Southern army, but not one was lighted." [2] Whatever was written afterward of Negro loyalty to rebel masters, those masters
during the war were obsessed by the possibility of slave insurrection, and their reaction to any suggestion of arming the
slaves by the North was as extreme as that obsession was profound.
    Some indication of what might happen to Negroes taken in

arms against the Confederacy was provided in early 1862. A Confederate general, N. G. Evans, reporting the capture of a band of Negroes thought to have attacked rebel pickets, wrote: "I think, after a due investigation, should any negroes be convicted, they should be hanged as soon as possible at some public place as an example. The negroes have evidently been incited to insurrection by the enemy." Those Negroes not directly implicated in the business, Evans proposed to put in irons and work under guard. Another Confederate general in the early summer of 1862 moved to counter the escape of Louisiana slaves, thus preventing their carrying military information to Union forces in the Department of the Gulf and returning with inflammatory messages for other slaves. General Ruggles prohibited the passage of all Negroes, slave or free, toward Union lines without passes or written permission from masters and local authorities countersigned by the highest military authority in the parish. "Every negro, slave or free," he directed, "who shall violate this order will be shot in the attempt unless he or she shall immediately submit to arrest." [3]

When Union Generals Hunter and Phelps began to recruit Negroes as soldiers in the middle months of 1862, the indignation of the South knew no bounds. To the people and leaders of the Confederacy this was the beginning of a movement to turn the slaves of the entire South against their masters. This was inciting slaves to revolt on a monstrous scale. Confederate War Department General Orders, No. 60, August 21, 1862, stated the official attitude of the South toward these officers who dared to put arms into the hands of slaves. Since Hunter and Phelps, the order announced, had "organized and armed negro slaves for military service against their masters, citizens of this Confederacy," and since the Union government had "refused to answer an inquiry whether said conduct of its officers meets its sanction," all the Confederacy would do to repress such action was adopt "such measures of retaliation as shall serve to prevent their repetition." Accordingly, it was ordered that Hunter and Phelps were no longer to be treated as "public enemies" but as "outlaws." The order did not stop there: outlawry was to be extended automatically to "any other commissioned officer employed in drilling, organizing, or instructing slaves, with a view

to their armed service in this war." And the punishment? Once
captured, he was not to "be regarded as a prisoner of war, but
held in close confinement for execution as a felon at such time
and place as the President shall order." [4]

Apparently the South felt that the only means of repressing
the crime of raising Negro troops against it was the outlawing
of all persons guilty of that crime. And, to the people of the
South, arming slaves was a heinous crime. It seems to have
been impossible for the majority of the people of the South to
see it in any other light. Even the preliminary Emancipation
Proclamation of September 22, 1862, was taken as a signal for
the beginning of a war of extermination against Southern whites.
Confederate General Thomas H. Holmes, commanding the
Trans-Mississippi Department, wrote to Union General Samuel
R. Curtis, ". . . the proclamation . . . apparently contemplates,
and the act of your officers in putting arms in the hands of
slaves seems to provide for, even that extremity," war to the
knife, and the knife to the hilt. The South, General Holmes
maintained, could not be expected to "remain passive, quietly
acquiescing in a war of extermination . . . without waging a
similar war in return." [5]

Noting a report from its Washington correspondent that
seventeen Negroes had been hanged in Culpeper County, Virginia, "charged with organizing an insurrection against the
whites," the New York *Times* commented on October 21, 1862,
that "Southern slave insurrections, on any formidable scale, are
quite impossible at present. The rebels will suffer from the
Emancipation, and the negroes will get the benefit of it, just as
our army advances." This was small reassurance to the extreme
anxiety and sensitivity of the South.

As Benjamin F. Butler mustered his regiments of Louisiana
Native Guards in the Department of the Gulf and affronted the
people of the Confederacy in an infinite variety of ways,
Jefferson Davis extended the outlawry order of August 21 to
include the Massachusetts radical and all commissioned officers
in his command as "robbers and criminals deserving death."
Davis directed that "all negro slaves captured in arms be at
once delivered over to the executive authorities of the respective
States to which they belong . . ." To discourage the spread of

Negro soldier enterprises, Davis further directed the execution of similar orders "in all cases with respect to all commissioned officers of the United States when found serving in company with armed slaves in insurrection against the authorities of the different States of this Confederacy." [6]

The publication of Lincoln's Emancipation Proclamation in final form on January 1, 1863, aroused the ire of Jefferson Davis fully as much as had Butler's nefarious conduct in Louisiana. "We may well leave it to the instincts of that common humanity which a beneficent Creator has implanted in the breasts of our fellowmen of all countries," Davis told the Confederate Congress, "to pass judgment on a measure by which several millions of human beings of an inferior race, peaceful and contented laborers in their sphere, are doomed to extermination, while at the same time they are encouraged to a general assassination of their masters by the insidious recommendation 'to abstain from violence unless in necessary self-defense.' Our own detestation of those who have attempted the most execrable measure recorded in the history of guilty man is tempered by profound contempt for the impotent rage which it discloses." And what course of action would the Confederate president now follow? "I shall," he told his Congress, "unless in your wisdom you deem some other course more expedient[,] deliver to the several State authorities all commissioned officers of the United States that may hereafter be captured by our forces . . . that they may be dealt with in accordance with the laws of those States providing for the punishment of criminals engaged in exciting servile insurrection." Enlisted men, Davis suggested, ought to be treated "as unwilling instruments in the commission of these crimes"; he directed "their discharge and return to their homes on the proper and usual parole." [7]

The Confederate Congress was not disposed to be so lenient. On May 1, 1863, by joint resolution it authorized Jefferson Davis "to cause full and ample retaliation to be made" for any and all violations of the laws and usages of war "perpetrated" by the United States. As part of this retaliation, the resolution directed that commissioned officers commanding, arming, training, organizing, or preparing Negroes for military service should "if captured be put to death or be otherwise punished

at the discretion" of a military court. Negro soldiers were to
"be delivered to the authorities of the State or States in which
they shall be captured to be dealt with according to the present
or future law of such State or States." [8]

Since the sessions of the Confederate Congress were habitu-
ally conducted in secret, it was not clear to the general public
for the first four or five months of 1863 how that body would
deal with the Negro soldier problem. The *National Intelligencer*
of February 18 reported on the basis of "files of Richmond
papers" that the House of Representatives was considering a
bill to provide for the sale of all Negroes taken in arms against
the Confederacy, "the proceeds to be divided among the captors." Such a bill seems never to have passed. Meanwhile, as
debate continued, Confederate field forces required a policy.
In April, as Lorenzo Thomas began organizing Negro regiments in the Mississippi Valley, Confederate Secretary of War
Seddon informed General J. C. Pemberton at Vicksburg that
the War Department had "determined that negroes captured
will not be regarded as prisoners of war." [9]

What had been determined in Richmond was not at all clear
in the Deep South, as a letter signed "Mississippian" complained in the Atlanta *Southern Confederacy* of May 7. "We
would respectfully enquire of the Confederate Congress," this
communication began, "what, specifically, has been done, or
provided, to protect the country from the evils, and future
dangers, of permitting the Yankees to arm our slaves against
the white race of the South? We fear this matter has not sufficiently impressed itself upon the Government." And what solution did "Mississippian" offer? "Measures of retaliation, the
most sure and effective," he insisted, "should long since have
been adopted and put into execution to stop this inhuman, and
to us dangerous practice. If the war long continues," he argued
with considerable prescience, "a large negro force may be
organized against us. This will be a great gain to the enemy.
It will weaken and imperil the South." Not in a military sense
only. "The negroes thus corrupted," he warned, "will not only
be worthless as servants, if recovered, in all future time, but
they will be the most effective tools of the Northern incendiary.
This hellish scheme of the foe must be arrested!—We beg to

call the attention of the Government, of the press, and of the people to this most vital subject . . . What has been done?" The author of this letter may perhaps have been cheered when the news of the joint resolution of May 1 finally reached Mississippi.

That news stirred General David Hunter to write President Lincoln that he considered the action of the Confederate Congress "only a formal announcement of what has for some time been the practice in the Western departments where many colored teamsters, laborers and servants employed by the army when captured by the enemy have been sold into slavery." Hunter maintained that "the flag should protect and cover all its defenders irrespective of their color," and he suggested that, in retaliation, all rebel prisoners "and more particularly those of the aristocratic caste should be held as hostages to be hung man for man with any who may be executed by the rebels" under the joint resolution.[10] But Lincoln was not yet ready to go that far.

In December of 1862 the United States Senate had asked the secretary of war for information on "the sale into slavery of colored freemen captured or seized by rebel forces." Stanton replied that the War Department had received no such information, official or otherwise.[11] But in February, 1863, the capture and sale into slavery of two colored servants with the 42nd Massachusetts Infantry at Galveston, Texas, were reported to the War Department. The endorsement of General Ethan Allen Hitchcock, federal commissioner of prisoner exchanges, on this report reflects the dilemma of the Union government: ". . . it seems impossible," he wrote, "to do anything in this case except as a result of success in the war." [12]

Events during June and July of 1863 brought the Negro prisoner problem into sharp focus. Out of the fighting around Port Hudson and at Milliken's Bend came persistent reports of murdered Negro soldiers. General Grant attempted to investigate the alleged hanging of a number of colored soldiers, a white captain, and a white sergeant. To General Richard Taylor, commanding Confederate forces at Delhi, Louisiana, Grant wrote: "I feel no inclination to retaliate for the offense of irresponsible persons, but if it is the policy of any general invested with the command of any troops to show 'no quarter' or to punish with death prisoners taken in battle, I will accept the

issue. It may be you propose a different line of policy toward
black troops and officers commanding them, to that practiced
toward white troops." Grant was not the man to mince words or
deal in subtleties. "If so, I can assure you," he told Taylor,
"that these colored troops are regularly mustered into the service
of the United States. The Government and all officers serving
under the Government are bound to give the same protection to
these troops that they do to any other troops." Grant expressed
the rather naïve hope that there had been "some mistake in the
evidence" given him or that "the act of hanging had no official
sanction, and that the parties guilty of it" would be punished.[13]

Before Grant had received Taylor's reply, Assistant Secretary
of War Charles A. Dana suggested to Stanton that the captured
Negroes had been "handed over to the State authorities, by
whom they will probably be sold." Dana reported that "the idea
of arming negroes" had occasioned great dismay among the
Southerners, who supposed that such action by the Union "must
be followed by insurrection with all its horrors."[14] This report probably caused no great surprise on the part of Mr.
Secretary Stanton.

General Taylor's reply to Grant denied the alleged hangings
and promised a full investigation. The Confederate told Grant
that he had consistently ordered his forces "to treat all prisoners with every consideration," but he pointed out that "as
regards negroes captured in arms, the officers of the Confederate
States Army are required, by an order emanating from the
General Government, to turn over all such to the civil authorities, to be dealt with according to the laws of the State wherein
they were captured."[15] While this letter reflects only unques-
tioning obedience to orders from higher authority, Taylor's
official report written the day after the battle of Milliken's Bend
indicates his personal attitude. After reporting his own casualties and "a large number of negroes . . . killed and wounded,"
he wrote, "unfortunately, some fifty, with two of their white
officers were captured." Another Confederate general, J. G.
Walker, expressed a similar attitude in his report of Milliken's
Bend: "I consider it an unfortunate circumstance that any
negroes were captured . . ."[16] Little wonder that the War De-

partment should have recorded that two officers captured at Milliken's Bend on June 7, 1863, had been murdered.[17]

Grant's reply to Taylor's letter merely expressed the Union general's personal relief at the Confederate's denial of the alleged hangings. Grant did not feel authorized, he told Taylor on July 4, to say what the Union government might demand in regard to its Negro troops; this was a subject upon which he was "not aware of any action having been taken." [18] Perhaps the fall of Vicksburg on that Glorious Fourth had caused Grant to forget the rather definite position he had taken in his June 22 letter to Taylor. The demands of the closing phases of the Vicksburg campaign must have prevented Grant from familiarizing himself with "Instructions for the Government of the Armies of the United States in the Field," promulgated in War Department General Orders, No. 100, April 24, 1863, with the president's endorsement. Here the Union government had taken a definite position.

These Instructions were the fruit of the concentrated efforts of a special board of general officers and one civilian, Francis Lieber, professor of history and political science at Columbia College. Lieber, an authority on international law, performed the major work of writing the Instructions, the first modern code of laws for land warfare, although Henry W. Halleck and Ethan Allen Hitchcock aided appreciably by keeping the professor's Germanic prolixity in bounds. After the war, General Order 100 lived on to serve as the basis for most subsequent codes including the regulations, still in effect, drawn up by the Hague Conventions of 1899 and 1907.[19]

The Instructions dealt with the Negro soldier problem in at least three phases. Paragraph 43 maintained that slaves immediately became free men "under the protection of the military forces of the United States" and could not then be re-enslaved even by their former owners. Paragraph 57 specifically included the Negro soldier within the usages of war and endowed him with belligerent status in unmistakable language: "So soon as a man is armed by a sovereign government, and takes the soldier's oath of fidelity he is a belligerent; his killing, wounding, or other warlike acts are no individual crimes or offenses." Speaking directly to the Confederate policy, the order declared:

"No belligerent has a right to declare that enemies of a certain class, color, or condition, when properly organized as soldiers, will not be treated by him as public enemies." Paragraph 58 treated the problem of enslavement; it was clearly designed as an answer to the Negro prisoner problem. "The law of nations knows no distinction of color," the paragraph stated, "and if any enemy of the United States should enslave and sell any captured persons of their Army, it would be a case for the severest retaliation, if not redressed upon complaint." The question remained, what kind of retaliation? Paragraph 58 answered: "The United States cannot retaliate by enslavement; therefore death must be the retaliation for this crime against the law of nations." [20]

The trouble with these paragraphs was that they were part of a unilateral declaration. It would be hard to show how the Confederate States of America (so called) were bound to observe them. They did put the position of the United States clearly and strongly, but, as the *National Intelligencer* of June 24 pointed out, they did not preclude "the necessity of any formal warning by our Government, in case the ferocious threats of the rebels are carried out." The Washington paper asserted that few persons even knew of the existence of General Order 100, let alone the pertinent paragraphs, and that, "while the Government may have defined its position upon the record, it has not yet done so in any way likely to impress the rebels with a proper sense of what we suppose to be its stern determination in this matter. A formal announcement from the highest authority is still needed." Since even Major General U. S. Grant seems not to have known of the existence of the order, the *Intelligencer* argument is a strong one. But the highest authority, President Lincoln, was not yet ready to make the formal announcement that the newspaper maintained was essential.

Meanwhile the Northern press dug into the alleged murders of Negro prisoners at Milliken's Bend. The *Intelligencer* of June 24 maintained that Grant had issued an order "declaring that hereafter, should any soldier, whether white or black, wearing the uniform of a United States soldier, be captured and executed, retaliatory measures will be adopted by him [Grant], and rebel soldiers in his hands will be treated in like manner." A month earlier Colonel James Williams of the 1st Kansas Colored Volunteers had taken precisely that line of reason and action when the Missouri guerrilla leader Livingston had killed one of his Negro soldiers taken near Sherwood, Missouri.[21]

The Cincinnati *Daily Commercial* of July 28 broadened the scope of horror and spread the story wider by reprinting a dispatch from a New York *Times* correspondent at Port Hudson. "I am sorry to say," this New York newsman wrote, "that rumors are afloat, borne out, unfortunately, too strongly by facts, that our colored soldiers who have fallen into the hands of the rebels have not received the treatment recognized by civilized nations. In other words," he elucidated, *"we could find no negro prisoners in Port Hudson, and there were none in the hospital.* The simple question is—*Where are they?* I leave each one to draw his own conclusions, merely saying that this is a matter fully warranting the investigation of our authorities."

On June 27 the *National Intelligencer* reprinted an editorial that had originated in the Atlanta *Southern Confederacy.* Discussing the suggestion that Southern troops "should seek chiefly to capture, not slay, the negro soldiers in order to return them to slavery," the *Confederacy* pointed out with a gory sort of humor that "it is the fortune of war that much evil must be done that good may come, and it is impossible, in the heat of conflict, to discriminate. The death of an able-bodied negro is certainly a loss and an evil, but a soldier is not to stop to estimate a negro's value when he meets him in battle, for if he devotes himself to capturing negroes, Yankee bullets are all the time threatening him." The Atlanta paper expressed grave doubts of the value of Negroes "whether Northern freedmen or Southern slaves," once they had been seduced and polluted by contact with the Yankees; they then could "scarcely become useful and desirable servants among us." The *Confederacy* concluded that Southern soldiers should, "and they certainly will, kill all indiscriminately that they can, Yankees, Dutch, negroes, and what not, whom they meet in battle; but if any negroes are captured, it would be better than hanging to sell them to Cuba or Brazil."

As a practical way around "a disagreeable dilemma," Lieu-

tenant General Kirby Smith, commanding Confederate forces
in the Trans-Mississippi West, ordered that Negro troops and
their white officers be given no quarter. The Confederate War
Department declined to sustain him in that extreme position
and pointed out "that a different policy than that suggested . . .
is recommended." Oddly, there was no reference to the joint
resolution of May 1. "Considering the negroes as deluded vic-
tims," the assistant adjutant general, H. L. Clay, wrote, "they
should be received and treated with mercy and returned to their
owners." Clay had an interesting reason. "A few examples
might perhaps be made," he suggested warily, "but to refuse
them quarter would only make them, against their tendencies,
fight desperately." [22] How right Clay was time would disclose.

*   *   *

On the Atlantic seaboard the problem was complicated by
the presence of the 54th Massachusetts Infantry. When the Confederates showed their intention to treat Northern freedmen as
they did Southern slaves taken in arms, a storm of protest broke
about the president.[23] Frederick Douglass refused to continue
his recruiting efforts, and on August 1 he wrote a long letter
of explanation to George L. Stearns. Confessing that his faith
in Lincoln was "nearly gone," Douglass asked, "How many
54ths must be cut to pieces, its mutilated prisoners killed, and
its living sold into slavery, to be tortured to death by inches,
before Mr. Lincoln shall say, 'Hold, enough!' " [24]
Although Douglass had not learned of it before writing to
Stearns, Lincoln had said "Hold, enough!" on July 30.
Denouncing the enslavement of "any captured person on
account of his color" as a "relapse into barbarism and a crime
against the civilization of the age," Lincoln proclaimed that his
government would "give the same protection to all its soldiers"
and would punish offenses by retaliation as set forth in General
Order 100. He ordered that "for every soldier of the United
States killed in violation of the laws of war a rebel soldier shall
be executed, and for every one enslaved by the enemy or sold
into slavery a rebel soldier shall be placed at hard labor on the
public works, and continued at such labor until the other shall
be released and receive the treatment due to a prisoner of

war."[25] The prisoners from the 54th Massachusetts were not enslaved, although they were held in close confinement in the Charleston jail and in the Florence stockade until the end of the war.

Lincoln's action in ordering retaliation was generally hailed with approval. Typical of favorable Union newspaper comment was a Memphis *Bulletin* editorial reprinted in the Nashville *Sunday Press* of August 9. The *Bulletin* hailed the presidential proclamation and denounced the "insufferable arrogance" of the Confederacy in presuming "to consider the black soldiers as without the pale of civilized warfare." Not content to leave the matter there, the Memphis editor suggested that "In garrisoning the South, after the main rebel armies are scattered, the colored troops will be one of our main sources of reliance, and we look to see their regiments brought to the most perfect state of efficiency to accomplish this immense and otherwise impossible task."

The Nashville *Press* agreed with its Memphis neighbor that the national government was obliged to extend its protection to all its soldiers. "The national uniform on the person, and the 'Star Spangled Banner' overhead," it maintained, "must obliterate all colors." But the Nashville editor thought the suggestion of colored occupation troops was going it a little strong. "We cannot suppose that the Bulletin man has consulted the Administration, or anybody else, upon this subject," the *Press* editor wrote: "Negro garrisons to keep the peace in the subjugated South! Whew!" He would live and learn.

Frederick Douglass went back to his recruiting activities and had an interview with President Lincoln to discuss the whole problem of fair treatment for Negro troops. Colonel Charles Lowell wrote Mrs. Robert Shaw that he considered the president's order "one immediate good out of Rob's death and out of the splendid conduct of this regiment. Negroes at Port Hudson had been treated just as barbarously," he maintained, "but it passed unnoticed by the Administration,—they could not pass this over: I wish the President had said a rebel soldier shall die for every negro soldier sold into slavery. He ought to have said so."[26] It is reasonable to conclude that Colonel Lowell had been reading General Order 100.

The official positions of the North and South on the treatment of captured Negro soldiers created a gigantic deadlock. The Confederacy would not retreat from the extreme position of its Congressional resolution of May 1. The North was committed to Lincoln's policy of retaliation for whatever acts the South should commit in line with that resolution. The immediate result was a breakdown in the cartel for the exchange of prisoners. This breakdown had already begun with the Union discovery that the thousands of Confederate prisoners taken at the fall of Vicksburg and Port Hudson, released on parole to await exchange, had disregarded their parole. The Louisville (Ky.) *Daily Journal* of September 6, 1863, reported that "The government will take a firm and honorable position on this question: no exchange other than soldier for soldier, of any description, will be consented to." The *National Intelligencer* had two days earlier reprinted an editorial from the Richmond *Enquirer* which set forth Southern opinion of what the Louisville paper called "a firm and honorable position." "The Federal Government," exclaimed the *Enquirer*, "has planted itself insolently upon the demand that our runaway negroes, when taken in arms against their masters, shall be treated as prisoners of war, and shall be exchanged against white men. Confederates have borne and forborne much to mitigate the atrocities of war; but this is a thing which the temper of the country cannot endure."

The Cincinnati *Commercial* reported on September 21 that "A general exchange of prisoners will soon commence, except colored soldiers and their officers, and a corresponding number of rebels in our possession." The *Commercial* was whistling in the dark. Somewhere in that dark, Negro soldiers captured by the Confederacy got lost.

*   *   *

In December of 1863 General Benjamin F. Butler—still posted as an outlaw by the Richmond government!—was named a special agent of prisoner exchange under Ethan Allen Hitchcock.[27] Butler had convinced himself at least, and perhaps also Stanton, that the Union could exchange for all its prisoners in Southern prisons and still have enough rebel prisoners to ensure just treatment to its Negro soldiers and their officers. Statistically, Butler's position looked strong: the Union held some 26,000 captives, the Confederacy only half that number. According to Butler's calculations, exchange could be resumed on a man-for-man basis and still leave 13,000 Confederate hostages for the security of Union Negro troops.[28] After three months of difficulties with the Confederates, his own secretary of war, and General Hitchcock, Butler finally met with Judge Robert Ould, the Confederate commissioner for prisoner exchange. The two men came close to an acceptable modus operandi. Ould went so far as to agree that all free Negroes could be treated as prisoners of war. But there remained the stumbling block of the recaptured slaves.[29]

It seems clear that, for practical military reasons—the favorable Union balance of prisoners—Grant was unwilling to resume the exchange of prisoners in the spring of 1864. Had the Confederacy yielded on the recaptured slaves, there remained the question of the Vicksburg paroles. Had that been settled, there was still the Union ace in the hole—Butler's outlawry. Discussions never reached the point at which that card could have been played. With active campaigning resumed in the middle months of 1864, discussions broke down completely.[30]

The Southern position was that "slaves were property, and that property recaptured from an enemy in war reverts to its owner, if he can be found, or may be disposed of by its captor in any way he sees proper." [31] Just such an attitude toward Negro soldiers was reflected in the report of Colonel W. Pinckney Shingler to Brigadier General Hunton in March, 1864. Shingler wrote that one of his lieutenants had brought in four Negro soldiers taken near Williamsburg, Virginia. He wanted to know whether "to sell them and give the proceeds to the command capturing them." The colonel went on to tell the general that he had "directed Lieutenant Hume not to report any more such captures..." [32]

The South would have been happy if the entire Negro prisoner problem had never come up in the first place. Howell Cobb, who was having a difficult time finding food for Union prisoners in Georgia, asked the Confederate War Department to try to arrange an exchange for all except recaptured slaves. Secretary of War Seddon wrote him: "I doubt... whether the exchange

of negroes at all for our own soldiers would be tolerated [by
Southerners]. As to the white officers serving with negro troops,
we ought never to be inconvenienced with such prisoners." [33]

The Union could assent to the Southern demands only by a
palpable breach of faith with the Negro soldier, and for over a
year the deadlock dragged along until military facts forced a
waiving of the fundamental argument without agreement ever
having been reached. The excess of prisoners in Union hands
became so great as to be burdensome, and in the last few months
of the war exchange was resumed. In his report of March 1,
1865, Secretary of War Stanton was able to state: "The general
exchange of prisoners effected under the instructions of this
department by Lieutenant General Grant is in the course of dili-
gent execution, and it is hoped that all of our prisoners who are
in the hands of the rebels will soon be returned." [34] The war was
over before Negro prisoners were returned.

The intransigence of the Confederacy worked only to her disadvantage. Instead of discouraging Negroes from entering the
Union Army and deterring officers from accepting commissions
in colored regiments, the policy of the South had the effect of
turning the movement into a crusade and of making the Negro
soldier a stubborn fighter who would seldom surrender. A
letter in the Chicago *Tribune* of March 26, 1864, underscored
this. The writer commented that the 60,000 Negroes then in
the army had done well to enlist. They had known that they
would not be treated as prisoners of war, but they had enlisted
anyway. "Now bear in mind," the letter concluded, "that up to
this writing no colored prisoners taken with arms in their
hands have been exchanged by the rebel authorities, this notwithstanding the efforts of the Government to secure such a
result."

How many Negro soldiers and their officers lost their lives
because of the Confederate policy it is impossible to state. The
Official Army Register lists four officers as having been
"murdered" after their capture by rebel forces: Captain Heath
and Lieutenant Conn at Milliken's Bend; Captain Charles G.
Penfield of the 44th U.S. Colored Troops, "captured by Captain
Harbey of Forrest's command, and murdered December 22,
1864"; and Second Lieutenant John A. Moulton, 67th U.S.

Colored Troops, "captured by the enemy and executed at Mount Pleasant Landing, near Port Hudson, La., May 15, 1864." [35] There is no comparable list for the Negro enlisted men. There are only the figures after the word "missing." There is no sure way of finding out who they were or how they died.

*   *   *

In his report of the capture of Fort Pillow, Tennessee, on April 12, 1864, Nathan Bedford Forrest wrote that "the loss of the enemy will never be known from the fact that large numbers ran into the river and were shot and drowned." The Union garrison, Forrest reported, was "composed of about 500 negroes and 200 white soldiers (Tennessee Tories)." He estimated the Union losses as "upward of 500 killed." The Mississippi, he wrote with evident satisfaction, "was dyed with the blood of the slaughtered for 200 yards," and he expressed the hope "that these facts will demonstrate to the Northern people that negro soldiers cannot cope with Southerners." [36] Forrest's estimates, set down three days after the assault on Pillow, were inflated. The fort had been manned by some 577 officers and men: 295 members of the first battalion of the 13th Tennessee Cavalry, and 262 members of the first battalion, 6th U.S. Colored Heavy Artillery, and of a section of Battery D, 2nd U.S. Colored Light Artillery. [37] The report of the investigation carried out by Benjamin F. Wade and D. W. Gooch for the Committee on the Conduct of the War under authority of the joint resolution of April 21, 1864, stated flatly that 300 Union men had been "murdered in cold blood after the post was in possession of the rebels, and our men had thrown down their arms and ceased to offer resistance." [38]

It has been denied that there was an actual massacre at Fort Pillow, and the report of the Committee on the Conduct of the War has been shown to be heavily interlarded with errors of fact, hearsay set down as evidence, differences of opinion in testimony on similar points of fact, and exaggerations in style and content obviously designed more to stir human emotions than to convince human reason. It has been charged that the fort and its garrison did not surrender until after the fighting was over, that the garrison was drunk and neglected to lower the flag or throw down their arms in token of surrender, that the burial details were composed of Union troops under Union officers, a fact which clears Forrest's men of the charge that they buried Negro wounded alive.[39] While the extent of the massacre was exaggerated by Wade and Gooch, and while Union casualties may have amounted to less than two hundred killed, wounded, and missing,[40] still the testimony of some of the officers and men who survived shows that there was "indiscriminate slaughter" of Union troops, particularly of Negroes, after the fort had fallen.

As soon as the news of Pillow reached Washington, Stanton wired General William T. Sherman at Nashville to "direct a competent officer to investigate and report . . . the facts in relation to the alleged butchery of our troops at Fort Pillow." Sherman immediately wired Brigadier General Mason Brayman, commanding at Cairo, Illinois, and that officer began his investigation on April 16, five days before any Congressional action had been initiated. The next day General Brayman, an Illinois railroad lawyer before the war, wrote Sherman that "proof of horrid barbarities in ways without example" was already being accumulated.[41]

On April 23, Sherman reported to Stanton that the military investigation was proceeding. Sherman's observations on the Fort Pillow affair are significant, considering that he was no "ultra" and of all the major Union commanders probably the least favorable to Negro troops. "I know well the animus of the Southern soldiery," he told Stanton, "and the truth is they cannot be restrained. The effect will be of course to make the negroes desperate, and when in turn they commit horrid acts of retaliation we will be relieved of the responsibility. Thus far negroes have been comparatively well behaved, and have not committed the horrid excesses and barbarities which the Southern papers so much dreaded." Sherman suggested that, rather than set "a fixed rule" for the guidance of its forces in the field, the Union "let soldiers affected make their rules" as the war progressed. "The Southern army," he observed grimly, "which is the Southern people, cares no more for our clamor than the idle wind, but they will heed the slaughter that will follow as the natural consequence of their own inhuman acts." [42]

On April 28, General Brayman sent his first report to Stanton: it included some twenty-four enclosures, the testimony of twenty-six military, naval, and civilian personnel. Of these, twenty-two had been in Fort Pillow during the assault and capture. Five men, all members of the 13th Tennessee Cavalry, testified that they had heard, during the final assault, such cries as "kill the last God damn one of them," and "Kill them, God damn them; it is General Forrest's orders." [43] On May 4, General Brayman sent Stanton the testimony of nine more participants in the fight, all members of the 6th U.S. Colored Heavy Artillery—seven Negroes and two white first sergeants.[44] The pictures painted by the statements of the thirty-five witnesses interviewed by Brayman's investigating officers are horrible, red with charges that Forrest's men repeatedly shot unarmed men who had their hands raised in token of surrender or were on their knees in attitudes of supplication. Even if the charges of murdering some wounded Negroes and burning or burying others alive are set aside, there is still plentiful evidence of "indiscriminate slaughter." Whatever is said in mitigation, Fort Pillow remains "the one serious blot" on Forrest's record as an otherwise superb cavalry commander.[45]

It has been asserted again and again that Forrest did not order a massacre. He did not need to. He had sought to terrify the Fort Pillow garrison by a threat of no quarter, as he had done at Union City and at Paducah in the days just before he turned on Pillow. If his men did enter the fort shouting "Give them no quarter; kill them; kill them; it is General Forrest's orders," he should not have been surprised. Most damaging of all, however, is his own report written three days after the capture of the fort. There is no suggestion that his men were "out of control." There is, on the contrary, a kind of gory exultation in the river "dyed with the blood of the slaughtered," presumably including those who were shot in the river, to which they had fled before the fury of the attack.[46]

Early in May, President Lincoln and his cabinet took up the Fort Pillow case. Recommendations for action varied. The cautious Seward suggested that Confederate prisoners be confined as hostages until their government should either explain or disavow the massacre and give pledges against repetition.

Stanton advised that rebel officers be held as hostages, that
Forrest and all members of his command involved in the affair
be excluded from amnesty and exchange, and that their de-
livery for punishment be demanded of the Richmond government, in default of which Lincoln should take action against
the officer hostages. Attorney General Bates condemned retaliation as "avowedly revenge . . . wholly unjustifiable, in law and
conscience, unless adopted for the sole purpose of punishing
past crime and of giving salutary and blood-saving warning
against its repetition." Secretary of the Interior Usher also condemned retaliation on innocent men, but urged that prisoners
taken from Forrest's command be "set apart for execution."
But, Usher cautioned, the Union was "on the eve of an impending battle," and he therefore advised against "any extreme
action in the premises" until the outcome of Grant's offensive in
the Wilderness should become clear. This view seems to have
impressed the cabinet; at any rate, discussion of Fort Pillow
apparently never concerned it again.[47] Negro soldiers, even as
Sherman had suggested in his first report to Stanton, were left
to their own devices.

Those devices included, among the Negro troops at Memphis
at least, the taking of an oath "on their knees" to avenge Fort
Pillow and to show Confederate troops no quarter. Made desperate, as Sherman had predicted, Negro troops fought with
no idea of surrendering. Reports of the Union disaster at Brice's
Cross Roads in June show that colored troops engaged there
kept firing until their ammunition was expended, then fought
with bayonet and clubbed musket, and finally either picked up
new weapons and ammunition from the road along which the
rest of the Union forces were fleeing, or died.[48]

There were also reports of the shooting of captured and
wounded Negro soldiers in the battle of Poison Spring, in
Arkansas, six days after Fort Pillow had fallen. There the 1st
Kansas Colored suffered its heaviest losses of the war: 117 dead
and 65 wounded. A large foraging party of white and colored
troops out of Camden was cut off and cut up by Confederates
of Cabell, Maxey, and Marmaduke's commands.[49] A clue to the
attitude of some trans-Mississippi Southerners toward Negro
soldiers is provided by John N. Edwards, a member of Jo

Shelby's division, in his description of another engagement at Mark's Mill, Arkansas, on April 25. "The battlefield," Edwards recalled, "was sickening to behold. No orders, threats, or commands could restrain the men from vengeance on the negroes, and they were piled in great heaps about the wagons, in the tangled brushwood, and upon the muddy and trampled road." [50]

In the case of Poison Spring, the effect was immediate and measurable. The 2nd Kansas Colored, sister regiment to the hard-hit 1st, reacted to the massacre news by resolving to take no Confederate prisoners in the future. They had only to wait a fortnight for a chance to test their resolution. At Jenkins Ferry, on the Sabine River in Arkansas, the 2nd Kansas Colored fought its most distinguished action of the war on April 30. Relieving the 50th Indiana, which had expended most of its ammunition in a hotly contested rearguard action, the Kansas Negro regiment fought for almost two hours without gaining any advantage. Colonel Samuel J. Crawford, finding himself under fire from a rebel battery of three guns, asked for and was given permission to charge. The battery was quickly overrun by his colored troops shouting "Remember Poison Spring!" Confederate casualties were high—about 150 killed or mortally wounded; the 2nd Kansas Colored lost only 15 men killed, and 55 others were wounded. One prisoner was taken, by mistake, but Crawford had him returned to his own lines with a warning to his comrades. [51]

The results were roughly the same everywhere: Negro soldiers only fought more stubbornly and ferociously, and as they assaulted Confederate lines their battle cry became, east of the Mississippi, "Remember Fort Pillow!" and in the West, "Remember Poison Spring!" Of course the Confederate government did not order its troops to give no quarter to Negro soldiers. But, as one distinguished Southern historian has explained it, "if the wishes of the private soldiers who fought them had prevailed, no quarter would have been granted." Many, if not most, Confederates probably agreed with Jerome Yates of Mississippi, who wrote his mother: "I hope I may never see a Negro Soldier," he said, "or I cannot be...a Christian Soldier." [52]

That the South did not indiscriminately murder all Negro

soldiers taken prisoner is patent. Lieutenant O. O. Poppleton
of the 111th U.S. Colored Troops informed Benjamin F. Butler
in January, 1865, that he had a copy of the Mobile *Advertiser
and Register* containing a notice printed by command of Major
General D. H. Maury. It listed by name some 575 colored soldiers of the 106th, 110th, and 111th U.S. Colored Troops who
were then at work on the defenses of Mobile. These men had
been captured in September, 1864, by forces under Forrest's
command at Athens and Sulphur Branch Trestle, Alabama. The
notice in the Mobile paper included not only the names of the
prisoners but those of their alleged owners, who were directed to
come in to Maury's headquarters "to receive the pay due them."
In a second letter to Butler, Poppleton enclosed a later issue of
the same newspaper containing a similar list of 569 colored
soldiers of the same three regiments. Lieutenant William T.
Lewis of the 110th U.S. Colored Troops had a paper of even
later date, Poppleton reported, "containing the names of nearly
300 more soldiers of the same command, also at work on the
defenses of Mobile." This publication of the names of colored
prisoners, recaptured slaves, was a regular Confederate practice
required by action of the Richmond Congress, approved October 13, 1862, and published as General Orders, No. 25,
March 6, 1863, by the Confederate adjutant and inspector
general.[53]

When he learned that the Confederates were working captured Negro soldiers under fire in the trenches near Fort Gilmer,
on the James River in Virginia, General Butler "determined to
try the virtue of retaliation for wrong." With Grant's permission, he ordered an equal number of Confederate prisoners put
to work in his own forward trenches. One week later the experiment was crowned with success: the Negro prisoners were withdrawn from the hazardous and illegal activity. Butler then
rescinded his order and restored his Confederate prisoners to
safety.[54]

Retaliation—"the sternest feature of war," Francis Lieber
called it in General Order 100—worked in limited circumstances only. As an effective countermove to Confederate
policy and practice it was, with some few exceptions, a complete failure. Perhaps Ethan Allen Hitchcock had said the last

word on the Negro prisoner problem in August, 1863, when Gideon Welles notified the War Department that three Negro seamen had been captured and were being closely confined in Charleston.

"There have been other cases like this," Hitchcock wrote sadly, "in which [I have] been compelled to report [my] opinion that they can only be effectually reached by a successful prosecution of the war." After all, Hitchcock admitted, "the rebellion exists on a question connected with the right or power of the South to hold the colored race in slavery; and the South will only yield this right under military compulsion. The facts complained of ... appeal in the strongest manner to the loyal people of the United States to prosecute this war with all the energy that God has given them." [55]

*   *   *

Southern policy and practice toward Negro soldiers did not have their desired effect. They may have discouraged the faint-hearted from enlisting in the ranks of colored regiments and they may have dissuaded white officers whose hearts were not in the work from seeking commissions in those regiments. But the officers and men who made up those regiments and saw combat against the Confederates fought with a courage and determination fired by the knowledge that failure might lead to death or slavery. The Union policy of retaliation also was a failure simply because its application was practically impossible. Lincoln himself admitted this in his address to the Sanitary Fair in Baltimore on April 18, 1864, immediately after he had heard the first reports from Fort Pillow. "Having determined to use the Negro as a soldier," he said, "there is no way but to give him all the protection given to any other soldier. The difficulty is not in stating the principle, but in practically applying it." [56]

How many Negroes, North and South, realized that the Confederates did not consider them soldiers protected by the uniform they wore, it is impossible to tell. It is probable that Negroes were not soldiers very long before they became aware of their unenviable situation either through actual experience or through the usual channels of service rumor. Whether many of them realized at length that there was little the Lincoln administration could do to protect them in the event of their capture, it is also impossible to discover. Whatever their awareness of their peculiar military standing, Negroes continued to enlist in thousands and tens of thousands till the end of the war finally came. They fought to win freedom for themselves and for their fellow men, but to the average Negro soldier in the ranks the issue must have been far less freedom than mere survival. Negro soldiers and their officers were bound together in a heightened esprit de corps and in a determination to die before surrendering that is rare in military annals. The policy of the Confederacy contributed in large measure to that spirit and that determination.

X. *"There seems to be inequality and injustice . . ."*

> It is of little consequence to a dying man whether any one else is to die by retaliation, but it is of momentous consequence whether his wife and family are to be cheated of half his scanty earnings by the nation for which he dies. The Rebels may be induced to concede the negro the rights of war, when we grant him the ordinary rights of peace, namely, to be paid the price agreed upon.
>
> —THOMAS WENTWORTH HIGGINSON, 1864

Gerrit Smith was disappointed.

The York State abolitionist and philanthropist, true to the radicalism that had led him to support John Brown, had early advocated arming the Negro. A practical radical, he offered $3,000 to George Stearns in March of 1863 to help equip the 54th Massachusetts. But he quickly became disillusioned with Negro troops, not in their military performance but in their lack of what he considered the proper crusading spirit. He told William Lloyd Garrison of his disappointment on April 26, 1863: "they stand out for Pay, Bounty, &c.— Only one among them all seems capable of being moved by the purpose of redeeming his race—and he is a fugitive slave." [1] Gerrit Smith knew and admired Frederick Douglass, but if he thought Douglass advocated that his race fight without the pay and allowances of white soldiers he was mistaken.

James Montgomery, a member of the same radical school as Brown and Stearns and Smith, never made the same mistake. But then Montgomery was closer to the subject. He was at Beau-

fort, South Carolina, while Gerrit Smith was comfortably isolated from the realities of war at Peterboro in the peaceful hills
of central New York.

From Beaufort, Colonel Montgomery wrote to Mrs. Stearns
on April 25, the day before Smith penned his lament to Garrison. However hardheaded and practical Smith may have been
as a businessman, Montgomery was the more hardheaded and
practical in the business of understanding men. "Finding it
somewhat difficult to induce the negroes to enlist," the Jayhawker told Mrs. Stearns, "we resorted to the draft." But there
was no denunciation of the Negroes for their reluctance to
volunteer. "The negroes re-indicate their claim to humanity,"
Montgomery commented, "by shirking the draft in every possible way; acting exactly like *white men* under similar circumstances: Hence, I conclude, they are undoubtedly *human*. The
only difference that I notice is, the negro, after being drafted,
does not *desert*; but, once dressed in the uniform of a soldier,
with arms in his hands, he feels himself a man; and acts like
one." [2]

Unlike Gerrit Smith, Montgomery realized that the Negro
was adjusting to the mores of the white civilization that domi-
nated him. It was not so much that the Negro was "incapable of
being moved by the purpose of redeeming his race" as that he
was joining a contest between two groups of the dominant white
race. Despite the fact that his destiny was to be decided by that
contest, and that he was one of the pawns on the board, the
Negro perversely (as Smith saw it) supposed that his participation would be on the same terms as those already established
for the white contestants. Gerrit Smith expected the Negro to
have a higher standard of service and sacrifice than his white
contemporaries. James Montgomery was satisfied to discover
that the Negro standard was roughly the same as that of the
white civilization that had caught him.

James Williams was disappointed, too.

The colonel of the 1st Kansas Colored Volunteers was disappointed and disillusioned, not so much by the performance
of his Negro soldiers as by the performance of the federal
government in what he considered *its* part of the contract and,
more particularly, of the Paymaster General's Department. In

the spring of 1863 the men of the 1st Kansas Colored were hard at work building up the fortifications of Fort Scott, the great hub of Union defense and offense in the upper trans-Mississippi West. But morale in the regiment was low and, contrary to Montgomery's experience in South Carolina, desertions plagued it. Williams was a practical man after the manner of Montgomery. Instead of condemning his men out of hand, he assessed the situation and found a reasonable basis for their dissatisfaction and disaffection. He told Colonel C. W. Blair, post commander at Fort Scott, of what he considered a justifiable cause for the regiment's poor spirit: "my men have never received one cent of bounty or of pay although they have now been in the Service nearly 10 months."And Williams took his case to a higher court: he wrote General James G. Blunt, commanding the Army of the Frontier, that his troops felt "sorely troubled and grieved about the pay" as well they might, since the white troops about them were paid with a fair degree of regularity. Williams reported "a restlessness and insubordination" among his men which he considered "the natural results of these long trials and sufferings." To counter what he called a "mutinous" spirit, Williams took his men off work on the fortifications and moved his regiment out of Fort Scott proper in order to give his "whole time to the discipline of the Regiment." [3] Marching orders in early May probably helped Williams save his regiment from disintegration, and in July the organization enjoyed its first payday. By that time some of the men of the regiment had been in uniform a little more than a year. Over a score had died without even the small comfort of a single payday.

Robert Gould Shaw was probably the most disappointed of all.

His regiment had enlisted "on the express understanding that they were to be on precisely the same footing as all other Massachusetts troops." And yet, when the 54th was mustered for pay on June 30, 1863, the paymaster on St. Helena Island was "inclined to class [it] with the contraband regiments, and pay the men only $10." That was $3 less than white privates received from the same paymaster. Shaw's indignation knew no bounds. If the paymaster did not change his mind, the young colonel wrote Governor Andrew, "I shall refuse to have

the regiment paid until I hear from you on the subject." In
Shaw's opinion, his troops should either be "mustered out of
the service or receive the full pay which was promised them." [4]
   Before Governor Andrew could reply to the Shaw complaint,
the regiment had gone into action on James and Morris islands.

*   *   *

   Throughout the Civil War, American Negroes serving in the
Union Army labored under a double disadvantage: the South
refused to recognize them as soldiers and the North refused to
grant them financial status equal to that enjoyed by white
troops. Slowly and with marked reluctance the Union came to
recognize this inequity in pay and allowances. It took two years
of sustained effort by prominent officers of Negro troops, with
help from governors, newspaper editors, and senators, to
achieve partial victory in the Army Appropriation Bill of 1864.
Complete success did not crown their efforts until after the war
had been won.
   Negro soldiers and their spokesmen argued for equality in
financial treatment on two basic assumptions. The first of these
was that, since they served with white soldiers, ate the same
food, wore the same uniform, worked, fought, and died just as
the whites did, they were entitled to the same pay. And since
the Negro soldier did his soldier's job at substantially greater
personal risk than that of his white contemporaries in the Union
Army, it seemed only minimum justice to him to be paid what
the rest of the Union Army drew. The second basic assumption
was that Secretary of War Stanton had promised Negro soldiers
standard army pay in his original authorization to General
Rufus Saxton, the first definite War Department authorization
for the enrollment of Negroes as soldiers.
   This second assumption, which had less weight than the first,
was based on the third paragraph of Stanton's orders of August
25, 1862, in which he directed Saxton to raise five thousand
"volunteers of African descent." These volunteers and their
officers, the orders read, were "to be entitled to and receive the
same pay and rations as are allowed by law to volunteers in
the service." [5] Volunteers in the service at the time were entitled to $13 per month, $3 of which constituted a clothing

allowance, and one ration per day. Unfortunately, Secretary Stanton had shaky legal authority for this "promise" to General Saxton. The only law applicable to the Negro regiments that Saxton was empowered to raise was the Militia Act of July 17, 1862, Section 15 of which provided that colored recruits would be paid "ten dollars per month and one ration, three dollars of which monthly pay may be in clothing." [6] It was on the basis of this legislation that Negro troops were paid for the next two years.

The radicals in Congress had managed to fight through a law authorizing the president to employ Negro soldiers at his discretion, but at the same time they had made it clear that such Negroes were to be second-class soldiers when payday came. Secretary Stanton may have been motivated by the most generous of intentions, but his hands and the hands of the paymaster general were tied by Congress. The secretary of war may have pledged the faith of the federal government in the orders of August 25, as Colonel Thomas Wentworth Higginson charged, but to his question, "is not Congress bound, in all decency, either to fulfill [that pledge] or to disband the regiments?" [7] Congress continued to answer with a stubborn "No!"

It was on the other basic assumption (that Negro soldiers performed duty similar to that of white troops and at greater risk and thus were entitled to the pay of white troops) that some success was finally achieved. When Negro troops had been first proposed and recruited, it was pretty widely understood that they would be used as labor battalions, as service and garrison troops, that they would not be used in the full capacity of soldiers but only as auxiliary forces. White soldiers would continue to bear the brunt of battle; more white troops than before could appear on the fighting fronts, released from rear area and garrison duty in the forts by their Negro auxiliaries. These fighting troops, it was fairly thought, should naturally draw higher pay than garrison and service troops.

There were logical reasons for this point of view. Doubt was widespread that Negroes would be reliable in battle or that they could learn the duties of field soldiers in sufficient time to bear a part in the actual fighting before the South was brought to terms. Because of their being accustomed to the heat and

fevers of the South, it was argued that the logical role for
Negro troops would be in relieving white soldiers from the work
of building fortifications and manning artillery in captured
Confederate forts. It was further argued that, in order to prevent a degeneration of the war into savage barbarity, Negro
soldiers should be kept within the definite limits of fortifications
and out of close contact with their former masters.

Underlying most of this thinking was an awareness of the
sensitivity of Northern white soldiers to the charge that they
had been unable to bring the South to her knees without calling
on the Negro for help on the field of battle. Anti-Negro sentiment
in and out of the army added to the strength of that reasoning.
The prejudices against Negro soldiers clearly evident among
the white troops in the Department of the South during the
summer of 1862 could not be overlooked or lightly considered.
Equal pay to Negro soldiers would in effect place former slaves
on the same level with freeborn Northern whites, and this idea
could hardly be tolerated by large segments of the Northern
population, particularly in the lower economic strata where
competition with cheap Negro labor was both feared and hated.
As an example, the *National Intelligencer* of October 17, 1862,
reported that the packinghouse workers of Chicago had pledged
"not to work for any packer, under any consideration, who will,
in any manner, bring negro labor into competition with our
labor." To these Chicago workingmen, the obvious purpose of
employing Negroes in the packing houses was to reduce white
wages "to the lowest possible standard."

After Negro soldiers had proved in combat that they were
willing and able to carry the soldier's full burden and that they
could make efficient and courageous combat troops, this thinking had to be revised. The raising of regiments of free Northern
Negroes, such as the 54th and 55th Massachusetts, also argued
for a re-evaluation of thinking that had been based exclusively
on plans to arm fugitives from Southern slavery. As Colonel
Robert Shaw was quick to inform Governor Andrew, the officers
and men of the 54th keenly felt the discrimination in pay.
Andrew as quickly wrote Shaw to tell the regiment that there
had been a mistake and that "the Secretary of War will cause
right to be done as soon as the case is presented to him and

shall be fully understood." [8] Shaw and the 54th, however, had moved to the assault of Fort Wagner before the governor's letter reached the Department of the South.

Certain legal doors had already been closed on the case before Governor Andrew had the opportunity to present it to the secretary of war. When the Bureau for Colored Troops was established in May, 1863, Stanton, with his usual thoroughness, had asked the solicitor of the War Department, William Whiting of Boston, for an opinion as to what pay those troops should receive. Whiting, a patent lawyer and moderate Republican, after studying the Militia Act of 1862, concluded that the Negro should be paid as a laborer and not as a soldier. The War Department published this decision as part of General Orders, No. 163, June 4, 1863. The final paragraph announced that "Persons of African descent who enlist . . . are entitled to 'ten dollars per month and one ration; three dollars of which monthly pay may be in clothing.'" Stanton suggested to Governor Tod of Ohio late in June that "For any additional pay or bounty colored troops must trust to State contributions and the justice of Congress at the next session." [9]

Governor Andrew, not satisfied with correspondence, went to Washington in September for talks with Lincoln and various cabinet officers, and while he did secure assurances of fair treatment, he found the national capital so upset by the news of the Chickamauga disaster that action on the Negro soldier pay problem was impossible to secure. As a stopgap measure, Andrew then asked for and got action from the Massachusetts legislature: state money was appropriated to make up the difference in pay for the men of the 54th and 55th. But the men of those regiments were adamant and refused to accept this compromise solution to their problem. A spokesman for the 54th condemned the offer "to pay this regiment the difference between what the United States Government offers us and what they are legally bound to pay us" as tantamount to advertising "us to the world as holding out for *money* and not from *principle*,—that we sink our manhood in consideration of a few more dollars." [10] And, acting on principle, the Massachusetts regiments refused to accept *any* pay until it should be made equal by national legislation to that received by the white troops with whom they fought and died. As a result, they served for some eighteen months without pay other than the $50 bounty given each recruit by the state of Massachusetts upon enlistment.[11]

While Negro soldiers suffered humiliation because of the pay situation, at least they had food, clothing, and occasional shelter. Their families did not always fare so well. In the majority of Northern states, local or state aid was granted the dependents of soldiers in the armies, but state aid was not immediately extended to the families of Negro soldiers. Characteristically, Massachusetts seems to have led the way. Mary Livermore, nurse and worker with the Sanitary Commission, recorded several instances of state assistance to Chicago families of soldiers of the 54th. Governor Andrew, when he learned of the desperate need of some of these families, gave Miss Livermore "*carte blanche* for the relief of the families living in Chicago whose husbands and fathers were enlisted in the 54th." [12] Not until July, 1864, however, did the federal government make any provision for the wives and families of Negro soldiers who had been killed in action or had died of wounds or disease while in federal service. Then, finally, widows and orphans of Negro soldiers were declared entitled to pensions—"provided such widows and orphans were free." [13]

Negro soldiers served under a further financial disadvantage: they were not, until the middle of 1864, entitled to receive the federal bounty of $100 granted to white volunteers from the third month of the war. Curiously enough, Negro recruits were forbidden this small fortune even before their reception into the Union Army had been authorized by the War Department. On August 19, 1862, Assistant Adjutant General Thomas Vincent notified Lieutenant Charles S. Bowman, disbursing officer at Fort Leavenworth, Kansas, that "Recruits for negro regiments will under no circumstances be paid bounty and premiums." General Benjamin F. Butler managed to secure War Department authority for a $10 bounty for Negro recruits in Virginia at the end of November, 1863, but this was limited to Butler's command.[14]

Congress and the War Department seem to have been more interested in conciliating the sensitivities of Border state owners of slaves recruited into the Union Army than in meeting the just demands of Negro soldiers already in the service or of the families of Negroes who had already given their lives in that service. Recruiting instructions issued by presidential order in October, 1863, appointed boards to examine claims of loyal slaveowners whose property had become soldiers of the Union. Where claims were found valid, such owners were entitled to receive compensation "not to exceed the sum of three hundred dollars, upon filing . . . a valid deed of manumission and release, and making satisfactory proof of title, and any slave so enlisted shall be free." [15] These instructions carried into effect to some degree the president's earlier plan of compensated emancipation.

In his annual report for 1863, Secretary of War Stanton urged Congress to correct the inequity of Negro soldiers' pay. "The colored troops," he pointed out, "have been allowed no bounty, and, under the construction given the department [by Solicitor Whiting], they can only, under existing law, receive the pay of ten dollars per month, white soldiers being paid thirteen dollars per month, with clothing and a daily ration." Stanton spoke directly to the point: "There seems to be inequality and injustice in this distinction, and an amendment authorizing the same pay and bounty as white troops receive, is recommended." Nor did he base his recommendation on mean, legalistic grounds. "Soldiers of the Union," he declared, "fighting under its banner, and exposing their lives in battle to uphold the Government, colored troops are entitled to enjoy its justice and beneficence." [16]

Stanton had carried the case to the highest tribunal. The whole problem lay in the lap of Congress, as Stanton had suggested to the governor of Ohio in June. Both Stanton and Lincoln had implied as much to Frederick Douglass during their interviews with him in midsummer of 1863. Lincoln had suggested that, since Negroes "had larger motives for being soldiers than white men . . . they ought to be willing to enter the service upon any condition," and he had explained that their unequal pay "seemed a necessary concession to smooth the way to their employment at all as soldiers." Ultimately, the president had reassured Douglass, "they would receive the same." [17]

No one could say with any assurance how the Congress would act or when. As the tribunes of the people turned to the task of "equalizing the pay of soldiers," they demonstrated a tendency to be parsimonious and niggardly. The first bill they considered would have granted full soldiers' pay to Negroes only from the beginning of 1864! John Andrew and Thomas W. Higginson and other champions of the Negro soldier went into indignant action to try to get something a little more like the justice and beneficence Stanton had recommended.

Colonel Higginson, in his usual incisive language, set forth the case for United States colored troops in a letter to the New York *Tribune* in January, 1864: "The public seems to suppose that all required justice will be done by the passage of a bill equalizing the pay of all soldiers for the future." This was, for his regiment and others of early origin, "but half the question." He reminded the public that his men had then "been nearly sixteen months in the service, and for them," he insisted, "the immediate issue is the question of arrears." Referring to the initial War Department orders to Saxton, he argued that every man in his regiment understood the matter thoroughly, even if the public did not: every man had "volunteered under an explicit *written assurance* from the War Department that he should have the pay of a white soldier." Further, Higginson insisted, "He knows that for five months the regiment received that pay, after which it was cut down from the promised thirteen dollars per month to ten dollars, for some reason to him inscrutable."

The colonel maintained that there was "nothing mean or mercenary" about most of his men and that, if they could be convinced that the government actually needed the money, they "would serve it barefooted and on half-rations, and without a dollar—for a time." Unfortunately, however, his troops saw white soldiers all around them receiving hundreds of dollars in bounties for re-enlisting "from this impoverished Government, which can only pay seven dollars out of thirteen to its black regiments." Here he referred to the paternalistic practice of withholding the $3 uniform or clothing allowance instead of paying it in cash as was the custom with white soldiers. Federal delay, Higginson concluded, "has already inflicted untold suffering, has impaired discipline, has relaxed loyalty, and has begun to implant a feeling of sullen distrust in the very regiments whose early career solved the problem of the nation, created a new army, and made peaceful emancipation possible." [18]

James Montgomery, colonel of the 2nd South Carolina, urged similar arguments on Senator Henry Wilson of Massachusetts, chairman of the Committee on Military Affairs. "I can certify, most conscientiously," Montgomery wrote, "that the troops under my command have been second to none in efficiency; while their loyalty and fidelity might put to the blush some who boast of white skins. Could Honorable Senators have seen, as I have seen them; toiling in the trenches before 'Wagner,' mounting guns, digging, carrying shot and shells for weeks and weeks together; and this under a storm of shot and bursting shells, I know they could not, and would not, withhold so simple an act of justice." [19]

The Chicago *Tribune* early took an interest in the campaign for equal pay for colored troops, and on January 28, 1864, it argued editorially that no additional legislation was necessary to achieve that end. "The fact is," the Chicago paper maintained, "the chief disability of the black race, lies in prejudice and not in law." The blame lay with Stanton. "The War Department at the very outset," the *Tribune* urged, "could have found no legal bar to obstruct any order it chose to make, recognizing no distinction in its troops of whatever color. All that was required was to take down the barriers of false pride, and caste, and the black soldier and white would stand shoulder to shoulder on the common ground of devotion to country."

Unfortunately, the War Department had, through its solicitor, Mr. Whiting, made the fatal distinction in compliance with the Militia Act of 1862. While Stanton might have corrected the inequity by reversing or disregarding the decision of his solicitor, he had chosen rather to let Congress solve the problem. President Lincoln seemed satisfied to go along with the Stanton choice despite the steady pressure of John Andrew in the spring of 1864. [20] Even Attorney General Edward Bates supported Andrew's position and that of the Chicago *Tribune*.

Bates's opinion of April 23 discovered a way around the limita-
tions of the Militia Act as interpreted by Whiting, and the
attorney general went so far as to inform the president that his
"constitutional obligation to take care that the laws be faithfully executed" made it his duty "to direct the Secretary of
War to inform the officers of the Pay Department of the Army"
to end the inequality in soldiers' pay.[21] Notwithstanding this
strong encouragement to action, Lincoln continued to do nothing
in the matter.

The Chicago *Tribune* continued to do what it could, and on
May 1 it published an editorial clearly showing what the
double standard in pay meant. The Negro soldier "deserves
equal pay with the best," the *Tribune* insisted, "and has been
promised it. What he receives is this:

	white	colored
Sergeant Major	$21	$7
Quartermaster Sergeant	21	7
First Sergeant	20	7
Sergeant	17	7
Hospital Steward	30	7
Corporal	13	7
Private	13	7
Chaplain	100	7

The white soldier is permitted to purchase his clothing himself," the editorial explained, "but from the ten dollars of the
colored, three are reserved for this purpose." The *Tribune* gave
the editorial the title "Read and Blush." There is, however,
little indication that many members of Congress read the item
and no evidence to show that they blushed.

The bill finally passed in June granted equal pay to Negro
soldiers—retroactive to January 1, 1864. Stubbornly refusing
to solve the problem of arrears in pay, Congress provided that
"all persons of color who were free on the 19th day of April,
1861, and who have been enlisted and mustered into the military service of the United States, shall from the time of their
enlistments be entitled to receive the pay, bounty, and clothing

allowed to such persons by the laws existing at the time of their enlistment"—providing the attorney general approved! [22]

This was no solution at all. It simply called on Edward Bates to repeat his decision of two months earlier. This the attorney general did on July 14, and on the next day Stanton issued the necessary order to his paymaster general. On August 18, 1864, the adjutant general's office issued Circular 60, directing commanders of Negro regiments to find out which of their men had been free on April 19, 1861, "the fact of freedom to be determined in each case on the statement of the soldier, under oath, taken in connection with the most reliable information that can be obtained from other sources." [23]

This ruling and directive failed to solve the problem of back pay for all the men of a single colored regiment. Even the Massachusetts regiments had in their ranks men who had not been free in any strict legal sense in the first week of the war. Colonel Edward N. Hallowell, commanding the 54th, devised a way out of the dilemma. Since the circular had failed to provide any particular form of oath, he administered this one to his men: "You do solemnly swear that you owed no man unrequited labor on or before the 19th day of April, 1861. So help you God." This was called the "Quaker Oath" and even those men of the 54th who were fugitive slaves took it as freemen "by God's higher law, if not by their country's." [24] The muster rolls of the companies of the 54th and 55th Massachusetts with the magic word "Free" written after the name of every man who had taken the Hallowell oath went up to Washington for approval, and in October of 1864 the men were mustered for pay, the full pay of soldiers in the service of the United States, retroactive to the time of their enlistment. [25]

Of course this was no solution for other Negro regiments, whose back pay was still withheld from them by the inadequacy of the law. Thomas W. Higginson's indignation knew no bounds. His soldiers, few if any of whom had been free on April 19, 1861, were thus by the peculiar character of the legislation deprived of the arrears in pay which he had all along claimed for them and which were justly due them. He again addressed himself to the editor of the New York *Tribune*:

"No one can possibly be so weary of reading of the wrongs done by the Government toward the colored soldiers as I am of writing about them. This is my only excuse for intruding on your columns again." His apologetic tone quickly disappeared as he developed his argument. He pointed out that the men of his regiment were "volunteers, every one," and he argued that "they did not get their freedom by enlisting" under the terms of the Emancipation Proclamation; "they had it already. They enlisted to serve the Government, trusting its honor." That trust had been betrayed. "Now the nation," Higginson charged, "turns upon them and says: Your part of the contract is fulfilled; we have had your services. If you can show that you had previously been free for a certain length of time, we will fulfill the other side of the contract. If not, we repudiate it. Help yourselves if you can."

Colonel Higginson admitted that the law might at least do justice to most of the men of the Massachusetts regiments and "take their wives and children out of the almshouses," but toward his own regiment, "which had been in service and under fire months before a Northern colored soldier was recruited, the policy of repudiation," he maintained, "has at last been officially adopted." What could his men now do in the face of this official repudiation? "There is no alternative for the officers of the South Carolina regiments," he wrote, "but to wait for another session of Congress." Meanwhile, they would have to continue "to act as executioners for those soldiers who, like Sergeant Walker, refuse to fulfill their share of a contract where the Government has openly repudiated the other share." Walker had been shot for having the men of his company stack arms and refuse to continue to serve as soldiers until they had received the pay they understood had been promised them; he was found guilty of inciting to mutiny. Wearily Higginson concluded that "If a year's discussion . . . has at length secured the arrears of pay for the Northern colored regiments, possibly two years may secure it for the Southern." [26]

Higginson was right. Section 5 of the Enrollment Act of March 3, 1865, finally brought belated justice to the South Carolina and other Negro regiments recruited in the South before January 1, 1864, in the shape of a provision for their full payment from the date of their original enlistment.[27] The war was over by the time the colored soldiers in this category finally drew their arrears in pay.

*   *   *

It is impossible to measure the harm caused by the federal government's shortsighted and parsimonious policy toward the pay of colored troops. It is impossible to measure human suffering, humiliation, distrust, or the cancer of disloyalty bred of the conviction of having been treated unfairly. It does seem obvious, however, that, had the federal government—Lincoln, Stanton, or the Congress—seen fit to correct the inequalities in the pay of Negro troops more promptly, the results might have been apparent in a measurable increase in Negro enlistments. The adjutant general of Illinois in October of 1863 told Major Foster of the Bureau for Colored Troops that, if "no greater inducements can be offered to enlist these men than the sum named," Governor Yates could not be very optimistic about the prospects for raising a colored regiment in Lincoln's own state. "The colored men of this State," the Illinois official wrote Major Foster, "are generally a good class and can command at home readily from $12 to $15 per month." [28] And without running the risk of death or enslavement. Without the obvious inequity of the distinction in pay, Sergeant Robert Walker would not have been shot for mutiny and there would have been far fewer reports of impaired discipline and relaxed loyalty, such as Higginson made.

It should have been clear to the nation by the fall of 1863 that Negro soldiers were ready and willing to share all the dangers of the soldier's life in full measure, and that their contribution to saving the Union was worth at least $36 per man per annum over what was being paid them. There is no good explanation for the reluctance of the Union to admit its error in this regard and to correct it. The amount of money involved was too small by comparison with the amounts being spent every day of the war to explain the injustice of Negro pay on the basis of Congressional or War Department economy. That it was an error in judgment and an injustice is plain. That the error should have been corrected earlier and ungrudgingly is obvious. That the injustice was stubbornly maintained was unworthy of the cause for which all soldiers, Negro and white, struggled.

XI. *"taking life and honor in their hands . . ."*

> Courage is cheap; the main duty of an officer is to take good care of his men, so that every one of them shall be ready, at a moment's notice, for any reasonable demand.
>
> —THOMAS WENTWORTH HIGGINSON, 1864

It is an old military maxim that the performance of any military organization, whether company, regiment, brigade, or division, is in some measure a reflection of the character and ability of its commander. This probably was more true of combat during the Civil War than it is today, when warfare has become more a matter of mass action and coordination of all arms than of small unit operations in which combat success depends in large part on the decisions of the unit leader and his control over and relationship with his men. This is not to say that there is no longer opportunity for individual leadership and initiative in the lower echelons of the modern army. On the contrary, company-grade officers, lieutenants and captains, can still find far more room for the use of individual intelligence and imagination, in garrison and in combat, than is generally supposed. The stereotype of the inflexible military machine, closely geared from highest to lowest command, bound round with regulations, circulars, orders, and directives, and crowding out not only personal initiative but personal integrity, is highly overworked and grossly misleading.[1] But it is a fact that with the slow growth of administrative centralization and standardization, with technical advances in methods of communication, and with continued coordination of the various arms and ser-

197

vices, the scope of individual action by the unit commander has steadily decreased since the days of the Civil War.

In those days of the bayonet assault and the cavalry charge, before the invention of barbed wire, machine gun, coaxial cable, and divisional combat teams, the individual unit commander was a vitally important military figure. Units themselves were much smaller than their counterparts today and were as often called and popularly known by their commanders' names as by their official numerical or muster-roll designation.[2] Regiments and even companies were frequently isolated from the rest of their brigades and divisions and were in many instances self-supporting in the field for long periods of time. Means of communication were few and unreliable, even after the organization of the Signal Corps as a separate branch of the service. The writing of detailed battle orders and the long-range planning of campaigns were in rudimentary stages of development, and the now-ubiquitous duplicating machine had still to be invented. Orders were written out by military clerks or issued orally at staff meetings rather than "cut," as they are today. Occasionally, orders were printed for distribution, but this practice was generally limited to the echelons from brigade up. On the regimental level and below, where battles are fought and won or lost, the chain of command had its weak links, and the difference between victory and defeat was often measured by the character and ability of the regimental commander and the experience and intelligence of his company officers.

In those days of personal leadership, when officers literally led their men in the field, the need for good officers was paramount. And so, in view of their vital importance to the army and to the nation, it is hard to understand why the problem of officer selection was given little attention during the early years of the Civil War. For the most part, the selection of officers was left to chance and the fortunes of local, state, and national politics. Volunteer regiments were usually officered by the men who had raised them, with little or no regard to their military experience or the lack of it. There were many instances of political and social preferment. Many a man, whether a congressman like John Cochrane of New York or a Jayhawker like James Montgomery and Charles Jennison of Kansas, became a colonel by securing authority from his state governor to raise a regiment. On the company level, popular election was the general rule.

Augustus Chetlain had been a successful merchant in Galena, Illinois, and when Galena raised a company of infantry in April of 1861, Chetlain was elected its captain at the suggestion of U. S. Grant. Chetlain was mustered in as captain on May 2— and became a lieutenant colonel of the 12th Illinois Infantry on the next day. In the prolonged absence of its colonel, Chetlain led the 12th through the winter campaign against Forts Henry and Donelson and became colonel in name as well as fact on April 27, 1862. Dan Sickles of New York took a more direct route—he rose from private to colonel in about two months.[3]

Aside from what brief and uneven training some men had received as militia officers, the majority of Union officers were remarkably innocent of military affairs. Critics accused Daniel Ullmann of conducting battalion drill with the aid of a card on which he had written the necessary commands in proper sequence, and more serious complaints can be discovered almost without number. Civil War newspapers are full of advertisements for such helpful guides as Hardee and Casey's *Tactics* and manuals on a variety of military subjects, from rifle marksmanship to field sanitation. It is clear that most Union officers, with the obvious exception of the professionals from West Point, had to learn their duties through "on-the-job training" at the joint expense of their men and the country.[4]

One explanation of this rather haphazard approach to the problem of providing officers for a rapidly expanding army is found in the traditional American distrust of, and even disdain for, professional military men. We had maintained a token standing army and a military academy more on sufferance than because of any high regard for either. We had maintained the Revolutionary beliefs that one American is as "good" as any other, that an officer class is autocratic by nature and has no place in a democratic scheme of things, that the average American is familiar from boyhood with weapons and outdoor life and can quickly become a soldier equal to and even the superior of trained professionals. We had proved the pragmatic value of these beliefs to our own satisfaction against the best troops of

Great Britain in two wars and against the armies of Mexico in
1847. So far as Americans were concerned, there was nothing
mysterious about the military art. Our whole military history
testified to that. Our greatest military leaders had been civilians: Washington, the Virginia farmer; Nathaniel Greene,
the Rhode Island Quaker; Andrew Jackson, the Tennessee cotton
planter and horse racer. Of course, as a sort of Continental
Line, we possessed a leavening of officers, regular and militia,
with the experience of the Mexican War less than fifteen years
behind them. We had never considered the problems arising
from the event of a civil war in which Americans would fight
Americans on fairly even terms.

With the coming of this civil war there was no immediate
departure from established American practice. At the start the
South had the advantage of finding its best military leaders
almost at once. The North lost costly years trying one unskill-
ful general after another on the Union Army. The South had
also the advantage of an aristocratic respect for an officer class
and a tradition for hierarchical social gradations infused with a
clannish willingness to follow the man on horseback, the beau
sabreur. The South maintained a romantic myth of warfare in
the spirit of Sir Walter Scott's novels, while the more mechani-
cally and pragmatically inclined North rather quickly came to
look on war as an interruption of normal business pursuits and
at length as an unpleasant business to be organized and planned
along practical lines in order to get it over with as soon as
possible. But it is hard to break with established custom, particularly in military affairs, and for a long time the volunteer
armies of the North blundered along with what officers they
could find by the uncertain and faulty methods of political appointment and popular election. It was not until the use of
Negro troops approached reality that an opportunity arrived
for a clean break with the past and for the inauguration of a
system for selecting officers, from company to field grade, on
the basis of merit and ability, by examination before boards of
experienced military men.

This system did not spring full blown from the head of any
one man. A typically American product of this most American
of wars, it gradually emerged through practical experimenta-

tion and testing in the theaters of war. The most surprising thing about the system is that it emerged as rapidly and as well developed as it did. Its actual period of evolution was only a few days more than one year. In eighteen months it was fully matured and had survived the tests of combat.

*   *   *

When David Hunter began to recruit his 1st South Carolina Volunteers in May of 1862 he faced a major problem in finding officers for his black companies. Obviously, the customary methods of officer procurement would not answer his needs. His troops were to be recruited from a slave population widely regarded as "the most degraded negroes in the South" by reason of their long isolation on the Sea Islands, where one generation had followed another to the cotton fields, cut off from the outside world and with no infusion of new blood to check the slow human erosion of inbreeding.[5] If these black men were to be made into effective soldiers, the best officers available would be essential, men not only intelligent in the ways of war, in the use of rifle and bayonet and in platoon and company evolutions, but also aware of the revolutionary nature of their work and convinced of its significance and worth. Hunter looked over the means at his disposal and made a decision dictated by military necessity and of far-reaching importance: he would officer his regiment "from the most intelligent and energetic of our noncommissioned officers; men who will go into it with all their hearts."[6] This decision is the point of departure for any discussion of the selection of officers for Negro troops in the Union Army. Before Appomattox and the war's end, probably five thousand "intelligent and energetic" white noncommissioned officers from volunteer regiments of the Union Army had won shoulder straps in regiments of United States Colored Troops.

To command the ten companies of the 1st South Carolina, Hunter selected ten sergeants. Five had been sergeants in the engineers, generally recognized as the most highly trained branch of the army at that time. The other five came from Pennsylvania infantry regiments serving in the Department of the South. While Hunter's efforts were abortive, Thomas Wentworth Higginson found some of his sergeants leading the com-

panies of the 1st South when he took command of the regiment
in November, 1862. Foremost among them was Captain Charles
Trowbridge of Company A, former sergeant of engineers, ultimately mustered out with the rank of lieutenant colonel.[7]

Other methods were used to procure officers for Negro troops
before the final definitive system was perfected. In Louisiana
and in Kansas there was a lack of system and selection similar
to that prevailing in the officering of white volunteer regiments.
When Butler decided to raise colored troops in Louisiana, he
found colored officers already commissioned by the state's Confederate governor, Thomas Overton Moore, and some of these
Butler adopted along with their organizations.[8] Of the three
colored regiments Butler mustered in, Horace Greeley reported,
the first had "all its line officers colored," the second had "its
two highest officers White; all the rest colored," and the third
"was officered by the best men that could be had, regardless of
color." F. E. Dumas, a "free negro, wealthy, brave, and loyal,"
brought in a company of his own slaves and was straightway
commissioned captain; he eventually was promoted to major
for gallantry in action.[9]

Out in Kansas, where Lane, Jennison, and Montgomery took
up the work, there was no system of officer selection beyond
individual interest and political connection. Men with abolitionist sentiments tended to head recruiting activities, regardless of the extent of their military experience. Lane and Blunt
persuaded Benjamin Van Horn, for instance, against his protests of lack of military ability and inclination, not only to go
out and recruit a company of Negroes but also to command
them. Colonel James Williams of the 1st Kansas Colored had
been a captain known principally for his abolitionism; it was
entirely fortuitous that he should have developed into an effective regimental commander. Colonel Samuel Crawford, however,
insisted on competent, hard-working officers when he took command of the 2nd Kansas Colored; he required that they "make
good in drill, discipline, and military appearance, or hand in
their resignations." With immediate results, too; as Crawford
recalled later, "we soon had a number of vacancies." [10]

Daniel Ullmann was more careful than Lane and Blunt in his
selection of officers to command the Negro troops of his brigade.

He was especially concerned to find men with combat experience, and a large proportion of those who went to Louisiana with him were "war worn Veterans who had been in many a well fought battle." [11] But in Ullmann's view, the task ahead required more than military proficiency, important though that was. His General Orders, No. 7, June 10, 1863, shows clearly not only what the New York brigadier expected of his officers but also what he hoped for and thought about the Negro soldier. Pointing out to his officers that they were engaged "in a special, peculiar, and difficult service," Ullmann reminded them that they had been selected for "qualities which . . . eminently qualify them for this duty, namely: accurate knowledge of the drill, long experience in the field, patience, diligence, and patriotism." He warned his officers that they would find "the constant exercise of all these qualities necessary." Then he outlined his understanding of the military mission of his organization and gave what must have seemed extremely unorthodox instructions for the accomplishment of that mission. "You are brought into contact with a race, who, having lived in an abnormal condition all the days of their lives, are now suddenly elevated into being soldiers of the United States fighting against their oppressors, as well for their own liberties as for the integrity of the republic. They are to be molded by you into drilled and disciplined troops. You cannot display too much wisdom in your conduct, both as regards yourselves and them," he warned his officers. *"Let the law of kindness be your guide.* Thus acting, you will soon obtain their confidence; you will find them docile, impressionable, fully imbued with the spirit of subordination (one of the highest attributes of a soldier), possessed of a deep appreciation of kindly treatment and of keen perception, which enables them quickly to discover any flaw in the conduct of their superiors."

Ullmann was confident that Negroes would make good soldiers if properly trained and intelligently led, and he was filled with the conviction that the army had a definite role to play, above and beyond its strictly military functions, in uplifting the freedmen. "You have the materials," he told his officers, "crude though they now may be, but perfectly malleable, to make the best of soldiers. Perform your duty conscientiously, and our

beloved and once happy country will not only have a body of
soldiers, who will enthusiastically aid her in fighting her battles,
but she will also have the proud satisfaction of knowing that
she has, at last, taken a practical step towards the elevation of a
hitherto degraded and oppressed race." [12] This is the clear and
definite expression of a man whose heart was in the work. As
Ullmann conceived this work, officers for Negro regiments
would have to be carefully selected. None but the best could
hope to live up to his expectations.

On January 26, 1863, when Ullmann was just beginning the
work of finding "officers of the right stamp," the War Department authorized Governor John Andrew to recruit colored
troops in Massachusetts. Since these troops were to be state-
controlled, Andrew was given the responsibility of finding officers, and he was careful to secure the elite of the North. "The
officers and men are both carefully picked," he wrote Stanton in
April. "We have aimed at getting officers of high character,
making careful selections out of many candidates." [13] Besides
setting an unusually high standard in the selection of white
officers for his colored regiments, Governor Andrew also waged
a long struggle for authority to commission individuals from
the ranks in recognition of meritorious conduct. Three Negro
soldiers of the 54th and three of the 55th won promotions in
this manner. [14]

But Massachusetts made no direct contribution to the evolution of a system of officer selection. The fact that Andrew was
successful in securing unusually good officers is important as
an instance in which the older, more customary system did
function well and as a monument to the character and determination of Governor Andrew himself. The Massachusetts experience, however, has little relation to a discussion of the gradual
unfolding of a selective system by the central authority of the
War Department and devised to provide officers, not for one
or two specific regiments but for all organizations of colored
troops as they were needed.

*   *   *

In the spring of 1863 the War Department matured such a
selective system, in the light of the past experience of Hunter

and Higginson on the Atlantic coast and of the contemporary experience of Ullmann in New York and Louisiana. In its final form, this system was of a dual nature. It was designed to meet the needs of two different methods of recruiting and organizing Negro regiments: one, the system inaugurated and developed by Adjutant General Lorenzo Thomas in the Mississippi Valley and, two, the parallel system of raising colored regiments in the Northern and the Border states under the direction of the Bureau for Colored Troops, which was set up in the War Department in May.

Thomas telegraphed Stanton on April 4, 1863, from Memphis that he had authorized General Stephen A. Hurlbut to raise six companies of Negro soldiers "and select the officers." Hurlbut, Thomas told the secretary of war, "knows intelligent Sergeants who will make good Captains." [15]

That there were many "intelligent Sergeants" in the Union armies in the Mississippi Valley is clear from an analysis of the special orders Thomas issued to announce the formation of colored regiments. His Special Orders, No. 13, Helena, Arkansas, April 7, is typical. "The following Officers, Non-commissioned officers and Privates," the order read, "are announced as the Officers of the 1st Regiment of Arkansas Vols. of African Descent," and it listed the white personnel: seven sergeants, one first lieutenant, and two privates were promoted to the rank of captain; six sergeants, two corporals, and two privates were made first lieutenants; and two sergeants, two corporals, and six privates were given the shoulder straps of second lieutenant. Of the thirty line commissions issued in this one order fifteen, or 50 per cent, went to sergeants. [16]

In his telegram of April 4, Thomas reported to Stanton that he had authorized Hurlbut to select the officers necessary for his Negro companies. This is somewhat misleading and requires explanation. Hunter had selected his own officers, and so had Ullmann; the new War Department system made an important change by establishing machinery for the selection of officers instead of leaving it to the slow and tedious process of individual selection by the authority of one man who was subject to the usual human frailties in addition to the demanding responsibilities of leading a division in the field. Thomas described this machinery in a letter to General Frederick Steele on April 15. After explaining the reasons for the new policy to Steele and asking him to announce it to the troops of his division, Thomas wrote: "It is the wish of the War Department that each Division Commander interest himself in the officering and recruiting of two regiments; the officers to be selected by a Board of Officers appointed by the Division Commander to determine on the fitness of the applicants, and to assign them to positions, without regard to present rank, merit alone being the test." White soldiers were to be appointed to fill all the commissioned ranks of each regiment, the positions of first sergeant, and the noncommissioned grades. Those recommended by the boards for appointment were to be mustered out of their old regiments and mustered into their new colored organizations "as fast as companies, battalions, and regiments are organized." [17]

Thomas indicated the make-up and method of organization of the divisional examining boards in another letter to General John A. McClernand. "In the Divisions," the adjutant general explained, "the plan has been to institute a board of one officer from each Brigade to examine the several applicants and make a roster for the Regiment and this being approved is sufficient." Thomas made it clear to McClernand, though in dubious grammar, that he wanted no slipshod examinations: "I desire none but those well qualified and whose heart is in the work." [18]

This system of examination and appointment of candidates by divisional boards was widely used in the field, from South Carolina to the Frontier. In August, 1863, General John Beatty of Ohio, serving with George H. Thomas on the Tennessee River near Stevenson, Alabama, was appointed president of such a board. "The time was," he recorded in his journal, "when we thought it would be impossible to obtain good officers for colored regiments. Now we feel assured that they will have as good if not better officers than the white regiments." And he found obvious reasons for optimism. "From sergeants applying for commissions," he wrote, "we are able to select splendid men—strong, healthy, well informed, and of considerable military experience. In fact, we occasionally find a noncommissioned officer who is better qualified to command a regiment than nine-tenths of the colonels." Beatty knew colonels, he wrote, "who could not obtain a recommendation from this board for a second lieutenancy."

Commissions in Negro regiments attracted many applicants. In less than two weeks after General Beatty's board went to work the number of aspirants to shoulder straps had reached eight hundred. Beatty's board seems to have been anything but an easy touch: of the first 120 applicants examined, "perhaps forty" were recommended for commissions. Still, the board had its human and humorous moments. On August 31 the applicants included "a sergeant, fifty years old at least, but still sprightly and active; not very well posted in the infantry tactics now in use, but of more than ordinary intelligence." The day's candidates had not impressed Beatty and his board very favorably: the sergeant's age was against him, the others were "entirely too ignorant." But it turned out that the sergeant, a member of a Michigan regiment, recognized the president of the board as an old acquaintance.

"... You are the son of James Beatty," the sergeant said. "I have carried you in my arms many a time. My mother saved your life more than once. Thirty years ago your father and mine were neighbors. I recollect the cabin where you were born as well as if I had seen it but yesterday."

The board considered the sergeant's case. Colonel Hobart thought "his early associations had evidently been bad; he was entirely too old, anyway." But the colonel supposed that the board "should have to do something for the sergeant." After all, Hobart pointed out, "He had rendered important service to the country by carrying the honored president of the board in his arms, and but for timely doses of catnip tea, administered by the sergeant's mother," General Beatty might have died unknown. Hobart suggested a second lieutenancy. Beatty suggested a first lieutenancy, and the board concurred. That evening General Beatty had a long conversation with the sergeant, Daniel Rodabaugh, and discovered that he had served five years in the regular army in the Florida, or Seminole, War, two years in Mexico, and another two years in the Civil War. Beatty concluded that he "richly deserve[d] the position for which we recommended him." [19]

However well the system of divisional boards worked in the field, some other method had to be devised to provide officers for colored regiments raised in the North. This other method was announced on May 22, 1863, with the publication of War Department General Orders, Nos. 143 and 144. Number 143 established the Bureau for Colored Troops and directed that "Boards will be convened at such posts as may be decided upon by the War Department to examine applicants for commissions to command colored troops, who, on application to the Adjutant General, may receive authority to present themselves to the board for examination." These boards had authority over the selection of recruiting officers for colored troops as well as over appointments to line and field positions. Provision was made for the promotion of "meritorious commissioned officers . . . to higher rank if they prove themselves equal to it." [20]

General Orders, No. 144, prescribed rules to guide the boards. They were to sit from nine to five daily, six days a week, and examine only applicants with authority from the adjutant general to appear before them. To gain this permission, an applicant was required to present "satisfactory recommendations of good moral character and standing in the community" in which he lived or, if a soldier, he must have testimonials from his commanding officers. These recommendations had to be filed in advance with the Bureau for Colored Troops. The rules were quite explicit: each applicant was to receive "a fair but rigorous examination as to physical, mental, and moral fitness to command troops," and the boards were directed to specify for what grades of commission applicants were fit and to classify them by numbers "according to the merit of proficiency." Appointments to each grade were to be made "only . . . from the candidates approved by the Board[s], and in the order of merit recommended by" them. With a note of quiet finality the instructions stated that "the report of the Board, if adverse, shall be conclusive; and no persons rejected by it shall be reexamined." [21]

The numerous reports of the various boards and the voluminous correspondence carried on by the Bureau for Colored Troops show clearly that the examining boards followed these instructions to the letter, despite occasional pressure from state governors and members of Congress. One board, demonstrating what in academic circles is referred to as the military mind and what in military circles is called the administrative mind, even took literally the instructions to sit daily from nine in the morning to five in the evening until the president of the board, Colonel Daniel Huston, had secured permission from the bureau to adjourn in the middle of the day for lunch.[22]

The bureau seems to have exercised great care in the choice of officers to sit on these boards of examination, and regular army officers were generally used. The best known and busiest board was that which sat in Washington, and for its presiding officer the War Department selected Major General Silas Casey, a regular army officer and graduate of the military academy at West Point in 1826, who had served in the Florida wars of 1837 and 1842 and in the Mexican War. In the latter conflict Casey received brevet promotions twice in less than a month for "gallant and meritorious conduct" in the battles of Contreras and Churubusco and again in the fighting at Chapultepec. He had been a member of a board of officers to revise American infantry tactics during the 1850's, and the manual finally adopted for general use in 1862 carried his name.[23] Colonel Henry Van Rensselaer, an academy man of the class of 1831 and a member of the Inspector General's Department, presided over the board in Cincinnati, and Colonel Daniel Huston, another West Pointer of the class of 1847, who had won two brevet promotions for his actions at Wilson's Creek and in the siege of Vicksburg, headed the board in St. Louis. Additional boards were later established in Davenport, Iowa, and New Orleans. Finally, with a touch of wry Yankee humor that seems almost overdrawn, a sixth examining board was set up in Richmond, Virginia, early in April, 1865. General Casey himself went south to supervise.[24]

To secure an examination for a commission an applicant wrote directly to the Bureau for Colored Troops for authority, sending with his letter of application the requisite recommendations and testimonials. If the bureau found the applicant's papers and records in order, a letter of permission was issued. Major C. J. Stalbrand, chief of artillery, 3rd Division of the XVII Corps, received a typical letter of permission early in

January of 1864. "Under authority of the Secretary of War," the bureau directed the major, "you are hereby permitted to appear for examination before the Board now sitting at No. 212 'F' Street of which Major General Silas Casey is President." The letter warned Major Stalbrand that the "Government makes no allowance on account of traveling, or other expenses, in consequence of this permission." To this particular letter the bureau added an enlightening explanatory note: "On receiving leave from your Commanding Officer to avail yourself of the above permission, you will proceed directly to the place designated, and file with the Board this authority for your examination. You will report to the Board daily until examined; and on the conclusion of your examination, will immediately rejoin your command. Any failure to comply with these directions will subject you to trial for 'absence without leave,' besides forfeiting your chance for appointment." [25] The bureau obviously wanted it understood that there was no easy road to a commission in the colored troops; it also wanted to keep to a minimum applications motivated by a desire for a change from the deep mud and dead horses of Northern Virginia to the comparatively pleasant surroundings of the capital.

Every day the bureau sent lists to the various boards notifying them of the persons to whom authority to appear had been issued that day. On December 28, 1863, the bureau notified General Casey that letters of authority to appear before the Washington board had that day been issued to the following:

> Smith, Pvt. A. J., Co. "C". 22d Mass. Vols.
> Wilder, Pvt. Geo. E., Co. "A". 15th Mass. Vols.
> Hull, Sergt. A. B., Co. "E". 44th N.Y. Vols.
> Ayars, Pvt. Wm. H., Co. "B". 124th N.Y. Vols.
> Gray, Sergt. Jos., Co. "E". 15th Conn. Vols.
> Miller, Sergt. C. H., Co. "F". 9th N.Y. Art'y
> Williams, Pvt. H. C., Co. "C". 16th Conn. Vols.

The bureau at the same time notified the Cincinnati board that a letter had been sent Private H. H. Chew of Company G, 39th Illinois Volunteers. And the St. Louis board was sent a list of sixteen persons to whom authority to appear had been granted that day. These sixteen included three civilians, two captains, two lieutenants, seven sergeants, one corporal and one private. Two of the civilians had Missouri addresses; the third came from Connecticut. The military personnel represented nine different organizations from four Midwestern states.[26]

At the end of each week the bureau sent each board a recapitulation of the number of letters of authority issued in the six days immediately preceding.[27] The boards in turn furnished the bureau with weekly reports of the names of applicants examined and the results of those examinations. Finally, the bureau placed on file the names and addresses of all candidates recommended for appointment in the order recommended, and as positions were found the candidates were appointed. The candidate then reported to the proper officer, was mustered in, and assumed the duties of his new position.

Not all candidates appointed to positions in colored regiments accepted those proffered appointments. On January 26, 1864, Major Charles Foster, in charge of the Bureau for Colored Troops, sent out letters of inquiry on five officers who had been appointed to various regiments of U.S. Colored Troops about a month earlier but who had not yet reported for duty. These letters, all but one of which were directed to the commanding officer of the appointee's former organization, all ended on this note: "I am directed to request you to call upon him for his immediate acceptance of the [appointment], or he will be considered as having declined." [28] Reasons for declining appointments were several, but the foremost reason was probably failure to win promotion. The bureau in some cases did not even bother to appoint candidates recommended by the examining boards only for rank in the colored troops equal to that already held. The bureau's records are sprinkled with instances of "nonavailability" in the cases of field and line officers recommended for lower or equal grades in Negro regiments.[29]

Every indication is that the examining boards played no favorites and were uniformly severe in their examinations. In a letter to Governor O. P. Morton of Indiana, suggesting that the governor send candidates to Cincinnati for examination for commissions in the Negro regiment being raised in Indiana, Major Foster warned that "it should be borne in mind that it will be necessary to have examined a larger number than is neces-

sary to officer the regiment as in all probability about forty per
cent of the parties examined will be rejected." And there was
no appeal to rejection by the boards. In reply to an inquiry
about the rejection of one E. K. Wardewell, Major Foster
merely reminded Senator Henry Wilson of Massachusetts that
"re-examinations are forbidden by General Orders Number 144,
War Department, current series," and asserted in clipped military language, "It is believed that the interests of the service
will be promoted by a strict adherence to the order above referred to." On another occasion Colonel Huston of the Cincinnati board forwarded to the bureau a letter from Brigadier
General Thomas Ewing requesting reconsideration in the case
of a rejected private of the 11th Kansas. To this request Foster
was typically unyielding, pointing out that to consider the
"many applications for re-examinations" which the bureau received "would lead to great embarrassment." [30]

While rejected applicants had no second chance, candidates
who had qualified for any commissioned grade might on occasion be reconsidered by the boards for advancement to a higher
grade. Private D. S. Munger of the 6th Michigan Cavalry was
examined on February 15, 1864, and recommended for appointment as second lieutenant, first class. On the next day he
was reconsidered, passed for appointment as first lieutenant,
third class, and he was eventually assigned in that grade to the
23rd U.S. Colored Troops. Sergeant Lindley C. Kent of the 4th
Delaware Volunteers had a similar experience: after his first
examination on February 27, 1864, he was rated for appointment as second lieutenant. Then he was reconsidered on March
1, found qualified as a first lieutenant, and in that grade appointed to the 32nd U.S. Colored Troops. When the New York
Union League Club requested the appointment of Lieutenant
Colonel N. B. Bartram of the 8th U.S. Colored Troops as colonel
of the 20th, New York's first Negro regiment, the bureau
directed Bartram to "appear before the Board for examination
with a view to his appointment" in accordance with the request. [31]

The bureau's instructions to Major Thomas Duncan, president of the board of examiners at Davenport, Iowa, provide a
clear view of what the examiners looked for in their examina-

tions. Although the bureau did not consider it necessary "to trammel the Board with definite and positive instructions as to the qualifications which should be required for the several grades," it did provide some general rules to be followed in determining the qualifications of the various applicants. "A Lieutenant," the bureau suggested, "should understand the school of the soldier, all company movements, know how to read and write, and understand the four ground rules of Arithmetic." More was expected of a captain: he "should be perfectly familiar with company movements, the School of the Battalion, and be reasonably proficient in the English branches." The bureau suggested "great care" in recommending field officers: "they should in addition to the qualifications required for lower grade be conversant with brigade evolutions, and be possessed of general acquirements, sufficient to enable them to discharge the duties of their positions in such a manner as to do credit to the Service. A fair knowledge of the U.S. Army Regulations should be required for all grades." [32]

Now these may sound like fairly simple requirements, but appearance before these examining boards was not considered an easy matter by the officers and men of the Union Army or by the civilians also eligible to try for commissions in Negro regiments. The fact that roughly 40 per cent of all who attempted the examination were rejected testifies to the strictness of the boards. Before these boards, as before the divisional examining boards set up by Lorenzo Thomas's orders in the Mississippi Valley, sergeants and other enlisted ranks did well. Board records show that one private, George W. Baird, qualified for and was appointed to a colonelcy in the 32nd U.S. Colored Troops; three sergeants became lieutenant colonels, and so did three majors. While captains rose to colonelcies and majorities in good number, sergeants rose to captaincies. Between June, 1863, and August, 1865, of 480 persons recommended to the rank of captain by examining boards, 120, or 25 per cent, had been sergeants. Sergeants and privates each provided 28 per cent of the 650 first lieutenants recommended by the boards in the same period. Of the more than one thousand second lieutenants recommended in those two years, 26 per cent had been sergeants and 33 per cent had been privates. [33]

These statistics are not entirely accurate, for several reasons. For one thing, they do not take into account the officers appointed on the recommendation of the divisional examining boards operating in the field. They are taken from reports of the six boards sitting in Washington, Cincinnati, St. Louis, Davenport, New Orleans, and Richmond. These six boards appointed some twenty-three hundred officers, while Lorenzo Thomas lays claim to having been instrumental in appointing over twenty-eight hundred.[34] But on the basis of the special orders issued by Thomas announcing the organization of colored regiments in the valley, it is reasonable to assume that the enlisted men of the white volunteer armies performed as creditably before the divisional boards as they did in the Northern cities. A second reason for the inaccuracy of these figures and percentages is more difficult to overcome and defies reasonable estimation. Each of the six city boards examined a large number of civilians—or "citizens," as they were usually recorded. These "citizens" were in large part veterans of the earlier stages of the war, but the task of tracking down their service records to discover their former grades in the Union Army is simply beyond the scope of this book.

*   *   *

War Department policy was distinctly unfavorable to the appointment of Negro officers. In spite of this, about one hundred Negroes held commissions at various times during the Civil War, over three-fourths of these in the Department of the Gulf, where Butler mustered in the first three Louisiana regiments. Nathaniel Banks reported to Stanton early in 1863 that these regiments had white field and staff officers and Negro line officers, whom he was replacing "as vacancies occur, by white ones, being entirely satisfied that the appointment of colored officers is detrimental to the service." Banks maintained that Negro officers would convert "what, with judicious management and good officers, is capable of much usefulness into a source of constant embarrassment and annoyance." He argued that their appointment would demoralize both white and colored troops, but he went into no detail in support of his position.[35]

Lorenzo Thomas also objected to the selection of Negro officers, and he withdrew Daniel Ullmann's authority to organize further colored regiments because the latter had asked for colored officers after the Adjutant General had registered his "express disapprobation" of the proposal. Thomas held the view that the appointment of colored officers would be "highly injurious to the organizations already authorized with entirely white officers." [36]

Against such opposition in high places, it was extremely difficult for Negroes to win commissions. Stephen A. Swails, the New York first sergeant of Company F of the 54th Massachusetts, was commissioned as second lieutenant on March 11, 1864, by Governor John Andrew, the recommendation being made by his colonel and brigadier according to form. But Swails was not mustered as a lieutenant until January 17, 1865, although he meanwhile served as an officer. The rub was that to be mustered as an officer he had first to be discharged as a sergeant, and the War Department persistently disallowed his discharge. It took John Andrew ten months to persuade Stanton to the justice of the commission. Swails was promoted to first lieutenant on April 28, 1865. Apparently encouraged by his success in the Swails case, Governor Andrew commissioned as second lieutenants two more Negro sergeants on the same date: Frank M. Welch of Connecticut, Swails' successor as first sergeant of Company F, and Peter Vogelsang of Brooklyn, regimental quartermaster sergeant. All three officers were mustered to their new grades on June 3. Within three weeks, both Welch and Vogelsang were promoted to first lieutenancies. [37]

Eight sergeants of the 55th Massachusetts were commissioned as second lieutenants, but only three were actually mustered in as officers. Four were not mustered in "on account of the muster out of the regiment." C. L. Mitchell of Boston failed of muster "because of los[s] of foot at 'Honey Hill,' November 30, 1864," although he was not discharged from the service until October 20, 1865. W. H. Dupree, J. F. Shorter, and J. M. Trotter, all first sergeants from Ohio, were commissioned in May, March, and April, 1864, respectively, but were not mustered as officers until July 1, 1865. [38]

Unique in Civil War annals was an independent battery of light artillery raised at Leavenworth, Kansas: all three of its officers were colored. H. Ford Douglass of Chicago was its captain, W. D. Matthews its first lieutenant, and Patrick H. Minor its second lieutenant. Captain Douglass was one of the first Negro soldiers in the Union Army, having been accepted in Company G, 95th Illinois Volunteers, in 1862. He had even urged Frederick Douglass to follow his example, to "lay down the quill and take up the sword."

The Rochester editor declined to follow Ford Douglass's advice "until our own unbiased judgment and the action of the Government shall make it our duty and our privilege to become a soldier." What Frederick Douglass wanted was "a call from Washington requesting us to raise a regiment in the State of New York and furnishing the money to do it with..." But such a call never came. In the summer of 1863, while he was in Washington to see Lincoln and Stanton about Negro prisoners of war and the pay problem, Douglass got the impression that the secretary of war offered him a commission as "assistant adjutant to General Thomas, who was then recruiting and organizing troops in the Mississippi Valley." Back in Rochester, Douglass waited for his commission in vain; the government, he feared, "was still clinging to the idea that positions of honor in the service should be occupied by white men, and that it would not do to inaugurate just then the policy of perfect equality." He wrote the War Department for his commission and was simply directed to report to General Thomas. Douglass wrote again to Stanton that he would report to Thomas on receipt of his commission, "but it did not come," he recorded afterward, "and I did not go to the Mississippi Valley as I had fondly hoped." In his stead, his son, Frederick, helped recruit colored troops in that region.[39]

Another distinguished American Negro leader, Martin R. Delany, had more success with the War Department than Douglass: he was commissioned a major of infantry and sent to the Department of the South to aid Saxton in the recruitment and organization of the 104th Colored Troops. His commission was issued on February 26, 1865, and he was mustered in at that rank the next day. Delany had ambitious plans for the raising of what he called an "armée d'Afrique" but the war was over before the work had been well started. He was instrumental in the recruitment of the 104th and 105th U.S. Colored Troops, but had no opportunity for field service with either of those organizations. Shortly after the end of the war he was detailed for duty with the freedmen and continued on that duty with the rank of major until early 1868.[40]

In addition to these individual Negro officers who can be identified by name, there were also a few colored surgeons and a large number of colored chaplains. Alexander T. Augusta, surgeon of the 7th U.S. Colored Troops, was probably the best known of the Negro surgeons, since he took the initiative in demanding the right to ride on Washington street cars despite his color. His letter of protest at having been denied entrance to a car and forced to walk in the capital mud occasioned considerable debate in the Senate on February 10, 1864, when Charles Sumner introduced a resolution to redress the "outrage." The resolution carried by a vote of 30 to 10.[41]

According to the records of the examining boards, the fact of color did not always disqualify otherwise acceptable applicants for commissions. One James B. Schermerhorn, a civilian, was approved for appointment as a second lieutenant on July 22, 1864, and assigned to the 20th U.S. Colored Troops in spite of the notation after his name that "this man stated that he is of African descent." [42]

*   *   *

By the end of 1863, War Department efforts to organize Negro regiments were being hampered by a lack of able officers to train and command the colored recruits. Up to December 26, 1863, a total of 1,051 applicants had come before the examining boards, and of these 560 had been passed while 491, or almost 47 per cent, had been rejected. Of the rejects, 372 were officers, noncommissioned officers, and privates from the army. The War Department was concerned over the situation. Were the boards too exacting in their examinations? Should the examinations be somewhat less severe to let more candidates through? Or was there some other alternative? Out of these questions came the forerunner of the Officer Candidate School, a Free Military Academy to prepare candidates for the ordeal of meeting the board.

Toward the close of 1863, Major General Silas Casey, president of the Washington examining board, suggested to the Philadelphia Supervisory Committee for Recruiting Colored Regiments that a few weeks of concentrated study "of the principles and details laid down in the books on Tactics and Army Regulations" would enable many more candidates for commissions to pass the board. The Philadelphia committee, of which Thomas Webster was chairman, accepted the challenge, got together a faculty, published a prospectus, devised a thirty-day course of study, and on December 26 opened its Free Military School for Applicants for the Command of Colored Troops at 1210 Chestnut Street. John H. Taggart, formerly colonel of the 12th Pennsylvania Reserve, was its chief preceptor, and the faculty included Colonel Albert L. Magilton, a West Point graduate, and Captain Levi Fetters of the 175th Pennsylvania as professors of infantry tactics and army regulations. John P. Birch and A. E. Rogerson, both Masters of Arts, were professors of mathematics, geography, and history. The illustrious name of James Buchanan appeared also in the prospectus, as "messenger," followed by the parenthetic clarification "colored" to prevent confusion with the former president of the United States.[43]

Within two months the school was in full swing and doing an effective job. On March 7, General Casey wrote Chairman Webster to congratulate him on the success of the enterprise and to inform him that his Washington board had yet to reject one of the school's graduates. Even the secretary of war wrote Mr. Webster to give the school his "cordial approval." "Sufficient success has already attended the workings of the institution," Stanton wrote, "to afford the promise of much usefulness hereafter in sending into the service a class of instructed and efficient officers." This was more than polite rhetoric, of which Stanton usually stood in short supply. To March 31, 1864, the school had sent 94 students to Casey's board, and all but four had been recommended for commissions.[44]

With that kind of performance record, the Free Military School attracted wide attention in a short time. The first edition of its prospectus—8,000 copies—disappeared in less than three months, and a second edition became a necessity. Major Foster, chief of the Bureau for Colored Troops, began to receive requests for thirty days' furloughs to permit military personnel to attend the school. At first the bureau discouraged the idea, since "the demands upon the rank and file of the Army [made] it absolutely necessary that details for special service, or for special purposes, be restricted to the lowest possible limit." Foster "thought, and hoped," that the school would be "filled with worthy officers and soldiers . . . discharged or mustered out of service." Of the first 94 graduates examined by Casey's board, 39 were listed as "civilians" with the notation that "Many of these had previously been in the three months', nine months' and three years' service, from which they had been honorably discharged." [45]

But the pressure for special treatment of ambitious officers and men of the army continued. On March 23, Foster wrote Webster that the department would consider special applications in individual cases, with "the consent of local commanders and Department commanders." Despite this, Foster on the next day refused F. E. Spinner's request for such a furlough for a Private Barlow of the 157th New York Volunteers on the ground that "the interest of the service would not be promoted by granting furloughs for the purpose mentioned." [46] Five days later the Bureau for Colored Troops and the War Department finally yielded on the point, and General Orders, No. 125, announced that "Furloughs, not to exceed thirty days in each case, to the non-commissioned officers and privates of the Army who may desire to enter the free military school at Philadelphia, may be granted by the commanders of armies and departments, when the character, conduct, and capacity of the applicants are such as to warrant their immediate and superior commanders in recommending them for commissioned appointments in the regiments of colored troops." [47]

Three days before this order was published the new policy had gone into operation with the granting of thirty-day furloughs "for the purpose of visiting Philadelphia" to a corporal and a private of the 21st Connecticut. From the end of March on, the bureau was able to answer all requests for such furloughs by simply referring them to the general commanding the army or department concerned. [48]

In its first three months of operation the school received no less than 1,691 applications, of which 843 were approved. At the end of March half that number, 422, were or had been on the school rolls; the other half were either on their way to Philadelphia or waiting for enabling furloughs. Of the 422 entered in the school, 72 had withdrawn by the end of March, 56 had been dropped, 90 had been approved for commissions by Casey's board, 4 had been rejected by that body, and the remaining 200 were hard at their studies and drill. Candidates from Pennsylvania were most numerous in every category: applications had been approved for 167 Keystone State men; of these 29 had withdrawn, 26 had been dropped, 27 had been approved for commissions, 2 had been rejected, and 83 were still enrolled in the school. Altogether 17 states and the District of Columbia were represented, as well as a dozen foreign states and territories from Canada to the East Indies.[49]

Under the command of Colonel Taggart, the candidates were divided into four classes depending on their degree of military proficiency. First classmen studied Casey's *Tactics*, Volume III, Evolutions of the Brigade; second classmen studied the School of the Battalion, third classmen the School of the Company, and fourth classmen began at the bottom with the School of the Soldier. Classes were held six days of the week with classroom work from nine to ten-thirty each morning, drill from ten-thirty to noon, followed by dress parade; afternoon sessions included an hour and a half of classwork and an equal amount of drill time, followed by the practically inevitable dress parade. Evenings were devoted "chiefly to the study of mathematics" with the exception of advanced students of the first class, who met with Colonel Taggart for instruction in brigade evolutions. Candidates had Saturday evenings and Sundays free, but aside from that brief respite, their thirty days must have been full of activity in the classroom and on the drill ground. Text books were provided by the school, but candidates were expected to pay for the food. "Good board," the prospectus assured them, "can be had at from $3.50 to $5 per week."

To give its most promising upperclassmen actual experience with colored troops, the school made arrangements with Colonel Louis Wagner, commander of Camp William Penn near Philadelphia, "the largest camp existing for the organization and disciplining of Colored Troops," to permit students "to sojourn temporarily at the camp and exercise the functions of officers, in assisting to drill and train the Regiments that may be organizing there." [50]

Without ever becoming an actual part of the Union Army, the Free Military School of Philadelphia, grandfather of the Officer Candidate School, was geared into the army's machinery and played a large role in the preparation and selection of officers for colored troops.

*   *   *

In view of the difficulties and opposition Daniel Ullmann had encountered in finding officers for his brigade in the first months of 1863, it must have gratified all who were interested in the Negro soldier movement to see the great change that had taken place by the spring of 1864. At the end of April of that year, Major Foster had on his books the names of 513 candidates recommended for commissions by the various examining boards and awaiting appointments, that number in addition to the hundreds of officers already serving in colored regiments east and west. [51] Popular interest, in and out of the army, had been stirred by the opportunity existing in the officer requirements of the Negro regiments. The War Department policy of throwing open the way to commissions to all who could pass the boards had had its desired effect. Anti-Negro feeling in the Union armies seems to have been materially reduced by the process of making participation in the organization and use of Negro troops attractive to the white rank and file. The program was composed of just the right mixture of idealism and materialism: a man could have a part in a great military, educational, and humanitarian experiment and at the same time improve his own situation. Something of this mixed motivation is apparent in the letter a young lieutenant just out of West Point wrote to his parents in November of 1863. The "examination is rigid and none but good officers are allowed," John R. Winterbotham breathlessly told his family, "and they are much better than Volunteer officers, and the darkeys make splendid troops and I shall be devilish well satisfied if I can get a

Lieutenant Colonelcy, which I am going to aim for and try my best under the circumstances to obtain." [52]

Daniel Ullmann observed the change with the bitterness of the zealot who has seen his crusade become crowded with men less zealous than himself. "Among the minor scenes of the drama," he wrote after the war, "it was pleasing to see how rapidly the foulest-mouthed revilers became enthusiastic and patriotic admirers and laudators; how jaundiced eyes were cleared to see Colored Troops only in rainbow tints, when Commissions in the Field, Staff and Line began to flutter in the air, thickly as autumn leaves. Not a few Colonels, and some Generals, of Colored Troops," he charged, "were once their intensely disgusted haters. Such alas, is ever the history of some classes of humanity, when the assertion of a great principle is weak, especially when it takes the form of action, none but men of earnest conviction are willing to meet the opprobrium of its support, but when, by their determined energy, it battles its way to power, no one can count the number of those who were 'always its friends.' " [53]

There was more than one reason for seeking a commission in the colored troops. Aside from the more obvious advantages of being an officer—social distinction, better pay, better food and quarters—there was the realistic consideration of increased chance of survival. It has been calculated that the proportionate Civil War battle losses of enlisted men to officers was 16 to 1. It has been asserted that "throughout the army, the officers were far less apt to succumb to the fatalities of disease than were their men," the proportionate losses here being estimated as 82 to 1 among white troops and 214 to 1 in the colored troops. [54] Naturally an officer's chances were better than an enlisted man's, because in most situations the officer could eat better, enjoy better quarters, and bathe and change his clothing more often than the usually dirty and often lice-infested enlisted man.

But the officers' corps of the Union Army did not exactly constitute a refuge for the sybaritic. Company officers lived and died with their men, in the mud of Virginia and the sweltering heat of the Deep South. And for the officer with Negro troops there were other risks. There was the social stigma attached to serving with colored troops, in the Border states at least, although the situation was reversed in the Northeast. The Louisville *Journal* of November 30, 1863, discussing the report that Captain James W. Conine had been made colonel of the 5th U.S. "Negro Regiment," commented: "Conine formerly resided in Lexington, was a member and the drill officer of John Morgan's Rifle Company, and was at the time understood to be in full sympathy with the majority of the company who were secessionists. He suddenly left for Cincinnati, however, and was appointed a Lieutenant and Adjutant of the Second Kentucky." How explain this defection? "He is a Northern man by birth. We congratulate him upon the *proud* position to which he has been *elevated,* as the commander of a 'nigger' regiment." Not all colonels were automatically honored in Kentucky.

Far more compelling than any threat of social ostracism, however, was the widespread fear in the North and along the Border that officers of Negro troops would be denied the rights of prisoners of war if taken in battle. Jefferson Davis, the Confederate Congress, and various Confederate generals in the field had, of course, encouraged that fear. Kirby Smith ordered that Negro troops and their white officers be given no quarter; this in June of 1863 when Hunter and Phelps had already been outlaws in Confederate eyes for a full year. In popular imagination and in military reality, it took a special brand of courage to serve with Negro troops. Probably not many officers had the kind of brash bravery that Lieutenant Lemuel D. Dobbs of the 19th U.S. Colored Troops demonstrated when he was captured by the Confederates in the crater of Petersburg on July 30, 1864. Indignant when some other captured officers gave their captors the numbers of white regiments in the same action, he announced with more valor than discretion: "Lemuel D. Dobbs, Nineteenth Niggers, by ———." [55]

There was an uneasy feeling in the North over the possible fate of officers killed or wounded in battle, but the reaction to the burial of Robert Gould Shaw in the same ditch with his men was a healthy one. Shaw's death provided a tremendous stimulus to the crusading ardor of the North, just as his acceptance of the command of a Negro regiment had helped immeasurably to elevate the whole movement in public opinion. Still it is doubtful if many men sought commissions in the

colored troops to die gloriously and be buried with their men.
There were probably many men who, like William Henry
Harrison Ladd, a New York corporal, chose to remain without shoulder straps in the comparative safety of the white
volunteer regiments.[56]

In the spring of 1864 another colonel of a Negro regiment
was killed in battle under rather clouded circumstances, and
this must have given pause to candidates awaiting assignment
and applicants awaiting examination. Colonel C. W. Fribley of
the 8th U.S. Colored Troops was left dead on the field after the
battle of Olustee, Florida, in February. Following an exchange
of letters between Brigadier General Thomas Seymour, commanding Union forces at Jacksonville, and General William
Gardner, C.S.A., through which Seymour attempted to recover
Fribley's body or at least some of his personal belongings for
his widow, Gardner wrote, "I have the honor to forward through
you to the widow of the late Colonel Fribley, an ambrotype,
supposed to be the one referred to in the memorandum accompanying your communication" of February 25. "Traces have
also been discovered," Gardner continued, "of his watch, a
letter from his wife to himself, and his diary, and steps have
been taken to recover possession of them. If successful, the two
former articles will be forwarded." Then the Confederate
general made his personal position clear: "That I may not be
misunderstood, it is due to myself to state that no sympathy
with the fate of any officer commanding negro troops, but com-
passion for a widow in grief, has induced these efforts to
recover for her relics which she must naturally value." [57] There
were reasons enough to justify the words of Charles W. Eliot
on the Shaw Monument on Boston Common: "The white officers,
taking life and honor in their hands, cast in their lot with men
of a despised race unproved in war and risked death as in-
citers of servile insurrections if taken prisoners, besides en-
countering all the common perils of camp, march, and battle."

*   *   *

Whatever mixed emotions may have led men to seek commissions in the Negro forces of the Union, it is clear that the
selective system for officering those forces did produce leaders

substantially better qualified than those who led the white volunteer army in the first two years of the war. In drawing this conclusion, it is necessary to weigh the facts that candidates had to meet rather strict requirements and to pass an examination generally regarded as severe, that many officers appointed to company and field grade under the traditional system did not measure up to the standards of the examining boards, and that Negro organizations were uniformly praised for the cleanliness of their camps, the neatness of their persons, and their general excellence on parade. Even today these are considered among the criteria of well-disciplined, well-trained, and well-led troops.

It may be asked if their officers were really better than their counterparts in white regiments or whether their men only made them look better. If these Negro troops had been regular soldiers of long training and experience, the question would have more force. But in almost every case Negro regiments were formed from the rawest and least likely material available: from hordes of ignorant freedmen and fugitive slaves. They were mere human clay ready to be molded as their officers desired and were able. Negro soldiers were more willing to be led than whites, and they were much more dependent on their officers. Born and reared in slavery, the vast majority of them lacked the individualism and independence of will that characterized the white soldiers of the Union Army. For this reason especially, they required the best officers, men who could mold the raw clay into the forms of military efficiency, men who not only knew their duties but could drill and train and lead their men diligently and patiently.

Not all the seven thousand-odd officers who led the Negro troops of the Union were paragons of virtue and courage or even of intelligence. A colonel of a Louisiana regiment was dismissed from the service "for cowardice in front of the enemy, in the . . . engagement at Milliken's Bend, La." Another colonel had to be advised by Major Foster that maintaining his headquarters in a Philadelphia tavern, nine miles from the camp of his regiment, was "inconsistent with regulations and usage, and . . . highly prejudicial to the interests of the service." [58] There were other instances of conduct out of keeping with the respon-

sibilities of the work in hand, of drunkenness, absence from
duty without leave, and all the other occupational diseases of
the soldier. But the fact that these offenses were often punished
with speed and justice is a further indication of the high standards of the U.S. Colored Troops. Lorenzo Thomas, in September, 1863, dismissed a captain of the 3rd Mississippi Volunteers
of African Descent for "drunkenness and conduct unbecoming
an officer and a gentleman." Benjamin F. Butler, in the following March, handled another case of drunkenness in his own
distinctive style: he required the lieutenant involved to serve
for three months as a private soldier under the watchful eye of
the general himself to prove his character and self-control.[59]

That some instances of misconduct went unpunished is indicated in a letter from the colonel of a New York regiment.
He was aware that the chief difficulty in making colored troops
as effective as possible was the problem of officer selection. He
was inclined to think that "Although the Department strives to
have none but those of the highest qualifications, yet, even then,
rough and severe brutal officers are to be found in command of
them. I have had repeated instances of absolute brutality told
me by persons who have witnessed it." In his opinion, he wrote,
"some remedy is required more than is now furnished by the
Army Regulations; for the negro knows not where or to whom
to apply for redress." [60]

In sharp contrast to these brutal officers were Thomas Wentworth Higginson, James Beecher, Thomas J. Morgan, Robert
Gould Shaw, Norwood P. Hallowell, and Daniel Ullmann, who
recognized not only their military responsibilities to the men of
their regiments but went even further to help those men prepare
for the lives they would lead as free men after the war was
over. They set high standards of personal leadership and strove
night and day to look after their men, to train them as soldiers,
to teach them to read and write, and by example to show them
the best of the white civilization in which they were caught.

Aside from departures from the norm that must be expected
and guarded against in any large human endeavor, the selective
system that provided the bulk of the officers for colored regiments more than proved itself. Contemporary statements, in
newspapers and in letters and diaries written by Union officers,

rather uniformly praise the quality of the officers selected and make flattering comparisons of them with the commissioned ranks of the white volunteers. Horace Greeley thought that the system secured "a higher state of average character and efficiency ... than had been attained in the (too-often hasty and haphazard) organizations of our White regiments." Fred Shannon, a pioneer in exploring the administration and organization of the armed forces of the Union, was convinced that the officers for Negro troops "were more carefully chosen than the officers for any other branch of the volunteer service." [61] The Chicago *Tribune* of January 18, 1864, discussing the method of applying for examination for commissions in colored troops, warned that "None but first class officers are accepted, and the examination is just as rigid" whether given to civilian or soldier.

It is significant that seasoned officers expressed eagerness to command Negro troops after the experiment had been in successful operation for a year or more. West Pointer John R. Winterbotham of Chicago was unstinting in his praise of Negro troops and their officers until he discovered that General Silas Casey considered him too young (he was twenty) to become a lieutenant colonel of colored troops. Captain Alfred Lacey Hough of General George Thomas's staff wrote his wife that he was "really looking anxiously for the time" when he would command a Negro regiment of his own. Unfortunately, Hough was prevented from that pleasure and opportunity because Thomas would not release him.[62] Of even greater significance is the fact that plans for reorganization of the army after the war uniformly included some similar system of examination both for appointment to commissioned rank and for promotion in the commissioned grades.[63]

Without some system for the selection of proper officers on the basis of merit and ability, there can be little doubt that the use of Negro soldiers in the Union Army could not have been successful. Leadership of the highest quality was essential to turn the freedmen into disciplined soldiers who could stand up to the cavaliers of the Confederacy, their former masters, whether led by Douglas Cooper, John Bell Hood, Kirby Smith, Nathan Bedford Forrest, or Robert E. Lee. The system was

successful in providing the best leadership available. The system
was also successful in attracting wide support for Negro troops
by placing a premium on the participation of the best white
soldiers and junior officers in the great experiment. Finally, it
pointed the way to future military use in the United States of
a program of officer appointment and promotion based on personal proficiency and demonstrated ability. From a military
point of view, the selection of officers for Negro regiments during the Civil War made a clean break with the customs of the
past and showed the efficacy of selective officer procurement
from the ranks. From a social and humanitarian point of view,
the system provided leadership for a difficult experiment, and
the success of that experiment was in large measure a reflection
of the quality of that leadership.

XII. *"We looks like men a-marchin' on . . ."*

No doubt there were reasons why this particular war was an especially favorable test of the colored soldiers. They had more to fight for than the whites. Besides the flag and the Union, they had home and wife and child. They fought with ropes around their necks, and when orders were issued that the officers of colored troops should be put to death on capture, they took a grim satisfaction. It helped their esprit de corps immensely. With us, at least, there was to be no play-soldier.

—THOMAS WENTWORTH HIGGINSON

General Thomas F. Meagher and the officers of his Irish Brigade gave a banquet in New York's Irving Hall on January 13, 1864, for returned veterans of that dashing organization. The evening's program included speeches, testimonials, toasts, and songs, all in the finest Irish tradition. Among the songs sung that night was a new one, hailed as the work of that literary genius, Private Miles O'Reilly, and designed to fit the old Irish tune, "The Low-Backed Car." Aside from the brogue in which it was written and the air to which it was sung, the new song had little to do with Ireland or the Irish—little directly. It was titled "Sambo's Right to be Kilt," and it argued a fundamental question with Gaelic logic.

> Some tell us 'tis a burnin shame
> To make the naygers fight;
> An' that the thrade of bein' kilt
> Belongs but to the white;
> But as for me, upon my soul!

> So liberal are we here,
> I'll let Sambo be murthered instead of myself
> On every day in the year.
>> On every day in the year, boys,
>> And in every hour of the day;
>> The right to be kilt I'll divide wid him,
>> An' divil a word I'll say.

The second verse continued the argument in the same vein but moved from the general to the particular.

> In battle's wild commotion
> I shouldn't at all object
> If Sambo's body should stop a ball
> That was comin' for me direct;
> And the prod of a Southern bagnet,
> So ginerous are we here,
> I'll resign, and let Sambo take it
> On every day in the year.
>> On every day in the year, boys,
>> And wid none o' your nasty pride,
>> All my right in a Southern bagnet prod
>> Wid Sambo I'll divide!

With great good nature and irresistible logic, Private O'Reilly's song moved on to its majestic close.

> The men who object to Sambo
> Should take his place and fight;
> And it's betther to have a nayger's hue
> Than a liver that's wake an' white.
> Though Sambo's black as the ace of spades,
> His finger a thrigger can pull,
> And his eye runs sthraight on the barrel-sights
> From undher its thatch of wool.
>> So hear me all, boys darlin',
>> Don't think I'm tippin' you chaff,
>> The right to be kilt we'll divide wid him,
>> And give him the largest half! [1]

The songs seems to have become popular almost immediately, especially with the Irish, many of whom had been determined in their resistance to recognition of the Negro's right to fight.

O'Reilly's verses put the argument into language that anyone could understand; they emphasized the practical value of the Negro soldier in fundamental terms. Of course there was no Private Miles O'Reilly—that was the pen name of Charles G. Halpine, "talented literary gentleman" of New York who for a time served on the staff of Major General David Hunter in the Department of the South. While Hunter worked to make soldiers of Negroes, Halpine worked to win their acceptance as fighting men. "Sambo's Right to be Kilt" helped to break down popular opposition to colored soldiers. The behavior of those soldiers did the rest.

*   *   *

The accomplishments of the first half of 1863 were numerous and of outstanding importance. The recruitment of Negro soldiers had been systematized under War Department control; officer procurement had been regularized; centers had been established in the North for the reception and training of Negro recruits; and in Washington the Bureau for Colored Troops had been established to control the whole widespread machinery. The main outlines of the colored troops program had emerged. While there were to be departures from these outlines in some details, organizational and procedural decisions made during the first half of 1863 were to serve as guideposts for the raising of Negro regiments for the rest of the war.

When Lorenzo Thomas went into the Mississippi Valley in the spring of 1863, his plan of organization had envisaged Negro regiments with white officers, white first sergeants, and white noncommissioned staff officers, such as regimental sergeants major and quartermaster sergeants. Other sergeants and corporals below first sergeant were to be "selected and appointed from the best" of the enlisted men "in the usual mode of appointing noncommissioned officers." [2] But among the hordes of fugitive slaves and freedmen along the Mississippi from which Thomas drew the enlisted men of his regiments there was an almost complete lack of Negroes who could read and write and who had any leadership ability. The vast majority had been slaves and the sons of slaves. It took time for such men to accustom themselves to positions requiring the giving of orders; they had done little but take orders all their lives. This presented a problem in the selection of noncommissioned officers. The adjutant general readily found a solution: he requested the secretary of war to permit colored men drafted in the Western states to be sent to the Department of the Gulf in order that noncommissioned officers might be appointed from the most intelligent of these to the regiments of former slaves.[3]

An adaptation of this plan was followed in Negro regiments raised from the slaves of Maryland and Virginia. The Bureau for Colored Troops instructed General William Birney, commanding at Camp Stanton, Bryantown, Maryland, that the War Department intended "to have recruited from among the more intelligent colored men of the North" sufficient numbers to fill Birney's regiments to maximum strength, in order to make sergeants and corporals of these Northern Negroes more accustomed to the exercise of initiative and less dependent on directions from superiors than slaves. Many Negro regiments in the Southwest had white noncoms in addition to white first sergeants, however, the white soldiers having enlisted in colored organizations with the intention of winning stripes and better pay by the transfer.[4]

The Thomas system of recruiting was relatively simple. After explaining the government policy to the officers and men of the Union armies in the Mississippi Valley, he asked each division commander to organize at least two Negro regiments. Led on by the tempting bait of promotions and commissions, junior officers and enlisted men presented themselves to divisional examining boards and, as soon as they had been recommended for appointment, went to work recruiting their men. As a result of this activity, it is impossible to state with any accuracy how many Negro regiments were filled by voluntary enlistment and how many by simple impressment.

Thomas himself seems to have been a trifle callous on the matter. General John M. Schofield, commanding at St. Louis, was planning an expedition into Arkansas in the summer of 1863, and Thomas requested him to "collect as many blacks— men, women, and children—as possible." The men, Thomas wrote, "you can organize into regiments, and I will commission such officers for them as you may designate." The adjutant general seems to have been unconcerned with how the men were secured as long as the regiments were manned. Negroes were to be "collected" and the able-bodied organized as soldiers. Shades of the "trade" on the Gold Coast in the eighteenth century! Thomas was, however, concerned about the quality of officers appointed to lead them. "You will of course," he warned Schofield, "be careful to give me only such officers whose hearts are in the work." [5]

By whatever means the Negroes were recruited, the raising of colored regiments went ahead encouragingly in the summer of 1863. The Cincinnati *Daily Commercial* of July 25 reported: "The War Department is pushing the organization of colored troops vigorously. The successes of our forces in the West"— the news of the fall of Vicksburg and Port Hudson and the opening of the Mississippi was still on everyone's lips—"have given a new impetus to enlistment among the blacks, and by autumn it is estimated that 100,000 negroes will be in arms in the Valley of the Mississippi."

In the Ohio Valley the work did not move so speedily. The *Daily Commercial* of July 30 reported that progress was slow in the Buckeye State. "The first colored regiment," the paper noted, "is not yet complete. There are, we believe, three hundred and fifty colored men in Camp Delaware, sworn into service. It is desired to increase this number to at least six hundred and fifty, as a minimum regiment, to be filled up in the South with contrabands. They cannot take the field till this number has been attained." The *Commercial* happily pointed out that "The cost of recruiting this regiment so far, has been much less per man than that of any regiment which has left the state." It was not hard to explain the slowness of Negro recruiting in the North. Among the "many influences to deter colored men from entering the service," the *Commercial* listed the absence of a bounty, the draft on the colored population to provide men for gunboat and transport duty, the demands of the army for servants, teamsters and the like, and the lack of provision for the families of those who joined. That black men would fight there was no doubt in Cincinnati, at least not in the editorial

office of the *Commercial*. "They do fight and fight bravely," the
paper asserted; "they are obedient, submit to the most rigid
discipline, and acquire the knowledge essential to a good soldier with an aptitude that has surprised the most sanguine."

However reluctant Ohio Negroes may have been to enter the
service, there was ready evidence that a good number of Negroes
from other parts of the country were rallying to the colors. The
National Intelligencer of August 6, 1863, gave a lengthy list of
colored regiments organized or organizing. Actually organized
and equipped at the end of July were fourteen infantry regiments and a battery of artillery:

Two Massachusetts regiments,	in the field
Two South Carolina regiments,	" " "
One North Carolina regiment,	" " "
One Philadelphia regiment,	ready for service
One Washington regiment,	" " "
One Kansas regiment,	in the field
Two New Orleans regiments,	" " "
Four Mississippi and Tennessee regiments,	" " "
One Rhode Island artillery company,	" " "

In the course of organization, according to the *Intelligencer*,
were twenty-four additional regiments:

One Philadelphia regiment, nearly half full
One Baltimore regiment
One Virginia (Fortress Monroe) regiment
One North Carolina (Newbern) regiment
Two South Carolina regiments
One Ohio (Camp Delaware) regiment
One New Orleans regiment
Sixteen Mississippi and Tennessee regiments

Incomplete though these figures are—Banks' and Ullmann's
regiments are rather slighted—they serve to give an impression
of the way the movement had spread and was being pushed,
from the North to the Deep South, from tidewater to the Great
Valley. Precisely one year earlier, on August 6, 1862, the
National Intelligencer had carried the news of the president's
refusal to authorize the arming of Negro soldiers.

*   *   *

The story of the varied experiences of George L. Stearns, the recruiting agent originally appointed by Governor John Andrew to collect men for the 54th and 55th Massachusetts, sheds light on the methods used and the difficulties of the work. Stearns had set up a widespread recruiting organization made up of salaried agents in most of the larger Northern cities and of sub-agents paid a per capita fee for the men they brought into the service. Stearns offered the services of this organization to the War Department, and on June 13, 1863, he went to work as recruiting commissioner for colored troops with the rank of major. He began in Philadelphia and in four weeks had raised eight hundred men for the Third U.S. Colored Troops. Dissatisfied with War Department interference with his personally organized system and impatient with red tape, Stearns "took measures to raise a fund by subscription" so that he might continue to operate in his own way. The operation of the draft in July, 1863, interfered with his recruiting, he reported, since colored men were more interested in becoming paid substitutes than in enlisting without a bounty. So widely accepted was the practice of hiring substitutes that even Lincoln's secretary, John G. Nicolay, furnished a replacement when he was drafted on a visit to Democratic New York in 1864. Nicolay's substitute was a Negro from North Carolina, Hiram Child, who later died in battle.[6]

Major Stearns urged that the government pay the authorized recruiting fee of $2 per capita to "colored men of ability [to] encourage them to devote themselves to the work," on the ground that "their advocacy of the service [would] create a general impression on the race favorable to the service." These Negro recruiting agents, Stearns suggested, would "venture within the enemy lines, prompted by hatred of slavery and the desire to earn money." He thought it reasonable to expect them "soon to demoralize the slave population everywhere within the enemy's lines."

The Boston recruiter made a trip to Maryland and Virginia to assist General William Birney, son of James Birney, the noted abolitionist, in raising regiments on the Eastern Shore and to discuss recruiting with General J. G. Foster at Fortress Monroe. In the course of this trip Stearns discovered that a Washington order for the impressment of all able-bodied Negroes at Fortress

Monroe as laborers in the Quartermaster Department had driven many to flight. If such impressment could be ended, Stearns thought, large numbers of Negroes would come out of hiding and might be obtained for the army as soldiers, especially if the regular recruiting fee were paid them.[7] He concluded that eight or ten regiments might be raised in Maryland and "as many more in General Foster's department."

Stearns was insistent on two points: selected recruiting officers and an end to impressment. Since army officers were "so fully occupied with their duties that they [had] not sufficient time to attend to this work," he recommended that selected officers be detailed to recruiting service and be furnished adequate funds to pay all expenses including the $2 fee for the recruits. Emphatically he urged that "the impressment of colored men be discontinued everywhere. The ablest of them run to the woods, imparting their fears to the slaves, thus keeping them out of our lines, and we get only those who are too ignorant or indolent to take care of themselves. I feel sure," he told Stanton, "we can get more men by fair enlistment, or by hiring them at wages as laborers, in three months than we can by combining it with impressment." He had reliable information that some three hundred Negroes in the Department of the South had been frightened away from the Union lines by impressment orders previous to the arrival of General Gillmore to replace Hunter in early June. Those Negroes, Stearns maintained, were hidden in the woods, "visiting the plantations by night and returning to their hiding places before daylight." For all the good he had been able to initiate, Hunter's extremist practices were still hurting the cause.

On the conclusion of his Maryland-Virginia trip, Stearns was ordered to report to General Rosecrans at Nashville to take charge of recruiting colored troops in the Department of the Cumberland.[8]

There was a world of difference between the methods of the two outstanding recruiters of Negro soldiers for the Union. General Lorenzo Thomas was blunt, unsubtle, direct in the old army manner. He announced a policy and expected the army to comply. If Negro soldiers were required, then he would see to it that Negro soldiers were provided as quickly as possible and with no sentimental nonsense about the feelings of the

Negroes involved. Major Stearns, on the other hand, was a rare combination of shrewd Boston business man and radical, a man who knew the power of money, how to get it and how to make it work for him and for his causes. At the same time he had a practical concern for the personal feelings of the people with whom he was working; his deepest instincts seem to have been humanitarian.

"Our citizens yesterday saw, for the first time, a regiment of colored troops marching through the streets of Nashville." So the Nashville *Daily Press* of October 3, 1863, announced the arrival of the new era. "The regiment is the one, we understand, recently recruited in this city by Major Starnes [Stearns]. These soldiers were 'armed and equipped as the law directs,' and attracted more attention than any body of troops that ever kept time to martial music in Nashville. They were officered by white men, but the novelty of armed negro troops elicited many remarks about the policy of the Administration in raising them—both *pro and con*." Five more colored regiments were to follow this first one before Major Stearns left the scene of his Tennessee labors. By the end of the war the Volunteer State would be credited with 20,000 Negro troops.

In Tennessee, Stearns found wide-scale impressment of Negroes and a completely chaotic recruiting situation. Notwithstanding the odds against him, he went to work with a will and was successful in bringing some semblance of order and organization to the raising of colored troops in middle Tennessee. His insistence on bounties for Negro recruits made him unpopular with the War Department, and his continued objections to impressment and the almost exclusive use of Negro soldiers for fatigue duty made him unpopular with army officers in the field. Finally, toward the end of 1863, he resigned from the service, but not before he had done a great deal to establish the work on a solid basis. He was able to swing public opinion from opposition to encouragement of the colored troops program, and he found time and energy to do much more besides. He established a camp for contrabands near Nashville and organized a school for colored girls in the city. At his encouragement, chaplains of Negro regiments made "the instruction of the regiment a part and the principal part of their duty." Among the teachers brought

down from the North after Stearns had begun Negro education
in Tennessee was Mrs. Charles Fribley, widow of the late colonel
of the 8th U.S. Colored Troops.[9]

Stearns' recruiting methods in the Department of the Cumberland were built around his earlier system which had worked so
successfully in filling the 54th and 55th Massachusetts. His paid
agents held public meetings at various points throughout the
department and by personal appeals and the wise use of colored
assistants they soon had a steady stream of recruits flowing
toward Nashville. Then, as organizations were begun, Stearns
ordered "frequent scouts" or recruiting expeditions by these
nascent regiments. "Upon these scouts all who desired, of the
negroes found on the way, were recruited; none were pressed." [10]

When Stearns first began his work in Tennessee, Captain R. D.
Mussey, 19th U.S. Infantry, was detailed as mustering officer
for colored troops with directions to cooperate with the major.
On Stearns' resignation, Mussey was appointed commissioner in
his place by Lorenzo Thomas.[11] The choice was excellent. Captain Mussey continued the work as he had learned it under
Stearns' direction, with healthy results for the whole service, and
he became colonel of the 100th U.S. Colored Troops, "composed
of the first colored men openly recruited in Kentucky." Evidence
of the good influence of Stearns on Mussey is obvious throughout
the comprehensive report the colonel made of his operations in
October of 1864. "I regard and have regarded," Mussey wrote,
"the organization of colored troops as a very important social,
humanitarian, as well as military measure, and as a providential
means of fitting the race freed by this war for their liberty."
Nor was Mussey content merely with holding that high view himself. "I have endeavored," he concluded his report, "to impress
this view upon the officers appointed to these organizations, and
upon the men themselves, showing them that their recognition as
men would follow the soldier, and I have now, after a year's
labor in this department, more hope and more faith than ever
in the capacity of the negro to make a good soldier and a good
citizen." [12]

While Stearns, and after him Mussey, labored in Tennessee,
Lorenzo Thomas was the supreme War Department authority in
the Mississippi Valley for the recruitment and organization of

colored troops. In the Northern states, the Bureau for Colored Troops alone controlled or delegated authority to control similar operations there. War Department authority to raise Negro regiments was issued through the bureau to state governors and to public and private organizations. As those governors and organizations went ahead with the work, they kept in close touch with the bureau, making frequent reports and relying on the bureau to settle all questions of policy. The bureau appointed officers to these regiments as they were needed, thus ensuring the selection only of officers who had passed the examining boards established by General Order 143.

Once a regiment was raised to minimum organizational strength, the bureau ordered it to report to the commanding general of the department to which it was assigned, and it then passed from bureau control to the direct control of the army in the field. General Order 143 had directed that colored regiments be "numbered ad seriatim, in order in which they are raised" and designated U.S. Colored Troops. Accordingly, the Massachusetts and Rhode Island regiments were the last raised in the North bearing state designations, with the exception of one Connecticut and one Michigan infantry regiment and the Fifth Massachusetts Cavalry of which Charles Francis Adams, Jr., finally became colonel. While Northern states thereby lost some degree of recognition for their contribution to the war effort, they did get credit on their draft quotas for Negro recruits raised, and state pride was somewhat soothed by the care the Bureau for Colored Troops took to see that state agencies had an opportunity to select the officers for the regiments they raised from lists of available personnel furnished by the bureau. State governors were invited to recommend individuals, civilians as well as soldiers, for examination by the several boards, and from the lists of candidates passed by these boards the final selection of officers was made.[13] While the operation of the Bureau for Colored Troops seems to have been remarkably independent of political pressure, the bureau showed equally remarkable patience in catering to state and local pride and crotchets. The voluminous correspondence between Major Foster and Governor Buckingham of Connecticut during the organization of the 29th Connecticut Infantry (colored) provides the best example of this patience and spirit of accommodation on the part of the bureau.[14]

Through the centralized control and direction of the bureau a fair degree of uniformity in recruitment and organization was achieved. It was in the employment of Negro regiments that all uniformity disappeared.

*   *   *

Departmental and divisional commanders followed largely the dictates of tactical situation and personal prejudice in the use they made of Negro troops. The result was that in some departments colored troops were permitted to do the work of soldiers, meeting the enemy in the field shoulder to shoulder with white Union regiments, while in other departments Negroes were detailed to whatever heavy fatigue duty, railroad or fortification construction was required. It may be argued, as indeed it was during the Civil War, that Negroes were better suited to hard physical labor in the South than their Northern white comrades-in-arms, and that their incorporation into the military service had been primarily intended to free white troops from garrison and fatigue duty for the active pursuit of Confederate forces. Certainly there were many in the Union government, from the president on down, who had originally held that view. Commenting on the employment of Negro troops, the *Annual Cyclopaedia* for 1863 observed: "As may be inferred from the language of the President's proclamation, it was at first expected that the colored soldiers would be employed almost exclusively in post and garrison duty. Emergencies, however, soon occurred in which it was found necessary to bring them into the field, and even when but partially disciplined they acquitted themselves so well as to elicit the commendations of generals in command, and to cause their being placed in several instances in the lead in assaulting columns."

The *Annual Cyclopaedia* referred specifically to the fighting around Port Hudson and Milliken's Bend in May and June, to Fort Wagner and to the defense of Helena, Arkansas, in July. It spoke in glowing terms of Negro soldiers' willingness to follow their officers "even in charges or assaults of great peril, far more readily than white soldiers," but expressed the opinion, common at that time and since, that "when deprived of their commanders

[they] would not in general fight independently so well as those troops who have had more education." [15]

Despite such generalizations in praise of the fighting qualities of Negro troops, army commanders were slow to be convinced, and the contribution of these troops to the war effort varied from command to command. In the trans-Mississippi West, where their recruitment and organization had begun earliest and their commanding officers had not hesitated to use them, Negro soldiers were offered frequent opportunities to show their ability. During the month of May, 1863, troops of the 1st Kansas Colored Volunteers and the 2nd Arkansas Colored Volunteers participated to the satisfaction of their commanders in small engagements at Center Creek, Missouri, and near Island No. 65 in the Mississippi, respectively. [16] In early July the 1st Kansas Colored played a prominent role at Cabin Creek, Indian Territory, when a mixed force of Texans and Indians were driven from strong positions by assaulting infantry after strong artillery preparation. [17] One excellent reason for the wide use of Negro soldiers in the District of the Frontier is explicit in the comment of the Leavenworth *Daily Conservative* of July 17, 1863, in discussing the fight at Cabin Creek: *"All reports from the lower country are to the effect that we have to rely mainly upon colored soldiers."* Another excellent reason was the fact that General James G. Blunt, who commanded the District of the Frontier, had earlier worked with Jim Lane in organizing the 1st Kansas Colored, and he was not at all hesitant about using Negroes in battle. His most sanguine hopes were realized on July 17, 1863, at Elk Creek, or Honey Springs. After a forced march, Blunt's mixed force of whites, Indians, and colored troops struck a superior force of Texans and Indians at daybreak. After a twenty-minute exchange of fire at fifty yards' range the Confederates broke and ran. [18]

In October of 1863 the 2nd Kansas Colored found opportunity to show their mettle when the Missouri guerrilla leader, Quantrill, surprised the small garrison at Baxter Springs while the Union soldiers were eating. The garrison, consisting of two companies of Wisconsin cavalry and one company of Negroes, had to break through the enemy lines to get their weapons, but after an hour's hard fighting the camp was cleared of Confederates. In his report of the engagement, Lieutenant James B.

Pond of the 3rd Wisconsin Cavalry, commanding the post, wrote:
". . . the darkies fought like devils. Thirteen of them were
wounded the first round, and not one but fought the thing
through." [19] The fact that their opponents were Quantrill's notorious raiders probably spurred the Negro troops to a supreme
effort. There could have been little doubt in their minds as to
their fate in case of defeat.

In the Department of the Tennessee and in the Department of
the South, Negro soldiers were widely used for fatigue purposes
during the summer and fall of 1863. For example, so great were
the demands for fatigue details on his command, the 12th U.S.
Colored Troops (Major Stearns' first Tennessee regiment), that
Colonel Charles R. Thompson had no time to drill and instruct
his men. He asked General James A. Garfield that the regiment
"be stationed at some post where they can all be together"
and have some opportunity to learn to function as a regiment.
Thompson maintained that "the regiment and the reputation of
the officers are not safe while the command is kept in the field."
Ten days earlier, on September 4, General Rosecrans had directed that "Colonel Thompson's regiment . . . must be left together as much as possible," and that "it never be divided so
that less than a third of the regiment shall be by itself until he
has had sufficient time to thoroughly organize." [20] In spite of this
order, the returns for the Army of the Cumberland on September
20 showed the 12th (then designated the 1st Middle Tennessee)
at Elk River Bridge with 14 officers and 301 enlisted men, while
the regimental aggregate strength, present and absent, was shown
as 949.[21] This indicates that slightly more than two-thirds of the
regiment were still on duty away from the regimental camp.

Lieutenant Colonel Theodore Trauernicht, commanding the
13th U.S. Colored Troops (then the 2nd Middle Tennessee Colored Infantry), had a somewhat similar complaint. He was
encamped in mid-October some thirty miles from Nashville
with his men constantly on picket or fatigue duty, guarding a
section of railroad, entrenching their positions, and foraging
in the neighborhood. Trauernicht's regiment was at about half
strength, and his camp was on the perimeter of a region under
federal control. His tactical position was most insecure. "The
necessity for completing the organization of the regiment im-

mediately is very plain," Trauernicht wrote Major Stearns. "If in our present state we can do no good service here, we might as well have remained in camp in Nashville, and in my opinion much better, as we are now simply on outpost, constantly in danger, with no chance to improve our drill and discipline." [22] There can be no doubt that there was plenty of work for colored soldiers in Middle Tennessee and elsewhere, but the disadvantages and dangers of sending an undermanned regiment out to an advanced and isolated position without drill or training in the duties of soldiers are obvious. Nevertheless, Trauernicht's experience seems to have been more typical than unusual.

When Major Stearns ordered Thomas J. Morgan to Gallatin, Tennessee, to organize the 14th U.S. Colored Troops in November, 1863, Morgan began with some two hundred Negroes who, "raw and untutored as they were, did guard and picket duty, went foraging, guarded wagon trains, scouted after guerrillas, and so learned to soldier by soldiering." Despite these practical difficulties, Morgan had his regimental organization completed in two months; all its noncommissioned officers, he proudly recalled, were colored, from sergeant major to corporal. But even before the regiment was full, General George H. Thomas ordered six of its companies to duty at Bridgeport, Alabama, where they were kept "very busily at work with but little opportunity for drill." As the result of his "earnest efforts to get the regiment united and relieved from so much labor, in order that they might be prepared for efficient field service as soldiers," Colonel Morgan secured an order from General Thomas uniting the organization at Chattanooga. There the regiment became something of a showpiece, or, as Colonel Morgan put it, "an object lesson to the army" with precise retreat parades which "helped to revolutionize public opinion on the subject of colored soldiers." But even though General Thomas himself congratulated the 14th's colonel on its excellent drill, heavy demands for work details weakened the regiment and made Morgan almost despair of ever "being ordered to the field." [23]

Even Adjutant General Thomas seems to have been rather cavalier with some of the raw Negro troops he raised in the Mississippi Valley. His special orders announcing the organization of the 9th Regiment Louisiana Volunteers of African

Descent (later designated the 63rd U.S. Colored Troops) directed that "As fast as Companies are organized they will be detailed as Guards to the respective Contraband Camps in the Department of the Tennessee, and for the protection of such negroes as may be employed by proper authority on plantations, woodyards, &c within our lines." [24] What opportunity the regimental officers were able to discover for making the companies into anything like a military organization remains a mystery. But, at least, the men of this particular regiment were to be given something other than uninterrupted fatigue duty.

There were two brigades of Negro regiments in the Department of the South in August of 1863. Colonel James Montgomery commanded the 4th Brigade of General Terry's division on Morris Island; it consisted of his own 2nd South Carolina (later designated the 34th U.S. Colored Troops), the 54th Massachusetts, and the 3rd U.S. Colored Troops. Brigadier General Edward A. Wild commanded an "African Brigade" on Folly Island which included the 55th Massachusetts, the 1st and 2nd North Carolina Colored Volunteers (later designated the 35th and 36th U.S. Colored Troops), and one company of the 3rd North Carolina. This brigade had been transferred from the Department of Virginia and North Carolina to Folly Island early in August.[25]

Since the tragic failure of the assault against Fort Wagner on July 18, the Union Army of the South had settled down to the slow and galling work of siege operations and the digging of parallels or entrenchments approaching the Confederate positions. Naturally it was the Negro troops who came in for their share of labor in the trenches. An order dated August 31 relieved the 3rd U.S. Colored Troops "from duty in the trenches, under the direction of Major T. B. Brooks," and directed that the regiment would "hereafter be subject to such details as the commanding officer of the brigade may direct." The same order sent the battle-scarred 54th Massachusetts into the trenches. "The whole of the available force of the regiment," the order required, "will be divided into four equal reliefs, which will succeed each other at intervals of eight hours each ... No other details will be made from this regiment until further orders." [26]

The Major Brooks referred to was assistant engineer in charge of the work of digging counterentrenchments and parallels working toward the Confederate fortifications. Fortunately he kept a journal, and under the date of August 31 he wrote: "The Third U.S. Colored Troops, who have been on fatigue duty in the advanced trenches since the 20th instant, were relieved today by the Fifty-fourth Massachusetts Volunteers (Colored), it being desirable to have older troops for the important and hazardous duty required in the advance at this period. Infantry officers commanding fatigue details inform me that it requires much more effort to make the men work than fight under the same fire." [27]

Apparently the assistant engineer had an inquiring mind. At any rate, he decided that the operations he was directing afforded an opportunity for close examination of the Negro soldier in action. Accordingly, he drew up a circular asking engineering officers working under him and over both white and colored troops to answer a few questions. It was, in short, a questionnaire. Major Brooks stated his reasons clearly: "As the important experiment which will test the fitness of the American negro for the duties of a soldier is now being tried, it is desirable that facts bearing on the question be carefully observed and recorded." In his opinion, in no military operation of the war had colored troops "done so large a proportion, and so important and hazardous fatigue duty as in the siege operations" on Morris Island. He asked the officers to give "impartial and carefully prepared" answers to these questions:

I. Courage, as indicated by their behavior under fire.
II. Skill and appreciation of their duties, referring to the quality of work performed.
III. Industry and perseverance, with reference to the quantity of work performed.
IV. If a certain work were to be accomplished in the least possible time, *i.e.*, when enthusiasm and direct personal interest are necessary to attain the end, would whites or blacks answer best?
V. What is the difference, considering the above points, between colored troops recruited from the Free States and those from the Slave States?

The major received six replies to his questionnaire, which he summarized as follows:

I. ... the black is more timorous than the white, but in a corresponding degree more docile and obedient, hence more completely under the control of his commander, and much more influenced by his example.

II. ... the black is less skillful than the white soldier, but still enough so for most kinds of siege work.

III. ... the black will do a greater amount of work than the white soldier, because he labors more constantly.

IV. The whites are decidedly superior in enthusiasm. The blacks cannot be easily hurried in their work, no matter what the emergency.

V. ... colored troops recruited from Free States are superior to those recruited from Slave States. [28]

Brooks pointed out that the average percentage of sick among the colored troops during siege operations was 13.9, "while that of the white infantry was 20.1 per cent." Negroes performed fifty-six hours of fatigue duty to forty-one by the whites, but at the same time the whites did all the grand-guard duty, which was considered, Brooks recorded, "more wearing than fatigue." [29]

A Captain Joseph Walker, an amateur sociologist of the New York Volunteer Engineers, submitted an additional statement of his own on the performance of Negro troops. "To me," he wrote, "they compare favorably with the whites; they are easily handled, true and obedient; there is less viciousness among them; they are patient; they have great constancy. The character of the white ... runs to extremes; one has bull-dog courage, another is a pitiful cur; one is excessively vicious, another pure and noble. The phases of the character of the white touches the stars and descends to the lowest depths. The black character occupies the inner circle. Their status is mediocrity, and this uniformity and mediocrity, for military fatigue duty, I think answers best." [30]

In his report to General Gillmore, commanding the Department of the South, Major Brooks declared that the 4th New Hampshire Volunteers, a white regiment, had done "the most and the best work." Next in order of accomplishment he rated the 54th Massachusetts and the 3rd U.S. Colored Troops.[31]

Excessive fatigue duty for colored troops caused concern to others besides those troops and their commanders. Toward the end of 1863, Amos Lawrence and thirty-four other prominent Bostonians raised the question in a petition directed to Secretary Stanton. This petition recommended that the unemployed of the Southern states be drawn upon as far as possible to fill up the ranks of the Union armies in order that "the well-paid and productive classes of the loyal States" might be spared the burden— and, presumably, continue to man the machinery of New England's textile mills. The petitioners also asked War Department authority to raise sums of money by subscription to be used as bounties in the "disaffected States" and to send state agents into the South to recruit against Northern draft quotas. Finally, the gentlemen strongly objected to the impressment of either white or colored soldiers except in emergencies and advocated "that stringent orders shall be issued that the black troops shall be treated as soldiers, and only called upon for their share of the fatigue and police work of the whole Army." [32]

General Lorenzo Thomas also became aware of the inequity in the allotment of fatigue details, and in early December he wrote General Frederick Steele: "I hope that you will require no more labor from the Colored Troops than from the other soldiers under your command." [33] The problem remained unsolved, but it was at least recognized as a problem. There was a large body of opinion in the North in favor of using the Negro soldier as a soldier instead of holding him exclusively to labor. That much the Negro soldier had been able to achieve by his courage and sacrifice in action against the enemies of the Union.

*   *   *

By the end of October, 1863, Major Charles W. Foster, chief of the Bureau for Colored Troops, was able to report the existence of 58 regiments of Negro troops in the Union Army with a total strength, including officers, of 37,482. These organizations had been raised in fifteen different states and the District of Columbia: nine Union states including Maryland and Tennessee, and six Southern states belonging to the Confederacy but partially or wholly occupied by Union forces. Louisiana led all the rest with twenty-one regiments raised through the combined, if not coordinated, efforts of Ben Butler, Nathaniel Banks, Daniel Ullmann, and Lorenzo Thomas. Tennessee was second with five regiments, South Carolina third with four. Connecticut, Indiana, Illinois, Kentucky, and New York had not yet contributed to the effort, although 1864 was to see Negro regiments from these states added to the number already in the field. The machinery of the Provost Marshal General's Department was geared into the recruitment of colored troops by a series of orders instructing Colonel J. B. Fry, the provost marshal general, to have his officers in various states "enlist into the service of the United States for three years or during the war all suitable colored men who may offer themselves for enlistment." [34]

As 1863 drew to a close the procedure and machinery for recruiting colored troops was thoroughly developed. In Massachusetts colored recruits and drafted men went to Readville, the camp at which the 54th and 55th had trained. Connecticut recruits were assembled and organized at New Haven. New York's Negro regiments were assembled at Riker's and Hart's islands in the East River. Delaware, New Jersey, and Pennsylvania recruits were collected and organized at Camp William Penn, outside Philadelphia. Other major training centers for Negro troops were Camp Stanton at Bryantown, Maryland; Camp Delaware, Ohio; and Benton Barracks, Missouri, which received and organized all colored recruits from Iowa, Minnesota, and Missouri. [35] In West Florida, in the fall of 1863, Brigadier General Alexander Asboth undertook the work of organizing colored troops under authority from Adjutant General Thomas, and in December Brigadier General Augustus Chetlain replaced Major Stearns in Tennessee and Western Kentucky. [36]

The Nashville *Daily Times and True Union* of February 27, 1864, gave some indication of the strength of Union sentiment in Tennessee, reprinting a story from the Memphis *Bulletin*. Discussing the activities of General Chetlain, the *Bulletin's* editor commented: "We are gratified to learn that while Tennessee has furnished 30,000 white troops in the Union Army, she has given equally as good a report of herself in regard to the formation of colored troops. Already upwards of twelve thousand colored troops have been enlisted in our State and the work goes bravely on." Stearns and Mussey had not struggled in vain. "In the middle district of Tennessee there is a perfect *furore* in this matter, and regiments are being formed at the rate of five hundred men per week. By the middle of the summer," the editor optimistically predicted, "we shall have upwards of one hundred thousand colored troops in the field." The prediction was not far off the mark.

The loyal men of Kentucky did not share this attitude at all. They long protested the recruiting of Negroes, not only in Kentucky itself but even as close to them as the northern part of Tennessee. A group of leading Kentuckians petitioned the secretary of war in December of 1863, submitting a list of suggestions "believed to be the proper remedy for the evils complained of by the citizens of Southern Kentucky." They wanted recruiting camps for colored troops at Clarksville and Fort Donelson, Tennessee, removed "to points farther South of the Kentucky Border —say Columbia and Jackson." If that suggestion would not suit the War Department, then they asked that "officers of camps in Tennessee be forbidden to receive Kentucky negroes within their lines." Kentuckians were losing too much slave property to Union recruiting officers. As a palliative, they suggested that "descriptive lists or certificates be given to every citizen of Kentucky (except those in the rebel army or otherwise notoriously connected with the rebel Government) whose slave has been enlisted." Certificates were ultimately developed ("Forms No. 1, Colored Bureau") to be "awarded whenever the owner desires," presumably in response to this Kentucky request. But it is significant of Stanton's reaction to the Kentucky petition that he raised no effective protest against the appointment of General Chetlain as recruiting commissioner for West Kentucky. And Chetlain was not the most considerate recruiter in the world. As he put it, his method was "simple." He would send "a company of colored troops, fully equipped . . . to a certain section of the state, with orders to bring in all colored men found of suitable age and of apparent good health and physique. After an examination by an army surgeon, all the rejected were sent back to their homes. The owners of those accepted as fit for service had a receipt given to them, with the proviso inserted that all owners would when the time came be paid by the government, $300, for each slave, provided they proved their loyalty to it." By July 4, 1864, Chetlain's Negro soldiers, splendid in new uniforms and white gloves, and with ten rounds of ammunition per man, paraded through the streets of Louisville.[37]

The Chicago *Tribune* wasted no sympathy on Kentucky's sensitivity and concern for her diminishing slave property. Commenting caustically on a letter from Governor Bramlette to a Captain Edward Cahill, who had requested and been flatly denied permission to recruit free colored men in Kentucky, the *Tribune* of January 29, 1864, simply asserted that Kentucky must and should recruit colored soldiers. The governor's letter, in the Chicago view, did not reflect the sentiments of the common, nonslaveholding people of the state, but only of the aristocrats.

The *Tribune* played an active role in the raising of the Illinois Negro regiment, the 29th U.S. Colored Troops. On January 3, 1864, the paper insisted that the "colored people of the State owe it to themselves to fill up this regiment if possible before the month of January shall close" in order to "count so much against the impending draft." Taking a starkly practical turn, the paper argued that every man in the city of Chicago ought to be personally interested in filling the quota and so securing "himself from the chance of being drafted." Appealing for funds to finance the raising of the 29th, the *Tribune* on January 13 addressed itself frankly "to our benevolent patriotic citizens who wish to avoid the draft."

From the Mississippi Valley, meanwhile, Lorenzo Thomas had reported the results of his labors to the secretary of war in late December: 29 regiments with an aggregate strength of 20,830. These organizations had been recruited, since April 1, 1863, from the colored population of the six Southern and Border states of Alabama, Arkansas, Louisiana, Mississippi, Missouri, and Tennessee. They did not include Butler's, Banks', or Ullmann's Louisiana regiments or those recruited by Stearns and Mussey in Middle Tennessee. General Thomas estimated that some five thousand colored soldiers had died of disease and wounds or had been killed or captured in the nine-month period. "Several thousand" had been "rejected before muster on account of disease or malformation." He asserted, with understandable satisfaction, that the number of deserters had been encouragingly low and that "the majority of the freedmen manifest a partiality for the military service, and are undoubtedly happy and contented in their position in the Army."

The adjutant general confessed that he had met many difficulties in his work, chiefly the tendency of the slaveholders to "run off the slaves to Texas, Georgia, and other points, at present beyond our reach." While he was somewhat dissatisfied with the numbers of colored troops he had been able to raise, he optimistically forecast the continued organization of colored infantry and cavalry regiments, with the latter mounted on mules in the absence of a supply of more suitable mounts. He concluded with the assertion that the organization of Negro troops in the valley had cost the national government little or nothing, and he spoke highly of the officers who had been selected to recruit and command the colored regiments.[38]

In his annual report to the president in early December, Secretary of War Stanton had announced that over fifty thousand Negroes had already been organized as Union soldiers and that "the number will rapidly increase as our armies advance into the rebel States." Stanton thought that the program had "been retarded, first, by the military operations in progress; and, second, by the removal of the slaves into the interior beyond reach of our recruiting agents." The latter obstacle, he hoped, would "soon be entirely overcome." There was no doubt in Stanton's mind about the practicality of the full military employment of Negroes. As infantry, artillery, and cavalry, he maintained, they had proved their ability.[39]

President Lincoln also was satisfied that the policy of drawing on the colored manpower of the nation for soldiers was proving its worth. In his third annual message to Congress he reported that "Of those who were slaves at the beginning of the rebellion full 100,000 are now in the United States military service, about one-half of which number actually bear arms in the ranks, thus giving the double advantage of taking so much labor from the insurgent cause and supplying the places which otherwise must be filled with so many white men." Aside from their mere replacement value, Lincoln suggested that they had military potential. "So far as tested," he reported, "it is difficult to say they are not as good soldiers as any." Conscious of the reiterated

Southern arguments against their military use, Lincoln pointed out that "No servile insurrection or tendency to violence or cruelty has marked the measures of emancipation and arming the blacks." [40]

In the first half of 1863 the major outlines of the administration policy and program had emerged, and by the end of July of that third year of civil war, Negro soldiers had demonstrated what they could do if permitted to do soldiers' work. During the rest of 1863 the organization of Negro regiments continued apace, as the program broadened and techniques of applying it were developed and adapted to suit the opportunities and requirements of various situations. In the Mississippi Valley recruiting Negroes was often little more than impressment. In the trans-Mississippi West and along the Atlantic seaboard the same practices generally obtained. But in the North an entirely different approach was necessarily employed. From state to state this approach had its variations: state governors assumed the initiative in Massachusetts, Rhode Island, Ohio, Illinois, and Indiana, while in Pennsylvania and New York committees of private citizens undertook the work of sponsoring Negro organizations. In the Border states the military generally took up the work: General Birney in Maryland and Virginia; Major Stearns, Colonel Mussey, and General Chetlain in Tennessee and Kentucky.

Rather rapidly the whole organizational framework grew, spreading out across the country from the heart and brain in the Bureau for Colored Troops in the War Department. The government and the War Department had come around to permitting the Negro to become a member of the Union Army—indeed, they were now actively seeking him out and even stealing him for that army. Hostile opinion gradually softened against the Negro soldier as he proved his fighting qualities in the evening twilight at Fort Wagner and the bright morning of Honey Springs—and as the federal government granted credit for Negro recruits against state and county draft quotas. Private Miles O'Reilly's arguments were, after all, practically unanswerable.

*   *   *

Perhaps the best evidence of the change in Northern sentiment toward the Negro in Union blue was the way New York City took to its heart its first Negro regiment, the 20th U.S. Colored Troops, in March of 1864. New York had been slow to join the growing throng of Northern states in recruiting and organizing Negro regiments. There were many prominent men in the Empire State seeking authority to raise Negro troops under New York auspices, but Governor Seymour, a Democrat with little love for Lincoln and the Union, refused his cooperation. Perhaps Seymour was wise in holding back when he did. Anti-Negro feeling in New York was appallingly strong, as the nation had been made aware by the bloody draft riots of July, 1863, when colored children were made the immediate object of the mob's unreasoning viciousness. Certainly John A. Kennedy, superintendent of the metropolitan police, had been wise in seeking War Department assistance to change the plans of the officers of the 55th Massachusetts Infantry, who had originally arranged their itinerary from Readville to the South by way of Broadway.[41] The sight of a full regiment of colored men in new blue uniforms parading through New York would certainly have had anything but a quieting effect on the mob spirit of the city.

Failing in their efforts to gain Governor Seymour's assistance, the New York Association for Colored Volunteers was formed by Peter Cooper, General Daniel Sickles, Colonel John Cochrane, William Cullen Bryant, Henry J. Raymond, P. T. Barnum, David Dudley Field, Park Godwin, and a host of other metropolitan leaders in military, literary, and cultural activities. But before this association had secured War Department authorization for a regiment, the Union League Club was so authorized on December 3, 1863. The association accepted the Union League's request for cooperation, and the two organizations proceeded to the work with a fat subscription fund raised from all strata of New York society.[42] The regiment was mustered into service on Riker's Island in the East River on February 9, 1864, and on February 27 General Halleck was informed that "the 20th Regiment United States Colored Troops . . . will be ready to march by March 5."[43]

Before the regiment was permitted to leave New York, the city insisted that it parade through streets that nine months be-

fore had seen the bodies of Negroes hanging from every lamp-
post for blocks. The ovation the city gave its regiment was
tremendous. At a reception in Union Square, Charles King,
president of Columbia College, addressed the officers and men
of the regiment and presented them with a flag on which were
emblazoned a conquering eagle, a broken yoke, and the armed
figure of liberty. With the flag he presented a parchment scroll
signed by the wives and daughters of members of the Union
League Club who had had the banner made for the regiment.
The signatures on the scroll included the proudest names in
New York society—Astor, Beekman, Colyer, Fish, Jay, Luding-
ton, Van Rensselaer, Wadsworth, and Wetmore—and one other
that must have stirred the thoughts of all the great throng that
crowded Union Square—Mrs. Robert Gould Shaw.[44]

The New York *Times* editorial on March 7 must have come
close to expressing what was in many a Gotham heart that day:
"There has been no more striking manifestation of the marvelous
times that are upon us than the scene in our streets at the departure of the first of our colored regiments." The editorial reviewed the course of the previous nine months and described the
procession of the Negro troops "in solid platoons, with shouldered muskets, slung knapsacks, and buckled cartridge boxes,
down our gayest avenues and our busiest thoroughfares with
waving handkerchiefs, flowers, acclamation. . ." The contrast
was overwhelming. "It is only on such occasions," the *Times*
concluded, "that we can at all realize the prodigious revolution
which the public mind everywhere is experiencing. Such developments are infallible tokens of a new epoch."

*   *   *

All across the North other tokens of the new epoch were visible
as state after state raised Negro regiments during the winter of
1863-64 and sent them south to meet the spring and the armies
of the Confederacy. Connecticut, New York, Pennsylvania, Ohio,
Indiana, Michigan, and Illinois sent their colored soldiers forth
to battle, and in the theaters of war more and more regiments
were organized under the stimulus of federal recruiting agents
and commanding generals with authority from the Bureau for
Colored Troops.

The actual number of colored troops credited to Northern nonslaveholding states far exceeded official expectations. On February 11, 1863, Joseph C. G. Kennedy, the superintendent of the census, wrote Secretary of the Interior J. P. Usher that, on the basis of the census figures for 1860, there were 48,191 free colored males between the ages of eighteen and forty-five in the nonslaveholding states, of whom 9,631 should be available as soldiers if they should come forward in the same proportion as the white volunteers. New York, for example, showed 10,208 free colored men in the military age group, of whom, Kennedy concluded, 2,041 ought to make soldiers. Kennedy was, of course, making his calculations before the Union had resorted to the use of the draft to fill up its depleted ranks. Pennsylvania had had 10,844 free Negroes of military age in 1860, of whom 2,169 should have come forward as soldiers. Massachusetts, with 1,973 free colored men in 1860, could have been expected, according to Kennedy's reckoning, to produce 394 Negro soldiers.[45] By the end of the war, however, New York was credited with 4,125 colored recruits, twice what Kennedy had forecast. Pennsylvania had raised 8,612, nearly four times the Kennedy estimate. And Massachusetts, thanks in large part to the efforts of George Stearns and his recruiting network, had provided the Union with 3,966 colored soldiers, ten times what the superintendent of the census had calculated as her probable contribution.[46]

The number of colored soldiers raised by Northern state recruiting agents in the South was insufficient to explain this wide difference between the forecast and the actual contributions. Aside from the fact that the draft did broaden the base of the population groups contributing soldiers to the Union forces by augmenting voluntary choice, two other explanations are possible. One is that the vast number of fugitive slaves coming north from 1861 on through the war swelled the number of men available for Negro regiments raised in the North. The other is the good possibility that American Negroes, aware of the stakes for which they fought, came forward in proportionately greater numbers than did the white volunteers on whom Kennedy based his calculations. While the total number of free colored men of military age in the entire United States had been reported in the census of 1860 as 90,955, of whom, according to Kennedy's ratio, perhaps 18,000 should have made themselves available for military service, by mid-1865 the free states alone had raised nearly 75,000 colored troops in addition to the 99,000 recruited by the federal government.[47] It may be that the explanation is simply a matter of economics. Certainly the Negro stood on the bottom rung of the ladder within easy grasp of the provost marshal general's men and the draft officials; he was in no position to buy himself out of military service or to hire a substitute. On the contrary, he was often the hired substitute fighting in the white man's place.

Under the authority of the act of July 4, 1864, Northern states sent recruiting agents into Confederate areas occupied by Union armies, with the undistinguished result that 1,045 agents managed to recruit only 5,052 colored soldiers. These were credited to the states whose agents enrolled them. So great a failure was this effort that the act of March 3, 1865, repealed the authority for it.[48] The provost marshal general, in his report for 1865, expressed an opinion widely shared by many military men and historians: "No material advantage to the service resulted from this undertaking." [49]

So impatient did General William T. Sherman become with the nuisance of recruiting agents depleting his supply of Negro laborers that he ordered the arrest of any recruiter who might enter his lines without specific authority from his own officers. This was directed at federal agents appointed from the Bureau for Colored Troops, and, at Lorenzo Thomas's protest, the secretary of war had Sherman rescind his order even before the state agents had descended on the South to begin their unsuccessful work.[50] Perhaps Sherman's subordinates were not fully aware that the order had been rescinded; at any rate, one state recruiting agent, James T. Ayres of Illinois, found himself "Arrested . . . under the Charge of kidnapping niggers and sent under gard to Huntsville," by order of General Gordon Granger, one of Sherman's divisional commanders. When Ayres produced his authority as a recruiter, the charges against him were dropped and he was allowed to continue his discouraging work.[51]

In spite of the difficulties of raising Negro regiments in the South, with armies on the move and the Negro population torn loose from its moorings, Major Foster of the Bureau for Colored Troops was able to render a good report on the overall work in October of 1864. In the year since his first report, Foster wrote, "the organization and recruitment of colored troops had steadily advanced; many new regiments have been mustered in, and the older regiments, reduced by service, have been strengthened by volunteer enlistments and the assignment of drafted men and substitutes." On October 20, 1864, he reported, 140 Negro regiments were in federal service with a total strength of 101,950:

12 regiments artillery (heavy)	12,226
8 batteries artillery (light)	833
6 regiments cavalry	5,605
121 regiments infantry	83,386

This was an increase of 82 regiments and 62,243 men over the strength of colored troops Foster had reported in October, 1863. His total did not include losses by battle casualties, discharge, desertion, and disease, totaling 33,139, nor did it include the 1,624 men "transferred to the navy and other branches of the public service." Added to the number in military service these raised the total of officers and men in the colored troops from the date of first organization to 136,713.[52]

In his annual report for 1864, Adjutant General Lorenzo Thomas told of further progress. Since his first efforts in the Mississippi Valley in April of 1863, Thomas had organized or authorized the organization of 50 regiments in the states of Alabama, Arkansas, Florida, Kentucky, Iowa, Louisiana, Mississippi, and Tennessee:

4 regiments cavalry	4,800
6 regiments artillery (heavy)	10,800
4 companies artillery (light)	720
40 regiments infantry	40,000
Total	56,320

Thomas explained in his report that "all of the above regiments were organized on the maximum standard, and when entirely complete would give the specified number." He might better have written *"if* entirely complete . . ." Since most regiments had been ordered to duty before being filled to maximum strength, and since there had been the usual losses from combat, disease, and desertion, the actual strength of his 50 regiments was probably well below his 56,000. Thomas, himself, recognized this probability and estimated their aggregate strength as 50,000 at the time of his report.

He was not entirely satisfied with the results of his efforts, and in explaining this he touched on another familiar problem, that of the almost exclusive use of colored troops for fatigue duty and labor. "More troops would have been put into the Army," Thomas wrote, "but for the pressing demands of the several departments on the Mississippi, and for laborers with the troops operating in the field. The number of blacks used in this way, including cooks and servants, must be very large. Most of the labor," he reported, "is done by this class of men, and the forts on the Mississippi river have been mainly thrown up by them." In the army, too, it was Negro muscle that carried the heaviest burden of work "Where white and black troops come together in the same command," Thomas asserted, "the latter have to do the work. At first this was always the case, and in vain did I endeavor to correct it, contending that if they were to be made soldiers, time should be afforded for drill and discipline, and that they should only have their fair share of fatigue duty." He had not so contended in vain. "The prejudice in the army against their employment as troops was very great; but now, since the blacks have fully shown their fighting qualities and manliness, it has greatly changed." [53]

*   *   *

In the first two weeks of December two widely separated actions involving Negro troops presaged the larger role they were to be permitted to play as soldiers during the balance of the war. At Wolf River Bridge near Moscow, Tennessee, on December 3 and 4, the 2nd Regiment of West Tennessee Infantry of African Descent engaged Confederate forces commanded by Major General S. D. Lee so creditably as to win a unit citation from the corps commander, General Hurlbut. It is not surprising to find that the regimental commander, Colonel Frank A. Kendrick, had reported the conduct of his troops in glowing terms. "The majority of the men were for the first time under

fire," he wrote, "but their conduct did not disappoint my most
sanguine anticipation, as, after the first few rounds, they received and returned the enemy's fire with the steadiness and
deliberation of veterans." But even before he could have received Kendrick's proud report, Hurlbut had written Sherman
that "The affair at Moscow the other day was more spirited than
I thought. The negro regiment behaved splendidly." After he
had received full reports from subordinate commanders, speaking highly of "the soldierly qualities evinced by the Second
West Tennessee Infantry (AD) in this their first encounter with
the enemy," Hurlbut was moved to issue a general order com-
mending the regiment. "The recent affair at Moscow, Tennessee," proclaimed General Orders, No. 173, Headquarters, XVI
Army Corps, Memphis, December 17, 1863, "has demonstrated
the fact that colored troops, properly disciplined and commanded, can and will fight well, and the general commanding the
corps deems it to be due to the officers and men of the Second
Regiment West Tennessee Infantry of African Descent thus publicly to return his personal thanks for their gallant and successful defense of the important position to which they had been
assigned, and for the manner in which they have vindicated the
wisdom of the Government in elevating the rank and file of these
regiments to the position of freedmen and soldiers." [54]

On the same day that Hurlbut published his thanks and com-
mendation, Brigadier General Isaac J. Wistar wrote his report
of an expedition to Charles City Court House, Virginia, in which
another Negro regiment, the 6th U.S. Colored Infantry, had
performed a humble role in a satisfactory manner. General
Wistar merely stated, without rhetorical elaboration, the assignment given the colored troops participating in the expedition,
a Union raid in brigade strength up the peninsula toward Richmond. "At 4 a.m. on the 13th instant, the 6th U.S. Colored
Infantry, Col. J. W. Ames, marched from Yorktown, with ambu-
lances and a wagon loaded with rations, with instructions to
arrive at Twelve-Mile Ordinary, 24 miles distant, a sufficient
time before dark, to select a good defensive position, and throw
out pickets on both roads, which fork at that point." The report
disclosed that the assignment was "effected with complete success, notwithstanding a severe storm of wind and rain which

commenced suddenly during the process of ... execution."
Apparently General Wistar was pleased. "Col. Ames' colored
infantry did what was required of them," he wrote, "which
would be considered very severe duty (weather and roads considered), except in connection with the more arduous services
of the other troops." His cavalry had moved some 76 miles in
44 hours, and his white infantry 67 miles in 54 hours "over
deep and muddy roads." Still he thought the colored troops'
position at Twelve-Mile Ordinary "in readiness to receive and
guard prisoners and horses, issue rations, attend to wounded,
and do picket duty, on the return of the other exhausted troops,
was found of extreme advantage." [55] They had won no glory,
but they had done their job to the complete satisfaction of the
brigadier commanding.

That was enough.

XIII. *"... even the slave becomes a man ..."*

We called upon them in the day of our trial, when volunteering had ceased, when the draft was a partial failure, and the bounty system a senseless extravagance. They were ineligible for promotion, they were not to be treated as prisoners of war. Nothing was definite except that they could be shot and hanged as soldiers. Fortunate indeed it is for us, as well as for them, that they were equal to the crisis; that the grand historic moment which comes to a race only once in many centuries came to them, and that they recognized it ...

—NORWOOD PENROSE HALLOWELL, 1892
Colonel, 55th Massachusetts Infantry

"Gentlemen, the question is settled; negroes will fight."

This is the verdict pronounced by Major General George H. Thomas as he rode over the battlefield of Nashville in December, 1864, and observed "the bodies of colored men side by side with the foremost on the very works of the enemy." [1] Thomas was neither the first nor the last Union commander to reach that verdict.

Rufus Saxton had expressed the same opinion back in 1862. The behavior of Negro troops at Port Hudson, Milliken's Bend, Honey Springs, and Fort Wagner in mid-1863 had proved its validity. But throughout the war, whenever Negro soldiers fought, they had to prove it all over again. As late as April 13, 1865, four days after Lee had surrendered to Grant at Appomattox, Colonel Charles A. Gilchrist, commanding the 50th U.S. Colored Infantry, thought it necessary to conclude his report of the conduct of his troops in the siege and assault on Fort Blakely, guarding Mobile, with this statement: "The conduct of none could be criticized to their discredit, and the behavior of the men when constructing trenches under fire, than which there could scarcely be a more trying position, was a convincing proof that the former slaves of the South cannot be excelled as soldiers." Colonel A. Watson Webber, commanding the 51st U.S. Colored in the same operations, concluded his report in almost the same language: "There can be no doubt now, in the minds of their officers at least, but that our colored soldiers are brave and will fight." [2]

It is hard to realize, ninety years after the Civil War, how revolutionary the experiment of permitting Negroes to bear arms was considered, how fraught with imagined dangers to the Union cause, how galling to white pride, how difficult of popular acceptance. And yet today, ninety years after Appomattox, the same questions are still asked when Negro soldiers are mentioned: how did they behave? did they fight or did they run? did they dare to face their former masters? did they require white soldiers with them to sustain their courage—and perhaps to keep them from running? Now, as then, the Negro soldier is a stereotype in the public mind, and the actual performance of actual Negro soldiers, which shows the stereotype for what it really is, is still slow to be accepted. Only through steady repetition of steady soldierly conduct could the Negro soldier break the stereotype. Even with integration officially a fact in the armed forces of the United States, the stereotype lingers, and now as then Negro soldiers, airmen, seamen, and marines, officers and men alike, have always to prove themselves over and over again.

Daniel Ullmann was no social scientist, and yet some of his observations on Negro troops and popular conceptions regarding them are worth noting. The common error in judging them, Ullmann thought, was "to look at them as a unit, as a whole, as being all alike—the inferior specimens are selected as examples of all—" and he asked a searching question: "How would the white races stand such a test?"

Of the quality of colored troops Ullmann had this to say: "Now, I have commanded colored regiments, as good troops as need be, and I have commanded some indifferent, and some very inferior. In their abnormal state, they require good officers more than other soldiers. I have seen colored regiments—weak, disorganized, inefficient—which stripped of their miserable officers, and placed in the hands of men who both knew their duty and discharged it, were raised speedily to a high degree of discipline and effectiveness." Few readers with any military experience will disagree that Ullmann could have been speaking of white troops as well. "The privates of the Colored Troops," he continued, "were pretty uniformly reported to me to be sober, docile, subordinate, obedient, attentive, and, as soldiers, enthusiastic. As sentinels, and on general picket duty, they have no superiors. On a march, it was generally necessary to check them. Their powers of endurance none will question. As to their fighting qualities, it is surprising that doubts were so extensively entertained . . ." [3] Extensively, stubbornly, exasperatingly, and, it almost seems, eternally.

Despite their painfully accumulated battle record, there was widespread lack of agreement on the ability of the Negro soldiers throughout and after the Civil War. Although the problem had ceased to exist as far as the promulgation of national policy was concerned, the complex details of the problem continued to plague president, War Department, and Negro soldiers themselves. The insistent and persisting questions of the proper employment of Negro troops—as garrison soldiers, labor battalions, prison guards, infantry and cavalry in the field; of their pay; of their recruitment in the sensitive Border states; of their impressment into service, of their treatment when captured, of their ability to re-form and return to the fight after having once been driven back; of their self-control in the heat of battle— these and others of less importance continued to be asked even after the answers were obvious. The Nashville *Daily Union* came close to the heart of the matter when it asserted on August 1, 1863, that "Copperhead officers would have called [the 54th Massachusetts] cowardly if they had stormed and carried the gates of hell . . ." There were persons in the United States who simply refused to believe that Negroes could and would make good soldiers, for whom the evidence was never sufficient, the testimony of commanding generals never convincing. Their descendants have stubbornly survived to this day.

*   *   *

From the beginning of 1864 on through the rest of the war Negro soldiers were permitted to do soldiers' work. They had given definite indications during 1863 of what could be expected of them. If doubt still remained in some minds—as it did—their combat performance during 1864 and 1865 should have removed a great deal of it.

The increasing contribution of colored troops to actual fighting is clearly shown in the number of engagements in which they participated in the different years of the war. The *Official Army Register* in 1867 listed the total of "battles" in which colored troops took part as 250: 1 in 1862, 28 in 1863, 170 in 1864, and 51 in 1865.[4] This is patently an incomplete list: for example, it shows only one engagement for 1862, the minor engagement of Island Mound, Missouri, in which the 1st Kansas Colored made its debut as a fighting organization.[5] The *Official Records*, however, contain reports of a number of other engagements in the fall of 1862 in which Negroes fought: two expeditions by portions of the 1st South Carolina Colored and several operations in which Butler's Louisiana regiments took part. There are omissions in the listings for the other years also. The expeditions against Fort Fisher near Wilmington, North Carolina, in December, 1864, and January, 1865, are the most obvious of these omissions.

The *Army Register* list of "battles" deserves further criticism because it makes no differentiation as between minor skirmishes, brushes with Confederate pickets, affairs, and major battles, sieges, and campaigns. The operations around Petersburg, lasting from May, 1864, through April of the next year, are disposed of in this list as one "battle" and, aside from the number of colored regiments involved, there is no indication that this "battle" was of any greater significance than the skirmish at Magnolia, Tennessee, on January 7, 1865, in which the 15th U.S. Colored suffered no casualties at all.[6] One explanation of these errors is that when the *Register* was published in 1867 reports and records were still being collected and many were probably not available to the War Department compilers.

Frederick Dyer's well-known *Compendium*, published in 1908, drew on the relatively complete records published between 1880 and 1901 in the *Official Records*. Dyer listed 449 engagements in which colored troops fought, 200 more than the *Register*.[7] Of these, Dyer rated 39 as major engagements. He also took the trouble to differentiate between battles, campaigns, brushes, and affairs, so that his list is more meaningful and of greater value to any analysis of the combat contribution of the Negro.

For all its obvious faults, the *Army Register* list still has value. It shows clearly, if inaccurately, how the military employment of colored troops increased steadily from an extremely small number of engagements in the first year of their organization to a substantial number in 1863, and to wide use as combat troops in 1864. In 1862 the organization of Negro regiments was merely beginning. The idea was new, tentative, extremely unpopular. Accordingly, Negro soldiers were given few opportunities to show their fighting ability. In 1863 they were still on an experimental basis; they were still expected to make their contribution to the war by providing a labor force for the armies, by garrisoning forts, by relieving white troops for combat. Circumstances forced the issue: colored regiments in a few scattered actions demonstrated that as combat troops Negroes could perform with courage and skill and determination. After serving their apprenticeship in 1863, it was logical and natural that Negro soldiers should have found themselves more and more in action in 1864.

They continued to serve as garrison troops, of course, with and without the company of white soldiers. With the freeing of the Mississippi in 1863, the main theater of war shifted toward the east and the battle of behemoths in Virginia, but Union garrisons from Columbus, Kentucky, to Forts Jackson and St. Philip downstream from New Orleans, continued to be necessary, and Negro troops made up the bulk of them. General E. R. S. Canby's statement of "troops left in garrison on the Mississippi" in March, 1865, showed a total effective strength

of 27,876 Union soldiers. Of this total, 18,299—65 per cent—
were colored soldiers of 27 different regiments.[8] But this was
by no means the end of their participation in the closing rounds
of the war.

Instead, Negro soldiers won an enviable reputation by their
stubborn fighting with the Army of the Frontier under Blunt and
Schofield and Steele. They fought repeatedly against Forrest
in Tennessee and Mississippi. They aided materially in the defeat and demolition of Hood's army at Nashville. Nine Negro
regiments were in on the difficult assignment of reducing Fort
Blakely in the final assault on Mobile, and victory rode their
bayonets. Other Negro regiments fought in Florida, South
Carolina, Georgia, and North Carolina, but by far the greatest
number in any single theater of war were involved in the slow,
bloody work of wearing down the Army of Northern Virginia
from May, 1864, through April, 1865.

Mere numbers of colored troops engaged in Virginia in the
last twelve months of war are impressive. Thirteen Negro regiments fought at Chaffin's Farm at the end of September, and of
a total of thirty-seven Congressional Medals of Honor awarded
to participants in that two-day struggle, fourteen went to members of colored organizations.[9] Four of those same regiments
fought again at Darbytown Road on October 13, six at Fair
Oaks, five at Hatcher's Run, and five at Deep Bottom toward
the end of the month. Twenty-two regiments were at one time or
another engaged in the terrible and costly fighting before
Petersburg in 1864 and 1865. Fifteen regiments served in the
XVIII Corps of Butler's Army of the James; eight served in the
IX Corps of the Army of the Potomac, fifteen in the X Corps.
Finally, in December of 1864, the XXV Corps was organized
under General Godfrey Weitzel. Unique in American military
history, it was an entire army corps made up of Negro regiments, thirty-two in all. When the Confederacy had been defeated and the war was over, more than thirty Negro regiments
(substantially the whole XXV Corps) were transferred to the
Department of Texas for duty along the Rio Grande, to give
force to State Department protests against French interference
and the puppet empire of Maximilian in Mexico.[10] In the closing
years of the war, and particularly during the last twelve months

of conflict, the American Negro soldier proved himself worthy
of the uniform he wore and the flag he defended.

*   *   *

Charles Francis Adams, Jr., wrote of the Union fiasco of the
Petersburg mine on July 30, 1864: "All who dislike black
troops shoulder the blame onto them—not that I can find with
any show of cause. They seem to have behaved just as well and
as badly as the rest and to have suffered more severely." [11]
Adams's observation has value not for Petersburg and the battle
of the crater alone but for the performance of Negro soldiers
generally. If their battle record in the Civil War proves anything, it is that Negro soldiers measured up to the standard set
for American soldiers generally. It is obviously impossible to
discuss every engagement in which colored troops fought and
to analyze their varying behavior in action. Certainly, however,
examination of some of their engagements, major and minor,
ought to be of value in discovering what they did and how they
did it.

In the battle of Olustee, or Ocean Pond, 50 miles west of
Jacksonville, Florida, on February 20, 1864, three Negro and
six white regiments (plus smaller artillery and cavalry units)
were defeated by Confederate troops after a stubborn fight.
Colonel Joseph R. Hawley, commanding a brigade consisting
of the 7th Connecticut, 7th New Hampshire, and 8th U.S.
Colored Troops, wrote afterward: "... Colonel Fribley's black
men met the enemy at short range. They had reported to me
only two or three days before; I was afterward told that they
had never had a day's practice in loading and firing. Old troops,
finding themselves so greatly over-matched, would have run a
little and re-formed—with or without orders." The 8th U.S.
Colored was a new regiment; its men had never been in action
before. They "stood to be killed or wounded—losing more than
three hundred out of five hundred and fifty." [12] Of the eight
infantry regiments involved at Olustee, Fribley's command
suffered the highest number of men killed on the field, 48. The
regiment was second only to the hard-hit 47th New York Volunteers in total casualties: 310 killed, wounded, or missing in the

8th; 313 in the 47th New York. Total Union casualties at Olustee were 1,861.[13]

The 35th U.S. Colored and the 54th Massachusetts were at Olustee, too, brigaded together under Colonel James Montgomery. While the 35th (the 1st North Carolina Colored Volunteers) lost heavily in action—230 killed, wounded, or missing—the 54th seems at first glance to have come off with relatively light casualties: only 86. One of the 54th's officers described the regiment's part in the action in a letter to a Boston friend. His letter, written three days after the fight and published in the Chicago *Tribune* on March 9, 1864, came directly to the point: "We have had a fight, a licking, and a foot-race," the Massachusetts officer wrote. "We marched 110 miles in 108 hours, and in that time had a three hour's fight. Our regiment lost one man in every five—going in five hundred strong, and losing one hundred in killed, wounded, and missing ... When we returned to Jacksonville we were all crippled from severe marching." The letter rather emphasized the role of the 54th in the battle. "Before going into battle [we] were double-quicked for a mile, and as [we] went in Gen. Seymour said to Colonel Hallowell, 'the day is lost; you must go in and save the corps.' We did go in and did save it, checked the enemy, held the field, and were the last to leave—and covered the retreat."

Colonel Hallowell's report was in general agreement with this officer's letter, although he maintained that the regiment had double-quicked *two* miles to get into action. He listed the 54th's losses as 87: 13 killed, 66 wounded, 8 missing. He cited Sergeant Stephen A. Swails for "coolness, bravery, and efficiency during the action" despite a severe wound; the sergeant later became the first Negro to be commissioned in the 54th.[14]

Brigadier General Thomas Seymour, in command of the Union forces, had the difficult task of explaining his defeat. He reported: "The colored troops behaved creditably—the Fifty-fourth Massachusetts and First North Carolina like veterans. It was not in their conduct that can be found the chief cause of failure, but in the unanticipated yielding of a white regiment from which there was every reason to expect noble service, and at a moment when everything depended on its firmness." Seymour was referring to the 7th New Hampshire,

Colonel Hawley's brigade, which in the early maneuvering of the action failed to carry out Hawley's orders with the result that "All semblance of organization was lost in a few moments, save with about one company..." This regiment lost 208 in killed, wounded, or missing; the extent of its disorganization is suggested by the fact that it had the highest number of missing of any regiment engaged, 120 men. General Seymour suggested that its "misfortune arose, doubtless, from [its] having lately been filled with conscripts and substitutes, of a very inferior class." [15]

Lieutenant M. B. Grant, a Confederate engineer, had a curious observation in his report of the engagement: "As usual with the enemy, they posted their negro regiments on their left and in front, where they were slain by hundreds, and upon retiring left their dead and wounded negroes uncared for, carrying off only their whites, which accounts for the fact that upon the first part of the battlefield nearly all the dead found were negroes." That this is at least slightly exaggerated is indicated by the federal casualty lists: total Negro soldiers killed, 81; wounded, 365; missing, 157; total Negro casualties, 503.[16] Whatever the truth of the matter, the Negro troops themselves seem to have fought with valor if not with discretion.

The stubborn tenacity of Negro soldiers, motivated in part by their awareness that as prisoners they had no rights which Confederates were bound to respect, made them of considerable value as holding forces and as rear guards in withdrawals under superior enemy pressure. Lieutenant John Merrilies, serving with a battery of Illinois light artillery in the disastrous rout of the Sturgis expedition from Brice's Cross Roads on June 10, 1864, recorded the part of the colored troops in preventing Forrests's men from making the disaster more complete than it was. "The Cavalry... were formed in line on one flank," Merrilies wrote in his diary after he had reached a place safe enough for literary work, "and the Colored Brigade on the other, checking the onward rush of the enemy till the artillery had passed and then covering the rear of that and the ammunition train." As the Union forces retreated in vast disorder, more Negro soldiers won the admiration of the Illinois lieutenant. "The 59th U.S.C.," he wrote on June 13, "was also detailed

[with some cavalry] to cover the rear and altho the first fighting they have seen, they behaved, under very trying circumstances, with a coolness and confidence worthy of old troops."
Merrilies was particularly astonished at their indifference to
wounds. He had seen "numbers shot in the arms, hands, legs,
their clothing soaked with blood, marching along with the rest,
without a sign of pain." [17]

While Sturgis and his troops fell back in confusion upon
their Memphis base, other Union troops under Grant were
moving forward in Northern Virginia. Among them were Negro
regiments, finally permitted to play the soldier's role they had
long desired. The "Record of Events" sections of muster rolls
kept by company commanders in these regiments are a fruitful
source of information on the activities of some of these Negro
troops. The narrative of the operations of Company A, 30th U.S.
Colored, covering the period from April 30 to June 30, 1864,
shows the work of that unit in great detail. "The Company has
been on the march since May 4th," Captain Charles N. Swift
wrote on June 30. "Starting from Manassas Junction . . . and
arriving at Petersburg . . . or near there, June 28th, 1864, passing through Catlett's and Bristow Station, Warrenton Junction,
Rappahannock, Rapidan, Matapony, Pamunky, Chickahominy,
and James Rivers . . ." It was not all marching, either. "The
Company being on picket at Old Church . . . June 10th . . .
commanded by Lieutenant Bowen, were attacked by a body of
Rebel cavalry, (who had dispersed a Battalion of the 18th
Pennsylvania cavalry). The men held their ground and drove
the enemy away from their works." Proudly Captain Swift recorded these lines: "They received the praise of Gen'l Ferrero
commanding 4th Division 9th A[rmy]. C[orps]. No loss sustained by the company—the enemy carried away several
wounded." At the end of the two-month report period, the
company had been "under fire before Petersburg three days
and four nights, no loss." Although experts on the geography of
Virginia may dispute Captain Swift, he must have penned the
last line of the report with solid conviction: "The distance
marched by the company is nearly four hundred miles." [18]

What happens to a company of infantry that has marched

"nearly four hundred miles," much of it in the presence of the enemy? A comparison of the muster roll of Company A for the period February 29 to April 30 with the roll for May and June shows that this unit underwent a transformation similar to that of most combat outfits. The muster rolls show these remarks by the mustering officer, Colonel Delevan Bates, the regimental commander:

	April 30	June 30
Discipline:	good	good
Instruction:	progressive	progressive
Military appearance:	very good	fair
Arms:	very good	very good
Accoutrements:	good	very good
Clothing:	good	poor

While their appearance had slipped from "very good" to "fair" and their clothing had been worn from "good" to "poor," their arms had been maintained in very good condition, and they had learned in two months of campaigning to look after their equipment and keep it in top condition ready for instant use. In short, Company A no longer presented a crisp parade-ground appearance, but it had become a company of "poor, bloody infantry," seasoned by continued campaign and contact with the enemy. They needed all the seasoning they could get.

The muster rolls of Company E, 30th U.S. Colored, for the last eight months of 1864, throw much light on the kind of work these troops performed before Petersburg. The report for May and June is brief: "This regiment started from Manassas Junction, May 4 . . . We were rear guard until we reached the James River, June 17th. Ordered to the front. Went to rifle pits the morning of the 21st; came out the morning of the 25th." In view of the deadly action in which the 30th fought in the crater before Petersburg on July 30, the report for July and August is disappointingly brief and may reflect the grim humor of the infantry. "Since last muster," the company commander wrote, "have not had much marching to do. Have been in front of Petersburg the most of the time. Have built forts, thrown up breastworks, chopped timber, &c., &c. We have been on the front line at different times and for shorter or longer periods. The

Company was in the charge on the 30th of July, in which we were repulsed for some reason."

While it is not unusual for infantry to spend most of their time digging-in a position only to leave it almost at once and begin to dig-in another position, the Company K report for September and October, 1864, indicates that the colored infantry of the 30th may have been used in the construction of fortifications for other soldiers. At any rate, Company K was almost invariably ordered to move a few days after making its position safe and substantial. "From 1st September till 8th remained in camp near Curley House," the "Record of Events" section began, but it was only the calm before the storm. "The night of the 4th, received orders at 11 P.M. to build a breast work in our front, worked that night and the next two days. The 8th moved a mile to left and went into camp. Worked on forts and felling timber for several days. The night of the 25th ordered to move and went on line to left of Fort Warren. While there reconnoitered the enemy's line several times." But there was no rest for the infantry.

"About the 1st October," the Company K saga continued, "moved farther to left near the 'Yellow House.' Finally the 7th October were ordered on the newly acquired line west of the Weldon RR. and near the 'Peebles House.' We immediately commenced building breastworks, Forts, and felling timber. We were busy perfecting our line for two weeks. On the 26th were ordered to provide six days rations and sixty rounds cartridges, and be ready to move at 2 P.M. the 27th. Did not start till 6." Despite this unpromising, if typical, beginning, the expedition turned out to be more than the usual digging and felling timber. "Went west about two miles and half, where formed line, advanced, striking the enemy's line very suddenly, ascertaining their position and strength. While doing this, we had one officer mortally wounded and twenty men more or less seriously. We fell back 20 rods in the woods and threw up a temporary line which we held till next morning, when we fell back." [19] Nothing very glorious, just the usual hard, dangerous work of infantry in the Army of the Potomac.

Negro troops fighting before Petersburg had their moments, however. The Leavenworth *Daily Conservative* reported on June

21, 1864, from Virginia: "The hardest fighting has been done by the black troops. The forts they stormed were the worst of all. After the affair was over General [William F.] Smith [commanding the XVIII Corps] went and thanked them; told them he was proud of them, their courage and dash. He says they can't be excelled as soldiers and hereafter he will send them to a difficult place as readily as the best white troops." Smith praised their conduct in his report of the action, and in a proclamation of appreciation he called them to the attention of the entire corps. "They have stormed the works of the enemy and carried them," the proclamation concluded, "taking guns and prisoners, and in the whole affair they have displayed all the qualities of good soldiers." [20] With that sort of recommendation, Negro soldiers were bound to get soldiers' work. In midsummer a division of them were sent to a "difficult place"— into the crater blown in the Confederate lines early in the morning of July 30.

The original plan for this well-conceived but disastrously executed assault was to have Brigadier General Edward Ferrero's 4th Division of the IX Corps jump off immediately after the huge mine had been blown. Ferrero had two colored brigades: the first commanded by Colonel Joshua K. Sigfried, included the 27th, 30th, 39th, and 43rd U.S. Colored Troops; Colonel Henry G. Thomas commanded the second, which included the 19th, 23rd, 28th (one battalion of six companies), 29th, and 31st regiments. The division numbered about 4,300 men, 2,000 in Sigfried's brigade, 2,300 in Thomas's. "We were all pleased with the compliment of being chosen to lead the assault," Colonel Thomas recalled afterward. "Both officers and men were eager to show the white troops what the colored division could do."

The men had reacted curiously to the news that they would lead. As Colonel Thomas put it, "the news filled them too full for ordinary utterance." They sat silent in little circles in their company streets until a single deep voice began to sing, rather tentatively at first and then over and over with hardening conviction: "We-e looks li-ike me-en a-a-marchin' on, we looks li-ike men-er-war." Then the singer's circle took up the shout and it rapidly spread through the encampment until "a thousand voices were upraised." It must have been a magnificent, barbaric spectacle: the "dark men, with their white eyes and teeth and full red lips crouching over a smouldering campfire, in dusky shadow, with only the feeble rays of the lanterns of the first sergeants and the lights of the candles dimly showing through the tents." And the voices of a thousand Negro soldiers, making their own harmony, lifting the words up into the night sky like some great shapeless battle flag: "We looks like men a-marching on, we looks like men er war." "Until we fought the battle of the crater," Colonel Thomas remembered, "they sang this every night to the exclusion of all other songs." [21]

"It is an axiom in military art," Thomas wrote twenty years later, "that there are times when the ardor, hopefulness, and enthusiasm of new troops not yet rendered doubtful by reverses or chilled by defeat, more than compensate, in a dash, for training and experience. General Burnside, for this and other reasons, most strenuously urged his black division for the advance." The officers and men of the division were prepared: they drilled and rehearsed "certain movements to be executed in gaining and occupying the crest" of the enemy's lines. They were ready. But Burnside was overruled, and late in the afternoon of July 29, about twelve hours before the mine was to be detonated, the orders were changed. The golden moment was lost.

It was Ulysses S. Grant who ordered the change. Grant had sound reasons for disrupting the plans, as his testimony before the investigating Committee on the Conduct of the War shows. "General Burnside wanted to put his colored division in front," Grant stated, "and I believe if he had done so it would have been a success. Still," he admitted, "I agreed with General Meade in his objection to that plan. General Meade said that if we put the colored troops in front, (we had only that one division) and if it should prove a failure, it would then be said, and very properly, that we were shoving those people ahead to get killed because we did not care anything about them. But that could not be said if we put white troops in front." [22]

Call it a wrong decision based on right premises. It was a hard decision to make, but it was made. The next thing to be done was to select the white troops to put in front. No one seems to have considered postponing the action until a white division could be prepared for the assault. The three generals command-ing the white divisions making up the bulk of the IX Corps drew straws. General James H. Ledlie, commanding the battle-weary and understrength 1st Division drew the short straw. Time permitted only a brief reconnaissance of the position, and that after dark on the night of the 29th. Ledlie alerted his division and formed them just behind the Union battle lines at about midnight.

After all three white divisions had been committed, Ferrero's men were ordered into action around six o'clock on the morning of the 30th, about two hours after the mine had been "sprung." The white troops, worn down by fairly constant campaigning in the weeks just preceding the assault and unprepared by any special training or even instructions for the task before them, had not moved promptly to the attack with the explosion of the mine. Once in, they had milled about in confusion in the huge crater. The supreme error seems to have been made in delaying the first infantry attack for about half an hour after the explo-sion, long enough at any rate for the Confederates to recover somewhat from shock and surprise and to bring forces to bear on the breach in their lines.

The Negro brigades went in finally at about seven-thirty in the morning. The press of returning white troops in the covered ways, the only paths for forward movement, held them back, and the painful flood of wounded probably did their morale no good. But, once in, the Negroes forced their way through the troops in the crater and went some two hundred yards beyond, recovering some captured battle flags and taking prisoners. This success was only temporary. Many of their officers were shot down; "the men were largely without leaders, and their organi-zation was destroyed." A second assault was somehow mounted when Thomas's brigade went in, but this too came reeling back in disorder as more officers went down. Colonel Sigfried, com-manding the first brigade, maintained afterward that "Had it not been for the almost impassable crowd of troops of the other divisions in the crater and entrenchments, [the hill] would have been ours." The 4th Division suffered the heaviest casualties: 1,327, as compared with 654 in the 1st, 832 in the 2nd, and 659 in the 3rd. The total killed in the colored brigades was 195, as

compared with 227 killed in the three white divisions combined.
Officer casualties were extremely heavy, too: the IX Corps lost
50 officers killed, of whom 14 were in the 4th Division; 124 were
wounded, of whom 41 were with the colored troops; and 79 were
missing, 20 from the 4th Division.[23]

George L. Kilmer, an officer of the 14th New York Heavy
Artillery, 2nd Brigade, Ledlie's 1st Division, went into the
crater with the first wave and reported afterward that "The last
rally was when the colored division moved out from our works
in splendid order, which promised us success. Growlers were
now put to shame, and the most of the men fell into line, to go
forward. Some few declared that they would never follow
'niggers' or be caught in their company and started back to our
own lines but were promptly driven forward again." When the
colored assault halted, broke, and streamed back, Kilmer recalled, "pandemonium began. The bravest lost heart, and the
men who distrusted the negroes vented their feelings freely.
Some colored men came into the crater, and there they found a
worse fate than death in the charge." Long after the war Kilmer
recalled the horror of the scene. "It has been positively asserted," he wrote, "that white men bayoneted blacks who fell
back into the crater. This was in order to preserve the whites
from Confederate vengeance. Men boasted in my presence that
blacks had thus been disposed of, particularly when the Confederates came up." [24]

Newspaper comment on the Petersburg fiasco was divided
along political lines. The Leavenworth *Conservative* of August
3, 1864, gave credit to the colored troops for bravery in the
face of furious Confederate fire. The *Putnam County Courier*, a
stridently Democratic weekly published at Carmel, New York,
declared on August 6: "Nothing in the details of the battle yet
received tends to extenuate the conduct of the negro troops, or
to relieve the officers having immediate direction of the operation, from the accusation of blundering." The *Courier* cited the
New York *Tribune*'s own account of the assault to prove that the
Negroes had fallen back "in confusion through our lines, repulsed and demoralized."

The 17-day court of inquiry found that there had been some
blundering and cited Generals Burnside, Ledlie, and Ferrero,

Colonel Z. R. Bliss, commanding the 1st Brigade, 2nd Division, and General O. B. Wilcox, commanding the 3rd Division, for particular failures. Ledlie and Ferrero were especially criticized for having retired to a bombproof shelter behind the Union lines to beg "stimulants" from Surgeon H. E. Smith while their divisions were engaged in the crater.

The court asked rather pointed questions on the behavior of the colored division. Burnside's testimony seems frank and fair. "It is a fact," he admitted, "that the black troops broke and ran to the rear in considerable of a panic, which indicates misbehavior; but they went in late, found in the enemy's works quite a mass of our own troops unable to advance, and during their formation, and in fact during their advance between the two lines, they were subjected to probably the hottest fire that any troops had been subjected to during the day; and I do not know that it is reasonable to suppose that after the loss of so great a portion of their officers they could have been expected to maintain their position. They certainly moved forward as gallantly under the first fire and until their ranks were broken as any troops I ever saw in action." [25]

Colonel Thomas was as frank in his testimony. "They went up as well as I ever saw troops go up," he said of his colored soldiers, "—well closed, perfectly enthusiastic. They came back very badly. They came back on the run, every man for himself." That was not quite all the story. "It is but justice to the line officers," Thomas continued, "to say that more than two-thirds of them were shot, and to the colored troops that the white troops were running back just ahead of them." General J. F. Hartranft, commanding the 1st Brigade, 3rd Division, offered some explanation of what happened to the Negro soldiers. "They passed to the front just as well as any troops," he asserted, "but they were certainly not in very good condition to resist an attack, because in passing through the crater they got confused; their regimental and company organization was completely gone."

Colonel Thomas's report of the action, written three days after the battle, reflected frustration and bewilderment: "Whether we fought well or not, the scores of our dead lying as if mowed down by the hand of some mighty reaper and the terrible loss

of the officers can best attest." How his men felt about their
day's work cannot be stated accurately. But Thomas noted that
they never sang their marching song again.[26]

Captain James A. Rickard, who was with Thomas's own regiment, the 19th U.S. Colored Troops, argued that their crater
performance improved the status of Negro soldiers. "The charge
of Ferrero's division ... through a broken and demoralized division of white troops, then forming line inside the enemy's
works, and temporary capture of their interior works, with awful
losses in killed, wounded and *murdered,* is a record," Rickard
insisted, "to win back the previously prejudiced judgment of
the president, cabinet, generals, and officers of the Army of the
Potomac, who up to this time had thought negroes all right for
service in a menial capacity, but from henceforth to take responsible places, like the right flank of the army at Deep Bottom,
Va., and the storming of strong works like Forts Alexander and
Gregg." [27] Rickard was not merely exercising his own obvious
prejudice in favor of colored troops. The facts of combat in the
remaining months of 1864 bear out his assertions. He might
have added New Market Heights and Fort Gilmer while he was
about it.

In the actions around Deep Bottom, August 13 through 20,
Brigadier General William Birney's colored brigade of Major
General David Birney's X Corps did soldiers' work. There, four
regiments of colored troops fought; their casualties were relatively light as compared to those of the white brigades participating. But David Birney, the corps commander, reported that
they had "behaved handsomely" and were "in fine spirits." "In
front of one colored regiment," he wrote with evident satisfaction, "eighty-two dead bodies of the enemy were counted." [28]

The battle of the crater convinced Benjamin F. Butler, but
not in the way suggested by Captain Rickard. Butler, commanding the Army of the James, saw the Petersburg action as further
evidence that "in the Army of the Potomac negro troops were
thought of no value ..." With the qualified exception of Smith's
good use of Hinks' colored division in the assaults of June 15,
Butler felt that "negro troops had had no chance to show their
valor or staying qualities in action." His fertile mind grappled
with the problem and devised a plan of action. "I want to con-

vince myself," he told Grant in discussing this plan, "whether, under my own eye, the negro troops will fight; and if I can take with the negroes, a redoubt that turned [Winfield Scott] Hancock's corps on a former occasion, that will settle the question." The redoubt was the strong Confederate position at New Market Heights. On the night of September 28 the Army of the James, consisting of Birney's X Corps and Ord's XVIII Corps, moved to assault positions.[29]

Brigadier General Charles J. Paine's report of the actions of his 3rd Division of Ord's Corps told the story:

September 29.—The entire division, with the exception of the Tenth U.S. Colored Troops, moved from Deep Bottom, and was successfully engaged in the assault on the enemy's works, losing heavily in officers and men.

Birney's report for his colored brigade was only slightly more detailed:

September 28.—Moved across the Appomattox and James Rivers to Deep Bottom, Va.

September 29.—Moved out from Deep Bottom. In the afternoon participated in an assault on Fort Gilmer, a rebel earthwork near Chaffin's farm, which was unsuccessful.

September 30.—Took part in engagement at Fort Harrison, Chaffin's farm, in which the enemy were repulsed, with loss. The loss of the brigade in these two engagements amounted to 434 officers and men.[30]

The casualty reports were more extensive. The X Corps suffered a total of 963 killed, wounded, or missing. The 1st and 2nd divisions lost 533, while Birney's colored brigade of five regiments lost 430. The 7th U.S. Colored was the hardest hit: 20 killed, 76 wounded, and 129 captured or missing, a total of 235 casualties. Ord's XVIII Corps came through with 2,328 casualties, with General Paine's Negro 3rd Division suffering 1,302 of that total. The 5th U.S. Colored even exceeded the terrible losses of the 7th, with 28 killed, 185 wounded, and 23 captured or missing, a total of 236.[31]

What had happened in this two-day engagement or series of engagements, called Chaffin's Farm in the records, was more than the sum of the enormous Union casualties. Butler had his proof.

Under his personal command, the Negro division of the XVIII Corps, nine infantry (and one dismounted cavalry) regiments, stormed the works of New Market Heights in the early dawn of September 29. With the caps removed from the nipples of their guns so that there could be no confused or confusing firing during the advance, the Negro soldiers moved across a stream, up the slope, through two lines of obstructions, and into the fortifications. The garrison fled before the bayonet assault, and the works were in Union hands—at the cost of 1,000 casualties. Butler wrote afterward that, as he rode among the victorious, jubilant colored troops at New Market Heights, he "felt in [his] inmost heart that the capacity of the negro race for soldiers had then and there been fully settled forever." [32]

William Birney's brigade did not crown its efforts with the same success. His troops were not sent up New Market Heights but thrown against an even stronger position, Fort Gilmer, an important salient in the Confederate line. It was here that the 7th U.S. Colored suffered its heaviest losses. Four companies under Captain Julius A. Weiss were sent forward, after the 9th Maine had been repulsed at the same point. Confederate fire was fierce from Gilmer; what was even more murderous was enfilading fire from another fort on the right. Worst of all, immediately before Fort Gilmer was a ditch, seven to ten feet deep, twice as broad, which turned into a death trap. Although the Negro troops attempted to move forward, standing on each other's shoulders to reach the edge of the parapet, rifle fire at point-blank range and hand grenades rolled down among them soon forced their surrender. Of the men in the four companies, all but three were killed, wounded, or captured.[33]

For the rest of 1864, Negro regiments in the Army of the Potomac and in the Army of the James found full employment. With the first division of the X Corps, Birney's division of five colored regiments fought on the Darbytown Road on October 13, suffering 81 casualties. These were disproportionately light, since Birney's men were engaged only as skirmishers; the ten white regiments of the 1st Division were more heavily engaged and had a total of 315 casualties. The entire X Corps was fully engaged in the actions of Fair Oaks and Darbytown Road on October 27-28, and there the six regiments of the 3rd Division suffered 117 casualties, while the 24 white regiments making up the 1st and 2nd divisions lost, among them, 409. Here the Negro troops seem to have borne a fairly equal share of the battle burden and cost. In the same actions, the XVIII Corps also was heavily engaged, but the 3rd Division of six Negro regiments suffered only 196 casualties, as compared with 850 in the 19 white regiments making up the 1st and 2nd divisions. Ferrero's 3rd Division of the IX Corps, veterans of the battle of the crater, were in action on October 27-28 at Boydton Plank Road, or Hatcher's Run, and the Negroes seem to have borne more than a fair share of the cost. Ferrero's nine regiments lost 80 men altogether, while the other two divisions only 70 between them.[34]

On December 3, 1864, the XXV Army Corps was organized by War Department order from the colored troops of the Department of Virginia and North Carolina under Major General Godfrey Weitzel. This corps, the only all-Negro army corps in American military history, had varied duty during its short career. Large elements of it accompanied Weitzel and Butler on the amphibious expedition against Fort Fisher, guarding the approaches to Wilmington, North Carolina. The bulk of the corps "performed the usual fatigue, picket duty, &c." as 1864 ended, holding sections of the Union lines before Richmond.[35]

As the wheel of the year turned inexorably toward spring, it seemed that Negro troops had arrived. General Grant seemed to be impressed with their performance; as William Birney pointed out after the war, he showed his appreciation by "enlarging the line entrusted to us and ordering us out for review eight different times, for the inspection of General Prim, Secretary Stanton, President Lincoln, and other illustrious visitors." Birney and others were "inspired with hope" and "labored, with unflagging zeal," to get their troops ready "to respond to all the demands likely to be made" upon them when the blue hosts should be unleashed in the spring. Their hopes were insecurely founded. "Marching orders for the spring," Birney wrote bitterly afterward, "dispelled our illusions and scattered our hopes. We found our corps broken up, our divisions taken from General Weitzel and placed under strangers; our brigades scattered, our regiments ordered into temporary service with

white brigades, our fractured command placed in the rear and
on the flank. It was clearly not intended," Birney concluded,
"that the colored troops should win any glory in the last events
of the war." [36]

Certainly Birney had reasons for his personal bitterness. He
had demonstrated on numerous occasions that his Negro brigades and divisions could handle themselves creditably in any
kind of action, and the conduct of the final campaign of the
war must have been frustrating to his ambitions and hopes. But
Negro soldiers were not denied *all* participation in the closing
acts of the drama. The first Union troops to enter Charleston
after her fall included the 21st U.S. Colored, closely followed by
two companies of the 54th Massachusetts. That was appropriate
enough. Even more fitting was the entrance of Union forces into
Richmond—with Charles Francis Adams, Jr., leading the 5th
Massachusetts Cavalry (colored) in the van. A week later, still
"confounded at the good fortune" that had brought him there,
Colonel Adams wrote his father of his deep satisfaction: "To
have led my regiment into Richmond at the moment of its
capture is the one event which I should most have desired as
the culmination of my life in the Army." [37]

Adams and his Negro cavalrymen were not alone. Close behind came elements of Godfrey Weitzel's XXV Army Corps,
and when the news reached Chicago, the *Tribune* of April 6
could hardly contain its joy. "This war," the lead editorial proclaimed, "has been full of marked coincidence, and that by
which the representatives of an enslaved race bore the banner
of freedom into the birthplace and also the capital of the Rebellion, is not the least of the historical compensations of the
war. We can imagine the sable warriors of Weitzel rolling up
the whites of their visual orbs, and exhibiting an untarnished
display of nature's dentistry, as they passed the offices of our
contemporaries of the press—the Richmond *Sentinel, Examiner,
Whig,* and *Dispatch.* Perchance Richmond hears from their own
lips, for the first time, the 'wild warbling strains' of 'John
Brown's Soul is Marching On,' or sympathizes opportunely in
the sentiment so feelingly expressed by the venerable and aged
'Shady': 'Good-bye, Massa Jeff, good-bye, Massa Steben!' " To
the Chicago *Tribune* there was fine poetic justice in the great

occasion. "The survivors of those who fell in the disastrous assault of the 'crater' at Petersburg," it recorded approvingly, "have had the post of honor in the final consummation."

*   *   *

There were other posts of honor.

General Birney may have lamented the shabby treatment of Negro troops in Virginia, but elsewhere other regiments of their kindred marched along "like men er war." At Nashville in December and at Mobile in April, Negro soldiers had opportunities denied to Birney and his men. Best of all, they used those opportunities well.

Colonel Thomas Morgan of the 14th U.S. Colored Troops led his men into their first action at Dalton, Georgia, on August 15, 1864. This was the beginning of the regiment's combat history. They performed so satisfactorily at Dalton in helping to rout an attack by Confederate Cavalryman Joe Wheeler that the men of a white regiment "swung their hats and gave three rousing cheers" for Morgan's colored troops as they returned from the engagement. In late September the 14th stood face to face with Forrest's cavalry at Pulaski, Tennessee, and "stopped their progress." After varied duty from Chattanooga to Decatur, Alabama, during which the regiment saw real soldiers' work on several occasions, Morgan moved his command to Nashville in early December.[38]

As John Bell Hood's forces, battered by John Schofield at Franklin, approached Nashville, George H. Thomas assembled all available Union troops and prepared a suitable reception. Hood was desperate for food and supplies; Nashville, with its great Union storehouses, was a tempting prize. But Thomas, already "the Rock of Chickamauga," was about to become "the Sledge of Nashville." He concentrated his forces and organized his defenses so that when the weather changed on December 15, all was in readiness. With steady carefulness that had the North on edge with anxiety (and Grant impatient to the point of sending John A. Logan to replace Thomas), the loyal Virginian prepared the best battle plan of the entire war.

General James B. Steedman was in command of Thomas's left, a motley "provisional detachment" of quartermaster troops

and two brigades of colored troops, five regiments under Colonel
Morgan, three more under Colonel Charles R. Thompson. The
grand strategy was to open with a feint against Hood's right,
with Steedmans' troops delivering the blow. Once his left was
engaged, Thomas would deliver succeeding blows with his main
forces swinging wide and hard against Hoods' left. It worked
to perfection.

Steedman gave Morgan's colored brigade a prominent role,
and Morgan commanded the assault. Just as Thomas had
planned, Hood mistook Morgan's feint for the main Union attack and drew forces from his left. Thomas sent in his major
thrusts, and Hood's weakened left began to crumble. The first
day ended with the tide of battle running strongly against the
Confederacy. The second day settled the fate of Hood's army.
This was also the day of glory and high casualties for the colored
brigade under Colonel Thompson. His particular objective was
the strong Confederate position on Overton Hill. The plan of
battle called for a feint by Thompson's troops while the main
attack on the hill was begun on his right. But Thompson's
Negroes became excited as they moved forward in their first
battle and "what was intended merely as a demonstration was
unintentially converted into an actual assault." The white brigade on their right was repulsed, and Confederate fire was concentrated on Thompson's regiments. They lost 468 casualties.
Alarmed for his right, even as he had been on the first day,
Hood withdrew Patrick Cleburne's division from his left, and
the stage was set for a re-enactment of the Union successes of
the first day. Overton Hill was taken in the second assault, and
the whole of Hood's line was overrun.[39]

General Steedman, a prominent Breckinridge Democrat before the war, was frank in his appreciation of the role of the
Negro regiments. In reporting the casualties of his provisional
troops, he pointed out that "The larger portion of these losses,
amounting in the aggregate to fully 25 per cent of the men under
my command who were taken into action . . . fell upon the
colored troops. The severe loss of this part of my troops," he
explained, "was in their brilliant charge on the enemy's works
on Overton Hill . . . I was unable to discover that color made
any difference in the fighting of my troops. All, white and black,

nobly did their duty as soldiers, and evinced cheerfulness and
resolution such as I have never seen excelled in any campaign
of the war in which I have borne a part." [40]

In the last major campaign of the war, Negro troops again
"did their duty as soldiers." Nine colored regiments made up
the three brigades of General John Hawkins's 1st Division of
the "column from Pensacola" as the Union strangle-hold on
Mobile tightened. On April 9, 1865, six days after Adams's
cavalry and Weitzel's XXV Corps had entered Richmond and
a few hours after Grant and Lee had met at Appomattox, the
bayonets of Hawkins's division swept in through the tangled
abattis and over the ramparts of Fort Blakely. Of the seven
divisions in the Union forces engaged in the siege and capture
of Mobile, Hawkins's Negro division had the highest number
of casualties although his was the lightest division in point of
number of regiments. "The prisoners captured," he reported,
"amounted to 21 officers and 200 men—a small number, owing
to the fact that when we entered, many of the enemy, fearing
the conduct of my troops, ran over to where the white troops
were entering." [41]

*   *   *

To measure the contribution of the Negro soldier to final
Union victory in the Civil War involves more than counting
casualties and listing engagements. Actual combat takes a relatively small part of a soldier's time and energy. While some
organizations seem to have been kept pretty constantly in forward positions, others, although actively engaged in prosecuting
the war, found themselves in less harrowing situations, fighting
the boredom that is a constant in the soldier's equation, guarding prisoners, preparing fortifications, escorting wagon trains,
standing retreat parade for visiting dignitaries, drilling, working, and "wishing for the war to cease." It was like that with
all who fought in the Civil War, white or colored, Union or
Confederate. By and large, colored soldiers shared every kind
of soldiers' duty with their white comrades.

Had Negro soldiers been used uniformly throughout the
armies of the Union only as garrison troops, or labor battalions,
or assault infantry, the task of assessing their contribution would

be less difficult. As it was, their uneven employment in all the
variety of duties incident to the conduct of total war—civil war
at that—makes the task the more involved. In the trans-Mississippi West, colored troops were used as an integral part of the
Army of the Frontier, working, foraging, fighting, and dying,
side by side with white troops in Kansas, Missouri, Oklahoma,
and Arkansas, from 1862 on through the war. In the Mississippi Valley, Negro regiments were used as commanding generals saw fit and as the changing tactical situation demanded.
They fought against small bands of guerrillas or Forrest's rov-
ing columns; they garrisoned forts from Cairo to the Gulf; they
dug in the parallels approaching the Confederate fortifications
surrounding Mobile, and they came out of those parallels with
a shout in the last assault wave of the war. They protected contrabands chopping cotton on captured plantations. They worked
in the swirling waters of the Red River to build Colonel Joseph
Bailey's dams and save Porter's fleet in the ill-starred Banks
expedition of the spring of 1864. At the end of the war, Bailey,
then a general commanding a brigade of engineers at Mobile,
was careful to mention them by name in his final report. "No
troops during this war have labored more severely or ardu-
ously," he wrote of his engineers, "but those to whom most
credit is due are the Ninety-sixth and Ninety-seventh U.S. Colored Engineer Regiments. Night and day without complaint
those regiments worked, and it is difficult to comprehend how
they endured through it. The regiments manifest very great
care and ability in their organization and discipline. The officers of both, with two exceptions, now out of service, labored
assiduously. Of none of them can I do other than speak in the
highest terms." [42]

Captain J. M. Addeman of the 14th Rhode Island Heavy
Artillery (colored) served from the organization of his regiment through to the end of the war. It was the fate of the 14th
to have various garrison, picket, and outpost duty in the river
parishes of Louisiana, at Plaquemine and Donaldsonville. They
never knew the mingled panic and enthusiasm, the pain and
the glory of full combat with bugles and colors and three rousing cheers from the white regiment on their left. They lasted
out the war near Plaquemine, the officers caught in the routine

of reports, courts-martial, inspections, staff work, and the like, the enlisted men painfully learning to read and write in the regimental schools, building forts, standing guard, or doing picket duty. Their greatest enemies were not Confederates but "yellow jack," "breakbone fever," and boredom. But Nathaniel Banks complimented them in orders, and Thomas W. Sherman called them "a noble regiment." They wanted to fight, Addeman maintained: "The call was hopefully expected but disappointingly unheard. Yet," he asked, "may they not fairly claim to share in the glory of the result, and to them may not the words of the poet justly apply,—'They also serve who only stand and wait.'" [43]

Along the Atlantic coast Negro soldiers saw more mixed duty as occasion demanded. They sweated in the Union trenches around Charleston. They died in such ill-planned and badly executed battles as Olustee and Honey Hill. In Northern Virginia they fought, dug, entrenched, reconnoitered the enemy's lines, and fought again, as the need arose. They guarded Confederate prisoners at Rock Island, Illinois, at Point Lookout, Maryland, and on the Dry Tortugas. Negro soldiers, in whatever theater of war they found themselves, seem to have done everything that soldiers might conceivably be expected to do.

It is hard to find a fairer estimate than what Charles Francis Adams, Jr., wrote of their part in the crater at Petersburg: "They seem to have behaved just as well and as badly as the rest and to have suffered more severely." Adams, nearly half a century after the war, wrote bitterly of his personal disappointment at the conduct of his Negro troopers in the movement that carried them into the burning Confederate capital; it was "convincing proof," he declared, "that the negro was wholly unfit for cavalry service, lacking absolutely the essential qualities of alertness, individuality, reliability, and self-reliance." [44] But of the over-all performance of Negro soldiers, his earlier observation seems the fairer judgment.

* * *

In numbers alone Negro troops made a measurable contribution to the strength of Union arms. Under the draft call of December, 1864, some ten thousand colored soldiers were added

to the force already enrolled. On July 15, 1865, a total of
123,156 Negro soldiers were in the Union Army, organized
into 120 infantry regiments, 12 regiments of heavy artillery,
10 batteries of light artillery, and 7 regiments of cavalry. They
made up, at war's end, a good 12 per cent of the estimated
one million men then in the armies of the Union. The whole
number of colored troops recruited and organized during the
war is usually given as 186,017, but since that figure includes
7,122 officers, a more nearly correct total is 178,895. The exact
total will never be known, since records in some regiments
were incorrectly kept or lost and since some organizations may
have had their own rather irregular methods of securing re-
placements without either entering the casualties on the muster
roll or changing the names on the roll. Joseph T. Wilson insisted that sometimes "if a company on picket or scouting lost
ten men, the officers would immediately put ten new men in
their places and have them answer to the dead men's names."
Wilson asserted that this practice was followed in Missouri,
Tennessee, and Virginia. As a consequence, Wilson suggested,
the total number of colored troops who served in the Union
Army may run as high as 200,000.[45] But accepting the figure
of 180,000 as probable, Negro troops made up between 9 and
10 per cent of the total number of Union soldiers. Losses among
Negro troops were high: 68,178 from all causes were reported,
or over one-third of the total enrolled. Of these, 2,751 were
killed in action; the balance died of wounds or disease or were
missing. Disease took far more lives than bullets; this was true
of the entire Union Army, and of the Negro troops serving in
it, too. To cite an extreme case: the 56th U.S. Colored saw over
two years of service, chiefly post and garrison duty at Helena,
Arkansas, and participated in three minor engagements, with
a battle loss of 4 officers and 21 enlisted men killed or mortally wounded. But this regiment lost 6 officers and 647 men
from disease.[46]

Whatever duties they performed, Negro soldiers responded
to the Union call when war weariness and anti-Negro feeling
were at high tide in the North. Despite impressment, discrimination in pay and duty, and the constant threat of death or
return to slavery if captured, Negro soldiers did not desert in

abnormally large numbers. Some 14,887 went "over the hill" permanently, or roughly 7 per cent of the total desertions from the Union Army of over 200,000.[47] Negro soldiers worked hard and they fought hard; they improved themselves by study when more pressing demands of a military nature permitted; they were generally a challenge to their officers. It is not in the province of the historian to speculate on what might have been, but it is tempting to wonder how many Negro regiments might have been raised if the pay scale for colored troops had been the same as that for the rest of the Union Army from August, 1862—or even from January, 1863—through the war. It is tempting, too, to wonder how a hundred colored regiments, adequately armed and trained in the use of those arms, might have performed as an independent army corps under sympathetic and intelligent officers who appreciated their worth and their potential.

Hindsight and speculation on the basis of hindsight seldom win battles or campaigns. Soldiers are seldom adequately trained until a war is over. Conditions are never ideal. It is enough that they served as soldiers, that they were admitted finally into the ranks of armies organized to preserve the Union and to win freedom for the Negro. In summing up the part his colored troops had played in the battle of Nashville, Colonel Thomas Morgan used words appropriate to their role in the war: "Colored soldiers had fought side by side with white troops. They had mingled together in the charge. They had supported each other. They had assisted each other from the field when wounded, and they lay side by side in death. The survivors rejoiced together over a hard-fought field, won by common valor. All who witnessed their conduct gave them equal praise. The day we longed to see had come and gone, and the sun went down upon a record of coolness, bravery, manliness, never to be unmade. A new chapter in the history of liberty had been written. It had been shown that marching under the flag of freedom, animated by a love of liberty, even the slave becomes a man and a hero." [48]

The new chapter had been written. Negro soldiers had helped write it. And, as Frederick Douglass had foreseen in the opening weeks of war, they had helped themselves enormously by

their soldierly participation. As occasion provided, they had
learned their first lessons in reading and writing at company
and regimental schools. Of more significance, Negro soldiers
learned their first lessons in self-reliance and in the exercise
of authority, choice, and discretion. They bore arms like white
men, and as officers and noncommissioned officers they gave
orders, kept records, and shouldered new responsibilities. They
learned important lessons in loyalty to the Union, and after
the war they found respectful treatment and honor when, as
veterans of the Union Army, they joined the Grand Army of
the Republic. In the G.A.R., Negro veterans rose to positions
of trust and distinction: George Washington Williams in 1888
signed himself "Colonel and Late Judge Advocate in the Grand
Army of the Republic." Joseph Wilson became aide-de-camp
to the commander in chief of the G.A.R.[49]

In the period between the close of the Civil War and the
end of the century, the Negro veteran enjoyed wide respect
and some equality of treatment and consideration throughout
the North. In the rather florid language of Ben Butler, the
Negro soldier had "with the bayonet ... unlocked the iron-
barred gates of prejudice, and opened new fields of freedom,
liberty, and equality of right."[50] Opportunity was his after
the war: he served in state and local elective offices; he went
to constitutional conventions in Southern states; he went to the
Congress of the United States. He was permitted to become
an integral part of the regular army. As a part of that army
he helped to garrison the conquered South and to guard the
westward marches. As infantryman and especially as cavalryman on the western plains, he added new laurels to those won
at Petersburg, New Market Heights, and Nashville.

If there had been a better integrated and more widely accepted Negro soldier policy in the Lincoln administration and
in the Union Army earlier, very probably Negro soldiers might
have been allowed a larger share of what William Birney
called the "glory" of the closing campaigns. But the Negro
soldier had won glory enough. He had fought his way into
the Union Army by his courage and tenacity and sacrifice.
Once he had been officially recognized as a soldier, he had
fought to maintain his position as a soldier and to broaden

the scope of his military usefulness. As a soldier, he had gradually subdued much of the Negro's worst enemy, white prejudice. As a soldier in the Union Army, the American Negro proved his manhood and established a strong claim to equality of treatment and opportunity. In the 14th and 15th amendments to the Constitution of the United States, his manhood and his claim were recognized by the nation.

Had the Negro played a merely passive role as spectator during the Civil War, had he served only in his traditional menial capacity as cook and teamster and laborer, that national recognition of him as man and as citizen must have been postponed indefinitely. The Southern position that slaves could not bear arms was essentially correct: a slave was not a man. The war ended slavery. The Negro soldier proved that the slave could become a man.

NOTES ON SOURCES

Chapter I

1. Worthington Chauncey Ford, ed., *A Cycle of Adams Letters, 1861-1865*, 2 vols. (Boston, 1920), I, 77. Cited hereafter as *Adams Letters*.

2. David C. Mearns, ed., *The Lincoln Papers*, 2 vols. (Garden City, 1948), II, 531, April 8, 1861.

3. *The War of the Rebellion: Official Records of the Union and Confederate Armies*, 128 vols. (Washington, 1880-1902), 3 ser., I, 77, 78, 159. Cited hereafter as *Official Records*.

4. *Ibid.*, 107, 133.

5. *Ibid.*, 524, 526.

6. *Ibid.*, 609, 610, 626.

7. *Douglass' Monthly* (Rundell Memorial Library, Rochester, N.Y.), III (May, 1861), 451.

8. *Ibid.*

9. *Ibid.*

10. *Ibid.*, 454, 452.

11. Horace Greeley, *The American Conflict: A History of the Great Rebellion in the United States of America* ... 2 vols. (Hartford, 1866), II, 514, 515. Cited hereafter as Greeley, *American Conflict*.

12. Frederick Phisterer, comp., *New York in the War of the Rebellion, 1861 to 1865*, 3rd ed., 5 vols. (Albany, 1912), I, 22. In General Phisterer's opinion, "this appreciation of the struggle before the country and the loyal spirit the offer indicated, deserve to be placed on record."

13. The Shreveport *Daily News* (Bound volumes, Louisiana State University Library, Baton Rouge), May 21, 1861. The editorial was entitled "The Love they Bear."

14. *Official Records*, 1 ser., II, 593, April 23, 1861.

15. *Ibid.*, 1 ser., III, 373, May 14, 1861.

16. *Ibid.*, 1 ser., II, 46-49, May 26, 1861.

17. *Ibid.*, 662.

18. *Douglass' Monthly*, IV (July, 1861), 481.

19. *Congressional Globe*, 37 Cong., 1 sess., 32.

20. Allan Nevins, *Frémont, Pathmarker of the West* (New York, 1939), 480-501. See also T. Harry Williams, *Lincoln and His Generals* (New York, 1952), 34-37.

21. *Official Records,* 1 ser., III, 467.

22. Greeley, *American Conflict,* II, 239.

23. New York *Tribune,* July 28, 1861. Smith's letter was dated July 12.

24. John G. Nicolay and John Hay, *Abraham Lincoln, A History,* 10 vols. (New York, 1886), IV, Chapter 24 *passim* and especially 416-20. Cited hereafter as Nicolay and Hay, *Lincoln.*

25. Nevins, *Frèmont,* 504.

26. Benjamin P. Thomas, *Theodore Weld, Crusader for Freedom* (New Brunswick, N.J., 1950), 241.

27. Cited without documentation in Nevins, *Frèmont,* 507.

28. Greeley, *American Conflict,* II, 237.

29. *Official Records,* 4 ser., I, 409.

30. Cited in Greeley, *American Conflict,* II, 521, 522.

31. *Official Records,* 1 ser., IV, 569.

32. *Douglass' Monthly,* IV (September, 1861), 516.

33. Cited in Leavenworth (Kan.) *Daily Conservative,* Sept. 13, 1861.

34. For Butler's own story, see Benjamin F. Butler, *Autobiography and Personal Reminiscences of Major-General Benj. F. Butler—Butler's Book* . . . (Boston, 1892), 256 ff. Cited hereafter as *Butler's Book.* For Cameron's order directing the employment of fugitive slaves as laborers with the army, see *Official Records,* 3 ser., I, 243.

35. *Official Records of the Union and Confederate Navies in the War of the Rebellion,* 30 vols. (Washington, 1894-1922), 1 ser., VI, 252. Cited hereafter as *Official Records—Navies.* All citations are in Series I.

36. *Official Records,* 1 ser., VI, 176, 177.

37. *Official Records—Navies,* XII, 195 ff. See also Richard S. West, Jr., *Gideon Welles, Lincoln's Navy Department* (Indianapolis, 1943), 123, 127.

38. Greeley, *American Conflict,* II, 240 n.

39. *Official Records,* 1 ser., VI, 176, 177.

40. *Official Records—Navies,* XII, DuPont's reports, 261 ff., Sherman's reports, 288-90. See also West, *Gideon Welles,* 127.

41. Greeley, *American Conflict,* II, 240.

42. John B. Lance to Samuel J. Lance, Nov. 10. 1861, in Samuel J. Lance Papers, Department of Archives, Louisiana State University, Baton Rouge.

43. Howard K. Beale, ed., *The Diary of Edward Bates, 1859-1866* (Washington, 1933), 203.

44. Burton J. Hendrick, *Lincoln's War Cabinet* (Boston, 1946), 230.

45. Cited at length in Greeley, *American Conflict,* II, 242, 243.

46. A. Howard Meneely, "Three Manuscripts of Gideon Welles," *American Historical Review*, XXXI (April, 1925), 486-94.

47. Hendrick, *Lincoln's War Cabinet*, 232 ff. For instances of contract fraud under Cameron's regime, see Fred A. Shannon, *The Organization and Administration of the Union Army, 1861-1865*, 2 vols. (Cleveland, 1928), I, 64, 69, 120. For a complete analysis of Cameron's dismissal, see J. G. Randall, *Lincoln the President, Springfield to Gettysburg*, 2 vols. (New York, 1945), II, Chap. XVII, "Exit Cameron," 54-64.

48. Quoted in Leavenworth *Daily Conservative*, Aug. 30, 1861.

49. Greeley, *American Conflict*, II, 240.

50. *Ibid.*, 241.

51. *Official Records*, 1 ser., VIII, 370.

52. Greeley, *American Conflict*, II, 241, 242.

53. *Congressional Globe*, 37 Cong., 2 sess., 1, 18, 19.

54. *Ibid.*, 16, 33, 57-59, 60.

55. *Ibid.*, 130, 131.

56. James D. Richardson, comp., *Messages and Papers of the Presidents, 1789-1908*, 11 vols. (Washington, 1909), VI, 54. Cited hereafter as Richardson, *Messages and Papers*.

57. *Douglass' Monthly*, IV (September, 1861), 514.

58. Frederick Douglass, *The Life and Times of Frederick Douglass* ... (Cleveland, 1883), 410.

Chapter II

1. *Adams Letters*, I, 23.

2. *U.S. Statutes at Large*, XII, 354, March 13, 376-78, April 16, and 589-592, July 17.

3. *Congressional Globe*, 37 Cong., 2 sess., 185.

4. *Ibid.*, 334.

5. *Official Records*, 1 ser., X, Pt. 2, 109, Grant to Mason, April 16, 1862; *ibid.*, 31, Buell to Mitchel, March 11, 1862.

6. *Official Records*, 1 ser., VI, 264.

7. *Ibid.*, 1 ser., X, Pt. 2, 162, May 4, 1862.

8. *Ibid.*, 165, May 5.

9. Francis B. Heitman, *Historical Register and Dictionary of the United States Army* ... 2 vols. (Washington, 1903), I, 557. Cited hereafter as Heitman, *Register*. See also *Dictionary of American Biography*, 22 vols. (New York, 1928-36), IX, 400, 401. Cited hereafter as *DAB*.

10. *DAB*, XIV, 575-576, and Edward L. Pierce, "The Freedmen of Port Royal," *Atlantic*, XII (December, 1863), 298, 299, 300, 305, 306. See also the report of one of Pierce's teachers, a Negro protégé of John

Greenleaf Whittier, Charlotte Forten, "Life on the Sea Islands," *Atlantic*, XIII (May, June, 1864), 587-96, 666-76.

11. *Official Records*, 1 ser., XIV, 333.

12. *Ibid.*, 341.

13. For a comprehensive study of Lincoln's position on and efforts for compensated emancipation, see J. G. Randall, *Lincoln the President*, II, 141-49.

14. *Official Records*, 3 ser., II, 43.

15. *Ibid.*, 29, 30.

16. *Ibid.*, 31.

17. *Ibid.*, 57, May 13, 1862. For the full report, see *ibid.*, 50-60, *passim*, called by Chase "the Port Royal papers."

18. *Ibid.*, 60.

19. *Ibid.*, 59.

20. The Nashville *Dispatch*, May, 24, 1862. The *National Intelligencer*, May 28, reprinted a similar report by a correspondent of the Boston *Journal* which emphasized the giving of "free papers" and the choice of enlisting or returning to the plantations.

21. Quoted in the Nashville *Dispatch*, May 24.

22. Quoted in the *National Intelligencer*, May 27.

23. Quoted in the *National Intelligencer*, May 30.

24. Quoted in the *National Intelligencer*, May 30.

25. *Congressional Globe*, 37 Cong., 2 sess., Pt. 3, 2620, 2621.

26. *Official Records*, 3 ser., II, 148.

27. *Ibid.*, 197.

28. *Ibid.*

29. *Ibid.*, 198.

30. Nicolay and Hay, *Abraham Lincoln*, VI, 443

31. *Congressional Globe*, 37 Cong., 2 sess., Pt. 4, 3087, 3102, 3109.

32. *Ibid.*, 3121-3124 ff., 3127.

33. *U.S. Statutes at Large*, XII, 592, 599.

34. *Ibid.*, 599.

35. *Official Records*, 3 ser., II, 292.

36. *Adams Letters*, I, 169, July 28, 1862.

37. Quoted in the *National Intelligencer*, Aug. 5, 1862.

38. *Adams Letters*, I, 167, Henry to Charles Jr., July 19, and 171, Charles Jr. to Henry, July 28.

39. See *Ibid.*, II, 199, 217, 218. For a discussion of Adams's ideas of what the army might do in the way of preparing Negroes for citizenship, see Dudley Taylor Cornish "The Union Army as a School for Negroes," *Journal of Negro History*, XXXVII (October, 1952), 368-82.

40. *Adams Letters*, I, 171.
41. *Ibid.*, 172.
42. New York *Times*, Aug. 6, 1862.
43. *Ibid.*
44. Chicago *Tribune*, August 6.
45. Quoted in the *National Intelligencer*, Aug. 11, 1862.
46. *Official Records*, 3 ser., II, 346.
47. *Ibid.*, 174, June 24.
48. Nicolay and Hay, *Abraham Lincoln*, VI, 125.
49. New York *Times*, July 19, 1862.
50. *Adams Letters*, I, 174, 175.

Chapter III

1. Heitman, *Register*, I, 788. For a word picture of Phelps by an officer who served under him in Louisiana, see John William DeForest, *A Volunteer's Adventures, A Union Captain's Record of the Civil War* (New Haven, 1946), 9-11. Cited hereafter as DeForest, *Volunteer's Adventures*.

2. Benjamin F. Butler, *Private and Official Correspondence of General Benjamin F. Butler during the Period of the Civil War*, 5 vols. (Norwood, Mass., 1917), I, 519, Butler to Stanton, May 25, 1862. Cited hereafter as Butler, *Correspondence*.

3. *Ibid.*, 519-20. The *National Intelligencer* of Aug. 5, 1862, re-told the same story of the alleged failure of trained West Indian regiments at New Orleans in 1815, giving as its source the narrative of Captain J. N. Coke of the British Army, described as a "recognized authority on the attack on New Orleans."

4. *Ibid.*, 520.
5. *Ibid.*, 514.
6. *Ibid.*, 524-25, Page to Butler, May 27, 1862, and 553-54, Polycarpe Fortier to Butler, June 4, 1862.
7. *Official Records*, 3 ser., II, 174, Chase to Butler, June 24, 1862.
8. Butler, *Correspondence*, II, 41-42, Stanton to Butler, July 3, 1862.
9. *Ibid.*, 109, Butler to Mrs. Butler, July 25, 1862.
10. *Ibid.*, 125, Phelps to Butler, July 30, 1862.
11. *Ibid.*, 125-26.
12. *Ibid.*, 126, Davis to Phelps, July 31, 1862, and 126-27, Phelps to Davis, same date. Captain R. S. Davis was Butler's acting assistant adjutant general.
13. *Ibid.*, 143, Butler to Phelps (1), Aug. 2, 1862, and 143-44, Butler to Phelps (2), same date.

14. *Ibid.*, 142, Butler to Stanton, Aug. 2, 1862.

15. *Ibid.*, 148, Butler to Mrs. Butler, Aug. 2.

16. *Ibid.*, 145-46, Phelps to Butler, Aug. 2.

17. *Ibid.*, 192, Butler to Stanton, Aug. 14, 1862.

18. Greeley, *American Conflict*, II, 518.

19. *Butler's Book*, 491 ff.

20. *Official Records*, 3 ser., II, 173-74, Chase to Butler, June 24, 1862; and Butler, *Correspondence*, II, 131-34, Chase to Butler, July 31, 1862.

21. Butler, *Correspondence*, II, 164, Mrs. Butler to Butler, Aug. 8, 1862.

22. *Butler's Book*, 488, 489.

23. DeForest, *Volunteer's Adventures*, 43.

24. *Official Records*, 3 ser., II, 436-38.

25. *Ibid.*, 1 ser., XIV, 599, General Orders, No. 60, Richmond, Aug. 21, 1862.

26. *Ibid.*, 3 ser., II, 436-37.

27. Butler, *Correspondence*, II, 270, 271, Denison to Chase, Sept. 9, 1862.

28. *Official Records*, 4 ser., I, 625, 1020.

29. Christian A. Fleetwood, *The Negro as a Soldier* (Washington, 1895), 6.

30. Butler, *Correspondence*, II, 224, Butler to Stanton. Denison had written the news to Chase on Aug. 26, pointing out that he had urged "this matter upon Gen. Butler, but he had already decided upon it favorably." *Ibid.*, 229.

31. *Official Army Register of the Volunteer Force of the United States Army for the Years 1861, '62, '63, '64, '65*, Part VIII (Washington, 1867), 246, 248, 250. Cited hereafter as *Official Army Register*.

32. New York *Times*, Oct. 14, 1862.

33. *Douglass' Monthly* (January, 1863), 777.

Chapter IV

1. *Official Records*, 3 ser., I, 280-81, June 20, 1861.

2. *Ibid.*, 1 ser., III, 516.

3. *Congressional Globe*, 37 Cong., 2 sess., 334, 335, Jan. 15, 1862.

4. Leavenworth *Weekly Conservative*, Jan. 30, 1862. Lane addressed the Leavenworth Mercantile Library Association on Jan. 27.

5. New York *Times*, July 11, 1862.

6. "Robinson Papers," Manuscript Division, Kansas State Historical Society, Topeka.

7. Daniel W. Wilder, *The Annals of Kansas* (Topeka, 1886), 350.

8. *Military History of Kansas Regiments During the War for the Suppression of the Great Rebellion* (Leavenworth, 1870), 407. Cited hereafter as *Kansas Regiments*. See also Leavenworth *Daily Conservative*, Aug. 6, 1862.

9. *Official Records*, 3 ser., II, 294-95, Lane to Stanton, Aug. 5, 1862, and 295, Lane to Stanton, Aug. 6.

10. *Ibid.*, 314, Buckingham to Salomon, Aug. 6.

11. *Ibid.*, 417, Robinson to Stanton, Aug. 20, and 431, Stanton to Robinson, Aug. 21.

12. *Ibid.*, 445, Stanton to Lane, Aug. 23.

13. *Official Records*, 1 ser., XIII, 618-19, Sept. 8. A second complaint from one Edward N. Samuel of Clay County, Mo. (also a signer of the complaint just referred to), definitely linked the armed band to Lane through Jennison; see *ibid.*, 619, Sept. 8.

14. *Official Records*, 3 ser., II, 582, Stanton to Lane, Sept. 23.

15. *Kansas Regiments*, 407-8. See also Leavenworth *Daily Conservative*, Aug. 27, 1862.

16. Leavenworth *Daily Conservative*, Aug. 6, 1862.

17. *Official Records*, 1 ser., XIII, 618-19.

18. "Van Horn Manuscript," Manuscript Division, Kansas State Historical Society, Topeka, 21. This manuscript is a thirty-page autobiographical statement dictated by Benjamin F. Van Horn in 1909. Events described in it are well supported by military and contemporary newspaper reports.

19. New York *Times*, Oct. 12, 1862.

20. *Ibid.*, dateline, Kansas City, Oct. 8, 1862. The same report, *verbatim*, appeared in the *National Intelligencer*, Oct. 13.

21. *Kansas Regiments*, 408-9.

22. Chicago *Tribune*, Nov. 10, 1862, dispatch by *Conservative* correspondent.

23. Muster Rolls, Companies A, B, C, D, E, G, 79th (New) U.S. Colored Infantry [later official designation of the First Kansas Colored Volunteers], "Record of Events Sections, Returns for November, December, 1862." Microfilm from War Records Division, National Archives, Washington, D.C. Company G arrived at Island Mound too late to participate in the fighting.

24. *Official Army Register*, Pt. VIII, 256. Four companies were added to complete the regimental organization in the spring of 1863; see *Kansas Regiments*, 409.

Chapter V

1. *Official Records*, 3 ser., II, 152-53, Stanton to Saxton, June 16, 1862. These orders contained no mention of the employment of Negroes as soldiers.

2. *Official Records*, 1 ser., XIV, 377, Stanton to Saxton, Aug. 25, 1862.

3. David Donald, ed., *Inside Lincoln's Cabinet, The Civil War Diaries of Salmon P. Chase*, (New York, 1954), 96, 99. The questions were discussed in cabinet on July 21 and 22, 1862.

4. *Official Records*, 1 ser., XIV, 376, War Department, Special Orders, No. 202, Aug. 22, 1862.

5. *Ibid.*, 378, Halleck to Brannan, Aug. 26 and 28, 1862.

6. *Ibid.*, 380, 382; War Department Special Orders, No. 216, Sept. 1, assigned Mitchel; he assumed command in General Orders, No. 40, Hilton Head, Sept. 17, 1862.

7. *Ibid.*, 385, Mitchel to Stanton, Sept. 20, 1862.

8. *Official Records*, 3 ser., II, 683, Saxton to Stanton, Oct. 13, 1862.

9. *Ibid.*, 695, Saxton to Stanton, Oct. 29, 1862.

10. New York *Times*, Nov. 5, 1862.

11. *Official Records*, 1 ser., XIV, 191-92, Beard to Saxton, Nov. 10, 1862.

12. *Ibid.*, 189, Saxton to Stanton, Nov. 12, 1862.

13. New York *Times*, Nov. 17, 1862. The *Times* carried a fuller story on Nov. 18 based on Saxton's report to Stanton and an interview between the *Times* Washington correspondent and Chaplain Mansfield French, who had accompanied the expedition. The Chicago *Tribune* of Nov. 19 told of the expedition in glowing language, and its story included extracts from the reports of Beard and French.

14. *Official Records*, 1 ser., XIV, 193-94, Beard to Saxton, Nov. 22, 1862. See also Saxton to Stanton, Nov. 24, 1862; *ibid.*, 192-93. The Chicago *Tribune* of Dec. 2, 1862, told the story of this expedition fulsomely, including extracts from Beard's report.

15. Thomas Wentworth Higginson, *Army Life in a Black Regiment* (Boston, 1890), 2, 4. Cited hereafter as Higginson, *Black Regiment*.

16. Higginson, "Leaves from an Officer's Journal," *Atlantic*, XIV (November, 1864), 522, 521.

17. Charlotte Forten, "Life on the Sea Islands," *Atlantic*, XIII (May, 1864) 588. Miss Forten, Negro protégé of Whittier, was a teacher in the Sea Islands.

18. Higginson, "Leaves from an Officer's Journal," *Atlantic*, XIV (November, 1864), 526.

19. *Ibid.*, 747-48. For Miss Forten's description of the glorious day, see her "Life on the Sea Islands," *Atlantic*, XIII (June, 1864), 668-69. See also *The Journal of Charlotte Forten*, edited by Ray Allen Billington (New York, 1953), 153-57.

20. Forten, "Life on the Sea Islands," *Atlantic*, XIII (June, 1864), 670.

21. *Official Army Register*, Pt. VIII, 204.

22. Higginson, *Black Regiment*, 276. For Higginson's full discussion of the question of regimental priority, see "Appendix B" in *ibid.*, 272-77.

23. Edward L. Pierce, "The Freedmen of Port Royal," *Atlantic*, XII (September, 1863), 313.

Chapter VI

1. *Official Records*, 3 ser., III, 103.

2. Richardson, *Messages and Papers*, VI, 133 ff.

3. *Ibid.*, 158.

4. *Congressional Globe*, 37 Cong., 3 sess., Pt. 1, 23, 171.

5. *Ibid.*, Pt. 1, 282, 690, 695, and Pt. 2, 924.

6. *Address by Daniel Ullmann, L.L.D., Major General, U.S.V., before the Soldiers and Sailors' Union of the State of New York, on the Organization of Colored Troops and the Regeneration of the South, delivered at Albany, February 5, 1868* (Washington, 1868), 2. Cited hereafter as *Ullmann's Address*.

7. Generals' Reports of Service, War of the Rebellion, Adjutant General's Office, Returns Division (National Archives, Washington), XIV, 115, 117. Cited hereafter as Generals' Reports.

8. *Official Records*, 3 ser., III, 14. Ullmann was authorized on March 24, 1863, to add a battalion of six companies to his brigade; *ibid.*, 99-100.

9. Generals' Reports, XIV, 119, 121.

10. Charles Eugene Hamlin, *The Life and Times of Hannibal Hamlin* (Cambridge, 1899), 433.

11. Nicolay and Hay, *Lincoln*, VI, 454-55.

12. *Official Records*, 3 ser., III, 44. Included in report of Jos. C. G. Kennedy, Superintendent of the Census, Feb. 11, 1863, prepared for Secretary of the Interior J. P. Usher.

13. *Ibid.*, 46.

14. Special Orders, No. 78, Headquarters, Department of the Gulf, Camp near Baton Rouge, March 20, 1863 (extract—Paragraph 3). MS is Department of Archives, Louisiana State University, Baton Rouge.

15. The Stearns Collection, Kansas State Historical Society, Topeka, Montgomery to Stearns, Dec. 24 and 26, 1862.

16. *Official Records*, 3 ser., III, 14.

17. *Ibid.*, 20.

18. *Ibid.*, 116-17, Saxton to Stanton, April 4, 1863.

19. Henry Greenleaf Pearson, *The Life of John A. Andrew, Governor of Massachusetts, 1861-1865*, 2 vols. (Boston, 1904), II, 69-73. Cited hereafter as Pearson, *John Andrew*.

20. *Official Records*, 3 ser., III, 20.

21. *Ibid.*, 16, 38, 1112.

22. Andrew to Francis G. Shaw, Jan. 30, 1863, quoted in Pearson, *John Andrew*, II, 74, 75.

23. "Oration by Professor William James," in *The Monument to Robert Gould Shaw; Its Inception, Completion and Unveiling 1865-1897* (Boston, 1897), 78. Cited hereafter as *The Monument*.

24. "Address by Major Henry Lee Higginson delivered in Sanders Theatre, Cambridge, May 30, 1897," in *The Monument*, 30.

25. Edward W. Emerson, *Life and Letters of Charles Russell Lowell* (Boston, 1907), 234, 235. Cited hereafter as Emerson, *Charles Lowell*.

26. *Official Records*, 3 ser., III, 45.

27. Pearson, *John Andrew*, II, 81-82.

28. Luis F. Emilio, *History of the Fifty-Fourth Regiment of Massachusetts Volunteer Infantry, 1863-1865* (Boston, 1891), 12, 339, 364. Cited hereafter as Emilio, *54th Massachusetts*.

29. *Douglass' Monthly*, V (March, 1863), 801.

30. Quoted in Emilio, *54th Massachusetts*, 14.

31. *Ibid.*, 12-16, 19, 20, 24.

32. *Official Records*, 3 ser., III, 100-1.

Chapter VII

1. *Official Records*, 3 ser., III, 72, 82.

2. *DAB*, XVIII, 441; Fletcher Pratt, *Stanton, Lincoln's Secretary of War* (New York, W. W. Norton & Company, Inc., 1953), 180.

3. *Official Records*, 3 ser., III, 103, Lincoln to Johnson. *Ibid.*, 3 ser., IV, 921, Thomas to Stanton, Nov. 7, 1864. *Ibid.*, 3 ser., V, 124, Thomas to Stanton, Oct. 5, 1865.

4. *Ibid.*, 3 ser., V, 118.

5. Lorenzo Thomas, Orders and Letters (in Generals' Papers and Books, 140 vols., unnumbered, War Records Division, National Archives, Washington), 7, 8.

6. *Official Records*, 1 ser., XLVIII, Pt. 1, 1107-1110.

7. Thomas, Orders and Letters, 10.

8. *Ibid.*, 10, 14.

9. *Ibid.*, 15.

10. *Ibid.*, 18, 28, 35.

11. *The American Annual Cyclopaedia and Register of Important Events...1863* (New York, 1869), 26. Cited hereafter as *Annual Cyclopaedia.*

12. *Ibid.*

13. *Ibid.*

14. *Ibid.*

15. *Official Records,* 1 ser., XIV, 447.

16. *Ibid.*, 1 ser., XXIV, Pt. 3, 46, 47.

17. *Ibid.*, 157, Halleck to Grant, March 31, 1863.

18. *Ibid.*, 186, 187.

19. *Ibid.*, 1 ser., XXIV, Pt. 1, Grant to Halleck; *Ibid.*, 3 ser., III, 147, General Orders, No. 25, Department of the Tennessee, Milliken's Bend, La., April 22, 1863.

20. *Official Records,* 1 ser., XXIV, Pt. 1, 78.

21. Howard K. Beale, ed., *The Diary of Edward Bates, 1859-1866* (Vol. IV, *Annual Report of the American Historical Association, 1930,* Washington, 1933), 292.

22. Thomas, Orders and Letters, 44, April 22, 1863.

23. Pearson, *John Andrew,* II, 90.

24. See, Thomas, Orders and Letters, 28, 29, for a brief description of the method of selecting officers. On excessive fatigue duty, see *ibid.*, 59, Thomas to William W. Sanford, May 19, 1863. See also *Official Records,* 3 ser., IV, 921, 922, Thomas to Stanton, Nov. 7, 1864.

25. *Official Records,* 3 ser., V, 120.

26. Nicolay and Hay, *Lincoln,* VI, 465.

27. Quoted in full in Wilson, *Black Phalanx,* 119.

28. Generals' Reports, XIV, 127, 129-31.

29. Wilson, *Black Phalanx,* 119.

30. Paragraph V, General Orders, No. 47, Headquarters, Department of the Gulf, before Port Hudson, La., June 6, 1863, quoted in *ibid.*, 120.

31. Wilson, *Black Phalanx,* 120.

32. *Official Records,* 1 ser., XIV, 1020-21, General Orders, No. 17, Headquarters, Department of the South, Hilton Head, S.C., March 6, 1863.

33. Nicolay and Hay, *Lincoln,* VI, 455.

34. *Official Records,* 3 ser., III, 757.

35. Wilson, *Black Phalanx,* 119.

36. *Official Records,* 1 ser., XVIII, 659, Halleck to Foster, April 27, 1863, and 723, General Orders, No. 79, New Berne, N.C., May 19, 1863.

37. War Department, General Orders, No. 143, Adjutant General's Office, Washington, May 22, 1863, *General Orders Affecting the Volunteer Force, AGO, 1863* (Washington, 1864), 118-19.

38. *Official Records,* 3 ser., V, 661.

Chapter VIII

1. *Adams Letters,* I, 171, Charles Jr. to Henry, July 28, 1862; *ibid.,* II, 52, Charles Jr. to his father, July 22, 1863.

2. Higginson, *Black Regiment,* 58-60, tells the lively story of the first parade of Negro troops. For the original publication of Higginson's regimental history, see Higginson, "Leaves from an Officer's Journal," *Atlantic,* XV (January, 1865), 65-73. Ray Allen Billington, ed., *The Journal of Charlotte Forten* (New York, 1953), 159-65, is also helpful on this period of the regiment's development.

3. Higginson, "Leaves from an Officer's Journal," *Atlantic,* XV (January, 1865), 73.

4. Higginson recounted the tale of the expedition up the St. Mary's in *Black Regiment,* 62-96. It originally appeared as "Up the St. Mary's," *Atlantic,* XV (April, 1865), 422-36. For the official report, see *Official Records,* 1 ser., XIV, 195-98, Higginson to Saxton, Feb. 1, 1863.

5. *Official Records,* 1 ser., XIV, 196; Higginson, "Up the St. Mary's," *Atlantic,* XV (April, 1865), 432, 433.

6. *Official Records,* 1 ser., XIV, 195, 198.

7. Montgomery to Mrs. George L. Stearns, April 25, 1863, Stearns Collection, Kansas State Historical Society, Topeka. Higginson, "Up the St. John's," *Atlantic,* XVI (September, 1865), 312, 315.

8. *Official Records,* 1 ser., XIV, 423, Saxton to Stanton, March 6, 1863; *ibid.,* 227, Finegan to Jordan, March 14, 1863.

9. *Ibid.,* 226.

10. *Ibid.,* 226 ff., 837-38, Finegan to Jordan; 839-40, Beauregard to Finegan; 842, J. A. Seddon, Confederate Secretary of War, to Howell Cobb; 846, Beauregard to Cooper, Inspector General.

11. Higginson, "Up the St. John's," *Atlantic,* XVI (September, 1865), 314-19. Montgomery to Mrs. Stearns, April 25, 1863, Stearns Collection, Kansas State Historical Society, Topeka.

12. Higginson, "Up the St. John's," *Atlantic,* XVI (September, 1865), 319-25. *Official Records,* 1 ser., XIV, 432, Hunter to Halleck, March 27, 1863.

13. *National Intelligencer,* April 10, 1863, under head "Military Blunders in Florida."

14. *Official Records,* 1 ser., XIV, 435-36, April 1, 1863.

15. Generals' Reports, XIV, 133.

16. *National Intelligencer,* Aug. 24, 1863.

17. *Official Records,* 1 ser., XXVI, Pt. 1, 45.

18. Wilson, *Black Phalanx,* 214, 217.

19. *Official Records,* 1 ser., XXIV, Pt. 1, 95, 96, Dana to Stanton, June 8, 1863. *Ibid.,* Pt. 2, 447-48, Dennis to Grant, June 12.

20. *Ibid.,* Pt. 2, 467.

21. Charles Dana, *Recollections of the Civil War* (New York, 1898), 86-87. U. S. Grant, *Personal Memoirs,* 2 vols. (Hartford, 1885), I, 544. *Official Records,* 3 ser., III, 452-53, n. quoting Miller's letter as it appeared in the Galena (Ill.) *Advertiser.*

22. *Official Records,* 1 ser., XXII, Pt. 1, 322. *Kansas Regiments,* 410. See Regimental Letter and Order Book, 79th (New) U.S. Colored Troops (microfilm from War Records office, National Archives), for correspondence between Williams and Livingston on prisoner treatment.

23. *Official Records,* 1 ser., XXII, Pt. 1, 379, 380, 381. *Kansas Regiments,* 411, 412.

24. *Official Records,* 1 ser., XXII, Pt. 1, 449, 450. *Kansas Regiments,* 412. For an eyewitness account, see the Van Horn Manuscript, Kansas State Historical Society, Topeka; Van Horn commanded Company I of the 1st Kansas Colored at Honey Springs.

25. Cincinnati *Daily Commercial,* Aug. 12, 1863, quoting letter from Blunt dated July 25, 1863. Leavenworth *Daily Conservative,* July 17, 1863.

26. Emilio, *54th Massachusetts,* 24-31.

27. *Ibid.,* 31-33.

28. *Official Records,* 1 ser., XIV, 462, June 3, 1863.

29. Emilio, *54th Massachusetts,* 39-44.

30. Emerson, *Charles Lowell,* 261-62, 265-66.

31. Emilio, *54th Massachusetts,* 44-49.

32. *Ibid.,* 51-60.

33. *Ibid.,* 63-72.

34. *Ibid.,* 74-75.

35. *Ibid.,* 75-79.

36. *Official Records,* 1 ser., XXVIII, Pt. 1, 15-16.

37. James Ford Rhodes, *A History of the United States from the Compromise of 1850,* 7 vols. (New York, 1904-6), IV, 332-33.

38. Emerson, *Charles Lowell,* 286, 287.

39. Emilio, *54th Massachusetts,* 102-3.

40. *Official Records,* 3 ser., III, 696.

Chapter IX

1. *Official Records,* 2 ser., VI, 123, 124, 132, 134, 139, 145, 159.

2. Henry W. Grady, *The New South* (New York, 1890), 150-51.

3. *Official Records,* 1 ser., VI, 77-78; XVII, Pt. 2, 538.

4. *Ibid.,* 1 ser., XIV, 599.

5. *Ibid.,* 1 ser. XIII, 727, Oct. 11, 1862.

6. *Ibid.,* 2 ser., V, 797, Dec. 23, 1862. This proclamation was published by the Confederate War Department as General Orders, No. 111, Dec. 24, 1862.

7. *Ibid.,* 807-8, Jan. 12, 1863.

8. *Ibid.,* 940-41.

9. *Ibid.,* 867., April 8, 1863.

10. *Ibid.,* 712, May 27, 1863.

11. *Ibid.,* 9, 42.

12. *Ibid.,* 455, 456.

13. *Ibid.,* 1 ser., XXIV, Pt. 3, 425-26, June 22, 1863.

14. *Ibid.,* 1 ser., XXIV, Pt. 1, 110, June 26, 1863.

15. *Ibid.,* 1 ser., XXIV, Pt. 3, 444, June 27, 1863.

16. *Ibid.,* 1 ser., XXIV, Pt. 2, 459, 466.

17. *Official Army Register,* Pt. VIII, 152, 222.

18. *Official Records,* 1 ser., XXIV, Pt. 3, 469.

19. Frank Freidel, *Francis Lieber, Nineteenth Century Liberal* (Baton Rouge, La., 1947), 317-41. For the Regulations, see *Official Records,* 3 ser., III, 148-64.

20. *Official Records,* 3 ser., III, 153, 155.

21. Regimental Letter and Order Book, 79th (New) U.S. Colored Troops, correspondence between Williams and Livingston, May 20-23, 1863. *Kansas Regiments,* 410.

22. *Official Records,* 2 ser., VI, 22, 115.

23. Emilio, *54th Massachusetts,* 96.

24. Douglass, *Life and Times,* 418-20.

25. *Official Records,* 2 ser., VI, 163. The president's order was promulgated for the guidance of the Union Army in War Department General Orders, No. 252, July 31, 1863.

26. Douglass, *Life and Times,* 421-25. Emerson, *Charles Lowell,* 289-90.

27. *Official Records,* 2 ser., VI, 711-12.

28. *Ibid.,* 533. Butler to Stanton, Nov. 18, 1863.

29. *Ibid.*, 1122.

30. *Butler's Book*, 592-95. For the best examination of the whole complex problem of prisoner exchange, see William B. Hesseltine, *Civil War Prisons, A Study in War Psychology* (Columbus, Ohio, 1930), Chaps. V and X.

31. *Annual Cyclopaedia 1864*, 685.

32. *Official Records*, 2 ser., VI, 1022-23.

33. *Ibid.*, 2 ser., VII, 203.

34. *House Ex. Doc. No. 83*, 38 Cong., 1 sess., 6.

35. *Official Army Register*, Pt. VIII, 152, 217, 222, 240.

36. *Official Records*, 1 ser., XXXII, Pt. 1, 610.

37. *Ibid.*, 556.

38. *House Reports, No. 65*, 38 Cong., 1 sess., 6.

39. John L. Jordan, "Was There a Massacre at Fort Pillow?" *Tennessee Historical Quarterly*, VI (June, 1947), 99-133.

40. *Ibid.*, 111-13.

41. *Official Records*, 1 ser., XXXII, Pt. 3, 381, 395.

42. *Ibid.*, 464.

43. *Ibid.*, Pt. 1, 531, 532.

44. *Ibid.*, 534-40.

45. *DAB*, VI, 532.

46. *Official Records*, 1 ser., XXXII, Pt. 1, 545, 547, 525, 610.

47. Nicolay and Hay, *Lincoln*, VI, 481-84.

48. *Official Records*, 1 ser., XXXII, Pt. 1, 588, C. C. Washburn to N. B. Forrest, June 19, 1864, on the Memphis oath. *Ibid.*, XXXIX, Pt. 1, 126, 127, on Brice's Cross Roads.

49. *Ibid.*, XXXIV, Pt. 1, 743-57.

50. John N. Edwards, *Shelby and His Men; or, The War In the West* (Cincinnati, 1867), 279, 280.

51. Samuel F. Crawford, *Kansas in the Sixties* (Chicago, 1911), 117, 119-24. *Kansas Regiments*, 428-30. *Official Records*, 1 ser., XXXIV, Pt. 1, 697-99.

52. From *The Life of Johnny Reb, The Common Soldier of the Confederacy*, 314, by Bell Irvin Wiley, Copyright C 1943, used by special permission of the publishers, The Bobbs-Merrill Company, Inc.

53. *Official Records*, 2 ser., VIII, 26, 27, 109. *Ibid.*, V, 844.

54. *Butler's Book*, 607-8.

55. *Official Records*, 2 ser., VI, 171.

56. Roy P. Basler, ed., *Abraham Lincoln: His Speeches and Writings* (Cleveland, 1946), 749.

Chapter X

1. Harlow, *Gerrit Smith*, 436-37.
2. Stearns Collection, Kansas State Historical Society, Topeka, Montgomery to Mrs. Stearns, April 25, 1863.
3. Regimental Letter and Order Book, 79th (New) U.S. Colored Troops, Williams to Blair, undated, probably about April 21, 1863; Williams to Captain H. G. Loring, Blunt's acting assistant adjutant, April 21, 1863.
4. Emilio, *54th Massachusetts*, 47-48.
5. *Official Records*, 1 ser., XIV, 377.
6. *U.S. Statutes at Large*, XII, 599.
7. New York *Times*, Feb. 21, 1864, Higginson to the editor of the *Times*, from Beaufort, S.C., dated Feb. 14, 1864.
8. Pearson, *John Andrew*, II, 99.
9. *Official Records*, 3 ser., III, 252, 420.
10. Pearson, *John Andrew*, II, 99-104. Emilio, *54th Massachusetts*, 137.
11. Wilson, *Black Phalanx*, 134. Charles W. Eliot made the same assertion as part of the inscription on the Shaw Monument on Boston Common.
12. Mary A. Livermore, *My Story of the War* ... (Hartford, 1890), 599-600.
13. *Annual Cyclopaedia, 1864*, 36.
14. *Official Records*, 3 ser., II, 411, and III, 1102.
15. *Ibid.*, III, 938, War Department, Bureau for Colored Troops, Circular No. 1, Oct. 27, 1863.
16. *House Ex. Doc. No. 1*, 38 Cong., 1 sess., 8.
17. Douglass, *Life and Times*, 423.
18. Higginson, *Black Regiment*, 283-84.
19. Montgomery Collection, Kansas State Historical Society, Montgomery to Wilson, Jan. 22, 1864.
20. Pearson, *John Andrew*, II, 105-11.
21. *Official Records*, 3 ser., IV, 273-74.
22. Pearson, *John Andrew*, II, 112.
23. *Official Records*, 3 ser., IV, 565.
24. Emilio, *54th Massachusetts*, 220-21.
25. Pearson, *John Andrew*, II, 120.
26. Higginson, *Black Regiment*, 287-89.
27. *U.S. Statutes at Large*, XIII, 488.
28. *Official Records*, 3 ser., III, 865.

Chapter XI

1. Were all other evidence lacking, S. L. A. Marshall's classic narrative of the Korean conflict, *The River and the Gauntlet* (New York, 1953), provides ample refutation of the stereotype. Marshall makes some valuable observations on the fighting ability of Negro soldiers, too.

2. A full-strength Civil War infantry company mustered 101 officers and men or less than half the strength of an infantry company today. For examples of personal designations of units, see John T. Fallon, compiler, *List of Synonyms of Organizations in the Volunteer Service of the United States during the Years 1861, '62, '63, '64, and '65* (Washington, 1885).

3. Augustus L. Chetlain, *Recollections of Seventy Years* (Galena, Ill., 1899), 71-74, and Heitman, *Register*, I, 298. In the 12th Illinois, the field officers were elected by the company or line officers. For Sickles, see Edgcumb Pinchon, *Daniel Sickles . . .* (Garden City, N. Y., 1945), 152, 157, and Heitman, *Register*, I, 886.

4. Ullmann File, Generals' Reports, National Archives. See also W. T. Sherman to Lorenzo Thomas, April 24, 1863, *Official Records*, 3 ser., III, 165, for criticism of early selections of Union officers.

5. Charlotte Forten, "Life on the Sea Islands," *Atlantic*, XIII (May, 1864), 591. See also Edward L. Pierce, "The Freedmen of Port Royal," *Atlantic*, XII (September, 1863), 301.

6. *Official Records*, 3 ser., II, 30, Hunter to Isaac Stevens, May 8, 1862.

7. The complete list of Hunter's appointees was read in the House of Representatives on July 5, 1862, at the request of Charles S. Wickliffe of Kentucky. James E. English of Connecticut expressed surprise that "only one of these officers is from New England." *Congressional Globe*, 37 Cong., 2 sess., Part 3, 3123. See also Higginson, *Black Regiment*, 272-76.

8. One such commission was issued on May 2, 1861, to St. Albin Sauvinet, who had been "duly and legally elected Captain of 'Native Guards' (colored) 1st Div. of the Militia of Louisiana to serve for the term of War." In Officers' Records, National Archives.

9. Horace Greeley, *American Conflict*, II, 518. Wilson, *Black Phalanx*, 176, contains a roster of Negro officers of Louisiana regiments.

10. Samuel J. Crawford, *Kansas in the Sixties* (Chicago, 1911), 107.

11. Generals' Reports, XIV, 119-23.

12. *General Orders, No. 7*, Headquarters, Brigadier General Ull-

mann, New Orleans, June 10, 1863, Paragraph II. In Ullmann File, Officers' Records, War Records Office, National Archives.

13. *Official Records,* 3 ser., III, 111.

14. Emilio, *54th Massachusetts,* 330, 336. Burt G. Wilder, *The Fifty-fifth Regiment of Massachusetts Volunteer Infantry* (Brookline, Mass., 1919), 4, 5 n. 18. Cited hereafter, Wilder, *55th Massachusetts.*

15. Thomas, Orders and Letters, 10-11.

16. *Ibid.,* 17.

17. *Ibid.,* 28-29.

18. *Ibid.,* 52.

19. John Beatty, *Memoirs of a Volunteer, 1861-1863* (New York, W. W. Norton & Company, Inc., 1946), 229, 230-31, 236, 240-41.

20. *General Orders Affecting the Volunteer Force, 1863,* 118-19.

21. *Ibid.,* 119-20.

22. Letter Book, U.S.C.T., 8, Foster to Huston, Dec. 27, 1863. War Records Office, National Archives.

23. Heitman, *Register,* I, 289; *DAB,* III, 560.

24. Heitman, *Register,* I, 983, 559; Generals' Reports, VII, 517.

25. Letter Book, U.S.C.T., 2.

26. *Ibid.,* 12.

27. See, for example, Letter Book, U.S.C.T., 30-32, Foster to Casey, Jan. 2, 1864: 44 persons notified to appear before the Washington board since Dec. 26; Foster to Huston, same date, 38 persons notified to appear before the St. Louis board in the same period; and Foster to Van Renssalaer, same date, 5 persons notified to appear before the Cincinnati board.

28. Letter Book, U.S.C.T., 162-64, Foster to James Smith, Governor of Rhode Island, inquiring after Captain R. G. Shaw, appointed major in the 14th R.I. Heavy Artillery, Dec. 29, 1863, and Foster to Commanding Officers of 102d New York Volunteers, 54th Pennsylvania, 1st Michigan Colored Volunteers, and Camp Gamble, Ky.

29. *Ibid.,* 25, Foster to Smith, Dec. 31, 1863: "Lieutenant T. Fred Brown was recommended for 2nd Lieutenant. He has not been appointed; not being considered available, as that appointment would be no promotion." Many instances of nonavailability appear in List of Persons Who Have Passed the Examining Boards and Who Have Been Appointed or are Available for Appointment in the U.S. Colored Troops, War Records Office, National Archives. Cited hereafter as List of Persons Passed.

30. Letter Book, U.S.C.T., 82, 177, 87-88. Foster's letters to congressmen were uniformly crisp if not brusque. See Foster to Brandegee, Dec. 26, 1863; Foster to Grimes, Jan. 4, 1864; Foster to Colfax, Feb.

3, 1864; and Foster to Chandler, March 26, 1864, all in *ibid.*, 4, 41, 201-2, and 444.

31. List of Persons Passed, 202-3, 124-25, 204-5; Letter Book, U.S.C.T., 41.

32. Letter Book, U.S.C.T., 389, March 15, 1864

33. Statistics compiled from List of Persons Passed, *passim.*

34. *Ibid.* for rough total. The *Annual Cyclopaedia* for 1865 estimated 2,318 as the city boards' total, 32. For Thomas' report, see *Official Records*, 3 ser., V, 124, Oct. 5, 1865.

35. *Official Records*, 3 ser., III, 46.

36. Thomas, Orders and Letters, 122-123, Thomas to Banks, Sept. 11, 1863.

37. Pearson, *John Andrew*, II, 120 n. 2. Emilio, *54th Massachusetts*, 330, 336.

38. Wilder, *55th Massachusetts*, 4, 5 n. 18.

39. Williams, *Negro Troops*, 141; *Douglass' Monthly*, February, 1863, 786; Douglass, *Life and Times*, 425.

40. Frank A. Rollin, *Life and Public Services of Martin R. Delany, Sub-Assistant Commissioner Bureau Relief of Refugees, Freedmen, and of Abandoned Lands, and Late Major, 104th U.S. Colored Troops* (Boston, 1868), 166 ff.

41. *Congressional Globe*, 38 Cong., 1 sess., 553-55.

42. List of Persons Passed, 224-25.

43. *Free Military School for Applicants for Command of Colored Troops*... (Philadelphia, 1864), 3, 6, 8, 10. Cited hereafter *Free Military School.*

44. *Ibid.*, 11, 28.

45. Letter Book, U.S.C.T., 39; *Free Military School*, 28.

46. Letter Book, U.S.C.T., 422, 427.

47. War Department General Orders, No. 125, March 29, 1864, *Official Records*, 3 ser., IV, 207.

48. Letter Book, U.S.C.T., 441, 485-87, 489-90, and 547.

49. *Free Military School*, 8, 32.

50. *Ibid.*, 26, 18-19, 22, 7.

51. Letter Book, U.S.C.T., 589-90, April 29, 1864. Foster reported that he had available 3 colonels, 11 lieutenant colonels, 30 majors, 72 captains, 111 first lieutenants, and 256 second lieutenants, "most of these... serving in the Armies of the United States, as officers or enlisted men."

52. Winterbotham Letters, Chicago Historical Society, Lieutenant John Russell Winterbotham to his father and mother, Nov. 18, 1863.

53. *Ullmann's Address*, 3.

54. William F. Fox, "The Chances of Being Hit in Battle, A Study of Regimental Losses in the Civil War," *Century Magazine*, XIV (May, 1888), 106.

55. James H. Rickard, *Services with Colored Troops in Burnside's Corps*, Fifth Series, No. 1, in *Personal Narratives of Events in the War of the Rebellion* ... (Providence 1894), 29. Cited hereafter as Rickard, *Services with Colored Troops.*

56. Statement of Colonel Byron Ladd, commanding officer, Reserve Officers Training Corps, Kansas State Teachers College, Pittsburg, May, 1955. Colonel Ladd is the corporal's grandson.

57. *Annual Cyclopaedia, 1864*, 51, Gardner to Seymour, March 3, 1864.

58. Thomas, Orders and Letters, 121; Letter Book, U.S.C.T., 364-65, Foster to Scroggs, March 8, 1864.

59. Thomas, Orders and Letters, 129; Letter Book, U.S.C.T., 48, 458, Foster to Butler, March 29, 1864.

60. Henry O'Reilly, *First Organization of Colored Troops in the State of New York* ... (New York, 1864), 23, John A. Foster to Charles W. Darling, Jan. 23, 1864. Cited hereafter as O'Reilly, *Colored Troops.*

61. Greeley, *American Conflict*, II, 527; Shannon, *Union Army*, II, 162; reprinted by permission of the publishers, the Arthur H. Clark Company from Fred Shannon's "Organization and Administration of the Union Army."

62. Winterbotham Letters, Chicago Historical Society, Nov. 18, 1863, Jan. 10, 1864, and Feb. 22, 1864; Hough Papers, University of Colorado, Boulder, Civil War Letters, Hough to his wife, Feb. 6, 1864, and Autobiography, 34-35.

63. *Annual Cyclopaedia, 1865*, 34.

Chapter XII

1. Francis T. Miller, ed., *The Photographic History of the Civil War*, 10 vols. (New York, 1911), IX, *Poetry and Eloquence of Blue and Gray*, 176, 178. It may be significant of early Twentieth-century attitudes and understanding of the Negro soldier and his part in the war that in this ten-volume photographic history practically the only recognition of the existence of the Negro soldier is a few pages and four or five pictures under the subhead "The Lighter Side."

2. War Department, Adjutant General's Office, General Orders, No. 143, May 22, 1863, Paragraph 8.

3. *Official Records*, 3 ser., III, 706.

4. Letter Book, U.S.C.T., 234, Foster to Birney, Feb. 9, 1864; 371, Townsend to Thomas, March 10, 1864.

5. Thomas, Orders and Letters, 87, Thomas to Schofield, Aug. 5, 1863.

6. *Official Records*, 3 ser., III, 682-83, Stearns to Stanton, Aug. 17, 1863. Helen Nicolay, *Lincoln's Secretary, a Biography of John G. Nicolay* (New York, 1949), 219.

7. *Official Records*, 3 ser., III, 684.

8. *Ibid.*

9. *Official Records*, 3 ser., IV, 770-71.

10. *Ibid.*, 764.

11. *Ibid.*, 90.

12. *Ibid.*, 762-74.

13. *Official Records*, 3 ser., III, 873.

14. Letter Book, U.S.C.T., *passim.*

15. *Annual Cyclopaedia, 1863*, 427.

16. *Official Records*, 1 ser., XXII, Pt. 1, 320, May 9, 1863; 339-40, May 27.

17. *Ibid.*, 382.

18. *Ibid.*, 448.

19. *Ibid.*, 700.

20. *Official Records*, 1 ser., XXX, Pt. 3, 638, Sept. 4, 1863; 353, Sept. 4.

21. *Ibid.*, Pt. 1, 170.

22. *Ibid.*, Pt. 4, 482.

23. Thomas J. Morgan, *Reminiscences of Services with Colored Troops in the Army of the Cumberland, 1863-65*, Third Series, No. 13, in *Personal Narratives of Events in the War of the Rebellion, being Papers Read before the Rhode Island Soldiers and Sailors Historical Society* (Providence, 1885), 11, 12, 15, 16, 18, 19, 22, 24. Cited hereafter as Morgan, *Reminiscences.*

24. Thomas, Orders and Letters, 129, Special Orders, No. 59, Sept. 26, 1863, Memphis.

25. *Official Records*, 1 ser., XXVIII, Pt. 2, 62, 74, 75.

26. *Ibid.*, 72-73.

27. *Ibid.*, 298.

28. *Ibid.*, 328-29.

29. *Ibid.*, 329.

30. *Ibid.*, 330.

31. *Ibid.*, 270.

32. *Official Records*, 3 ser., III, 1162-63, Dec. 10, 1863.

33. Lorenzo Thomas, Letter Book, War Records Division, National

Archives, 1-2, Dec. 6, 1863. Cited hereafter as Thomas, Letter Book.

34. *Official Records,* 3 ser., III, 1115, 1162, 1163.

35. Letter Book, U.S.C.T., 97.

36. Thomas, Orders and Letters, 185; Chetlain, *Recollections,* 101.

37. *Official Records,* 3 ser., III, 1174-75; Chetlain, *Recollections,* 104-5.

38. *Official Records,* 3 ser., III, 1189, 1191, Dec. 24, 1863.

39. *Ibid.,* 1132.

40. Richardson, *Messages and Papers,* VI, 188-89.

41. O'Reilly, *Colored Troops,* 1-5; *Official Records,* 3 ser., III, 473, July 8, 1863.

42. O'Reilly, *Colored Troops,* 6-8, 14.

43. Letter Book, U.S.C.T., 328.

44. O'Reilly, *Colored Troops,* 15-18.

45. *Official Records,* 3 ser., III, 44, 45.

46. *Official Records,* 3 ser., IV, 1270.

47. *Ibid.*

48. *U.S. Statutes at Large,* XIII, 379, 491.

49. *Official Records,* 3 ser., V, 662.

50. *Official Records,* 3 ser., IV, 434, June 3, 1864, and 436, June 19.

51. John Hope Franklin, ed., *The Diary of James T. Ayres, Civil War Recruiter* (Springfield, Ill., 1947), 45.

52. *Official Records,* 3 ser., IV, 789.

53. *Ibid.,* 921-22.

54. *Official Records,* 1 ser., XXXI, Pt. 1, 583-85, Kendrick's report; 577, Hurlbut to Sherman; 583, John D. Stevenson to Hurlbut; 577, Hurlbut's General Orders, No. 173.

55. *Official Records,* 1 ser., XXIX, Pt. 1, 975-76.

Chapter XIII

1. Morgan, *Reminiscences,* 48.

2. *Official Records,* 1 ser., XLIX, Pt. 1, 294, 295.

3. *Ullmann's Address,* 5, 6.

4. *Official Army Register,* Part VIII, 321-42.

5. *Official Records,* 1 ser., LIII, 455-58.

6. *Official Army Register,* VIII, 339, Petersburg; 337, Magnolia.

7. Frederick Henry Dyer, *A Compendium of the War of the Rebellion* ... (Des Moines, 1908), 1720. Cited hereafter as Dyer, *Compendium.*

8. *Official Records,* 1 ser., XLVIII, Pt. 1, 1107-10.

9. *Official Records,* 1 ser., XLII, Pt. 1, 848-50.

10. Dyer, *Compendium,* 1720-40.

11. *Adams Letters*, II, 172.

12. Robert U. Johnson and Clarence C. Buel, eds., *Battles and Leaders of the Civil War*, 4 vols. (New York, 1888), IV, 80.

13. *Official Records*, 1 ser., XXXV, Pt. 1, 298.

14. *Ibid.*, 298, 315.

15. *Ibid.*, 290, 304, 298.

16. *Ibid.*, 341, 298.

17. Merrilies Diary, 3 vols., Chicago Historical Society, Manuscript Division, III, 17, 20.

18. Muster Rolls, Company A, 30th Regiment United States Colored Troops, from April 30 to June 30, 1864, Regimental Records, War Records Division, National Archives.

19. Muster Rolls, Company A. March-April, May-June, 1864; Company E, May-June, July-August, 1864; Company K, September-October, 1864; all companies of 30th U.S. Colored Troops, Regimental Records, War Records Division, National Archives.

20. *Official Records*, 1 ser., XL, Pt. 1, 705, 706.

21. Henry Goddard Thomas, "The Colored Troops at Petersburg," *Century Magazine*, XII (September, 1887), 777, 778.

22. *Ibid.*, 777; *Report of the Committee on the Conduct of the War on the Attack on Petersburg, on the 30th Day of July, 1864* (Washington, 1865), 5.

23. Thomas, "The Colored Troops at Petersburg," 778-81; *Official Records*, 1 ser., XL, Pt. 1, 246-48.

24. George L. Kilmer, "The Dash into the Crater," *Century Magazine*, XII (September, 1887), 775, 776.

25. *Official Records*, 1 ser., XL, Pt. 1, 118-19, Surgeon Smith's testimony; 73, Burnside's testimony.

26. *Ibid.*, 106, Thomas; 102, Hartranft; 599, Thomas's report; Thomas, "The Colored Troops at Petersburg," 778.

27. Rickard, *Services with Colored Troops*, 31-32.

28. *Official Records*, 1 ser., XLII, Pt. 1, 120, 678.

29. *Butler's Book*, 721-22, 730.

30. *Official Records*, 1 ser., XLII, Pt. 1, 108, 106.

31. *Ibid.*, 133-34, 134-36, 137.

32. *Butler's Book*, 731-33.

33. George R. Sherman, *The Negro as a Soldier*, Seventh Series, No. 7, in *Personal Narratives of Events in the War of the Rebellion*... (Providence, 1913), 21-22; *Official Records*, 1 ser., XLII, Pt. 1, 134.

34. *Official Records*, 1 ser., XLII, Pt. 1, 147, 148-50, 151, 157-59.

35. *Ibid.*, 113-14.

36. William Birney, *General William Birney's Answer to Libels*

Clandestinely Circulated by James Shaw, Jr.... (Washington, 1878), 8.

37. Emilio, *54th Massachusetts*, 282-83; *Adams Letters*, II, 261-62. General Weitzel's report (*Official Records*, 1 ser., XLVI, Pt. 1, 1227-28) gives the palm for being first into Richmond to the 4th Massachusetts Cavalry, a white regiment, but Adams was there among the first.

38. Morgan, *Reminiscences*, 28-38.

39. *Ibid.*, 38-47; Henry Stone, "Hood's Invasion of Tennessee," *Century Magazine*, XII (August, 1887), 612, 615.

40. *Official Records*, 1 ser., XLV, Pt. 1, 508.

41. *Official Records*, 1 ser., XLIX, Pt. 1, 110-15, 287.

42. *Ibid.*, 140.

43. J. M. Addeman, *Reminiscences of Two Years with the Colored Troops*, Second Series, No. 7, in *Personal Narratives of Events in the War of the Rebellion...* (Providence, 1880), 15, 25, 27, 30, 36-40.

44. *Adams Letters*, II, 172; *Charles Francis Adams, 1835-1915, An Autobiography* (Boston, 1916), 166. His men, contrary to the general performance of Negro soldiers in the Civil War, straggled badly on the advance and, what was worse, stole some horses, with the result that Colonel Adams was put in arrest for about two weeks. Adams seems not to have considered that he was assuming the extraordinary in expecting his troopers to be transformed from prisoner of war guards to well-behaved cavalry on their *first* road march. March discipline is extremely difficult to attain and usually requires time and patience; Adams seems to have had neither. To complicate matters the more, he was worn out physically and at the point of collapse, in no mood for nonsense. His last weeks with his regiment were his worst, and his judgment of Negro troops was permanently warped by that unhappy time. See *Adams Letters*, II, 267-70, for full particulars.

45. *Official Records*, 3 ser., V, 661-62; Wilson, *Black Phalanx*, 143. Major Foster of the Bureau for Colored Troops reported the aggregate as 186,097 officers and men, but an error in addition accounts for the increase. See *Official Records*, 3 ser., V, 138.

46. *Official Records*, 3 ser., V, 138; Fox, "The Chances of Being Hit in Battle," *Century Magazine*, XIV (May, 1888), 104-5; *Official Army Register*, VIII, 229; Dyer, *Compendium*, 1753.

47. *Official Records*, 3 ser., V, 1030.

48. Morgan, *Reminiscences*, 44-45.

49. Williams, *Negro Troops*, title page; Wilson, *Black Phalanx*, title page.

50. L. D. Reddick, "The Negro Policy of the United States Army, 1775-1945," *Journal of Negro History*, XXXIV (January, 1949), 18; *Official Records*, 1 ser., XLVI, Pt. 2, 71.

CRITICAL BIBLIOGRAPHY

The complex problem of the Negro soldier in the Union Army has never before been thoroughly explored. While the raw material is extremely plentiful, only three book-length studies have been made since Appomattox; the last of these appeared in 1888. Since then there have been a number of detailed examinations of various aspects of the whole subject, but no one has ever before attempted to make an exhaustive analysis of the material or to present anything like a complete treatment of the Negro's fight for the right to fight.

The first book to sketch out the story of this struggle within a struggle, this social revolution within a political revolution, was written by William Wells Brown, a Massachusetts Negro, under the title *The Negro in the American Rebellion;* this was published in Boston in 1867. Brown began his story with a discussion of the Negro in the American Revolution and the War of 1812, carried it forward through the slave insurrections led by Denmark Vesey and Nat Turner, and devoted a chapter each to the rise of the slave power and John Brown. As a history of the development of Union policy favorable to the use of Negro soldiers, Brown's work left much to be desired. Instead of tracing the development of that policy, Brown told a disjointed story of an anecdotal nature. He devoted brief chapters to a few individual regiments, such as the 54th Massachusetts and the 6th U.S. Colored Troops, to a series of vignettes on outstanding individual Negroes, and to discussions of a few battles in which colored troops fought, including Port Hudson, Milliken's Bend, Fort Wagner, Poison Spring, Fort Pillow, Honey Hill and Petersburg. Brown was handicapped by not having available to him the wealth of material contained in the *Official Records* published between 1880 and 1901. He based his book chiefly on newspaper dispatches and editorials augmented by occasional official reports, letters, and speeches, and by detailed accounts of some engagements provided him by "officers and privates of several of the colored regiments." Considering the material available to him in 1867, Brown made a creditable beginning. His work lacks documentation and by modern standards is overwritten, but it has value as the first attempt to tell the story of the Negro soldier's contribution to Union victory.

George Washington Williams, himself a veteran of the U.S. Colored Troops, turned out a much more scholarly work in 1888 with the publication of *A History of Negro Troops in the War of the Rebellion*. Williams gathered material for years before beginning to draft his history, from official sources and through correspondence with many Union officers who had worked in the movement or had commanded Negro troops. But with all his excellent material and preparation and in spite of his obvious ability and intelligence, his story of the evolution of Union Negro soldier policy is far from clear. There is far more information in his book than in Brown's, and it is occasionally documented, but in sum it is merely a more detailed treatment of the actual performance of Negro soldiers in combat than Brown had written. It is rich in battlefield anecdote and color, enlivened by reports from sometimes unidentified participants, but even more than Brown's book it is overwritten to the point of tediousness. Williams weakened his work by continually overstating the case for the Negro soldier; he tried too urgently to show that every Negro was a gallant hero.

A third full-length treatment of the role of the Negro as a Union soldier is Joseph T. Wilson's *Black Phalanx*. Like Williams, Wilson had served in the Union Army, first in the 2nd Regiment Louisiana Native Guards, later in the 54th Massachusetts. He appropriated page after page of military dispatches, and not infrequently he broke his narrative with long essays on the Negro soldier by officers who had formerly commanded colored troops. The work is accordingly very uneven; its value would have been greatly enhanced had Wilson documented his materials more fully. There is more information in Wilson's book than in either of its forerunners, but his organization is small improvement over Brown's. Perhaps the greatest contribution Wilson made was in his discussion of prejudice against the Negro, particularly in the Union Army; here he was writing from firsthand experience. On the gradual development of the Negro soldier policy of the Lincoln administration, the book is weak and does not approach the level Williams attained.

All three books suffer the common faults of weak organization, lack of documentation, lack of objectivity, and a constant tendency toward extravagant praise of Negro soldiers, on the one hand, and vindictive condemnation of those who opposed equality of military opportunity, on the other. It is perhaps too much to expect men who had themselves experienced the trials of Negro soldiers to use balanced judgment in the discussion of a subject which for them was either all right or all wrong with no gradations between. It is difficult at first to understand how Negro writers could find much praise for David Hunter in view of his rough-and-ready "recruiting" methods in South Carolina, and there

were other officers, too, who built up the strength of their colored
regiments by impressing Negroes at will. But neither Brown nor
Williams nor Wilson criticized Hunter, and it is seldom that they criticized other officers who used methods not far removed from those of
the slave catchers themselves. The explanation may be that for all the
suffering these officers caused individual Negroes and their families, in
the long run they did aid the major war effort by increasing the
number of Negro soldiers in the Union Army and by building their
own organizations into effective military units.

In 1938, Bell Irvin Wiley's *Southern Negroes* appeared, with several
chapters devoted to a brief, critical review of the Negro soldier's story.
More recently, in 1953, Benjamin Quarles published his comprehensive study, *The Negro in the Civil War*, with the Negro soldier given
prominent position. Neither volume isolated the Negro soldier question,
analyzed it as a self-contained problem, or gave it the attention it has
long deserved. As their titles indicate, neither writer intended to do
those things.

Since 1888 no one has attempted any fuller explanation than
Williams' of the steps through which the Union reached the point of
using Negro soldiers, of the slow development of policy, and of the
performance of Negro troops in the Civil War. During this long period
the materials necessary to such an examination have steadily continued
to become available. It is now possible to view the Civil War through
the perspective of three generations of American history, and the amount
of material still relatively unexamined or completely unused is challenging. The establishment of the National Archives in the 1930's was
a great encouragement to students to examine the vast hoard of relevant
records available in Washington. Steadily growing collections of state
historical societies and similar groups also have helped those interested
in exploring and re-examining various aspects of the Civil War. Con-
tinuous publication of biographies of Civil War leaders, civil and
military, North and South, and of a variety of special studies have
further helped. Many materials unavailable to the men who wrote in
the closing decades of the nineteenth century are now within relatively
easy reach of whoever desires to examine them.

The foundation stones of any study of the American Civil War are,
of course, the 128 volumes of the monumental *War of the Rebellion: A
Compilation of Official Records of the Union and Confederate Armies.*
Here the detailed story of the organization and recruitment of colored
troops and of their employment by the Union Army is available to the
patient researcher. The main lines and problematic variations in national policy are largely contained in Series 3, while the narrative of

the actual performance of Negro troops is scattered through the expanses of Series 1. Series 2, dealing with prisoners of war, contains a wealth of material on the Negro prisoner problem. While Brown to a slight extent and Williams and Wilson to a far greater extent used some of the official records which later appeared in these volumes, there is a great deal more that they did not use. In the *Official Records* is the bulk of the material necessary to any thorough analysis of the Union policy toward Negro soldiers and of their role in the Civil War.

Frederick Dyer's *Compendium of the War of the Rebellion* contains the best brief histories of all the Negro organizations serving in the Union Army. Although there are some obvious errors in the *Compendium*, particularly in the casualty reports, these appear to be chiefly the result of inefficient proofreading.

Fred Shannon's two-volume *Organization and Administration of the Union Army* still stands without a challenger almost a generation after its publication. In his treatment of Negro troops, however, Professor Shannon provides little more than a full outline of the development and application of the policy of raising and using those troops. He does not go into the details of the work of the Bureau of Colored Troops; indeed, no one has. He does not examine in any detail the various systems of selecting officers for colored regiments, although he speaks well of the results of the system of examining boards functioning in Northern cities. His primary purpose was to treat the organization and administration of the Union Army, and the organization of colored troops was only one segment of his whole problem.

To get to the heart of the Negro soldier problem it is necessary to go to the *Official Records*, to the biographies, autobiographies, diaries, and collections of the correspondence of the men who were engaged in or who were observers of the movement to include the Negro among the soldiers of the Union. It is necessary, too, to examine the records kept by the Bureau for Colored Troops and the records of Negro organizations on file in the War Records Division of the National Archives. For the political ramifications of the problem it is essential to consult the *Congressional Globe* for the war years, pertinent documents of House and Senate, and Richardson's *Messages and Papers of the Presidents*. Newspaper files are invaluable in tracing the ebb and flow of public opinion. In addition to almost constant newspaper discussion of the Negro soldier question there was, throughout the war and for years after, a steady and rewarding flow of articles in the magazines of the period.

While there are some biographical studies of the leaders of the movement to make the Negro a Union soldier, many of the key figures

still require attention. General David Hunter still remains a shadowy
figure, although Jim Lane of Kansas has been handsomely and fully
treated by Wendell H. Stephenson. Many of the leaders of the movement were not of the first rank in American military or political affairs,
and for the outlines of their lives and works it is necessary to turn to
the *Dictionary of American Biography*. Some, such as William Birney
and Daniel Ullmann, have left fairly complete notes and comments on
their contributions to the raising and employment of Negro soldiers in
their files among the Generals' Reports in the National Archives.

The Kansas State Historical Society has in its collections of correspondence at Topeka a store of information on James Montgomery,
Charles Jennison, and George L. Stearns. Thomas Wentworth Higginson showed a great deal of himself in his classic history of the 1st South
Carolina, *Army Life in a Black Regiment*, much of which originally
appeared in the *Atlantic Monthly* in 1864 and 1865. Ben Butler's *Book*
is of doubtful value because of its author's tendency to smooth over
wartime difficulties with the help of hindsight and to show himself in
a flattering light. The Butler *Correspondence*, which fills five large
volumes, is, on the other hand, extremely illuminating and valuable.
The *Cycle of Adams Letters*, edited in 1920 by Worthington C. Ford, is
particularly valuable to a study of the Negro soldier because Charles
Francis Adams, Jr., was an extremely acute observer of whatever went
on around him and wrote frequent and fulsome letters. Further, he
was an officer in the Union Army who saw at first hand the slow
evolution of the Negro soldier. He experienced the disgust of the white
army with Hunter's experiment and methods in the Sea Islands in
1862, but despite this unfavorable beginning Adams went on to become
at last the colonel of the 5th Massachusetts Cavalry, the first colored
regiment to enter Richmond. The writings of Frederick Douglass, the
first great American Negro leader, his *Monthly* and his autobiography,
are valuable for their eloquent presentation of the point of view of the
outstanding colored man in the United States during the period of the
war. For reasons difficult of explanation, neither Brown nor Williams
nor Wilson gave Douglass credit or room in their books.

Of primary importance are the manuscript records and correspondence in the War Records Division of the National Archives. Here are
the letter books of Lorenzo Thomas, the officers' files, the generals' reports, the correspondence of the Bureau for Colored Troops, the records
of Negro organizations, and the records of the examining boards for
officer candidates. While the Thomas correspondence has been used
widely—not a little of it is included in the *Official Records*, for the
most part in Series 3—the material in the generals' reports and in the

correspondence of the bureau has rarely been consulted previously. This is extremely valuable material in discovering the practices of the bureau in organizing Negro regiments, in dealing with state and national officials outside the army, and in its relations with the variety of organizations, public and private, to whom it granted authority to recruit colored troops. The officers' records are rich in the details of the multiple problems encountered in the work of recruiting Negro regiments, finding suitable officers, and combating prejudice in the higher echelons of the army. In the following pages, additional comments will indicate what use has been made of individual works and what particular value attaches to them.

PRIMARY MATERIALS, UNPRINTED

OFFICIAL

Generals' Reports of Service, War of the Rebellion, Adjutant General's Office, Returns Division, 22 vols., War Records Division, National Archives, Washington. In early 1864 and at various times after the end of the war to as late as 1872, the Adjutant General's Office requested all Union general officers to submit reports of their service during the Civil War. These reports contain much valuable information on the recruitment, organization, and use of colored troops as recorded by prominent officers from Casey to Ullmann. They vary in length, from the brief replies of Casey to the discursive essays of Chetlain, Ullmann, and Wild.

Letter Book, United States Colored Troops (Vol. II, Letters Sent, Adjutant General's Office, December, 1863—March, 1888, 21 vols.), War Records Division, National Archives. Contains clerks' copies of all communications from Bureau for Colored Troops from December, 1863, to war's end. This is a rich mine of information on the detailed workings of the bureau. All the minutiae of recruiting, organizing, officering, and mustering Negro regiments are discussed here, explained, and reiterated in letters to congressmen, governors, army officers, recruiting agents, candidates for commissions, and private citizens.

List of Persons Who Have Passed the Examining Boards and Who Have Been Appointed to or are Available for Appointment in the U.S. Colored Troops, War Records Division, National Archives. This 248-page legal-size ledger book contains a complete list of all personnel passed by boards sitting in Washington, Cincinnati, St. Louis, Davenport, New Orleans, and Richmond for commissions in colored regiments. Information here recorded includes, besides names, the former rank of all persons passed, former military organization or civilian address, date of examination, designation of board, regiment to which assigned, and remarks on availability or final disposition of each case. Invaluable to any analysis of the problem of officer selection for Negro troops.

Organizational Records, War Records Division, National Archives. These divisional, regimental, and company reports and muster rolls contain not only operational records and lists of all personnel in the various organizations reporting, but also valuable information on unit employment, strength, pay, health, and periodic rating by mustering officers. An almost inexhaustible supply of minute information on Negro regiments.

THOMAS, LORENZO, Adjutant General, United States Army. Orders and Letters of Brigadier General Lorenzo Thomas, April 1, to Nov. 24, 1863 (in Generals' Papers and Books, 140 vols., unnumbered), War Records Division, National Archives. This slim volume contains the record of Thomas' first trip to the Mississippi Valley to begin the organization of colored troops there and begins the record of his second mission on the same errand. His letters clearly show the problems he encountered and the steps he took to meet them. The orders show how Negro regiments were organized and list by name the regimental officers selected by divisional examining boards from the candidates for commissions in Colored Troops.

――――. Letters and Telegrams sent by L. Thomas, Adjutant General, Nov. 30, 1863, to July 7, 1864 (in Generals' Papers and Books), War Records Division, National Archives. This volume continues the record begun in Orders and Letters and is of equal value. It delineates Thomas' work in smoothing out recruiting problems in the Mississippi Valley, in disciplining officers when necessary, and in inspecting Negro organizations and plantations.

UNOFFICIAL

Alfred Lacey Hough Papers, unpublished manuscripts now in the possession of John Newbold Hough, Department of Classics, University of Colorado, Boulder. Hough was a Union officer serving on General George Thomas' staff; he remained in the regular establishment after the end of the war. His Civil War letters fill 250 typescript pages; they began in May, 1861, when Hough was a sergeant in the 19th Pennsylvania Volunteer Infantry and continued to February, 1865, by which time he was a major. His autobiography was written after the war when Hough was on duty with the regular army. Working from his old letters and diaries, Hough wrote sections of his story from time to time as occasion permitted.

Samuel J. Lance Papers, Department of Archives, Louisiana State University, Baton Rouge. A collection of letters and papers pertaining to the Lance family which includes valuable Confederate letters and records.

Merrilies, John, Diaries of the Civil War (also listed as the Merrilies War Diaries), three manuscript volumes, Chicago Historical Society, Manuscript Department. John Merrilies of Chicago served throughout the war with the 1st Regiment Illinois Light Artillery, rising from private to first sergeant to first lieutenant in Battery E. His diaries were kept in small ledger books, and they record the narrative of his service in the Mississippi Valley, around Vicksburg, and in Mississippi and Tennessee. Merrilies' descriptive powers were great, and his word pictures of the Union disaster at Brice's Cross Roads in June, 1864, and the rout that followed deserve a high place in the literature of the war. His disinterested reporting of the performance of Negro troops in action against Confederate forces commanded by Forrest contains high praise for their courage and tenacity.

Montgomery Collection, Kansas State Historical Society, Manuscript Division, Topeka. A small collection of letters received and sent by James Montgomery. Valuable for the light thrown on Montgomery's role in the movement to arm Negroes, for his relations with James H. Lane, Governor Charles Robinson, Charles Jennison, George L. Stearns, and other contemporaries.

Robinson Collection, Kansas State Historical Society, Manuscript Division, Topeka. A larger collection than the Montgomery correspondence, containing papers of Governor Charles Robinson of Kansas. Of particular value on the friction among Lane, Jennison, and Montgomery in the second half of 1862.

Stearns Collection, Kansas State Historical Society, Manuscript Division, Topeka. A fair-sized collection of the correspondence of George L. Stearns, Boston ship chandler and abolitionist, containing some papers relating to his activities with John Brown in the late 1850's and covering the Civil War period. Sheds further light on the quarrels of Lane, Jennison, and Montgomery.

The Van Horn Manuscript, Kansas State Historical Society. A typescript of some thirty legal-sized pages, this is Benjamin F. Van Horn's own sketch of his life as set down shortly after the turn of the century. Several pages tell in detail of his recruiting activities for General James G. Blunt and Senator Lane in Kansas in 1862 and of his adventures as lieutenant and captain of Company I, 1st Kansas Colored Volunteers.

Winterbotham Letters, Chicago Historical Society, Manuscript Division. The correspondence of Lieutenant John Russell Winterbotham of

Chicago, chiefly with his parents, on his activities as a young (20) staff officer in Corcoran's Legion, an organization of New York Irish, on active duty in Virginia in 1863 and 1864. The letters provide some insight into the role of family connections and social prestige in wartime Washington.

PRIMARY MATERIALS, PRINTED

GOVERNMENT PUBLICATIONS, FEDERAL

Congressional Globe, 1861, 1862, 1863, 1864, 1865. Government Printing Office, Washington, D.C.

FALLON, JOHN T., compiler, under direction of the adjutant general). *List of Synonyms of Organizations in the Volunteer Service of the United States during the Years 1861, '62, '63, '64, and '65* (Washington, 1885). An incomplete listing.

House Report No. 65, 38th Congress, 1st Session (Washington, 1864). Report of the Committee on the Conduct of the War on the Fort Pillow massacre.

General Orders Affecting the Volunteer Force, Adjutant General's Office, 1863 (Washington, 1864).

Official Army Register of the Volunteer Forces of the Army for the Years 1861, '62, '63, '64, '65, in 8 parts (Washington, 1867). Part VIII lists all Negro organizations and some of the engagements in which they participated. Of value for officers' rosters and casualties in officer ranks.

Report of the Committee on the Conduct of the War on the Attack on Petersburg, on the 30th Day of July, 1864 (Washington, 1865). Congressional investigation into the assault through the Crater.

RICHARDSON, JAMES DANIEL, *A Compilation of the Messages and Papers of the Presidents, 1789-1908*, 10 vols. and index (Washington, 1909).

The Statutes at Large, Treaties, and Proclamations of the United States of America, Vol. XII, Dec. 5, 1859, to March 3, 1863 (Boston, 1863); Vol. XIII, December 1863, to December, 1865 (Boston, 1866).

The War of the Rebellion: A Compilation of Official Records of the Union and Confederate Armies, 128 vols. (Washington, 1880-1901).

Official Records of the Union and Confederate Navies in the War of the Rebellion, 30 vols. (Washington, 1894-1922).

GOVERNMENT PUBLICATIONS, STATE

Military History of Kansas Regiments during the War for the Suppression of the Great Rebellion (Leavenworth, 1870).

PHISTERER, FREDERICK, compiler. *New York in the War of the Rebellion, 1861 to 1865*, 3rd ed., 5 vols. (Albany, 1912).

WILDER, DANIEL W. *The Annals of Kansas* (Topeka, 1886).

DIARIES, LETTERS, MEMOIRS, AND SPECIAL STUDIES

ADAMS, CHARLES FRANCIS, JR. *Charles Francis Adams, 1835-1915, An Autobiography* (Boston, 1916).

BASLER, ROY P., editor. *Abraham Lincoln: His Speeches and Writings* (Cleveland, 1946).

BEALE, HOWARD K., editor. *The Diary of Edward Bates, 1859-1866*, Vol. IV of the *Annual Report of the American Historical Association for the Year 1930* (Washington, 1933).

BEATTY, JOHN. *Memoirs of a Volunteer, 1861-1863* (New York, 1946). Valuable for detailed information on operations of divisional examining board for commissions in colored troops.

BILLINGTON, RAY ALLEN, editor. *The Journal of Charlotte Forten* (New York, 1953). Valuable for firsthand accounts of life on the Sea Islands during the beginnings of Negro recruiting by Hunter, Saxton, and Higginson.

BUTLER, BENJAMIN FRANKLIN. *Autobiography and Personal Reminiscences of Major-General Benj. F. Butler—BUTLER'S BOOK. A Review of His Legal, Political and Military Career* (Boston, 1892).

———. *Private and Official Correspondence of Gen. Benjamin F. Butler during the Period of the Civil War*, 5 vols. (Norwood, Mass., 1917), privately printed. More illuminating and trustworthy than *Butler's Book*.

CHETLAIN, AUGUSTUS L. *Recollections of Seventy Years* (Galena, Ill., 1899).

DANA, CHARLES A. *Recollections of the Civil War* (New York, 1898).

DE FOREST, JOHN WILLIAM. *A Volunteer's Adventures, A Union Captain's Record of the Civil War* (New Haven, 1946). Contains good material on the Phelps-Butler controversy, a valuable description of Phelps, and material on anti-Negro sentiment in the Union Army.

DONALD, DAVID, editor. *Inside Lincoln's Cabinet. The Civil War Diaries of Salmon P. Chase* (New York, 1954).

DOUGLASS, FREDERICK. *The Life and Times of Frederick Douglass, written by Himself...* (Cleveland, 1883). The full story of his life with special emphasis on the Civil War period and his role in the movement for Negro soldiers.

EMILIO, LUIS F. *History of the Fifty-Fourth Regiment of Massachusetts Volunteer Infantry, 1863-1865* (Boston, 1891). The best available regimental history, written by the captain of a company of the 54th.

FORD, WORTHINGTON CHAUNCEY, editor. *A Cycle of Adams Letters, 1861-1865*, 2 vols. (Boston, 1920).

FRANKLIN, JOHN HOPE, editor. *The Diary of James T. Ayres, Civil War Recruiter* (Springfield, Ill., 1947). Of value for its discussion of the problems of Northern state recruiting agents in the Deep South during the Civil War.

GRADY, HENRY W. *The New South* (New York, 1890). Of value in assessing the spirit of the South after the period of reconstruction, with attendant changes in wartime attitudes.

GRANT, ULYSSES S. *Personal Memoirs of U. S. Grant*, 2 vols. (Hartford, 1885). Of slight value on the subject of Negro troops.

GREELEY, HORACE. *The American Conflict, A History of the Great Rebellion in the United States of America, 1860-'65, Its Causes, Incidents, and Results . . .*, 2 vols. (Hartford, 1866). A contemporary account from a definite point of view.

HIGGINSON, THOMAS WENTWORTH. *Army Life in a Black Regiment* (Boston, 1890). The classic regimental history, written with insight, imagination, intelligence, and a masterful style.

JOHNSON, ROBERT UNDERWOOD, AND BUEL, CLARENCE CLOUGH, editors. *Battles and Leaders of the Civil War*, 4 vols. (New York, 1888). Of uneven value since it treats the Negro contribution to the war only occasionally and without much discussion of the fundamental problems or policy difficulties encountered. Written well after the war, it suffers from the usual memoir troubles of faulty memory and illuminating second thoughts.

KNOX, THOMAS WALLACE. *Camp-Fire and Cotton-Field: Southern Adventure in Time of War. Life with the Union Armies, and Residence on a Louisiana Plantation* (New York, 1865). Knox was a New York *Herald* correspondent who saw much of the war on the Mississippi River and for a time ran a captured plantation in Louisiana. Some few pages on Negro troops at Milliken's Bend and as plantation guards.

LIVERMORE, MARY A. *My Story of the War: A Woman's Narrative of Four Years Personal Experience as Nurse in the Union Army, and in Relief Work at Home, in Hospitals, Camps, and at the Front, during the War of the Rebellion . . .* (Hartford, 1890).

MEARNS, DAVID C., editor. *The Lincoln Papers, The Story of the Collection with Selections to July 4, 1861*, 2 vols. (New York, 1948).

MENEELY, A. HOWARD, editor. "Three Manuscripts of Gideon Welles," *American Historical Review*, XXXI (April, 1926), 486-494.

NICOLAY, JOHN G., AND HAY, JOHN. *Abraham Lincoln: A History*, 10 vols. (New York, 1890). Chapter XX in Vol. VI is of some value in regard to the slow emergence of administration policy on Negro soldiers.

WILDER, BURT G. *The Fifty-fifth Regiment of Massachusetts Volunteer Infantry* (Brookline, Mass., 1919). Brief and sketchy, with more material in footnotes than in the text.

WILLIAMS, GEORGE WASHINGTON. *A History of the Negro Troops in the War of the Rebellion, 1861-1865* ... (New York, 1888).

WILSON, JOSEPH T. *The Black Phalanx; a History of the Negro Soldiers of the United States in the Wars of 1775—1812, 1861—'65* (Hartford, 1888).

PAMPHLETS

BIRNEY, WILLIAM. *General William Birney's Answer to Libels Clandestinely Circulated by James Shaw, Jr., Collector of the Port, Providence, R. I., with a Review of the Military Record of the Said James Shaw, Jr., Late Colonel of the Seventh U.S. Colored Troops* (Washington, 1878). Good material on organization of colored troops and attitudes of their officers. Copy in Birney File, Generals' Reports, National Archives.

FLEETWOOD, CHRISTIAN A. *The Negro as a Soldier* (Washington, 1895). A brief review of the development and acceptance of Negro troops by a former sergeant major, one of fourteen Negro soldiers to receive the Congressional Medal of Honor during the Civil War.

Free Military School for Applicants for Command of Colored Troops, No. 1210 Chestnut Street, Philadelphia, Established by the Supervisory Committee for Recruiting Colored Regiments, John H. Taggert Late Colonel 12th Regiment Pennsylvania Reserves, Chief Preceptor, 2nd ed. (Philadelphia, 1864). Of very great value.

O'RIELLY, HENRY, *First Organization of Colored Troops in the State of New York to aid in Suppressing the Slaveholders' Rebellion* ... (New York, 1864). Traces the development of public opinion in favor of recruiting Negroes in New York. O'Rielly was secretary of the New York Association for Colored Volunteers.

Soldiers and Sailors Historical Society of Rhode Island, *Personal Narratives of Events in the War of the Rebellion:*

ADDEMAN, J. M. *Reminiscences of Two Years with the Colored Troops*, No. 7, Second Series (Providence, 1880).

MORGAN, THOMAS J. *Reminiscences of Service with Colored Troops in the Army of the Cumberland, 1863-65*, No. 13, Third Series (Providence, 1885).

RICKARD, JAMES H. *Services with Colored Troops in Burnside's Corps*, No. 1, Fifth Series (Providence, 1894).

SHERMAN, GEORGE R., *The Negro as a Soldier*, No. 7, Seventh Series (Providence, 1913).

ULLMANN, DANIEL, *Address by Daniel Ullmann, LL.D., Major General U.S.V., before the Soldiers and Sailors' Union of the State of New York, on the Organization of Colored Troops and the Regeneration of the South, delivered at Albany, February 5, 1868.* (Washington, 1868). Describes Ullmann's role; in Ullmann File, Generals' Reports, National Archives.

MAGAZINE ARTICLES

FITTS, JAMES FRANKLIN. "The Negro in Blue," *Galaxy*, III (Feb. 1, 1867), 249-55. Good material on early use of Negro soldiers in Department of the South and Louisiana; good discussion of anti-Negro sentiment in Union Army. Fitts was a Union officer with duty in South Carolina and Louisiana.

FORTEN, CHARLOTTE. "Life on the Sea Islands," *Atlantic Monthly*, XIII (May, June, 1864), 587-96, 666-76. Eyewitness accounts of muster-in of the 1st South Carolina and of life around its encampment at Beaufort.

HIGGINSON, THOMAS WENTWORTH. "Leaves from an Officer's Journal," *Atlantic Monthly*, XIV (November, December, 1864), 521-29, 740-48. The opening chapters of *Army Life in a Black Regiment* as they first appeared.

———. "Regular and Volunteer Officers," *Atlantic Monthly*, XIV (September, 1864), 348-57. Excellent critical essay on essential qualities of good officers.

———. "Up the St. John's," *Atlantic Monthly*, XVI (September, 1865), 312-25.

———. "Up the St. Mary's," *Atlantic Monthly*, XV (April, 1865), 422-36.

KILMER, GEORGE L. "The Dash into the Crater," *Century Magazine*, XII (September, 1887), 774-76. An account of the Petersburg assault and disaster of July 30, 1864, by an officer who participated.

PERKINS, FRANCES BEECHER. "Two Years with a Colored Regiment, A Woman's Experience," *New England Magazine*, XVII (January, 1898), 533-43. Valuable for information on eagerness of colored troops for education; details educational activity by Mrs. Beecher for the men of the 35th U.S. Colored Troops, Colonel James Beecher's regiment.

PIERCE, EDWARD L. "The Freedmen of Port Royal," *Atlantic Monthly*, XII (September, 1863), 291-315. Excellent account of educational mission to the Sea Islands with observations on recruitment, performance, and slow acceptance of Negro troops by white soldiers.

Stone, Henry. "Hood's Invasion of Tennessee," *Century Magazine*, XII (August, 1887), 597-616. Good account of battle of Nashville and colored troops' participation.

Thomas, Henry Goddard. "The Colored Troops at Petersburg," *Century Magazine*, XII (September, 1887), 777-82. Account by colonel commanding 2nd Brigade of Ferrero's colored division on July 30, 1864.

NEWSPAPERS

Atlanta (Ga.) *Southern Confederacy*, 1863. Bound newspapers, Tennessee Historical Society, Nashville. Of importance for discussions of Negro prisoner problem.

Carmel (N.Y.) *Putnam County Courier*, 1864. Newspaper room, Reed Memorial Library, Carmel. Valuable for expressions of anti-Negro and anti-administration opinion.

Chicago *Tribune*, 1861-65. Bound volumes, Chicago Historical Society. A pro-administration paper containing much good material on Negro soldiers.

Cincinnati *Daily Commercial*, 1863. Miscellaneous bound newspapers, Tennessee Historical Society.

Cincinnati *Commercial Advertizer*, 1862-63. Miscellaneous bound newspapers, Tennessee Historical Society.

Douglass' Monthly, 1861-63. Original and microfilm copies in Rundell Memorial Library, Rochester Public Library, Rochester, N. Y. Invaluable for point of view of free colored men in North.

Emporia (Kan.) *News*, 1861-63. Bound newspapers, Kansas State Historical Society, Topeka. Pro-administration and in favor of Negro troops.

Leavenworth (Kan.) *Conservative*, 1861-64. Bound newspapers, Kansas State Historical Society. Lane's paper.

Louisville (Ky.) *Daily Journal*, 1863. Miscellaneous bound newspapers, Tennesse Historical Society. A Union paper inimical to the idea of using Negroes as soldiers.

Nashville (Tenn.) *Daily Times and True Union*, 1863. Bound newspapers, Tennessee Historical Society.

Nashville *Daily Union*, 1863. Tennessee Historical Society. Pro-Union, favoring Negro soldiers.

Nashville *Dispatch*, 1862. Bound newspapers, Carnegie Library, Nashville.

Nashville *Republican Banner*, 1861. Bound newspapers, Tennessee State Library, Nashville.

New York *Times*, 1861-64. Microfilm in New York Public Library.

Excellent for considered and controlled editorial expression and discussion of question; good detail from correspondents in the field.

New York *Tribune*, 1861. Microfilm in New York Public Library.
Greeley's paper, sharply critical of the Lincoln administration, favorable to employment of Negro troops.

Savannah (Ga.) *Republican*, 1862. Miscellaneous bound newspapers,
Tennessee Historical Society. Good for Southern reaction to Union
employment of Negro troops.

Shreveport (La.) *Daily News*, 1861. Bound newspapers, Louisiana
State University Library, Baton Rouge. Good for Southern attitudes on
"loyal" Negroes.

Washington (D.C.) *Daily National Intelligencer*, 1861-64. Bound
newspapers, Library of Congress. Pro-Confederacy and anti-administration in policy, particularly for the first two years of the war. Highly
critical of Union policy toward Negroes, unfavorable to their employment as soldiers. Valuable for material on anti-Negro sentiment and
for reprints of news stories and editorials from a wide variety of newspapers, North and South.

SECONDARY MATERIALS

BOOKS AND SPECIAL STUDIES

*American Annual Cyclopaedia and Register of Important Events for
the Year[s] 1863 [1864 and 1865]. Embracing Political, Civil, Military, and Social Affairs* ... (New York, 1869, 1872, 1876). A valuable
yearbook.

BROWN, WILLIAM WELLS. *The Negro in the American Rebellion*
(Boston, 1867). The first treatment of the subject.

CORNISH, DUDLEY TAYLOR. "The Union Army as a School for
Negroes," *Journal of Negro History*, XXXVII (October, 1952), 368-
82.

DYER, FREDERICK HENRY. *A Compendium of the War of the Rebellion Compiled and Arranged from Official Records of the Federal
and Confederate Armies, Reports of the Adjutant Generals of the
Several States, the Army Registers and Other Reliable Documents and
Sources* (Des Moines, Iowa, 1908).

EMERSON, EDWARD W. *Life and Letters of Charles Russell Lowell*
(Boston, 1907). Colonel Lowell's letters to Robert Gould Shaw's sister
give insight to abolitionist feeling on 54th Massachusetts Infantry.

FOX, WILLIAM F. "The Chances of Being Hit in Battle, A Study of
Regimental Losses in the Civil War," *Century Magazine*, XIV (May,

1888), 93-133. Some discussion of and statistics on Negro casualties from combat and disease.

FREIDEL, FRANK. *Francis Lieber, Nineteenth Century Liberal* (Baton Rouge, La., 1947). Sets forth Lieber's part in preparation of General Order 100, Rules of Land Warfare.

HAMLIN, CHARLES EUGENE. *The Life and Times of Hannibal Hamlin* (Cambridge, Mass., 1899). Some information on Ullmann's project.

HARLOW, RALPH VOLNEY. *Gerrit Smith, Philanthropist and Reformer* (New York, 1939). Some references to Smith's aid to recruitment of 54th Massachusetts Infantry.

HEITMAN, FRANCIS B. *Historical Register and Dictionary of the United States Army from Its Organization, September 29, 1789 to March 2, 1903*, 2 vols. (Washington, 1903).

HENDRICK, BURTON J. *Lincoln's War Cabinet* (Boston, 1946). Of value on Cameron's departure from the cabinet.

HENDRICKS, GEORGE LINTON. "Union Army Occupation of the Southern Seaboard, 1861-1865," unpublished doctoral dissertation (on microfilm), Columbia University, 1954. Good detailed account of Hunter's recruiting methods and of drafting Negroes.

HESSELTINE, W. B. *Civil War Prisons: A Study in War Psychology* (Columbus, Ohio, 1930). Good material on prisoner of war problems.

JOHNSON, ALLEN, AND MALONE, DUMAS, editors. *Dictionary of American Biography*, 22 vols. (New York, 1928-36).

JORDAN, JOHN L. "Was There a Massacre at Fort Pillow?" *Tennessee Historical Quarterly*, VI (June, 1947), 99-133.

MARSHALL, S. L. A. *The River and the Gauntlet* (New York, 1953). Good discussion of behavior of Negro troops in Korean War.

MILLER, FRANCIS T., editor. *The Photographic History of the Civil War*, 10 vols. (New York, 1911). Scant material on Negro troops in Vol. IX.

The Monument to Robert Gould Shaw: Its Inception, Completion and Unveiling, 1865-1897 (Boston, 1897). Contains informative addresses by Henry Lee Higginson, William James, and Booker T. Washington.

NEVINS, ALLAN. *Frémont, Pathmaker of the West* (New York, 1955). Throws some light on Cameron's attitude toward the employment of Negro soldiers and on John Cochrane's connection with Frémont.

NICOLAY, HELEN. *Lincoln's Secretary, A Biography of John G. Nicolay* (New York, 1949).

PEARSON, HENRY GREENLEAF. *The Life of John A. Andrew, Governor of Massachusetts, 1861-1865*, 2 vols. (Boston, 1904). Good on 54th Massachusetts and pay problem.

PINCHON, EDGCUMB. *Daniel Sickles* ... (Garden City, N.Y., 1945).

PRATT, FLETCHER. *Stanton, Lincoln's Secretary of War* (New York, 1953). Some light on feeling between Stanton and Lorenzo Thomas.

QUARLES, BENJAMIN. *The Negro in the Civil War* (Boston, 1953). An excellent comprehensive study with some moving chapters on Negro soldiers; very helpful bibliography.

RANDALL, J. G. *The Civil War and Reconstruction* (Boston, 1937). Still the best one-volume history of the war.

———. *Lincoln the President, Springfield to Gettysburg*, 2 vols. (New York, 1945). The best available analysis of Lincoln's attitude and the slow maturation of policies.

REDDICK, L. D. "The Negro Policy of the United States Army, 1775-1945," *Journal of Negro History*, XXXIV (January, 1949), 9-29. Brief treatment of Civil War and Reconstruction periods.

RHODES, JAMES FORD. *A History of the United States from the Compromise of 1850*, 7 vols. (New York, 1904-1906).

ROLLIN, FRANK A. *Life and Public Services of Martin R. Delany, Sub-Assistant Commissioner Bureau Relief of Refugees, Freedmen, and of Abandoned Lands, and Late Major 104th U.S. Colored Troops* (Boston, 1868).

SHANNON, FRED A. *The Organization and Administration of the Union Army, 1861-1865*, 2 vols. (Cleveland, 1928).

STEPHENSON, WENDELL HOLMES. *The Political Career of General James H. Lane* in *Publications of the Kansas State Historical Society*, Vol. III (Topeka, 1930).

THOMAS, BENJAMIN P. *Theodore Weld, Crusader for Freedom* (New Brunswick, N.J., 1950).

WEST, RICHARD S., JR. *Gideon Welles, Lincoln's Navy Department* (Indianapolis, 1943).

WILEY, BELL IRVIN. *Southern Negroes, 1861-1865* (New Haven, 1938). Vol XXXI in *Yale Historical Publications*, Leonard Woods Labaree, editor. Several chapters sketch out the role of the Negro in the Union Army.

———, *The Life of Johnny Reb, The Common Soldier of the Confederacy* (Indianapolis, 1943).

WILLIAMS, T. HARRY. *Lincoln and His Generals* (New York, 1952). Good on Frémont and his emancipation proclamation. Excellent overall view of Lincoln as strategist.

BIBLIOGRAPHIC UPDATE

A revolution has occurred in the historiography of black Americans over the thirty years since *The Sable Arm* first appeared. The result has been that whole new chapters of our national experience have won scholarly attention and examination, and the historical profession itself has changed rather remarkably. Quite remarkably, in fact, in view of this 1951 statement: "A Jim Crow society breeds and needs a Jim Crow historiography. The dominant historiography in the United States either omits the Negro people or presents them as a people without a past, as a people who have been docile, passive, parasitic, imitative. This picture is a lie." At the time many historians dismissed that charge because it was radical and abrasive—and because it had been made by Herbert Aptheker, an avowed Marxist. Lamentably, his statement was not only radical and abrasive but also fundamentally true. Literally scores of volumes of our history—on the American Civil War, the war with Spain, and both world wars in this century—support Aptheker's allegation. Numerous examinations of our high school and college history textbooks provide detailed corroboration of his charge; until the late 1960s, the textbook treatment of black Americans ranged from partial, misleading, incomplete, and erroneous to outright omission. That is changed now, as a cursory view of the American history stacks of any good college library will show.

Nowhere is there a better, more comprehensive, and more thoughtful analysis of the slow unfolding of that revolution than August Meier and Elliott Rudwick's *Black History and the Historical Profession, 1915–1980* (Urbana: University of Illinois Press, 1986). The two Kent State historians have collaborated to produce some ten books of black social history, including one of the first textbooks designed for black history courses, *From Plantation to Ghetto* (1966). In this, their last volume together, they carefully explore and explain all the factors making for the profound changes in our historiography: the beginnings under Carter G. Woodson and his Association for the Study of Negro Life and History, founded in 1915, the year of that racist film, *Birth of a Nation;* the effects of the Harlem Renaissance of the 1920s and the Depression and the New Deal in the 1930s; the acceleration and broadening of interest in racial problems during the war years; and the great flood augmented by the Cold War and the Civil Rights Revolution. For Meier and Rudwick, the major turning point came in the 1950s, although some earlier landmarks stand out: Bell Wiley's *Southern Negroes, 1861–1865* (1938), Herbert Aptheker's *American Negro Slave Revolts* (1943), Gunnar Myrdal's monumental *An American Dilemma* (1944), and Benjamin Quarles's *Frederick Douglass* (1948). In the 1950s, more and more historians, both black and white, contributed valuable monographs touching all aspects of the black experience, most notably C. Vann Woodward's *Origins of the New South* (1951) and his classic *The Strange Career of Jim Crow* (1955), Benjamin Quarles's *The Negro in the Civil War* (1953), and John Hope Franklin's *The Militant South* and Kenneth M. Stampp's *The Peculiar Institution* (both in 1956). Franklin had already begun his distinguished career with his classic textbook, *From Slavery to Freedom* (1947). After that decade (which included both the school desegregation decision in 1954 and Little Rock three years later), the pace of research, writing, and publication on every phase of the history of black Americans picked up. That history became an integral part of the history of the United States of America, and black and white historians grew to respect each other and to associate professionally and socially beyond any credible 1951 forecast.

Two years before *The Sable Arm* appeared, Lee Nichols produced his solid account of the desegregation of United States armed forces during the Korean conflict, *Breakthrough on the Color Front* (1954). The subject is more significant than the book: it signaled the end of racial segregation in the U.S. armed forces, the end of three hundred years of official Jim Crow policy and practice developed to its most extreme and inflexible degree in this twentieth century. Certainly the combination of those events, desegregation of the armed forces and the unanimous decision of the Supreme Court in the Brown case, had a stimulating and liberating effect on historians, especially those just entering that profession after service in those armed forces of democracy.

Benjamin Quarles, hardly a new recruit to black history, led the parade into the 1960s with his illuminating study *The Negro in the American Revolution* (1961). With the Civil War centennial just getting under way, some significant books on black participation in that struggle appeared. James M. McPherson began his publishing career with *The Struggle for Equality: Abolitionists and the Negro in the Civil War and Reconstruction* (1964), a comprehensive and sensitive exploration based on thorough research and graced with a superb bibliography. He followed up on this with his ambitious and revealing work *The Negro's Civil War: How American Negroes Felt and Acted during the War for the Union* (1965), an impressive, original, and rich collection of contemporary eye-witness and participant accounts gleaned from black newspapers and correspondence.

In the same year, Peter Burchard contributed *One Gallant Rush: Robert Gould Shaw and His Brave Black Regiment,* an appreciation of the martyred hero and his 54th Massachusetts.

While the Civil War naturally drew wide interest, attention, and investigation, the most significant single volume published in the 1960s was Ulysses Lee's *The Employment of Negro Troops: U.S. Army in World War II, Special Studies,* released by the Center of Military History in 1966. It remains a landmark in the development of the new military history and a monument to Major Lee's long labors. To this day, every historian studying or writing about the black soldier in World War II must consult this long (over 700 pages) volume, again and again.

The Indian-fighting constabulary of the post–Civil War era attracted the attention of William H. Leckie, a young Air Force veteran whose curiosity about black troops sprang from his brief service with two hundred black airmen at the end of the war. That curiosity (like my own earlier) led to a doctoral dissertation and eventually a book, *The Buffalo Soldiers: A Narrative of the Negro Cavalry in the West* (1967). Arlen Fowler's experience as a young lieutenant parallels Leckie's: he encountered remnants of the 25th U.S. Infantry in 1952 "on the shady side of the hill" at Fort Hood, Texas. That stirred *his* curiosity and led to his doctoral dissertation and his book *The Black Infantry in the West, 1869–1891* (1971). It is a logical companion to Leckie's *Buffalo Soldiers.*

Another important book growing out of a doctoral study is *Desegregation of the U.S. Armed Forces: Fighting on Two Fronts, 1939–1953,* by Richard M. Dalfiume, published by the University of Missouri Press in 1969. Dalfiume set forth his thesis unequivocally in his subtitle. His interest in and respect for black troops grew from his experience as an enlisted man in the newly integrated army. While his sensitive study put in the shade an earlier brief survey by Richard J. Stillman II, *Integration of the Negro in the U.S. Armed Forces* (1968), it was a dozen years before Morris J. MacGregor, Jr., overtook Dalfiume with his encyclopedic *Integration of the Armed Forces, 1940–1965.* Published in 1981 by the Center of Military History, it is a significant piece of CMH's Defense Studies series.

Serious students of American history can never forget the tragic events of the late 1960s following on the heels of substantial achievements in voter registration, school integration, and passage of a sweeping civil rights act—the assassinations of Robert F. Kennedy and Martin Luther King, Jr. More than a score of American cities were in flames almost overnight. Far more than a score of American colleges and universities hastily offered their first courses in black history. It comes down to this: after the sixties the floodgates were wide open, and the seventies saw an impressive list of important, revealing, disturbing, and positively helpful collections of documents, explorations of broad and narrow subjects, and just plain solid historical monographs. For the most part, these were the work of academic historians, but there were others, too, among them a Kansas City newspaperman named John D. Weaver. His careful report, *The Brownsville Raid* (1970), was instrumental in stirring the Department of Defense to action in 1972, reversing the executive order that had discharged without honor 167 (only 153 finally) members of the First Battalion of the 25th U.S. Infantry for their alleged role in the 1906 affray. That tragic miscarriage of justice undergirded the steady deterioration of the black soldiers' position in the Regular Establishment, which reached its nadir in World War I.

Interest in and investigation of various aspects of black military history grew in the 1970s, with Fowler's book on the 24th and 25th U.S. Infantry in the West and Willard Gatewood's *"Smoked Yankees" and the Struggle for Empire: Letters from Negro Soldiers, 1898–1902* (1971), which brought a new dimension to that part of the black experience. John M. Carroll, out of his experience teaching black history, assembled an engaging potpourri of materials under the title *The Black Military Experience in the American West.* More important than those efforts is a series of bibliographical tomes produced by John Slonaker and his fellow-workers at Carlisle Barracks: *The U.S. Army and the Negro—A Military History Research Collection Bibliography* (1971) and later rich supplements. These are invaluable aids to serious research.

However rich 1971 was in the production of monographs and research tools, one cannot ignore 1974 as the richest in recent time in contributions to black history. Lorenzo J. Greene, *The Negro in Colonial New England,* makes a logical companion for Gary H. Nash's *Red, White, and Black: The Peoples of Early America.* Closer to our own time is Arthur E. Barbeau and Florette Henri's important and disturbing volume, *The Unknown Soldiers: Black American Troops in World War I,* a moving study of institutionalized racism. Marvin E. Fletcher examined a critical subject in a critical period and produced *The Black Soldier and Officer in the United States Army, 1891–1917,* and Jack Foner brought out his popular, readable, but undocumented *Blacks and the Military in American History.* In 1975 Henry Shaw, Jr., and Ralph W. Donnelly collaborated on *Blacks in the Marine Corps,* thus adding a new dimension to the field. And in that year Mary P. Motley produced *The Invisible Soldier: The Experience of the Black Soldier in World War II,* based on sixty-five interviews with black veterans of that war, the majority of them from the Detroit area.

Alan M. Osur wrote *Blacks in the Army Air Forces during World War II,* published by the Office of Air Force History in 1977. The following year

—

saw the publication of Alan L. Gropman's solid *The Air Force Integrates*. Forever enriching 1977 in the minds of military historians is an invaluable research tool: the thirteen-volume collection *Blacks in the United States Armed Forces: Basic Documents*, edited by Morris MacGregor and Bernard C. Nalty. Their materials, many reproduced in facsimile, are arranged chronologically and by period; Volume II, for example, treats the Civil War. Four years later, when MacGregor's *magnum opus* appeared, he once more teamed up with Nalty to develop a one-volume abridgment of the 1977 collection; this they called *Blacks in the Military: Essential Documents*. In 1982, Ira Berlin, Joseph P. Reidy, and Leslie S. Rowland joined forces to edit a sterling collection of materials: *The Black Military Experience*. It is the second of six volumes published by Cambridge University Press in the series *Freedom: A Documentary History of Emancipation*.

Nearly forty years ago, my adviser at Colorado, a Harvard Ph.D. who had been a graduate assistant to Frederick Jackson Turner, cautioned me as I began my research on Negro troops: "You may not find enough material." But everywhere I looked, I found material—pertinent, relevant, and rich. And today, thanks to that thorough-going revolution in American historiography, materials are far more easily found.

A final word: The book on my desk awaiting review is *Strength for the Fight: A History of Black Americans in the Military*, by Bernard Nalty, a historian in the Office of Air Force History. It is the best overall treatment of the subject I have seen. Black history, an integral part of American history, is here to stay.

DUDLEY T. CORNISH

San Francisco
September 1986